Unreal Engine 5 Character Creation, Animation, and Cinematics

Create custom 3D assets and bring them to life in Unreal Engine 5 using MetaHuman, Lumen, and Nanite

Henk Venter

Wilhelm Ogterop

BIRMINGHAM—MUMBAI

Unreal Engine 5 Character Creation, Animation, and Cinematics

Copyright © 2022 Packt Publishing

Group Product Manager: Rohit Rajkumar
Publishing Product Manager: Nitin Nainani
Senior Editor: Keagan Carneiro
Content Development Editor: Abhishek Jadhav
Technical Editor: Saurabh Kadave
Copy Editor: Safis Editing
Project Coordinator: Rashika Ba
Proofreader: Safis Editing
Indexer: Manju Arasan
Production Designer: Ponraj Dhandapani
Marketing Coordinator: Teny Thomas

First published: June 2022

Production reference: 2120722

Published by Packt Publishing Ltd.
Livery Place
35 Livery Street
Birmingham
B3 2PB, UK.

ISBN 978-1-80181-244-3

www.packt.com

I dedicate this book to the memory of my mother and father, Margaret and Daniel, who encouraged me to follow in my mother's footsteps to become a professional artist.

– Henk Venter

To my dad, Tiemen Ogterop, who was my rock of stability and always supported me unconditionally in any way he could. You had so much love to give. To my mum, who had fire in her belly and refused to give up during my childhood health problems. I owe you both the happy life I've had the privilege to experience. To my wife, June, and my daughter, Mila, who gave up some family time with her daddy so that he can teach others through this book. I love you to the end of time.

– Wilhelm Ogterop

Contributors

About the authors

Henk Venter is a senior 3D character artist with 22 years of experience in the 3D computer graphics industry. He is currently running his own 3D art production studio. He was the principal character artist at THQ Studio Australia and senior character artist at Electronic Arts in Montreal, Canada.

In the UK, he worked for Microsoft's Rare studio, Sumo Digital, and Eurocom . He has worked on multiple projects throughout his career, such as *Army of Two*, *Crackdown 3*, *Batman Begins*, *Kinect Sports: Rivals*, *Battleship*, *Megamind: Ultimate Showdown*, and *Boogie*, to name a few.

Wilhelm Ogterop has 24 years of experience in the 3D computer graphics industry and has worked as a character animator and lead animator for several UK and international game studios. Raven Software, Deep Silver, TT Fusion, Eurocom Entertainment, Instinct Games, Entrada Interactive, and Headfirst Productions are among the studios for which he has worked on-site and as a contractor.

Throughout his career, he has worked on a variety of interesting projects, including *Call of Duty: Black Ops III* (2015), *Call of Duty: Infinite Warfare* (2015), *Homefront: The Revolution* (2016), *Deadspace Extraction*, *Miscreated*, *The LEGO Movie Videogame*, *LEGO Legends of Chima*, *LEGO Lord of the Rings*, *LEGO City Undercover*, *Rio (Blue Sky Studios)*, *GoldenEye 007*, *Vancouver 2010* (the official video game of the Olympic Winter Games), *James Bond: Quantum of Solace*, *The Mummy 3: Tomb of the Dragon Emperor*, *Pirates of the Caribbean: At World's End*, *Call of Cthulhu: Dark Corners of the Earth*, and other unpublished projects.

About the reviewer

Varun Kumar Gupta is a junior technical artist at Technicolor Creative Studios. He is an accomplished 3D generalist and programmer and enjoys using his skills to contribute to the exciting technological advances that happen every day at Technicolor. He likes to spend his time contributing to open source, procedural content generation, and computer graphics as much as possible. He also works as a freelancer, dealing in concept art, short films, and 2D art whenever time permits. He graduated from Bennett University in 2022 with a bachelor's degree in computer science engineering. In his free time, he likes to draw, learn music (guitar and piano), and play video games.

Table of Contents

2
Modeling a Robot Drone Character

3
Let's Sculpt an Alien Plant!

4
UV Maps and Texture Baking

5

Texturing Your Models inside Quixel Mixer

Part 2 - Building Your Virtual Movie Set in Unreal Engine 5

6

Exploring Unreal Engine 5

7
Setting Up Materials in UE 5

8
Using MetaHuman to Create a Photorealistic Human for UE5

9
Building a Virtual 3D Movie Set in UE5

10
Adding Lighting and Atmospheric Visual Effects in UE5

Part 3: Character Rigging for Animation in UE5 with Control Rig

11
Alien Plant Joint Setup in Blender

12

Alien Plant Skinning in Blender

13

Robot Joint Setup and Skinning in Blender

14

Making a Custom Rig for Our Alien Plant with Control Rig

15

Creating a Control Rig with Basic IK Controls for the Robot in UE5

Part 4: Animation in UE5 Using Control Rig and Sequencer

16

Creating a Simple Swaying Animation Cycle in UE5 Sequencer

17

Creating Three Simple Animations for the Robot in UE5 Sequencer

18

Importing Motion Capture onto the MetaHuman Control Rig

19

Motion Capture Editing and Cleanup Using Control Rig and Sequencer

20
Using Sequencer to Construct Your Final Scene

Index
Other Books You May Enjoy

Preface

Unreal Engine 5 (**UE5**) offers beginners and seasoned professionals the ability to create detailed movie scenes with realistic human characters using MetaHuman, combining them with custom props and environments, plus built-in industry-standard animation tools to create state-of-the-art movie scenes in a fraction of the time compared to old methods. This book takes you through the entire 3D movie production pipeline using free (open source) software. This book can also be used as a foundation course in 3D computer art in general – a strong foundation that can be built upon and serve as a springboard toward a career in the field.

By following the step-by-step, beginner-friendly tutorials in this book, you'll learn how to create your own custom 3D assets in Blender and texture these 3D assets in Quixel Mixer. Next, you'll import these completed 3D assets into UE5 and use them to build a virtual 3D movie set for your 3D movie. You'll also populate your 3D movie set by using Quixel Megascans assets and create and customize your own photorealistic human character, using MetaHuman Creator and UE5. As you advance, you'll discover how to rig, skin, and animate these 3D assets and characters using Blender and UE5's new Control Rig. Finally, you'll explore the process of setting up your movie cameras and animation sequences and find out how to render out your 3D movie using UE5's Sequencer.

By the end of this Unreal Engine book, you'll have learned to combine different elements in UE5 to make your own movies and cinematics.

Who this book is for

This book is ideal for beginners to Unreal Engine or 3D animation and art in general who want to learn the entire process of creating 3D movies with UE5. Experienced 3D artists and animators new to UE5 will also find this book invaluable, as it covers cutting-edge techniques for making real-time 3D movies using Unreal Engine, Blender, Quixel Mixer, and Quixel Bridge. Experienced animators will learn how to move almost the entire animation pipeline into Unreal Engine. Prior experience with 3D software is not necessary, but any experience will be helpful in understanding the concepts easily.

What this book covers

Chapter 1, An Introduction to Blender's 3D Modeling and Sculpture Tools, will introduce you to the basic concepts of 3D graphics, and you will explore Blender's 3D modeling and sculpting tools.

Chapter 2, Modeling a Robot Drone Character, takes you through the complete process to create a 3D model of a Robot Drone character in Blender.

Chapter 3, Let's Sculpt an Alien Plant!, teaches you how to use Blender to create a 3D sculpture of an Alien Plant for your 3D movie set.

Chapter 4, UV Maps and Texture Baking, helps you understand how to UV-map your 3D models in Blender and then bake your textures in xNormal.

Chapter 5, Texturing Your Models Inside Quixel Mixer, takes you through the complete procedural texturing process in Quixel Mixer.

Chapter 6, Exploring Unreal Engine 5, introduces you to the basics of UE5's user interface.

Chapter 7, Setting up Materials in UE5, teaches you how to import your 3D models, set up their textures, and create materials in UE5.

Chapter 8, Use MetaHuman to Create a Photorealistic Human for UE5, takes you through the complete process of creating a custom MetaHuman character.

Chapter 9, Building a Virtual 3D Movie Set in UE5, teaches you how to build a virtual 3D movie set by using Nanite in combination with Quixel Megascans assets in UE5.

Chapter 10, Adding Lighting and Atmospheric Visual Effects in UE5, teaches you how to light your 3D movie set by using Lumen with custom lighting and add fog, light bloom, light shafts, and solar flares in UE5.

Chapter 11, Alien Plant Joint Setup in Blender, helps you to create a skeleton joint/bone chain for the Alien Plant to make it animated.

Chapter 12, Alien Plant Skinning in Blender, helps you understand how to skin the Alien Plant 3D model so that it can animate and move with the skeleton.

Chapter 13, Robot Joint Setup and Skinning in Blender, helps you to create a skeleton for the robot and teaches you how to skin it to the skeleton in a rigid way.

Chapter 14, Making a Custom Rig for Our Alien Plant with Control Rig, helps you understand how to create a simple custom **Forward Kinematics** (**FK**) animation rig with the new Control Rig tools in UE5.

Chapter 15, Creating a Control Rig with Basic IK Controls for the Robot in UE5, shows you how to create a simple custom **Inverse Kinematics** (**IK**) animation rig with the new Control Rig tools.

Chapter 16, Creating a Simple Swaying Animation Cycle in UE5 Sequencer, shows you how to animate your first simple animation with a custom Control Rig using Sequencer.

Chapter 17, Creating Three Simple Animations for the Robot in UE5 Sequencer, helps you to create some more simple animations using your custom robot Control Rig, Sequencer, IK, and additive animation layers.

Chapter 18, Importing Motion Capture onto the MetaHuman Control Rig, shows you how to find free motion capture animations and teaches you how to retarget them to the MetaHuman Control Rig.

Chapter 19, Motion Capture Editing and Cleanup Using Control Rig and Sequencer, helps you understand how to clean up, edit, and repurpose motion capture animation for your final movie.

Chapter 20, Using Sequencer to Construct Your Final Scene, will teach you how to construct your final movie scene with all the animated custom assets you created in this book, add cameras, and render your final movie.

To get the most out of this book

First of all, you need a computer that is powerful enough to run UE5. Even a lower-lever gaming PC or a modern laptop will be sufficient. You don't need previous experience with 3D software or Unreal Engine, but you will need to have basic computer literacy such as using the Windows operating system. For experienced 3D artists making the transition from other software packages to Blender or UE5, this book will help you to make the transition by showing you how to use the equivalent basic tools.

Software/hardware covered in the book	Operating system requirements
Unreal Engine 5.0.2	Windows 10, 11, or above
Blender 3.1	
Quixel Mixer 2021.1.3	
MetaHuman	

At the time of writing, all the software used in this book is free to download and use for individuals. There might be some licensing terms and conditions, but they are mostly for big studios working on big projects and don't affect individual users. At the time of writing, these are the download links:

- `https://www.unrealengine.com/`
- `https://www.blender.org/download/releases/3-1/`
- `https://quixel.com/mixer`
- `https://metahuman.unrealengine.com/`
- **Instant meshes:** `https://github.com/wjakob/instant-meshes`
- **Xnormal:** `https://xNormal.net/`

However, they should be easy to find with a quick internet search. Follow the installation instructions from the software websites.

The book is an equivalent of a foundation course on the most important elements of 3D art in general. We try to teach you the most important industry-standard ways of doing things in order to lay a solid foundation that you can build upon. See this book as the first step. We want to put the first tools in your toolbelt, but it is up to you to learn the subtleties of these tools.

Practice with these tools. Find and explore more tools. Explore the area or discipline you enjoy doing the most. In many cases, this also turns out to be the one you have a talent for. Put the time in, find a mentor, and you too can become a top craftsman and artist in this field.

Download the example files

You can download the example code files for this book from GitHub at `https://github.com/PacktPublishing/Unreal-Engine-5-Character-Creation-Animation-and-Cinematics`. If there's an update to the code, it will be updated in the GitHub repository.

We also have other code bundles from our rich catalog of books and videos available at `https://github.com/PacktPublishing/`. Check them out!

Download the color images

We also provide a PDF file that has color images of the screenshots and diagrams used in this book. You can download it here: `https://packt.link/EjXGU`.

Conventions used

There are a number of text conventions used throughout this book.

`Code in text`: Indicates code words in text, database table names, folder names, filenames, file extensions, pathnames, dummy URLs, user input, and Twitter handles. Here is an example: "The completed Robot Drone model, `RobotDrone_Blender_File.blend`, is available to download from the online repository."

Bold: Indicates a new term, an important word, or words that you see onscreen. For instance, words in menus or dialog boxes appear in **bold**. Here is an example: "The last tabs we will cover in this book are the **UV Editing Workspace** tab and the **Texture Paint Workspace** tab."

> **Tips or Important Notes**
> Appear like this.

Get in touch

Feedback from our readers is always welcome.

General feedback: If you have questions about any aspect of this book, email us at `customercare@packtpub.com` and mention the book title in the subject of your message.

Errata: Although we have taken every care to ensure the accuracy of our content, mistakes do happen. If you have found a mistake in this book, we would be grateful if you would report this to us. Please visit `www.packtpub.com/support/errata` and fill in the form.

Piracy: If you come across any illegal copies of our works in any form on the internet, we would be grateful if you would provide us with the location address or website name. Please contact us at `copyright@packt.com` with a link to the material.

If you are interested in becoming an author: If there is a topic that you have expertise in and you are interested in either writing or contributing to a book, please visit `authors.packtpub.com`.

Share Your Thoughts

Once you've read *Unreal Engine 5 Character Creation, Animation and Cinematics*, we'd love to hear your thoughts! Scan the QR code below to go straight to the Amazon review page for this book and share your feedback.

https://www.amazon.com/review/create-review/
error?asin=1801812446&

Your review is important to us and the tech community and will help us make sure we're delivering excellent quality content.

Part 1
Creating 3D Assets

In this part of the book, you will learn the complete process of creating 3D assets for use in Unreal Engine 5.

We will cover the following chapters in this section:

- *Chapter 1, An Introduction to Blender's 3D Modeling and Sculpting Tools*
- *Chapter 2, Modeling a Robot Drone Character*
- *Chapter 3, Let's Sculpt an Alien Plant!*
- *Chapter 4, UV Maps and Texture Baking*
- *Chapter 5, Texturing Your Models Inside Quixel Mixer*

1
An Introduction to Blender's 3D Modeling and Sculpting Tools

Welcome to the exciting world of 3D movie making!

We know you are super eager to start making your first 3D movie, but before you can do that, you need to get virtual actors, virtual sets, and virtual props, just like in a (virtual) Hollywood movie.

To create these 3D assets, you will need to learn how to use a piece of 3D software called **Blender**. This 3D creation suite is open source (free to use).

In this chapter, we will cover two approaches to creating 3D assets in Blender: 3D modeling and 3D sculpting.

I will start by explaining the very basic concepts of 3D modeling, then delve into the differences between 3D modeling and 3D sculpting and which is the best suited for a particular task.

After this, you will get a quick overview of how to use Blender by learning how to use the user interface, navigate in the 3D Viewport, view modes, and manipulate and select items.

Finally, we will briefly explore some of the most used 3D modeling tools, 3D sculpting tools, and modifiers that we will use in the practical exercises throughout the next four chapters.

> **Note**
> This chapter's purpose is to introduce you to the fundamentals of 3D graphics in general and the basic functionality of Blender's 3D modeling and sculpting tools. It is not meant as a practical chapter but rather as a reference of the tools that are used in Blender.

In this chapter, we're going to cover the following main topics:

- What is 3D modeling?
- Understanding 3D sculpting
- Introducing Blender
- Exploring Blender's modeling tools
- Using modifiers in Blender
- Exploring Blender's sculpting tools
- Other sculpting tools

By the end of this chapter, you will have a thorough understanding of the basic concepts of 3D modeling and sculpting.

You will learn the basics of Blender's functionality and learn about the 3D modeling and sculpting tools that you will use in the upcoming chapters.

Technical requirements

You will need the following hardware and software to complete this chapter:

- A computer that can run basic 3D animation software
- Blender, which can be installed from https://www.blender.org/download/

The Blender version that's used in this chapter is version 2.93.4. Even if your version of Blender is newer, the examples should still work without any problems.

Before we dive into the 3D movie-making process, you need to understand the basic concepts of 3D modeling.

The files related to this chapter are placed at `https://github.com/` `PacktPublishing/Unreal-Engine-5-Character-Creation-Animation-` `and-Cinematics/tree/main/Chapter01`

What is 3D modeling?

3D modeling is the process of creating 3D models by manipulating **Meshes** in 3D software.

A mesh (also called a polygon mesh) is a three-dimensional virtual object that is represented in a three-dimensional space in the 3D software.

A mesh is made up of components. These components are faces, edges, and vertices:

- A **face** is best described as a filled-in plane with at least three or more straight edges. Faces are made of two sub-component parts – edges and vertices.

- An **edge** is a connection between two vertices.

- A **vertex** (plural: vertices) is a point in a 3D space. Vertices are the smallest components of a mesh.

  These can be seen in the following diagram:

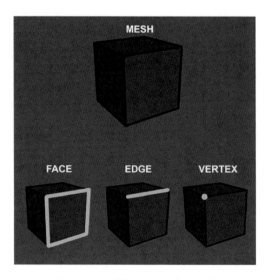

Figure 1.1 – The parts of a mesh

In this section, you learned about the basics of 3D modeling. This knowledge is an essential building block to learning more about 3D graphics.

In the next section, we will explore the fundamentals of 3D sculpting as a different approach to creating 3D assets.

Understanding 3D sculpting

So, what is 3D sculpting and how is it different from 3D modeling?

3D sculpting or **digital sculpting** can best be described as shaping or forming a 3D mesh with brush-based sculpting tools.

Imagine a traditional sculptor who is modeling in clay. Now, with modern computer graphics software such as Blender, you could sculpt much like a traditional sculptor but in a virtual three-dimensional space by using a pressure-sensitive graphic tablet and pen, or a mouse.

In Blender, we have many sculpting tools available that approximate the feeling of *digital clay*.

The benefit of a sculptural approach to creating models is that it can be more intuitive for creating organic shapes instead of using regular modeling tools (which are usually better suited for mechanical meshes or models of man-made structures such as buildings, vehicles, and so on).

Some examples of organic shapes for 3D sculpting include human bodies, creatures, animals, plants, rocks, and any other natural organic-shaped solid form. For 3D sculpting, we also use polygon meshes.

In this section, you learned about the basic concepts of 3D sculpting.

In the next section, you will learn about the essential functionality of Blender, which includes its user interface, navigation, and much more.

Introducing Blender

Blender is a 3D creation suite that can create almost any virtual scene or object.

We'll start exploring Blender by learning about the user interface that you see before you. Knowing what is where is the most essential starting point.

The user interface

As we open up Blender for the first time, we are greeted with a splash screen. This is a helpful menu to get you started when you have a particular project in mind. But for now, just close this menu. Once you've closed the splash screen, your view should look similar to what's shown in the following screenshot:

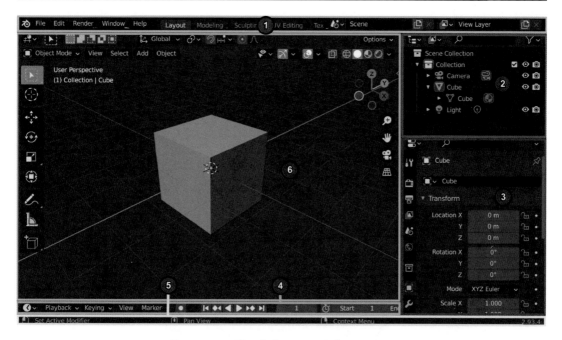

Figure 1.2 – Blender's user interface regions

The numbered areas in the preceding screenshot mark the different user interface regions that I will explain:

1. **Topbar:** This contains menus such as **File**, **Edit**, **Render**, and **Help**. On the right of that, we have tabs for selecting workspaces. These are like modes for the software, complete with menus and shortcuts. For example, if we want to move objects around the scene, we can use the **Layout Workspace** tab. Later, when we want to learn about the modeling process, we can switch over to the **Modeling Workspace** tab.

   And, as you have probably already guessed, for 3D sculpting, we can use the **Sculpture Workspace** tab. The last few tabs we will cover in this book are the **UV Editing Workspace** and **Texture Paint Workspace** tabs. Some of the other tabs that you will need for your future projects are the **Shading Workspace** and **Animation Workspace** tabs.

2. **Outliner:** This is a list representation of the various objects (meshes, curves, and so on) and elements (cameras, lights, and so on) in the scene. The Outliner can be used for selecting, deselecting, hiding, and organizing these objects and elements in the scene.

3. **Properties:** Here, we will find adjustable properties with tabs for adjusting active data, including the scene and its objects.

4. **Timeline:** This is used for scrubbing and manipulating animation keyframes.

5. **Status Bar**: This is where Blender displays contextual information about mouse and keyboard shortcuts and other statistical information.

6. **3D Viewport**: This is where you can view what is happening in your virtual 3D world.

In this section, you learned about the basic layout of Blender's user interface and its regions. In the next section, we will take an in-depth look at the various elements of the 3D Viewport.

Elements in the 3D Viewport

The 3D Viewport is where you can view what is happening in your virtual 3D world. The grid pattern shows you the floor plane. The floor grid plane is positioned at 0 on all three axes:

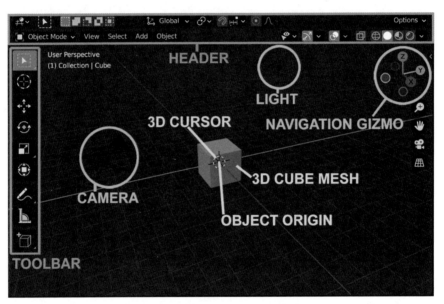

Figure 1.3 – The 3D Viewport's UI elements, shown with the Layout Workspace active

There are a few important items and regions in the 3D Viewport, as highlighted in the preceding screenshot:

- **The Header bar**: This menu bar acts as a container for menus and commonly used tools. Menus and buttons will change with the editor type and the selected object and mode.

- **Toolbar**: This menu bar contains a set of interactive tools that change depending on the workspace that's been selected. To show or hide the toolbar, press *T*.

- **Properties region**, also known as the **N-panel**: The Properties region can't be seen in the preceding screenshot because it is hidden by default. To open the Properties region, press *N*. This will open the Properties region on the right-hand side of the 3D Viewport. The Properties region holds settings for the 3D view and active object. It also provides numeric inputs for editing the **Transform** tab of your selected item (**Location, Rotation, Scale**, and **Dimensions**), as shown in the following screenshot. You can also use the Properties region to edit your 3D view's focal length and viewport clipping:

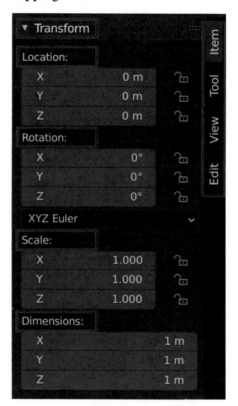

Figure 1.4 – The Properties region

By default, the 3D Viewport will show you some additional items that are automatically loaded on startup. These are the 3D cube mesh, the camera, and the light:

- The **3D cube mesh** is a model that provides a good starting point for many modeling tasks.

- The **camera** is a virtual camera that's used for renders inside Blender, while the **light** is a virtual light that's used to light our scenes. Neither of these will be used for our tutorial, so we can delete them.

- We also have the **object origin**. If we focus our attention on the 3D cube mesh in the center of our view, we can see that there is a tiny orange dot right in the center. This indicates the object origin point of our mesh. We will discuss why it is of importance later.

- The **3D cursor** is a red-and-white striped circle with crosshairs. This is a very useful tool that will be discussed later.

- Finally, we have the **Navigation Gizmo**, which can be found in the top-right corner of the 3D Viewport. You can use this gizmo to rotate your view of the 3D scene. We can either click and drag on the navigation gizmo to smoothly change our view, or we can click on one of the dots, which will immediately snap our view to one of the Orthographic views.

> **Note**
>
> **Orthographic views** are two-dimensional views of a 3D object or scene. These are usually front, back, right, left, top, and bottom Orthographic views.

In this section, you learned about the different elements of the 3D Viewport in Blender. So, now that you have an understanding of the basic user interface, let's continue our journey and learn more about the basics of Blender.

In the next section, we will explore how we can interact with items in the 3D Viewport.

Interacting with the 3D world in Blender

In Blender, there are three basic ways to navigate inside the 3D Viewport – that is, to change your viewpoint of the 3D scene.

Navigating around the 3D view

The following three methods change your viewpoint and can be used to navigate inside the 3D Viewport:

- **Zoom**: Use the mouse scroll wheel to zoom in or out from the object. Alternatively, you can use *Ctrl* + click and drag using the middle mouse button to zoom in or out.

- **Rotate**: Click and drag while pressing the middle mouse button. Hold *Alt* + click and drag using the middle mouse button to snap the view to the Orthographic view.

- **Pan**: Press *Shift* + click and drag using the middle mouse button to pan. Panning means moving the viewpoint from side to side.

Now that you understand how to change your viewpoint in the 3D scene, let's explore how we can interact with items in the 3D Viewport.

Selecting and deselecting items

Once you close the splash screen in Blender, the first thing you will see is a view with a 3D cube in the center.

By default, the 3D cube is already selected. We know this because the 3D cube is highlighted with an orange outline. If an item or component is deselected, it will have no orange outline.

> **Note**
>
> When an item is selected in the 3D Viewport, that same item will also be selected and highlighted in the Outliner. You could use the Outliner to select or deselect items. Any selected/deselected items will also be automatically selected/deselected in the 3D Viewport.

There are a few more ways to select or deselect items, objects, or mesh components in Blender:

- **Selecting items directly**: Left-click on an item or component directly to select it. To deselect an item or component, you should left-click anywhere in the 3D Viewport.

- **Selecting using the selection tools**: The select box (located at the top of the toolbar on the left, as shown in *Figure 1.3*) is the default tool that's used for selection. To use this tool, press the left mouse button and drag over the items or components you want to select.

- **Selecting multiple items**: If you want to select multiple items at once, you can add to your selection by holding *Shift* when you click on an item. Clicking on an already selected item while holding *Shift* will deselect that item from the rest of the selected items.

  To select all the items in your scene at once while in the **Layout Workspace** area, press *A* to select all. Pressing *A* twice in quick succession will deselect all the items in your scene.

- **Selecting mesh components**: By default, meshes in the **Layout Workspace** area are in **Object Mode**. To select a mesh component, you need to toggle **Edit Mode** so that it's on by pressing *Tab*.

The following diagram shows how to enter **Vertex**, **Edge**, or **Face Selection** mode by either using the icons shown (these can be found in the **Header** menu bar) or using the relevant numbers on your keyboard, as shown here:

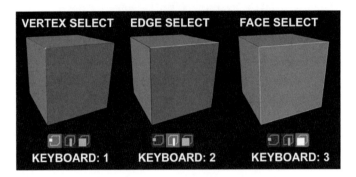

Figure 1.5 – How to select mesh components

To select any of these components for our tutorials, we will use the **Box Select** tool from the toolbar. Once selected, you can make a variety of edits. We will discuss how to do this later.

To toggle back to **Object Mode** (and leave **Edit Mode**), just press *Tab*.

- **Selecting linked mesh components**: There are times when you may want to select linked (connected) parts of your mesh that are a continuous mesh surface. Position your mouse cursor over the part you want to select and use the *Ctrl + L* shortcut. To deselect linked (connected) mesh components under your mouse cursor, press *Shift + L*.

In this section, you learned how to select and deselect various items and/or their components.

In the next section, we will explore the concepts of axes and transform orientations in Blender.

Axes and transform orientations

What are axes? In 3D graphics, an axis is an imaginary line in a 3D space that defines a direction. There are three axes – *X*, *Y*, and *Z* – that correspond to the left/right (*X*), front/back (*Y*), and up/down (*Z*) directional lines, as shown in the following diagram.

Axes have both a positive and a negative direction and are colored to make them easier to visually identify. The *X*-axis is red, the *Y*-axis is green, and the *Z*-axis is blue. In Blender and **Unreal Engine** (UE), the up direction is in the positive direction of the *Z*-axis:

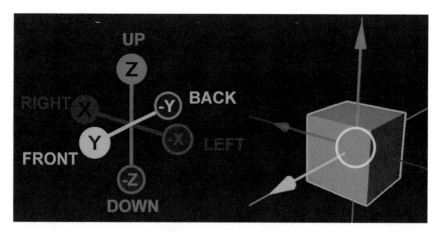

Figure 1.6 – (A) Blender's three axes: X, Y, and Z; (B) The cube serves as a reference to show how the three axes will appear on a 3D cube mesh

Now that you know what axes are, let's take a quick look at some of the other concepts you need to understand:

- **Transform**: Transforming an object/item means to move, rotate, or scale it. When you transform an object, you are automatically using the object's axes and the axes' orientation to transform it.

- **Orientation**: This describes the direction of the axes. The orientation of the axes changes, depending on the type of **Transform Orientation** that you choose. In *Figure 1.7*, you can see that the orientation of the red, green, and blue arrows (called the Object Gizmo) changes from *Figure 1.7*, part A, to *Figure 1.7*, part B.

> **Note**
> We will cover the Object Gizmo in more depth in a later section.

- **Transform Orientation**: This changes the behavior of transformations. In other words, the way that you transform/manipulate an object will change, depending on which **Transform Orientation** you choose to use. In this chapter, we will cover two of these **Transform Orientation** options – the **Global** axis and the **Local** axis.

To change your **transform orientation** using the **Transform Orientations** menu (drop-down menu), go to the **Header** bar and look for the icon with the word **Global** next to it. This menu is shown near the top area of the following screenshot:

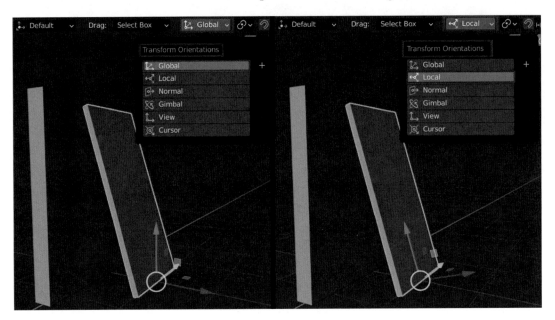

Figure 1.7 – (A) Using Global (Transform Orientations); (B) Using Local (Transform Orientations)

Let's take a quick look at the difference between the **Global** axis and the **Local** axis:

- **Global:** The orientation of the **Global** axis is aligned to the world/scene. In *Figure 1.7*, part *A*, I selected the **Global** axis **Transform Orientation** for the orange-outlined box. The **Global** axis **Transform Orientation** is set as the default for all objects/items in Blender. The orientation of the **Global** axis is fixed and cannot be changed. All items in Blender can share the same **Global** axis since it is the axis of the world/scene.

- **Local:** Each object/item in Blender has a **Local** axis that is unique to the object/item/component. When the object is transformed, the **Local** axis will follow along. In *Figure 1.7*, part *B*, I selected the **Local** axis, and you can see that the axes of the orange-outlined box are following a different orientation than when we used the **Global** axis. **Local** axes are adjustable, unlike the **Global** axes.

You've just learned about the concepts of axes, transforms, orientations, and how to switch between the **Global** axis and the **Local** axis using the **Transform Orientation** menu.

In the next section, we will go over the shortcuts that can be used to transform your objects. We will also explore how to use shortcuts to switch between the **Global** and **Local** axis **Transform Orientation**, to speed up your workflow.

Lastly, we will explore how to use Object Gizmos as another way to transform your objects.

Manipulating objects or their components

We can manipulate objects/components by either using shortcuts or Object Gizmos. We will explore how to use both these options now. Let's start by showing you how to manipulate using shortcuts.

Using shortcuts to manipulate objects/components

Let's look at the shortcuts for moving, rotating, and scaling objects/components:

- **Move**: Use the *G* shortcut to move your selected item up, down, left, or right (perpendicular to your current viewing angle). To constrain the movement to a **Global** axis, hold down the *X*, *Y*, or *Z* key (the axes' name keys) while using this shortcut. If you press the same axis key (*X*, *Y*, or *Z*) a second time, it will toggle a constrain for your movement to a **Local** axis.

- **Rotate**: Use the *R* shortcut to rotate your selected item in either a clockwise or anti-clockwise direction (perpendicular to your current viewing angle). The item will use the object's origin (as shown in *Figure 1.3*) as the pivot point for the rotation. To constrain the rotation to a **Global** axis, hold down the *X*, *Y*, or *Z* key (the axes' name keys) while using this shortcut. If you press the same axis (*X*, *Y*, or *Z*) a second time, it will toggle a constrain for your rotation to a **Local** axis.

- **Scale**: Use the *S* shortcut to scale your selected item up or down. The item will use the object origin (as shown in *Figure 1.3*) as the center for scaling. To constrain the scaling to a **Global** axis, hold down the *X*, *Y*, or *Z* key (the axes' name keys) while using this shortcut. If you press the same axis (*X*, *Y*, or *Z*) a second time, it will toggle a constrain for your scaling to a **Local** axis.

You've just learned how to use shortcuts to transform objects and their components and other items. You've also learned that you can constrain these transforms by using the *X*, *Y*, or *Z* keys (the axes' name keys) and that you can switch between the **Global** and **Local** axis by pressing these keys once for the **Global** axis, and twice for the **Local** axis.

In the next section, we will learn how to use Object Gizmos to transform/manipulate objects, components, or items.

Using Object Gizmos to manipulate objects/components

What are Object Gizmos? They are transform (manipulation) tools that appear in the 3D Viewport and are overlayed on the selected item when you choose one of the three manipulation modes (move, rotate, or scale) from the toolbar, as shown in the following screenshot.

Object Gizmos offer an alternative way (another alternative to using shortcuts) to transform/manipulate objects or their components in the scene. The benefit of using Object Gizmos is that you can constrain the movement or scale to two of the three axes during a transform (constrained to a two-dimensional plane). This isn't possible when using shortcuts:

Figure 1.8 – The toolbar, with descriptions of the icons next to them. I have highlighted the manipulation modes

Let's take a look at how we can activate any of the three Object Gizmos

- **Move:** Use the Space bar + *G* shortcut or click on **MOVE ICON** in the toolbar, as shown in the preceding screenshot, to move with the **Move** Object Gizmo.

- **Rotate:** Use the Space bar + *R* shortcut or click on **ROTATE ICON** in the toolbar, as shown in the preceding screenshot, to rotate with the **Rotate** Object Gizmo.

- **Scale:** Use the Space bar + *S* shortcut or click on **SCALE ICON** in the toolbar, as shown in the preceding screenshot, to scale with the **Scale** Object Gizmo.

Once you have selected a **Transform** mode (move, rotate, or scale), the Object Gizmos will be overlayed over your item, as shown in the following diagram:

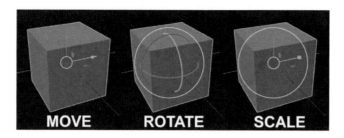

Figure 1.9 – The Object Gizmos overlaid over a 3D cube model for move, rotate, or scale

Inside the Move Object Gizmos, you can see that there are red, green, and blue arrows that point in three directions. These three directions represent the three axes. The red arrow represents the X-axis, the green arrow represents the Y-axis, and the blue arrow represents the Z-axis.

For example, if you want to move the cube in the X-axis direction, you should left-click and hold the red arrow and then move the mouse. This will move the cube in the X-axis direction. Then, you can release the mouse again when you want to stop moving it.

The small white circle in the middle of the Move Object Gizmo is to move the object in any direction that is perpendicular to your current viewing angle.

If you manipulate the small red, green, and blue planes near the center of the gizmo, it will constrain the movement to two of your chosen axes during a transform. For example, if you manipulate the red plane, the model's movement would be constrained to the Y-axis and Z-axis simultaneously. In other words, it would be constrained to a two-dimensional plane.

The Rotate Object Gizmo has red, green, and blue colored curves. The red curve represents the X-axis, the blue curve represents the Y-axis, and the green curve represents the Z-axis. Use these curves to rotate the selected object. The white circle that encompasses the colored curves allows free rotation in any direction that is perpendicular to your current viewing angle.

The Scale Object Gizmo has red, green, and blue lines with square endpoints that will scale the selected object in the X, Y, or Z directions, respectively. There are two white circles on this gizmo, and you can use either of them to scale freely on all three axes simultaneously. If you manipulate the small red, green, and blue planes near the center of the gizmo, it will constrain the scaling to two of your chosen axes during a transform (constrained to a two-dimensional plane).

In this section, you learned how to manipulate items/components using three types of object gizmos that are available.

In the next section, we will explore how to change the way that Blender displays meshes and other items by using different **View Mode** options.

View Mode

View Mode (or **Viewport Shading Mode**) is used to display an item/component in the 3D Viewport.

The different options in **View Mode** are **Solid View Mode**, **X-Ray View Mode**, and **Wireframe Viewport Shading Mode**:

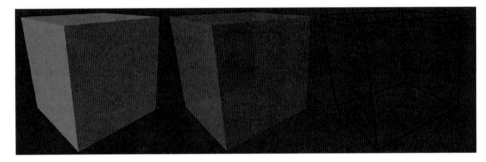

Figure 1.10 – Viewport Shading Modes – (A) Solid View Mode; (B) X-Ray View Mode; (C) Wireframe Viewport Shading Mode

> **Note**
>
> **Solid View Mode** is the default Viewport Shading Mode. In this mode, when you use the select box to select the components of a mesh, it will only select the components that are facing your current view (visible components). When you want to select mesh components on the other side of your current object (not visible in **Solid View Mode**), you need to activate either **X-Ray View Mode** or **Wireframe Viewport Shading Mode**.

The following shortcuts are used to toggle the View Mode options:

- Use *Alt* + *Z* to toggle X-Ray View Mode.
- Use *Shift* + *Z* to toggle Wireframe View Mode.
- Use *Z* to toggle the Shading Pie Menu, which contains the Solid, Wireframe and X-Ray Viewport shading modes.

You have just learned about the different Viewport Shading Modes and why these are essential when creating 3D assets. You need these to switch between Solid View Mode, X-Ray View Mode, and Wireframe Viewport Shading Mode to select mesh components on the non-visible side of your model.

This also concludes the *Introducing Blender* section. You now understand the user interface, Viewport navigation, how to select and deselect, and how to manipulate items with object gizmos.

In the next section, we will explore the 3D modeling tools that we will use in the next four chapters.

Exploring Blender's modeling tools

Let's take a look at the 3D modeling tools that we will use in our practical tutorials during the next four chapters. This section serves as a reference and is not meant to be a practical tutorial.

> **Note**
>
> In the *Further reading* section, you will find a link to download *Additional Content Volume 1 – More Blender Tools and Modifiers.pdf*. This is a document where I have covered a few more modeling tools and modifiers.
>
> When using Blender's modeling tools, either click outside the mesh in the 3D Viewport to apply the current tool, or press *Alt + A* to deselect the active edit; this will also apply the tool.

Extrude region

This tool extrudes a face, edge, or vertex, thus increasing the volume of the mesh and adding new geometry to it.

To use this tool, switch to **Edit Mode** by pressing *Tab*. Then, either select the **Extrude Region** tool icon from the toolbar or use the *E* shortcut to extrude:

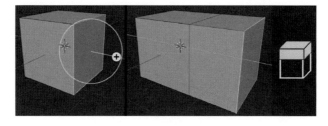

Figure 1.11 – (Left) Using the Extrude tool; (Right) The Extrude Region tool icon

If you're using the icon, left-click and drag the plus sign (or handle) to extrude the selected face/s out in a straight path.

Click and drag on the white circle to extrude in the screen space's direction (perpendicular to your current view).

Bevel

The **Bevel** tool is used to bevel your selected edge, vertex, or face. A bevel is used to smooth out edges and corners, as shown in the following screenshot.

To use this function, select the **Bevel** tool icon and the object's components that you wish to bevel. Then, click and drag on the yellow handle. The minimized Operator panel will appear in the bottom left of your 3D Viewport (below your mesh). It shows additional options when it is expanded (it is minimized by default). If you want to use a shortcut to bevel, press *Ctrl + B*:

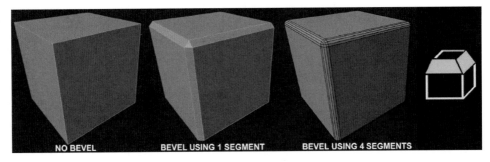

Figure 1.12 – (Left) Applying a bevel with a varying number of segments; (Right) The Bevel tool icon

The default **Bevel** contains one segment, but after completing your first bevel, you can add more segments inside the Operator panel to make the bevel more rounded.

If you've used the shortcut (*Ctrl + B*) to bevel, you can use your mouse's scroll wheel to increase or decrease the number of segments, without needing to use the Operator panel. If you beveled using the **Bevel** tool icon from the toolbar, then you must use the Operator panel to add more segments.

> **Note**
> The Operator panel only appears once. If you left-click outside the Operator panel in the 3D Viewport, the Operator panel will disappear, so make sure you've made all the edits that you want to in the Operator panel before it closes.

Loop Cut

The **Loop Cut** tool is used to add an Edge Loop to your mesh (an encircling loop of edges that connects back to its starting point):

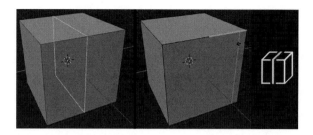

Figure 1.13 – (Left) Using the Loop Cut tool; (Right) The Loop Cut tool icon

To use this tool, select the **Loop Cut** tool icon from the toolbar, or use the *Ctrl + R* shortcut and follow these steps:

1. Click on the area you wish to add the Edge Loop to. A yellow edge will appear indicating that your Edge Loop is still in **Edit Mode**.
2. Click and drag the yellow Edge Loop to an area where you wish to place it.
3. Press *Alt + A* to deselect and apply the Loop Cut.

Let's move on to the next tool now.

Inset Faces

The **Inset Faces** tool is similar to the **Extrude** tool, but all the faces it creates are on the surface of the selected face and do not change the mesh's surface shape. To use this tool, either press *I* on your keyboard or select the **Inset Faces** tool icon from the toolbar:

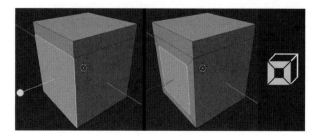

Figure 1.14 – (Left) Using the Inset Face tool; (Right) The Inset Faces tool icon

Merging faces, edges, and vertices

To collapse faces, edges, and vertices down to a single point, use the **Merge** function by pressing the *M* shortcut and choosing **At Center**:

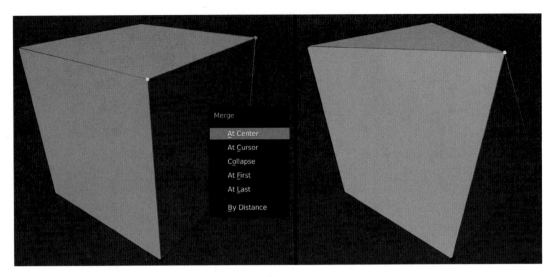

Figure 1.15 – Merging vertices

Proportional Editing

Blender has a great function to modify mesh components with a soft fall-off. If you manipulate a component in your mesh with **Proportional Editing** enabled, the mesh components will move with a soft fall-off:

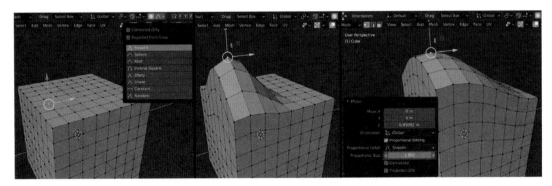

Figure 1.16 – (A) Selecting Proportional Editing; (B) Moving a vertex with Proportional Editing turned on; (C) Adjusting the fall-off

In the preceding screenshot, we can see what happens when we enable **Proportional Editing** in the Header bar. Alternatively, you can press *O* to toggle **Proportional Editing** on/off.

Immediately after your first modification, an Operator panel will appear in the bottom left of your 3D Viewport, with options to adjust the fall-off interactively.

In this section, you learned about different 3D modeling tools and **Proportional Editing** mode, which is used during 3D asset creation in Blender. These tools will come in very handy during our practical tutorial in *Chapter 2, Modeling a Robot Drone Character*.

Blender also has some other useful functions that give you more flexibility and options when you create 3D assets. These are called **modifiers**. We'll look at them in the next section.

Using modifiers in Blender

What is a modifier? Essentially, a **modifier** is like a mode (or function) that acts on a mesh's geometry, while allowing you to keep editing the geometry.

Modifiers are non-destructive, which means that you can toggle the modifier on or off at any time to revert to your original mesh. You can keep on modifying your mesh's geometry with the modeling tools since the modifier effect only acts on the mesh's geometry after you've made your edits.

Modifiers can act on their own or can be placed in a modifier stack in the **Properties** panel. When more than one modifier has been applied to the geometry, they can be re-arranged in any order to create a different result.

For example, if you put a **Bevel Modifier** on a 3D cube, and then you extrude some of the faces on that 3D cube, that **Bevel Modifier** will automatically bevel any new geometry's sharp edges.

In this section, you learned what modifiers are and what they are used for. In the next section, we will explore two of the modifiers that we will use for this book's practical tutorials. We will start with the **Mirror** modifier.

The Mirror modifier

Use the **Mirror** modifier to save time when constructing meshes that are symmetrical or have some symmetric parts on them.

With this modifier, you only need to model half of the symmetrical mesh; Blender will mirror it to the opposite side for you.

To use the **Mirror** modifier, follow these steps:

1. Delete half of the mesh (the side that will be mirrored to).

2. Make sure all the edges and vertices in the mirror center line of your mesh are in a straight line.

3. Now that the mesh has been prepared, let's add the **Mirror** modifier. Find the spanner icon in the **Properties** panel. You will see a collapsed drop-down menu, as shown in the following screenshot:

Figure 1.17 – The Add Modifier drop-down menu from the Properties panel

4. As soon as you click on **Add Modifier** in the drop-down menu, it will open and reveal all the modifiers that are available in Blender. Select **Mirror** from this list, as shown in the following screenshot:

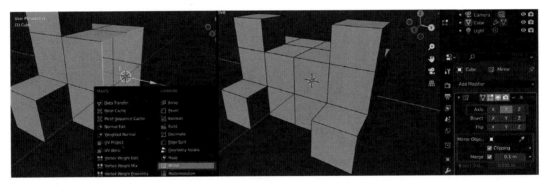

Figure 1.18 – (A) Selecting the Mirror modifier; (B) The settings for the Mirror modifier

5. Choose the correct axis to mirror your mesh. Then, turn on **Clipping and Merge** and change the amount to a number just high enough that it will merge the vertices in the center line.

In this section, you learned how to use the powerful **Mirror** modifier. You can choose to use it to act on your mesh while you do 3D modeling (to see the mirrored result in real time) or you can choose to apply the **Mirror** modifier after you complete a model. The choice is yours.

In the next section, we will explore the Subdivision Surface modifier.

> **Important**
>
> Before you use functions in Blender that add new geometry to your mesh (such as **Remesh**, **Dyntopo**, **Subdivision Surface Modifier**, or **Multiresolution Modifier**), you need to take your computer system's specifications (CPU, video card, and RAM) into account. The denser the geometry of the mesh becomes, the more system resources your computer will need.

Subdivision Surface modifier

This modifier adds a Subdivision Surface function (or mode) over your mesh's geometry to subdivide and smooth out the original shape while keeping the original mesh light in geometry (not having too many faces).

By doing this, you can keep editing the low-resolution mesh while seeing the smoothed shape update with the result. Like all modifiers, it can be toggled on or off:

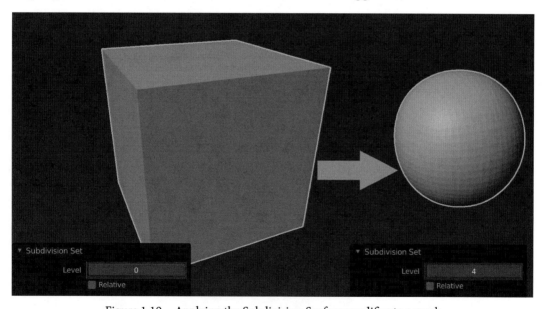

Figure 1.19 – Applying the Subdivision Surface modifier to a mesh

In the preceding screenshot, I used the **Subdivision Surface** modifier on a cube to turn the cube into a smooth-shaped sphere.

If you edit any of the original faces of the cube in **Edit Mode** (it will display as a Wireframe), the result of your mesh's edits will automatically be subdivided and smoothed by the Subdivision Surface modifier.

The keyboard shortcuts for this modifier are *Ctrl* + number (*0 to 5*).

The numbers *0* to *5* correspond to the subdivision level of the mesh in the modifier. You can switch between subdivision levels at any time.

The modifiers' **Subdivision Set** level can be found in the Operator panel, in the bottom left of the 3D Viewport. Using this menu is another way you can change the subdivision level of your mesh. To do so, click on the little arrows.

In this section, you learned how to use the **Subdivision Surface** modifier. With this, we have completed our introduction to the 3D modeling tools that are available in Blender.

In the next section, we will explore the other 3D asset creation method, known as 3D sculpting.

Using Blender's sculpting tools

You already understand the basic concepts of 3D sculpting. But now, let's explore how the 3D sculpting tools work in more detail. This section serves as a reference and is not meant to be practical.

Blender is excellent at 3D sculpting on meshes. When you select the **Sculpture Workspace** tab from the top bar, Blender automatically switches to **Sculpture Mode**, and the user interface changes to reflect this.

For this section, it is recommended that you use a graphics tablet and pressure-sensitive pen (also known as a stylus). That is because it makes sculpting more intuitive since we are primarily dealing with organic forms.

If you don't have a graphics tablet and stylus, don't worry – you can still follow along with the practical sculpture tutorial in *Chapter 3, Let's Sculpt an Alien Plant!*. Everything will still work, even if you are using a mouse instead of a stylus.

A good analogy of the digital sculpture experience would be to say that your stylus (or mouse) acts like a brush that deforms the digital clay (mesh). Depending on the tool you select, the brush affects the mesh differently.

You now know more about the **Sculpture Workspace** tab in Blender and the computer hardware that is used for 3D sculpting.

In the next section, we will explore the brush settings in detail.

> **Note**
>
> The sculpting brushes and tools that we will cover in this chapter are those that we will use in a tutorial in *Chapter 3, Let's Sculpt an Alien Plant!*. In the *Further reading* section, you will find a link to download `Additional Content Volume 1 – More Blender Tools and Modifiers.pdf`. This is a document in which I have covered more sculpting brushes and functions.

Brush settings

Because the basis of 3D sculpting is brush-based, we will first look at the brush settings.

The settings you should look at are **Radius**, **Strength**, and the positive or negative direction, which are indicated by + and - in the **Header** bar menu, respectively.

The default brush shortcuts are as follows:

- *F* for **Radius** (brush size).
- *Shift + F* for **Strength**.
- Hold *Ctrl* to toggle the negative (-) direction (inwards from the surface).
- Hold *Shift* to toggle the **Smoothing Function** while sculpting, as shown in *Figure 1.24*. This function works with the **Draw** brush, **Draw Sharp** brush and **Inflate** brush, which we will cover shortly. The **Smoothing Function** does not work on all brushes.

By default, the brush effect is in the positive (+) direction (pushes away from the surface):

Figure 1.20 – The Brush settings in the Header toolbar

You now have a good understanding of the brush settings that are used for 3D sculpting. In the next section, we will look at a function in Blender that is used to replace your geometry with new geometry.

Remesh

The **Remesh** function allows you to completely replace your existing mesh surface with a new, evenly spread-out mesh surface.

The reason you should use **Remesh** to replace your mesh's geometry is that during 3D sculpting, some of the geometry will become stretched (and give bad results for sculpting later). **Remesh** provides non-stretched geometry. Let's take a look at how we can use this function:

1. Click on **Remesh** in the **Header** bar, as shown in the following screenshot:

2. The density of this new mesh surface is dependent on the **Voxel Size** setting in the **Remesh** drop-down menu (the smaller the number, the denser the mesh). In the following screenshot, I have set **Voxel Size** to 0.1 for illustration purposes. The **Voxel Size** number you should use depends on what your computer system can handle, so adjust this number accordingly.

3. Use the *Ctrl + R* shortcut to apply a remesh to your mesh. Alternatively, you can press the **Remesh** button at the bottom of the **Remesh** drop-down menu (highlighted in the following screenshot). Here, the mesh on the left is the original mesh, while the mesh on the right-hand side has been remeshed using a **Voxel Size** of 0.1:

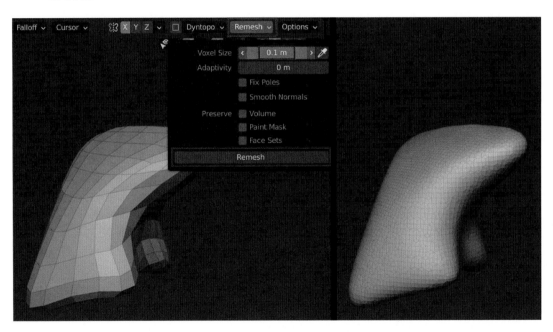

Figure 1.21 – (A) Applying Remesh to your mesh; (B) The result of using Remesh on your mesh

Figure 1.21, part *A*, shows a low geometric-density Sphere mesh that has been deformed. Because the face count is quite low, the mesh looks angular.

The Sphere mesh on the right-hand side has been remeshed with a higher density surface. This replaced the previous mesh surface with a new, evenly spaced-out mesh surface (the model on the right). Higher density surfaces are much better for 3D sculpting.

In this section, you learned how to use **Remesh** to replace stretched geometry or to provide denser geometry for your sculpts.

In the next section, we will explore how to use Blender's sculpting brushes.

Blender's sculpting brushes

In this section, we will go through all the 3D sculpting brushes that will be used in *Chapter 3, Let's Sculpt an Alien Plant!*.

Let's start with the **Draw** brush.

Draw brush

This is the default brush that is selected when you launch the **Sculpture Workspace**. This brush has a soft fall-off. Negative mode (-) pushes in the surface instead of pulling it out, as shown on the right-hand side of the following screenshot. To use this tool, either press *X* on your keyboard or select the **Draw** brush icon from the toolbar:

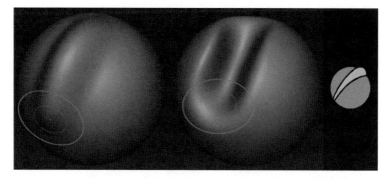

Figure 1.22 – (Left) Using the Draw brush; (Right) The Draw brush icon

Draw Sharp brush

This is used to carve sharp cuts. This brush has a sharp fall-off. Negative mode (-) pulls up a sharp crease on the surface instead of carving it in, as shown on the right-hand side of the following screenshot. To use this tool, either press *Spacebar + 1* on your keyboard or select the **Draw Sharp** icon from the toolbar:

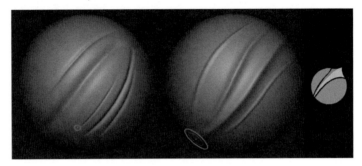

Figure 1.23 – (Left) Using the Draw Sharp brush; (Right) The Draw Sharp icon

The Brush Smoothing function

The **Draw** brush, **Draw Sharp** brush, and **Inflate** brush all have a smoothing function when you hold *Shift* while doing 3D sculpting:

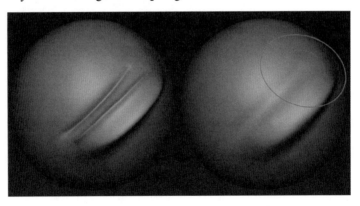

Figure 1.24 – Using the Brush Smoothing function

Inflate brush

This brush inflates the surface or deflates it in negative (-) mode. To use this tool, either press *I* on your keyboard or select the **Inflate** brush icon from the toolbar:

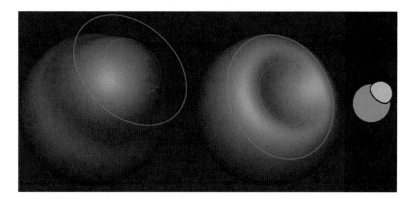

Figure 1.25 – (Left) Using the Inflate brush; (Right) The Inflate brush icon

Mask brush

You can paint a mask on an area on the surface of a mesh to block or limit the effect of manipulation of that area (by other brushes). To use this tool, press *M* on your keyboard or select the **Mask** brush icon from the toolbar. Holding *Ctrl* while painting will remove the masked area under the brush:

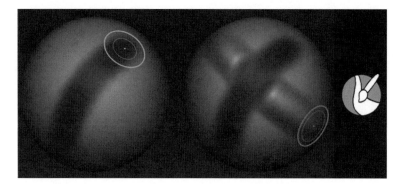

Figure 1.26 – (Left) (A) Painting a mask on a mesh; (B) The masking effect in action, demonstrated by brushing over the masked area with the Draw brush; (Right) The Mask brush icon

Pressing *A* brings up the **Masking** Pie menu, which contains many options for your mask, such as **Sharpen Mask, Grow Mask, Shrink Mask, Decrease Contrast, Invert Mask**, and **Clear Mask**.

In this section, you learned about the different brushes that will be used in the tutorial for *Chapter 3, Let's Sculpt an Alien Plant!*.

However, there are some more sculpting functions in the sculpting toolbar. We will explore these functions in the next section.

Other sculpting tools

There are two sculpting functions that we will use the most during our tutorial.

These aren't brushes; they act more like functions or modes. We'll start by looking at the **Line Project** tool.

Line Project tool

This tool is used to flatten an area of your mesh. To use it, you draw a guideline that tells the tool in which direction it should flatten a part of your mesh.

The shadowed side will be flattened toward the clear side, as shown in the following screenshot:

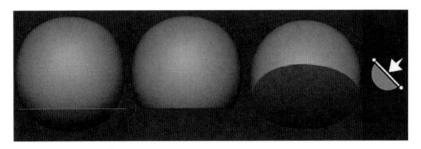

Figure 1.27 – (Left) (A) Drawing the guideline; (B) Observing the flattened mesh area; (C) Another view of the mesh; (Right) The Line Project icon

You now know how to flatten an area of a mesh if you need to. This function will come in very handy in *Chapter 3, Let's Sculpt an Alien Plant!*.

Next, let's look at another versatile sculpting tool – the Mesh Filter tool.

Mesh Filter tool

This tool applies an effect of your choice evenly across your entire mesh at the same time.

In the following screenshot, I used the Mesh Filter tool to apply a **Noise** effect to a mesh's surface. To copy what I have done on my mesh, select the mesh filter icon from the toolbar. In the drop-down menu that opens, select **Random**, as shown in the following screenshot:

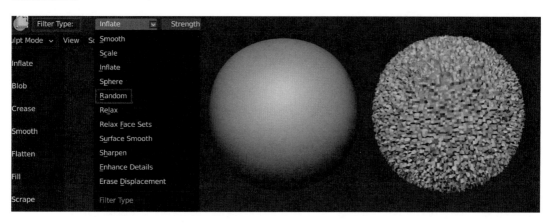

Figure 1.28 – (Left) The mesh filter drop-down menu in the Header bar; (Right) (A) A subdivided sphere on the left; (B) The same sphere with a Noise effect applied

The following screenshot shows the Mesh Filter icon:

Figure 1.29 – The Mesh Filter icon

You have just learned how to use the Mesh Filter tool to quickly add an effect (of your choosing from the drop-down menu) to your mesh.

Congratulations! You've completed all the sections in this chapter. With this knowledge, you can start the next chapter.

Summary

In this chapter, you learned about the basics of 3D modeling and sculpting. You've also gained a thorough understanding of the most used 3D modeling and sculpting tools, as well as some of the modifiers that we will use in the practical exercises.

Additionally, this chapter serves as a handy reference for the hands-on tutorials in *Chapter 2, Modeling a Robot Drone Character, Chapter 3, Let's Sculpt an Alien Plant!,* and *Chapter 4, UV Maps and Texture Baking.*

In the upcoming chapters, we will put some of the knowledge that you've gained about 3D modeling and sculpting to good use. Let's have a brief look at what's ahead.

In the next chapter, you will jump right into a mechanical Robot Drone modeling exercise for your 3D movie. This exercise will provide ample practice for sharpening your 3D modeling skills.

In *Chapter 3, Let's Sculpt an Alien Plant!,* you will sculpt an organic-shaped Alien Plant, which will provide plenty of 3D sculpting practice.

See you in the next chapter!

Further reading

- *Additional Content Volume 1 – More Blender tools and Modifiers.pdf:* `https://github.com/PacktPublishing/Unreal-Engine-5-Character-Creation-Animation-and-Cinematics/tree/main/Chapter01`.

2
Modeling a Robot Drone Character

In the previous chapter, you learned about all the different types of modeling tools in Blender. Now, we will continue our learning journey by jumping right into a practical, step-by-step modeling tutorial in which will create a mechanical Robot Drone character for your sci-fi-themed **3D** movie.

We will start off with the very basics by first setting up Blender's **Units**, then loading reference images (these will act as a guide for your modeling).

Afterward, we will proceed to block out the basic shape of the robot drone's body, before adding details and moving on to the other body parts of the model.

In this chapter, you will gain practical knowledge of 3D modeling by using some of the most powerful modeling functions Blender has to offer, such as creating basic meshes (called **primitives**), using extrusions, bevels, loop cuts, and insets, creating custom polygonal faces, and much more.

In this chapter, we're going to cover the following main topics:

- Preparing Blender's **Units**
- Modeling a Robot Drone character

Upon completion of this chapter, you will have both the knowledge and practical experience to start creating your very own 3D assets that you can use in your 3D movie in Unreal Engine 5.

Technical requirements

You will need the following hardware and software to complete this chapter:

- A computer that can run basic 3D animation software.

- A basic understanding of how to navigate and manipulate meshes in Blender. This was covered in *Chapter 1, An Introduction to Blender's 3D Modeling and Sculpting Tools*.

- You need to install Blender (**open source software**, or **OSS**) from `https://www. blender.org/download/`.

The Blender version used in this chapter is 2.93.4. Even if your version of Blender is newer, the examples should still work without any problems.

The files related to this chapter are placed at `https://github.com/ PacktPublishing/Unreal-Engine-5-Character-Creation-Animation- and-Cinematics/tree/main/Chapter02`

Preparing Blender's Units

Even though we are working with virtual 3D objects in 3D computer graphics, they still need to have an accurate scale (based on the scale/dimensions of real-world objects). This even applies to made-up things, such as the robot drone we will model in this tutorial.

3D software such as Unreal Engine calculates lighting and physics based on the scale of 3D assets. Another reason is that when you are building virtual 3D movie sets, it is a good idea to have a standardized scale for all your 3D assets—this way, it will make it easier to place them because they will have the correct size in relation to other items in the scene.

The scale of the scene and all the assets therein are set by using Blender's **Units** menu. Let's go through the steps to set up **Units**, as follows:

1. In the **Properties** panel, find the Scene Properties icon, as highlighted in the following screenshot. Click on this icon to open up the **Units** drop-down menu. Inside this menu, change **Unit System** to **Metric** and **Unit Scale** to 0.010000, as shown here:

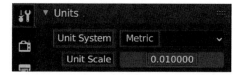

Figure 2.1 – Setting Unit System and Unit Scale

You will notice that the grid in the 3D Viewport now appears larger than before. This setting changes the way Blender navigates and views objects in the 3D view.

2. Press *N* to open the **Properties** region. Open the **View** tab on the right-hand border of the 3D Viewport. Inside this menu, you will see another view listed on top of the menu, as seen in the following screenshot. Change **Clip Start** to 0.01 m and change **End** to 200 m. Delete the **Cube** mesh, lights, and camera from your scene so that your default scene will be empty:

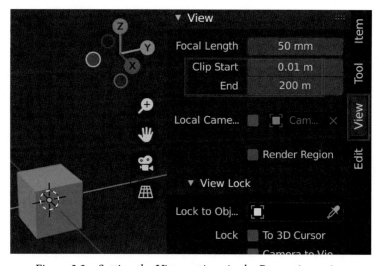

Figure 2.2 – Setting the View settings in the Properties region

3. We need to set Blender's **Startup File** so that Blender automatically uses the correct units, ensuring that every new project will start with the units already set up correctly. In the Topbar, navigate to **File | Defaults | Save Startup File**, as illustrated in the following screenshot. When you click on this, another menu will pop up and ask you to confirm your choice:

Figure 2.3 – Saving your startup file

All done! You've just set up Blender to use the correct units.

> **Note**
>
> At the time of writing, there was a **Unit Scale** issue when exporting models from Blender (version 2.93.4) to Unreal Engine 5. This seems to be a problem in the older versions of Blender only, and in some new export tests I've done, it seems to suggest that from Blender version 3.1.2 onward, **Unit Scale** works if set to 1.0. Regardless, a **Unit Scale** setting of 0.01 will work in any current version of Blender, so it is still the safest to use.

Now, all your new Blender projects will export 3D assets with the correct scale to other 3D software, such as Quixel Mixer and Unreal Engine.

> **Handy Tip**
>
> Use the following shortcuts for Orthographic views—**Front**: numpad *1*; **Back**: *Ctrl* + numpad *1*; **Right**: numpad *3*; **Left**: *Ctrl* + numpad *3*; **Top**: numpad *7*; **Bottom**: numpad *9*.

In the next section, we will load a Blender file that includes reference images for the robot-drone model, and we will get started on the modeling process.

Modeling a Robot Drone character

For those who'd prefer to skip the practical modeling tutorial and go on to *Chapter 3, Let's Sculpt an Alien Plant!*, the completed Robot Drone model (RobotDrone_Blender_File.blend) is available to download from the online repository here: https://github.com/PacktPublishing/Unreal-Engine-5-Character-Creation-Animation-and-Cinematics/tree/main/Chapter02

In *Chapter 1, An Introduction to Blender's 3D Modeling and Sculpting Tools*, you learned the theoretical functionality of Blender's modeling tools. Now, you will put all you have learned about 3D modeling into practice!

Let's start with a step-by-step modeling tutorial to create the mechanical body of the robot drone.

Modeling the shape of the body

To get started, we first need to load the Blender file with the reference images already prepared for us.

Download the following `RobotDrone_Reference.blend` Blender file from the online repository here: `https://github.com/PacktPublishing/Unreal-Engine-5-Character-Creation-Animation-and-Cinematics/tree/main/Chapter02`.

You will do all your modeling for this tutorial in this Blender file since I have prepared this file to contain all the reference images you will need. The reference images are placed on image planes that are in the scene. Let's take a look by following these steps:

1. Open this Blender file and take a look inside the **Outliner** panel. Here, you will find a folder named REF that contains four reference images that have been prepared for the front, side (using the **Right Orthographic** view), top, and the mechanical arm (also using the **Right Orthographic** view). See *Figure 2.4* for four reference images as they appear in your **Outliner** panel when you open the aforementioned Blender file.

2. The front, side, and top reference images only appear in Orthographic views and are set to be invisible in the Perspective view. The mechanical-arm reference image has been hidden. The following tip shows you how to toggle the visibility of the mechanical-arm reference image.

> **Handy Tip**
> To toggle the visibility of an item by using the **Outliner** panel, click on the eye icon. For example, in *Figure 2.4, Part A*, the **ARM REF** item has a closed-eye icon (see the highlighted icon in the screenshot). In *Figure 2.4, Part B*, I clicked on this closed-eye icon to turn it into an open-eye icon, which made the item visible (this toggles the item's visibility: closed eye = hidden/open eye= visible).

Figure 2.4 – Using the eye icon in the Outliner to toggle visibility

> **Handy Tip**
> To toggle the selectability of items by using the **Outliner** panel, click on the arrow icon, as shown in *Figure 2.5*. The first option shows the arrow icon in unselectable mode. The second option shows the arrow icon in selectable mode.

Figure 2.5 – Using the arrow icons in the Outliner panel to toggle selectability

In the next section, we will start blocking out the model—in other words, we'll start modeling with the rough approximate shapes.

Block-out shape

All right—we're now ready to get started on the model. Follow the next steps:

1. Change your view to **Top Orthographic** view by pressing the numpad key 7.

2. Create a **UV Sphere** mesh by pressing *Shift + A* and first selecting **Mesh**, then selecting **UV Sphere** from the menu.

3. Move, rotate, and scale the **UV Sphere** mesh to fit the curvature of the robot drone's outer shell that's shown in the reference image. Switch to different Orthographic views as needed. Match the **UV Sphere** mesh's position to the robot drone in the reference image, as seen in the following screenshot:

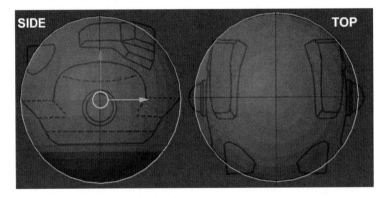

Figure 2.6 – Moving and scaling the Sphere mesh so that it fits the reference image

4. Let's delete the lower half of the **Sphere** mesh. With the **Sphere** mesh selected, press *Alt + Z* to turn on **X-Ray View Mode**. Now, press *Tab* to go into **Edit Mode**. Press *3* for **Face Select Mode** and make sure **Select Box** in the toolbar is used as the active selection tool (see *Figure 1.7* in *Chapter 1, An Introduction to Blender's 3D Modeling and Sculpting Tools*).

5. Press the numpad key *3* to use the **Right Orthographic** view. Select the lower half of the faces on the sphere, then press *Delete* on the keyboard and choose **Faces** from the pop-up menu that opens up. This will delete half of the faces on your sphere. See the following screenshot for how your mesh should look at this stage:

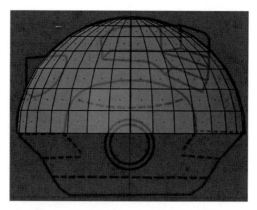

Figure 2.7 – Deleting half of the sphere

6. Select the Edge Loop on the bottom of the sphere (where you've just deleted the faces). Press *2* for **Edge Select** mode, then hold the *Alt* key and left-click on the edge loop that you want to select.

7. With the edge loop still selected, press *F* to fill the selected edges with a new face. You can leave **X-Ray View Mode** by pressing *Alt + Z* again (this toggles it on/off as needed).

8. Press *3* for **Face Select Mode** and then select the newly created face. Press *E* to extrude the selected face downward to the dotted line, as seen in the reference image in the following screenshot:

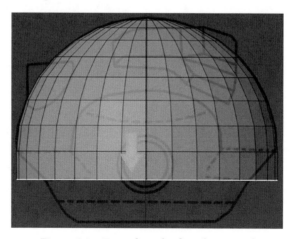

Figure 2.8 – Extruding the face downward

9. Continue the same process for the rest of the extrusions. Use the **Move** and **Scale** modes to modify the extruded faces to fit the silhouette outline of the robot drone, as shown in the following screenshot:

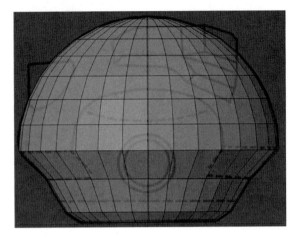

Figure 2.9 – Adding more extrusions and modifying them with Scale and Move manipulation

> **Handy Tip**
>
> Now is a good time to learn how to save your work. Saving your Blender file will allow you to save your progress and then load the file again later. To save, use the *Shift + Ctrl + S* shortcut. The Blender file **View** menu will open up. Select a name and a location to save your file. When you want to load this file later, use the *Ctrl + O* shortcut. The Blender file **View** menu will open up again. Choose the file you want to load. I advise you to save your work often and also to save different increments of your progress during practical tutorials.

10. At the very bottom of the mesh that was created by the face extrusions, select the bottom face. Press the *I* key to inset the face. Open the minimized **Operator** panel and change **Thickness** to 0.025 m.

11. Use the **Loop Cut** tool to add edge loops, indicated by orange lines in the following screenshot:

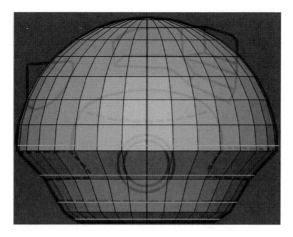

Figure 2.10 – Adding loop cuts

12. Press the numpad key *3* to change the view to the **Right Orthographic** view. Make sure **X-Ray View Mode** is turned off so that we only do the next step on one half of the mesh. We want to change the flow of the edges so that it follows the curvature of the robot drone's shoulder, as indicated by the yellow dots in *Figure 2.11, Part A*.

13. While still in the **Right Orthographic** view, select the vertices shown in *Part A* of the following screenshot (indicated by the yellow dots), then move each vertex individually so that the vertices match the curvature of the line shown in the reference image (see *Part B* of the following screenshot). The red arrows indicate which direction to move the vertices:

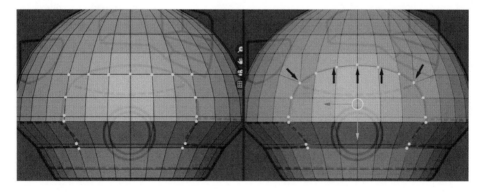

Figure 2.11 – (A) Yellow dots indicate which vertices need to be manipulated; (B) The vertices are moved to follow the curve of the reference image

Well done! You have just completed the block-out stage of the Robot Drone model and you have just learned how to extrude a mesh shape while also following a reference image as a guide. Then, you've learned how to use the **Inset** tool and the **Loop Cut** tool. Finally, you now also know how to manipulate individual vertices on a mesh surface.

In the next section, we will look at how we can fix some common issues we can sometimes encounter while modeling.

Fixing surface imperfections

Change your Viewport back to the **Perspective** view. Observe the mesh's surface around the part you've just modified. If you look closely, you will notice that the surface area of the top left and right sides have slight dents in them (the area is also indicated by downward-pointing arrows in *Figure 2.11, Part B*). Fixing this is really simple, as explained here:

1. Select a vertex in one of the dents. Press the comma key (,) to open the **Transform Orientation Pie** menu. In this menu, select **Normal** (this will enable the **Normal Transform Orientation** option).

2. Click on the **Move** icon in the toolbar to enable the **Move Object Gizmo** option. A **Move Object** gizmo will appear on the vertex you have selected. The (blue) *z* axis is oriented in the **Normal** direction. Click and hold the *z* axis and move it in the direction that is pointing away from the surface, to even out the surface dents (as shown in *Part B* of the following screenshot). Repeat the same process for the vertex in the other dent:

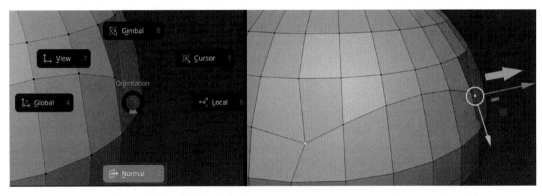

Figure 2.12 – (A) Using the Transform Orientation Pie menu to select the Normal orientation; (B) Using the z axis in the Normal orientation to move the vertex away from the surface

Both of the dented surface areas have now been fixed, and now, the surface looks great! You have just learned how to choose a **Transform** orientation to move, rotate, or scale a mesh component. In this case, you used the **Normal** direction, but there are many other options available.

In the next section, we will create a cavity shape for the shoulder of the robot droid.

Modeling the shoulder cavity

Let's continue detailing the model. We want to create a cavity in the body shape; this is where the shoulder (and arms) will be attached to. Proceed as follows:

1. Start by selecting the internal faces of the proposed cavity, then press *I* to inset these faces by 0.05 m, as shown in the following screenshot:

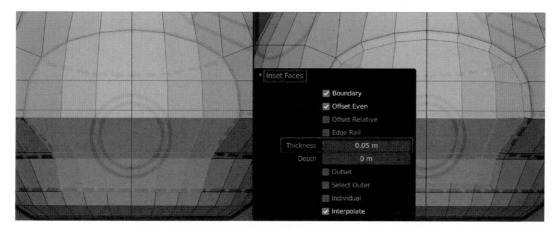

Figure 2.13 – (A) Selecting faces; (B) Using Inset on the faces

2. While keeping the newly inset faces selected, press *1* for **Vertex Selection Mode** to automatically select all the vertices of these inset faces.

3. Now, right-click anywhere in the 3D Viewport and select **Smooth Vertices** from the pop-up menu. This applies a smoothing function on the selected vertices. Repeat this five times. Your mesh should now resemble *Part B* of the following screenshot:

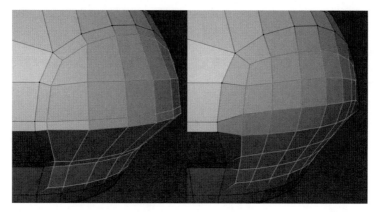

Figure 2.14 – (A) Selecting vertices; (B) Applying smoothing

4. With the vertices still selected, press the **Rotate** icon on the toolbar to activate the **Rotate Object** gizmo. Start to rotate the vertices very slightly on the y axis (the green circular handle on the gizmo) until the **Operator** panel opens up in the bottom left of the 3D Viewport.

5. Open this minimized **Operator** panel and change **Angle** to -12°, as seen in *Part A* of the following screenshot. Now, move the selected vertices -0.025 m on the X axis, as shown in *Part B* of the following screenshot:

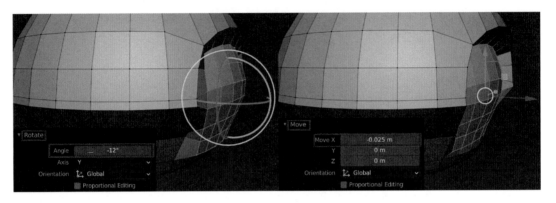

Figure 2.15 – (A) Rotating the selection; (B) Moving the selection

6. Extrude the faces inward by -0.006 m on the z axis, as seen in *Part A* of the following screenshot. Now, add a loop cut at a factor of -0.5 on the inside faces of the cavity, as seen in *Part B* of the following screenshot:

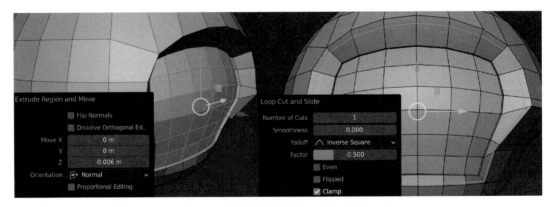

Figure 2.16 – (A) Extruding the faces; (B) Adding a loop cut

The body of the robot drone is starting to look really interesting. In this section, you've learned how to change the shape of a mechanical mesh surface by creating a cavity shape for the drone's shoulder.

In the next section, we will use the **Mirror** modifier to copy our work to the opposite side of the mesh. Then, we will take that model one step further by adding the last bit of polish.

Mirroring and adding polish to the mesh

The block-out for the robot drone's body is almost done, but we need to copy all the hard work that we have done on the body's left side over to the right side. Here's how we can accomplish this:

1. Delete the right-hand side of the mesh by selecting the faces on the right-hand side and then pressing the *Delete* key.

2. Use the **Mirror** modifier (as explained in *Chapter 1, An Introduction to Blender's 3D Modeling and Sculpting Tools*).

3. Apply the modifier by switching to **Object Mode**, then in the **Properties** panel, click on the **Modifier Properties** tab (as shown in *Part A* of the next screenshot). Inside the properties of the modifier, you will see a small downward-pointing arrow.

4. Click on this arrow, and in the drop-down menu that opens, select **Apply**, as shown in *Part B* of the following screenshot). Another quicker way to apply the modifier is by using the *Ctrl + A* shortcut while your mouse pointer is hovering over the modifier:

Figure 2.17 – (A) Selecting the Modifier Properties tab icon; (B) Clicking on the arrow and selecting Apply from the drop-down menu

> **Note**
> This process of applying a modifier can be used for all modifiers in Blender.

Now that the mesh has the cavity feature on both sides, it's time to move on to the polishing stage.

First, we will subdivide the model, then we will choose a selection of edges to bevel.

The reason we will do it this way is that the shape of the model is generally quite smooth already, even with only one additional level of subdivision, but some edges are still too sharp-looking and would need to be rounded off (beveled) manually. To do all this, just follow these simple steps:

1. Select the mesh. While in **Object Mode**, press *Ctrl + 1* to add a **Subdivision Surface** modifier with one level of subdivision to the mesh. Apply the modifier as you did for the **Mirror** modifier.

2. Select the edges that run around the middle of the body shape, but don't select the edges inside the cavities, as shown in *Part A* of the next screenshot. You can do this by holding *Ctrl* while selecting the beginning and then selecting the endpoint for the edges you want to select. This way, it will automatically select the edges between your beginning and end points.

3. Press *Ctrl + B* to bevel these edges and select a **Width** value of 0.0223 m and use two segments, as shown in *Part B* of the following screenshot:

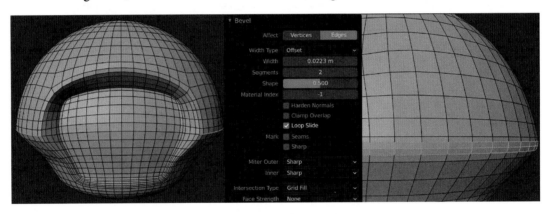

Figure 2.18 – (A) Selecting edges; (B) Adding a bevel

4. Press *Shift + Alt* and left-click to select the outer two edge loops of the cavity, as shown in *Figure 2.19, Part A*.

   Apply a bevel with a **Width** value of 0.0087 m and set the **Segment** value to 2, as shown in *Figure 2.19, Part B*.

> **Note**
> Holding *Shift* while selecting edge loops will add to your current selection.

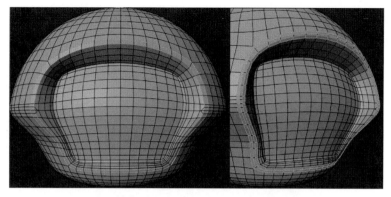

Figure 2.19 – (A) Selecting edge loops; (B) Adding a bevel

You have completed the body shape for the robot drone and have learned how to mirror your work from one side of a mesh to another side. You have also learned how to smooth out the shape of the mesh by using the **Subdivision Surface** modifier and by using the **Bevel** function on certain edges.

In the next section, we will create some eyes for the robot drone.

Creating eyes

Let's model some robot eyes for our robot drone, as follows:

1. Start by adding a **Cylinder** mesh by using the same method that you used when you added the **UV Sphere** mesh.

2. Move, rotate, and scale the **Cylinder** mesh to fit it over the reference image, as shown in the following screenshot:

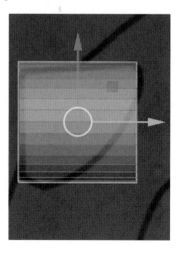

Figure 2.20 – Fitting the Cylinder mesh over the reference image

3. Select the inside vertices of the **Cylinder** mesh and scale and move them to create the shape shown in the following screenshot:

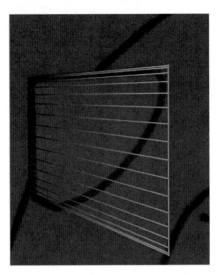

Figure 2.21 – Scaling the inside vertices

The result should look like the selected model in the following screenshot:

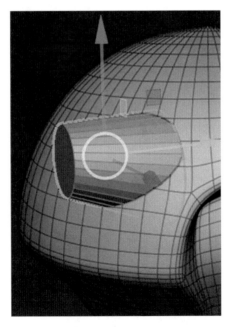

Figure 2.22 – The result

4. Select the outside edge loop of the **Cylinder** mesh and then bevel it. Select the inside face and then inset the face slightly, as shown in the following screenshot:

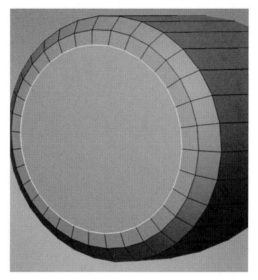

Figure 2.23 – Beveling the outer edge and insetting the inside face

5. Extrude the face inward and scale it down slightly, as shown in the following screenshot:

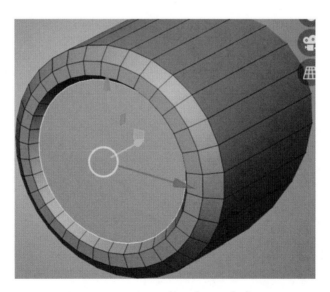

Figure 2.24 – Extruding the inside face

6. Continue to use the **Inset** tool to make eight more incremental insets. Make one last inset and select its vertices. Press *M* to open the **Merge** menu, then select **At Center** to merge them into one vertex. The end result can be seen in the following screenshot:

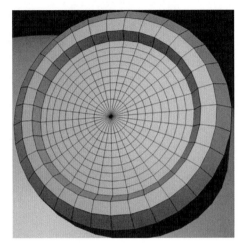

Figure 2.25 – Continuing to add eight more insets and merging the ninth inset so that it creates a vertex in the center

7. We want to turn the flat inner faces of the robot drone's eye into a bulging shape so that it looks like a lens. To do this, select the center vertex. Press *O* to turn on **Proportional Editing**, or you can click on the **Proportional Editing** icon in the **Header** bar. Move the vertex outward by -0.01 m in the *Y* axis. In the **Operator** panel, select **Sphere** as the shape for the **Proportional Falloff** setting, and set **Proportional Size** to 3.35, as shown in the following screenshot:

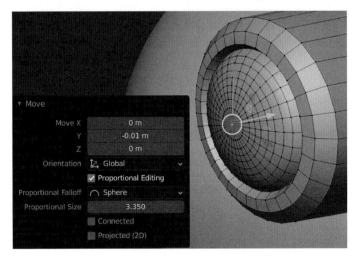

Figure 2.26 – Using Proportional Editing for the lens shape

8. For the last polishing step, bevel the sharp outer edges of the robot drone's eye, as shown in the following screenshot:

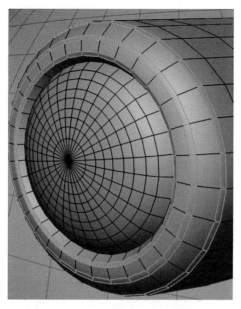

Figure 2.27 – Adding bevels

9. Now, you need to mirror the eye. With the robot drone's eye mesh selected, switch to **Object Mode**. Press *Ctrl + A* to bring up the **Apply Object Transformation** menu, and choose **All Transforms** to set the mesh's origin to the center of the scene. This is because Blender can use the point of origin as the center of the **Mirror** function.

10. Use the **Mirror** modifier to mirror the left-hand-side robot eye to the right-hand side (the **Mirror** modifier was covered in *Chapter 1, An Introduction to Blender's 3D Modeling and Sculpting Tools*).

You have just completed the robot drone's mechanical-robot-eye model. In this exercise, you've learned to create a bulging shape with the **Proportional Editing** tool and practiced how to refine the shape by adding more bevels and insets.

In the next section, we will create the robot drone's shoulders and shoulder ball joint. This is where the arms will be attached to.

Adding a shoulder and a ball joint

Now, we will quickly model the shoulder (made from a **Cylinder** mesh) and add a **Sphere** mesh that will be the ball joint. A ball joint is a mechanical joint in engineering that can rotate in any direction. Follow these next steps:

1. Create another **Cylinder** mesh. Move, rotate, and scale the cylinder into the position shown in the following screenshot. This cylinder is the robot drone's shoulder:

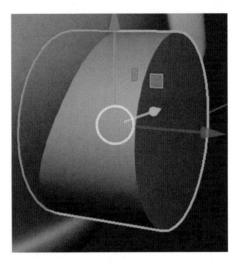

Figure 2.28 – Placing the cylinder that forms the robot drone's shoulder mesh

2. Select the outer face of the shoulder and inset it by 0.0106 m, as shown in the following screenshot:

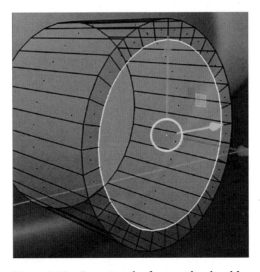

Figure 2.29 – Insetting the face on the shoulder

3. With the face on the shoulder still selected, extrude it inward by `0.06` m on the *x* axis, as shown in the following screenshot:

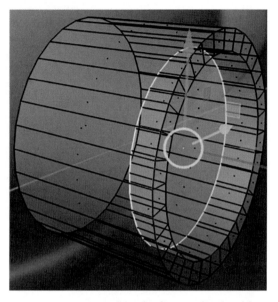

Figure 2.30 – Extruding the face on the shoulder

4. Now, select the outer edge loop of the shoulder and bevel the width by `0.0067` m, as shown in the following screenshot. The shoulder disk is now complete:

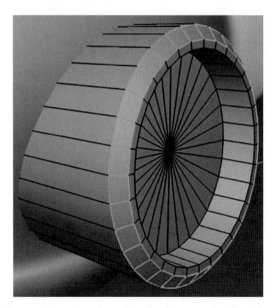

Figure 2.31 – Beveling the edge loop on the shoulder

5. Now, we will create a ball joint for the end of the shoulder. Create a **UV Sphere** mesh. This sphere will be the ball joint. Position the sphere halfway inside the shoulder, as shown in *Part A* of the following screenshot. Then, delete the faces that are hidden inside the cylinder, as shown in *Part C* of the following screenshot:

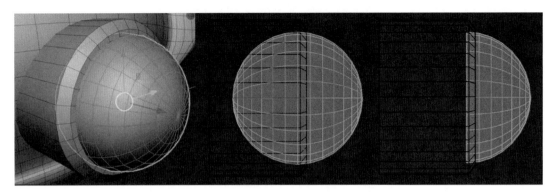

Figure 2.32 – (A) Adding the ball joint (sphere) to the shoulder disk mesh; (B) Wireframe side view of the same ball joint; (C) Wireframe side view of the ball joint with deleted faces

6. Mirror both the shoulder mesh and the ball-joint mesh to the right-hand side of the model by using the method that was explained in the *Creating eyes* section. The result should look like this:

Figure 2.33 – Mirroring the ball joint and the shoulder mesh

You have just completed the shoulder and ball-joint part of the model. In this section, you have learned to use extreme precision to position one mesh very accurately into another mesh. In the next section, we will explore how and why we can add some **KitBash** meshes to the model.

Attaching a KitBash mesh

So, what does **KitBash** mean? **KitBashing** (also called **model bashing**) is a practice whereby a model (or part of a model) is created from existing model parts to save production time.

This way, artists can rapidly add details to their model by using a library of pre-made smaller model parts.

As a 3D artist and 3D movie maker, you should organize and save bits of the models you create. This way, you can build up your own KitBash library.

I have prepared a `Kitbash_models.blend` KitBash model library file, which you can download from the online repository here: `https://github.com/PacktPublishing/Unreal-Engine-5-Character-Creation-Animation-and-Cinematics/tree/main/Chapter02`.

This file contains five KitBash model parts that you can use for your models. In the following screenshot, I am showing two views of this KitBash model library:

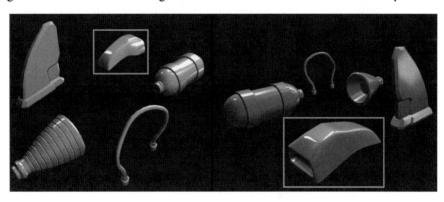

Figure 2.34 – KitBash model library

Load the `Kitbash_models.blend` file into Blender. Place any one of these KitBash models from the file onto the body of the robot drone. For the purpose of this tutorial, I have used the `Booster_V1` model from the KitBash model library (`Kit-Bash_models.blend`). This is the model that is highlighted by yellow rectangles in *Figure 2.34*.

It is advisable to place only one KitBash model on your robot drone; otherwise, you will have more models to UV unwrap and texture in the tutorial presented in *Chapter 4, UV Maps and Texture Baking*.

I loaded the `Booster_V1` model and positioned it in the place that was indicated in the reference image, and then I used the **Mirror** modifier to mirror it to the other side. The result of the mirrored `Booster_V1` model can be seen in the screenshot shown next.

Feel free to be creative and come up with some of your own interesting KitBash placements, using this representation as a starting point:

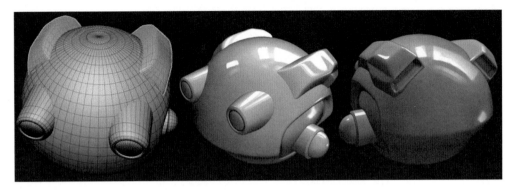

Figure 2.35 – The Booster_V1 model placed on the body and mirrored to the other side

In this section, you've learned how to save lots of production time by using a library of pre-made 3D assets to quickly add visual details to your models.

In the next section, we will start to model the mechanical arms of the robot drone.

> **Handy Tip**
>
> While going through the tutorials in this book, you will find it helpful to take a break every now and then, just to practice some of the new tools and techniques that you've just learned about. This is a good test for you, to see what you've learned so far and— more importantly—which information you've retained so far. Afterward, continue from where you left off with your chapter's project.

Modeling the arm

Let's start with the last part of the robot drone that we need to model—the arms. Proceed as follows:

1. Unhide the reference image for the mechanical arm in the **Outliner** panel. You will now see the mechanical-arm reference image is visible in the **Right Orthographic** view.

2. Create a **Cylinder** mesh. Move, rotate, and scale the **Cylinder** mesh into the position of the shoulder's black outline, as seen in the reference image indicated by the orange outline in the following screenshot. This cylinder will be the robot drone's shoulder disk:

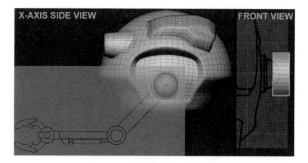

Figure 2.36 – Revealing the reference image and placing the cylinder for the shoulder disk

3. Select the outer edge loop of the shoulder disk and bevel it with one segment so that your shoulder disk looks similar to the model shown in the following screenshot:

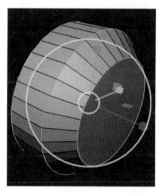

Figure 2.37 – Big bevel for the outer edge of the shoulder disk

4. Select the two outer edge loops on the shoulder disk and then bevel them by a small amount, using two segments as shown here:

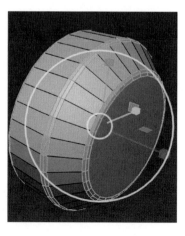

Figure 2.38 – Small bevels for the circular edge loops of the shoulder disk

5. Duplicate the shoulder disk. Move and scale it into the position of the elbow disk's black outline, as shown in *Figure 2.36*. This duplicated mesh will be the robot drone's elbow disk.

6. Extrude and bevel the right side of the elbow disk, as shown in the following screenshot:

Figure 2.39 – Extruding and beveling the elbow disk

7. Duplicate the elbow disk. Move and scale it into the position of the claw disk's black outline that is shown in the reference image. This duplicated mesh will be the robot drone's claw disk, as shown in *Figure 2.40*.

8. Create another small **Cylinder** mesh. Position this mesh to fit in the center of the claw disk.

9. Now, we will create and place rectangular-shaped meshes for the upper and lower arm. Create a **Cube** mesh. Move, rotate, and scale this mesh into the position of the upper arm's black outline that's shown on the mechanical-arm reference image.

10. Bevel the edges of this rectangular-shaped mesh, which used to be a **Cube** mesh before you scaled it.

11. Create another **Cube** mesh. Move, rotate, and scale this new **Cube** mesh into the position of the lower arm's black outline, as in *Figure 2.40*.

12. Bevel the edges of the rectangular-shaped meshes, as shown in the following screenshot:

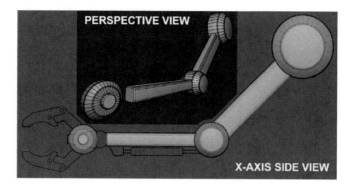

Figure 2.40 – Placement of all disks and rectangular shapes; note there is a small cylinder inside the wrist's disk

You've just created all required disk shapes and rectangular shapes for the shoulder, upper arm, elbow, lower arm, claw cylinder, and the small claw cylinder that is inside the claw cylinder, as shown in *Figure 2.40*.

You've learned how to accurately place geometry to match the reference image and add polish to these elements by beveling them.

In the next section, we will go on to model some of the smaller elements that can be seen in the reference image—the forearm piston, wrist ball joint, and claw disk holder.

Piston and wrist detailing

We now start on the mechanical arm's smaller details, as follows:

1. Create a **Cube** mesh. Position this mesh in the center of the wrist disk. This will be the claw disk-holder mechanism shown in *Figure 2.41, Tag A*.

2. Extrude the very front face of this **Cube** mesh and scale it down slightly. Then, modify the form of this **Cube** mesh to create the shape shown in *Figure 2.41, Tag A*.

3. Bevel the claw disk-holder mechanism.

4. Create a **UV Sphere** mesh. Move this mesh into the position shown in the reference image. This **UV Sphere** mesh is the wrist ball joint of the robot droid, as shown in *Figure 2.41, Tag B*.

5. Create another **Cube** mesh. Position this mesh at the bottom of the lower arm. This **Cube** mesh will be the forearm piston connector, as can be seen in *Figure 2.41, Tag C*.

6. Bevel the forearm piston connector. For this task, you would first need one big bevel applied to the outer edge near the piston. Then, bevel all the edges with a smaller-sized bevel.

7. Create two **Cylinder** meshes. One of the **Cylinder** meshes should be half as long as the other one, but it should be double in diameter.

8. Position these two **Cylinder** meshes so that the thinner cylinder is inside the center point of the wider cylinder to form the forearm piston, as shown in *Figure 2.41, Tag D*.

9. Place this forearm piston (the two **Cylinder** meshes) into the position of the piston's black outline.

10. Bevel the outer edge loops of the wider **Cylinder** mesh that is part of the forearm piston, as shown in *Figure 2.41, Tag D*.

Your model parts should now look like the models shown here:

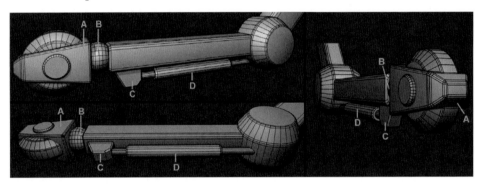

Figure 2.41 – Different views of the lower arm showing the four model parts (tags A-D)

You've just learned how to model a variety of mesh shapes and place them into accurate positions, according to what is shown in the preceding screenshot.

In the next section, we will start with the robot droid's claws.

Creating claws

If you look at the reference image, the robot droid's claws might look really complex, but they are actually really simple to model. Let me show you this method in the following steps. We will start on the far-left side of the upper claw:

1. Press the numpad key *3* to switch to the **Right Orthographic** view. Create a very small **Cube** mesh near the claw section of the reference image.

2. Switch to **Edit Mode** and **Vertex Selection Mode**. Press *A* to select all the vertices of the cube, then press *M* to merge and choose **At Center** from the pop-up menu, as illustrated in the following screenshot:

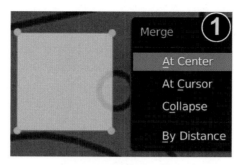

Figure 2.42 – Positioning the cube and selecting At Center merge

3. You will see that the **Cube** mesh has now been replaced by a single vertex, as shown in the following screenshot:

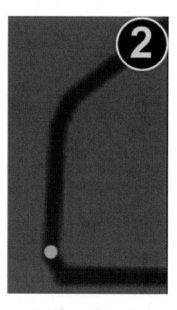

Figure 2.43 – The result is a single vertex

4. Press *G* for **Move Mode**. Then, move the vertex to anywhere on the outline of the claw that is shown in the reference image.

5. While still in **Move Mode,** press *E* to extrude the vertex. Move the mouse pointer to another spot close by on the outline of the claw. You will see that an edge is being drawn as you move your mouse pointer. Left-click to place a new vertex, as shown in the following screenshot:

Figure 2.44 – Extruding the vertex to create edges that follow the outline of the claw

6. Repeat the process to create more edges until you've traced the complete outline of the upper claw in the mechanical-arm reference image. Once you have traced all around the outline of the upper claw, place your last vertex close to the starting point.

7. Now, select two vertices that are close to each other and press *M* to merge them, as shown in the following screenshot:

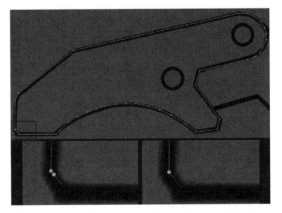

Figure 2.45 – Completing the outline trace and merging vertices that are close together

You've just learned how to draw a custom shape made out of edges, by using **Extrude Function** on a single vertex. In the next section, we will take this shape and create the front part of the claw from it.

Extruding the custom shape

You now have an outline made up of edges and vertices, but it doesn't have any faces yet. Let's learn how to add a face to the selected edges, then take it further by converting this new face into a full 3D shape in the following steps:

1. To create a face for the edges you made earlier, you just need to select all the edges and then press *F* to fill the edges with a face, as shown in the following screenshot:

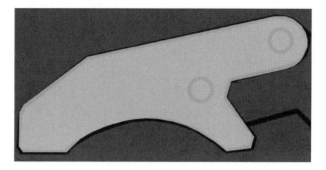

Figure 2.46 – Filling the edges to create a face

You have now created a custom face. This face is the shape of the front part of the upper claw. Let's give this face some thickness.

2. Select the face. Press *E* to extrude the face in the *x*-axis direction by 0.0125 m. Your custom outline made of edges will now have a solid 3D form, as shown in *Figure 2.47*.

3. Add small disks to areas where bolts are indicated in the reference image. Do this on both the left-hand and right-hand sides of the front part of the upper claw, as shown in *Figure 2.47*.

4. Repeat the same process for the inner part of the upper claw. To add some variation to the mesh shapes, you should make this part a bit thinner than the front part of the upper claw. The result should look like this:

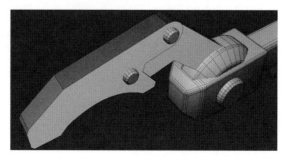

Figure 2.47 – Extruded faces for the upper claw

5. Now, we will bevel all the sharp angles of the claw to make it look like the other model parts. Fortunately, there is an easy way to select all sharp angles on your selected mesh. Switch to **Edit Mode** with edge selection activated. In the **Header** bar, navigate to **Select | Select sharp edges**.

6. All the sharp edges are now selected on your mesh. Now, bevel these edges slightly to complete this part of the model. Use the following screenshot as a visual guide for your bevel width:

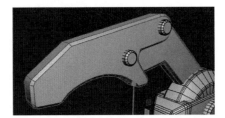

Figure 2.48 – Beveling sharp edges

7. With all these parts completed, switch to **Object Mode** and select all the different model parts of the upper claw, and press *Ctrl + J* to join them all together so that they become one mesh.

8. Keep the claw mesh selected. In the Header bar, navigate to **Object | Set Origin | Origin to Geometry** to set the origin of the mesh to the center of the geometry.

9. Use the *Shift + D* shortcut to duplicate the upper claw. Press *N* to bring up the **Properties region** menu. In the **Rotation** section of the **Properties region** menu, set the *y* axis to 180 to rotate the claw mesh, as seen in the following screenshot:

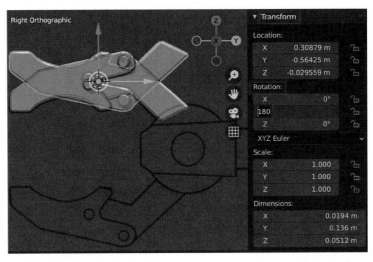

Figure 2.49 – Using the Properties region to type in the rotation of the duplicated claw

10. Manually move the duplicated claw mesh downward in the (blue) *z* axis so that it fits in the position of the outline of the lower claw shown on the mechanical-arm reference image, as illustrated here:

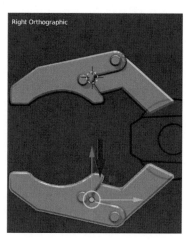

Figure 2.50 – Moving the duplicated claw to match the claw's outline in the reference image

With both the upper and the lower claw done, your claw model should now resemble the model shown in *Figure 2.50*.

11. Mirror each mesh part in the arm and shoulder to the right side (using the same method explained in the *Creating eyes* section). Your completed model should now look like the one shown in *Figure 2.51*.

12. Save the robot drone model in the Blender file format (`.blend`).

Congratulations! You have successfully completed the robot drone practical tutorial.

In this section, you have learned how to take a shape made up of edges and vertices and turn that into a full 3D mesh that you then polished off by adding smaller details such as bolts and bevels.

You've also learned to quickly select the sharp edges of your mesh so that you can bevel them. Take a look at the completed Robot Drone model here:

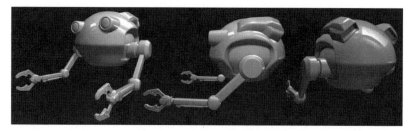

Figure 2.51 – The completed Robot Drone model from different viewing angles

Summary

You have now successfully completed your first practical modeling tutorial using Blender! Modeling tools work great for models such as robot drones because these tools are ideally suited for mechanical types of models, although there are no limitations to the kinds of 3D assets you can create by using these tools and methods.

One of the amazing skills you have now learned is the ability to follow reference images to guide your 3D modeling so that the final result is very accurate.

Furthermore, you've acquired other skills such as manipulating meshes in the 3D Viewport, extruding faces and vertices, beveling edges, and subdividing meshes to smooth out the block-out shape, and you've also learned how to build custom-shaped faces that you can then turn into 3D meshes.

You now have both the practical experience and theoretical knowledge from *Chapter 1, An Introduction to Blender's 3D Modeling and Sculpting Tools* to create your very own 3D assets for your 3D movie.

For creating organic types of models, there is a more efficient way to create them using a very different workflow...this method is known as **3D sculpture**.

In the next chapter, we will continue our journey by learning about 3D sculpture using Blender to create some amazing organic types of models.

You will be guided in a step-by-step practical 3D sculpting tutorial to create an Alien Plant 3D asset for your sci-fi-themed 3D movie.

3

Let's Sculpt an Alien Plant!

In *Chapter 2, Modeling a Robot Drone Character*, you learned how to utilize Blender's excellent modeling tools to create a Robot Drone character.

Modeling tools work great for mechanically shaped models (such as our Robot Drone), but when you want to create a model that has an organic form, 3D sculpting is the best method. That's because it is much more intuitive to use 3D sculpting tools to shape organic surfaces.

This practical tutorial will teach you how to create an organic model for your 3D movie set. So, let's learn how to do this by sculpting an Alien Plant model! These plants would look amazing in your *Alien Planet Surface* 3D movie set.

In this chapter, you will learn how to sculpt a mesh in Blender, as if it were a piece of virtual clay.

You'll be guided through the complete 3D sculpting process, which will start with setting up the reference image and the block-out stage of your model.

Next, you will learn how to combine all these parts into a single high-resolution mesh that you will sculpt on. Once your sculpted model is complete, you will learn how to convert it into a lower-resolution mesh for use in **Unreal Engine 5 (UE5)**.

In this chapter, we're going to cover the following main topics:

- Blocking out your model
- Fixing problem areas
- Adding secondary and tertiary forms
- Generating the low-resolution mesh

The techniques you will learn in this chapter are essential as a base for 3D sculpting in Blender. After completing this practical tutorial, you will have a solid understanding of the 3D sculpting workflow and its tools. You will be able to create 3D sculptures for use in **UE**.

Now that you know what we are going to cover in this practical tutorial, let's start by loading the tutorial file and creating the block-out shape of the model.

Technical requirements

You will need the following hardware and software to complete this chapter:

- A computer that can run basic 3D animation software
- Blender, which can be installed from `https://www.blender.org/download/`

  The Blender version that's used in this chapter is version 2.93.5. Even if your version of Blender is newer, the examples should still work without any problems.

- Instant meshes, which can be downloaded and installed from `https://github.com/wjakob/instant-meshes`

  Scroll down to the bottom and you will find a section called **Pre-compiled binaries**. Download the `.zip` file according to the operating system that you are using.

You can download the completed Alien Plant model, called `AlienPlant_LP.blend`, from this book's GitHub repository: `https://github.com/PacktPublishing/Unreal-Engine-5-Character-Creation-Animation-and-Cinematics/tree/main/Chapter03`.

Loading the file containing the reference image

First, let's take a quick look at the reference image that I've provided. It is a sketch of the Alien Plant that you will create for your Alien-Planet 3D movie set:

1. Download the `Alien_Plant_REF.blend` file from this book's GitHub repository: `https://github.com/PacktPublishing/Unreal-Engine-5-Character-Creation-Animation-and-Cinematics/tree/main/Chapter03`.

2. Upon opening this Blender file, you will see the reference image of the Alien Plant inside the 3D Viewport. You will also find the `AlienPlant_REF` item, listed in the Outliner panel. There is also a Cube mesh that has been prepared for this practical tutorial. The following figure shows what the reference image of the Alien Plant looks like:

Figure 3.1 – The reference image of the Alien Plant

Handy Tip

There is an easy way to identify the icons on the toolbar. Just hover your cursor over the right-hand side of the toolbar's edge until the two-directional arrow icon appears. Then, click and drag the toolbar to the right-hand side to expand it. Once the icons have rearranged themselves, drag the toolbar to the right once more to reveal the name of each icon on the toolbar.

In the next section, you will learn how to block out a model.

Blocking out your model

Blocking out means creating a mesh of the "rough approximate shape" of the model you want to sculpt. It can be created from low-resolution (low geometric density) meshes to create a base for the 3D sculpture.

In the next section, you will use the **Cube** mesh that has been prepared for you and extrude it into the shape of the Alien Plant.

Extruding and duplicating mesh parts

Now that you have loaded the Blender file containing the **Cube** mesh and reference image, we need to convert this **Cube** mesh into the rough approximated shape of the Alien Plant.

The easiest way to do this is by using the **Extrude** function on the **Cube** mesh's faces. We will do this in small incremental steps so that we can modify the position, rotation, and scale of the newly created geometry each time that we perform an extrusion. Let's get started:

1. Select the very top face of your **Cube** mesh.

2. Press *E* to extrude this face upward. Only extrude it by a small amount so that it matches the outlines of the Alien Plant's trunk; this is shown behind the **Cube** mesh in *Figure 3.2*, part *A*.

3. Adjust the rotation and scale of the newly extruded faces. Continue these extrusions and adjustments to the top of the plant, as shown in *Figure 3.2*, part *A*.

4. Refine the shape of the mesh by adding more Edge Loops by using the *Ctrl + R* shortcut. Then move, rotate, and scale the Edge Loops so that they match the shape of the plant's trunk and top, as shown in *Figure 3.2*, part *B*:

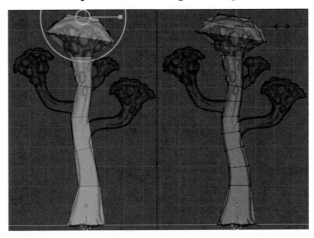

Figure 3.2 – (A) Extruding the Cube mesh's faces upwards to create the basic trunk shape; (B) Refining the form by adding more Edge Loops and adjusting them

5. Once your model looks approximately similar to the model in *Figure 3.2*, part *B*, it is time to move on to the next stage.

6. Press *Alt + Z* to toggle on **X-Ray Viewport Shading Mode** (toggle it on or off as needed). **X-Ray Viewport Shading Mode** allows you to select the mesh's components right through the mesh (on the opposite side of your current view).

7. Select the faces of the Alien Plant's head (the top) plus approximately six of the trunk's segments below the head.

8. Duplicate these faces by pressing *Shift + D*. Then move, rotate, scale, and edit the vertices of the duplicated mesh to fit it to the shape of the big branch that is shown on the bottom right-hand side of the reference image. This step is shown in *Figure 3.3*, parts *A* and *B*.

9. Repeat this process for the remaining two branches by duplicating this branch twice and manipulating it so that it fits the other two branches. The result of the model with the duplicated branches should look like the model shown in *Figure 3.3*, part *C*:

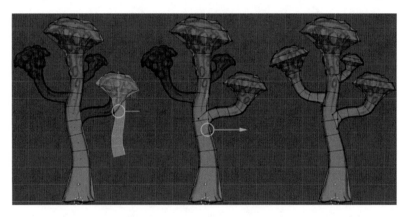

Figure 3.3 – (A) Duplicating the top part of the mesh; (B) and (C) Modifying the shape of the duplicated branches so that they fit the shape of the other branches

Now that we have the main shapes of our Alien Plant blocked out, we can see that it looks a bit too *mechanical* from the top and front Orthographic views since all the branches and the direction of the trunk's curvature are only in the *Y*-axis direction. See the *BEFORE* view in *Figure 3.4*.

10. Let's add some organic variation to the shape of the trunk. Select some of the mesh components. Press *O* to enable **Proportional Editing**, then rotate and move these selected mesh components into a slightly bent shape so that the trunk is bent in both the *X*-axis and *Y*-axis directions. The result should look like the *AFTER* view in *Figure 3.4*.

> **Note**
>
> To select all the linked components on a mesh, select one component on it and press *Ctrl + L* to use the **Select Link** function.

Now, you should have a mesh that resembles a more organic-shaped Alien Plant, as shown in the *AFTER* view in the following diagram:

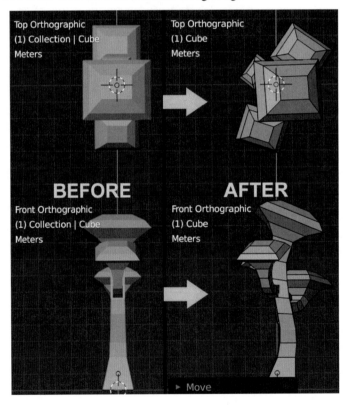

Figure 3.4 – Adjusting the shape of the trunk and rotating the branches

11. There is one last thing we need to do before our block-out mesh is completed. We need to add two Edge Loops very close to the bottom of the base of the trunk, as shown in the following screenshot:

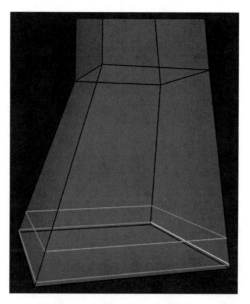

Figure 3.5 – Adding two Edge Loops to the base of the trunk

The block-out stage of the model is now complete and we're ready for the next stage! In this section, you learned how to create a block-out of a model and how to follow the shape of the reference image. You can use the same technique for any of your future 3D work.

In the next section, you will learn how to add higher geometric density to this mesh.

> **Important**
>
> Before you use functions in Blender that add new geometry to your mesh (such as **Remesh, Dyntopo, Subdivision Surface Modifier,** or **Multiresolution Modifier**), you need to take your computer system's specifications (CPU, video card, and RAM) into account. The denser the geometry of the mesh becomes, the more system resources your computer will need.

Subdividing the mesh

All the shapes of the Alien Plant have now been blocked out.

Since this mesh is still very *blocky* looking (because of its low-resolution geometry), we need to convert the mesh into a high-resolution mesh so that we can deform it with the 3D sculpting brushes. Follow these steps:

1. Select the model in **Object Mode** and press *Ctrl + 5* on your keyboard to turn the mesh into a smooth and rounded shape! By using that shortcut, you've automatically added the Subdivision Surface Modifier to your mesh, which is now visible in the **Properties** panel under the **Modifier Properties** tab:

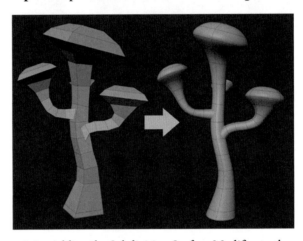

Figure 3.6 – Adding the Subdivision Surface Modifier to the mesh

2. Here, you will see that it lists **Modifier** as **Subdivision**. Set **Levels Viewport** to approximately four to five subdivisions.

3. Before you can sculpt the mesh, you need to apply the modifier to the mesh by using the *Ctrl + A* shortcut, while your mouse pointer is hovering over the modifier.

You will notice that the mesh's simple wireframe suddenly displays a lot of new faces. This is exactly what we want for 3D sculpting.

In this section, you learned how to subdivide the block-out mesh by using the Subdivision Surface Modifier and then used the **Apply** function to apply the modifier to the mesh.

The model is now prepared and has a high resolution (high mesh density).

In the next section, we will use the **Remesh** function on the model so that all the branches are joined up into one surface. Then, we can continue to the fun part: sculpting some of the big surface shapes – that is, making the primary forms.

Sculpting the primary forms

To start the 3D sculpting process, you need to use the **Remesh** function in Blender's **Sculpting Workspace**.

> **Important Note**
> The quoted figures for Remesh's **Voxel Size** should be used as a suggestion. The actual number depends on what your computer system can handle, so adjust these numbers accordingly.

Follow these steps:

1. Click on the **Remesh** button on the Header bar. The **Remesh** function was explained in *Chapter 1, An Introduction to Blender's 3D Modeling and Sculpting Tools*.

2. In the drop-down menu that opens, set **Voxel Size** to the approximate size of 0.02 m. The smaller the number, the higher the mesh's density.

3. Now, either click on the **Remesh** button at the bottom of the drop-down menu or use the *Ctrl + R* shortcut to remesh your mesh.

4. Once you've applied the **Remesh** function to your mesh, you will see that your mesh's surface has been divided into more faces (it has a much higher geometric density than before). You will also notice that the previously separate branch meshes have been combined into a single mesh.

   You can repeat this process any time your mesh becomes too blocky (or when it has a stretched topology). The remeshed mesh topology will replace the stretched mesh topology with a new, evenly divided mesh that works great for 3D sculpting.

5. Zoom in closer to where the branches join up with the trunk of the Alien Plant. Select the **Smooth** brush from the toolbar.

6. Press *Shift + F* to open the **Brush Strength** pop-up menu and set the amount to 0.3. Now, brush over the parts where the branches join the trunk. You will observe that this smooths out the sharp line where they joined up. The smoothed lines will create a great transition between the different surfaces, as shown in the following screenshot:

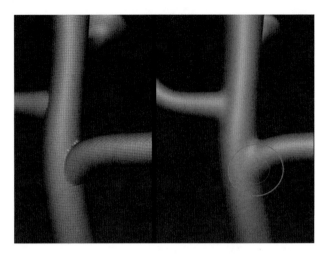

Figure 3.7 – Smoothing the joined parts

7. Now, let's move on to the base of the trunk. Zoom in closer and select the **Draw** brush from the toolbar. We will start our sculpting here. The shape of the trunk is a primary form since it is an important feature that we can notice even when we've zoomed out or are looking at the silhouette.

8. Set **Brush Strength** to 0.4 and start with medium-sized strokes. Brush gently over the base of the trunk to pull out the shapes.

If you want to push the surface inwards (in the negative brush direction), you can use the *Ctrl* button while sculpting, as shown in the following screenshot:

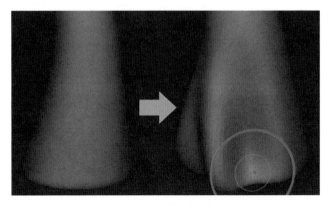

Figure 3.8 – Sculpting the base of the trunk

If you want to smooth the surface while sculpting, you can hold the *Shift* key while sculpting. This function works with the **Draw** brush, **Draw Sharp** brush, and **Inflate** brush.

You have just completed your first 3D sculpting exercise. You now know how to use the **Draw** brush, which is one of the most important sculpting tools in Blender.

You've practiced how to use the brush in both positive and negative directions, as well as how to use the **Smoothing** function. With more practice, your skill at handling the sculpting brushes will greatly improve.

In the next section, you will learn how to fix some common sculpting issues.

Fixing problem areas

From time to time, every 3D sculptor will encounter some common 3D sculpting issues. Let's look at how to fix some of these now.

Flattening an area of the mesh

Since you are sculpting the base of the trunk, parts of the geometry will move below the floor grid level. As seen to the left of the following screenshot, the base of the trunk is dipping below the dotted line.

To correct this, there is a handy tool in the 3D sculpting toolset called the **Line Project** brush. Let's learn how to use it:

1. With the **Line Project** brush selected, left-click and start to draw a line from the left toward the right-hand side.

2. Hold *Ctrl* while drawing to snap the line at an angle that's parallel to the floor grid.

3. Release the left mouse button once you have drawn the line past the base of the trunk. The overhanging part of the mesh will now be flattened out. You may have noticed that the area below the line is shaded darker than the area above the line. The **Line Project** brush will flatten the area of the mesh that is on the shaded side of the line, as shown in the following screenshot:

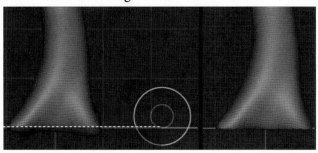

Figure 3.9 – Using the Line Project brush to flatten overhanging geometry

4.   Slightly smooth out the sharp edges of the base of the trunk.

In this section, you learned how to flatten a part of a mesh with the **Line Project** brush. Now, let's learn how to fix surface artifacts.

How to fix surface artifacts

Mesh surface artifacts are irregularities on the mesh's surface. These can be caused by various things, but one of the main effects is a surface that has strange pinching or smoothing errors, as shown in the following screenshot.

> **Important Note**
>
> The quoted figures for Dyntopo's **Detail Size** should be used as a suggestion. The actual number depends on what your computer system can handle, so adjust these numbers accordingly.

The following screenshot shows what surface artifacts can look like. As you can see, they cause unwanted surface details:

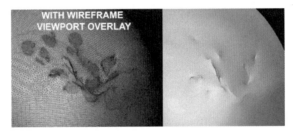

Figure 3.10 – An example of mesh surface artifacts.

(A) The Wireframe Viewport overlay turned on; (B) A regular view of the surface artifacts

If there are any artifacts on your 3D sculpture model's surface, follow these steps:

1.   Press *Ctrl* + *D* to toggle on the **Dyntopo** brush. Alternatively, use the **Dyntopo** button in the Sculpting Workspace Header bar, as shown in the following screenshot.

2.   Set **Brush Strength** to 0.

3.   From the **Dyntopo** drop-down menu, set **Detail Size** to 5.00 px:

Figure 3.11 – Use these settings to fix surface artifacts with the Dyntopo brush

4. Select the **Draw** brush and gently brush the problem area. This will add geometric detail while keeping the shape of the mesh intact. In the following screenshot, I used the **Dyntopo** brush with the **Draw** brush to replace the surface artifacts with new small triangular faces.

5. Smooth the problem area out slightly, as shown in the following screenshot. As you can see, the surface artifacts have been fixed:

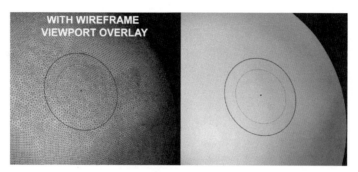

Figure 3.12 – (A) Brushing over the surface artifacts replaces them with small triangular faces;
(B) Smoothing them out

You've just learned how to deal with mesh surface artifacts. Now, let's start sculpting on the rest of the Alien Plant.

Adding secondary and tertiary forms

Now that the basic shape of the Alien Plant is complete, let's add some more details (called **secondary forms** in sculpting) to the upper parts of the Alien Plant:

1. Before we get started on the secondary forms, let's smooth the shading on the model. Make sure the Alien Plant model is selected, then switch to the **Layout Workspace** tab. Right-click anywhere in the 3D Viewport and select **Shade Smooth** from the menu that opened. Now, return to the **Sculpting Workspace** area.

2. Zoom into the upper part of the main trunk. Here, the plant has *alien-like spore sacks* that grow around the tops.

3. Select the **Inflate** brush from the toolbar and set **Brush Strength** to 0.85.

4. Gently brush in a circular motion until dome-like shapes form on the mesh's surface, as shown in the following screenshot. Continue sculpting more of these around the head and then move on to the other three plant heads. Try to cluster some of these domes together and keep some domes spaced apart. Vary the sizes of these domes. This will create an organic look; if you space them too evenly with uniform size, they will appear too *mechanical*:

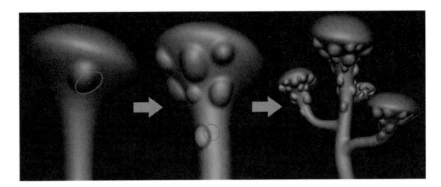

Figure 3.13 – Adding spore sacks to the Alien Plant

With that, you've learned how to use the **Inflate** brush to add dome-like details over a mesh surface. Now, let's learn how to use masking to quickly add some interesting details.

Using masking in 3D sculpting

The effect of masking in 3D sculpting is to define an area of the mesh that stops us from making modifications to it. Using masking in combination with other sculpting tools gives us a lot of new ways to deform a mesh.

Let's learn how to affect a whole area of a mesh globally (all at once) without the need to brush the surface:

1. Select the **Mask** brush since we want to mask out areas of the mesh.

2. Set **Brush Strength** to 1 and **Brush Radius** to 15.

3. Mask around the shapes of the domes, without brushing over them. Continue the mask around the plant heads. Mask the tops by using a bigger **Brush Radius**.

4. Once you've completed all four of the Alien Plant's heads, press *Ctrl + I* to use the **Invert Mask** function. You can see what the inverted mask looks like in *Figure 3.14*, right-hand side.

We used the mask in this way because it was quicker to paint the mask on the smaller surface area and then invert it, rather than to paint the mask over the bigger surface area:

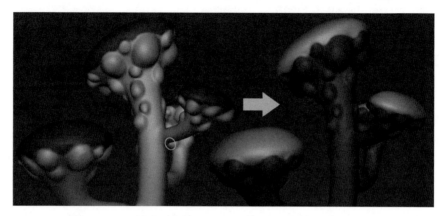

Figure 3.14 – (Left) Painting masks; (Right) Inverting the masks

Now, let's inflate parts of the mesh evenly but leave the masked parts alone.

5. Select the **Mesh Filter** tool from the toolbar. This will apply an effect (of your choosing) over the entire mesh or the parts of it that have not been hidden or masked.

6. From the Header bar, next to **Filter Type**, select **Inflate** from the drop-down menu.

7. Left-click on a space inside the 3D Viewport (but not on a menu) and drag the mouse to the right to apply the **Mesh Filter** effect. The further you drag your mouse to the right, the stronger the applied effect will be, as shown in *Figure 3.15*, part *A*:

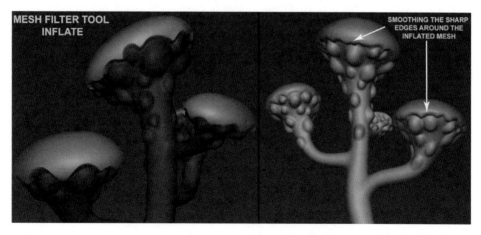

Figure 3.15 – (A) Using Mesh Filter to inflate the unmasked parts of the mesh;
(B) Smoothing the sharp edges

8. After you've inflated the mesh, as shown in *Figure 3.15*, part *A*, press *Alt + M* to apply the **Clear Mask** function. The model with the cleared mask should now look like the model shown in *Figure 3.15*, part *B*.

9. Use the **Smooth** brush with a low **Strength** setting and smooth out the sharp edges around all four plant heads.

10. Paint masks in the shape of big dots on all four plant heads.

11. Press *Ctrl + I* to apply the **Invert Mask** function.

12. Use the **Mesh Filter** tool to inflate the dots, but in the negative direction, so that the dots are going into the mesh instead of inflating outwards.

13. Press *Alt + M* to apply the **Clear Mask** function.

14. Smooth the edges of the submerged dots, as shown in *Figure 3.16*, part *C*:

Figure 3.16 – (A) Painting the masks;
(B) Inverting the mask and using the Inflate Mesh filter in the negative direction;
(C) Smoothing the sharp edges

In this section, you learned how to use masking in combination with the **Mesh Filter** tool to affect the mesh in unmasked areas.

The Alien Plant's surface is starting to look interesting and organic. If you look at the provided Alien Plant reference image, you will notice there are small nodules (protrusions) on the top of the plant's heads. These nodules release the spores from the spore sacks into the Alien-Planet's atmosphere.

> **Handy Tip**
>
> To spark your creativity while you are working on your 3D assets, it is useful to come up with an interesting backstory for your models, characters, and movie sets. Having a backstory allows your projects to come to life and be much more believable since they're filled with vivid details.

In the next section, you will learn how to sculpt the nodules in the Alien Plant model.

Sculpting the spore nodules

For this task, we will use the **Inflate** brush again, but this time on the inside of each of the recessed spots that you made in the previous section. Make sure that some of the nodules are more inflated than others and have varying sizes:

1. Once all the nodules have been inflated, remesh your sculpture with **Voxel Size** set to anywhere between `0.01` and `0.03`.

2. Use the **Draw** brush and hold *Ctrl* while sculpting to push in the centers of some of the nodules, as shown in *Figure 3.17*, part *C*:

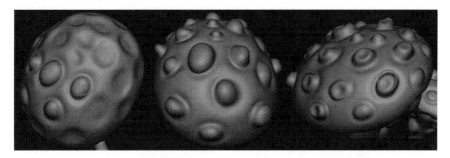

Figure 3.17 – (A) Sculpting the nodules; (B) Inflating the nodules;
(C) Pushing in the center parts

Your Alien Plant sculpture should now look similar to the following:

Figure 3.18 – The Alien Plant sculpture's progress thus far

In this section, you practiced how to sculpt some extra details inside the mesh. In the next section, we will start adding the final polish.

Adding the final polish to the sculpture

The Alien Plant looks great so far, so let's sculpt the finishing touches!

In terms of sculpting terminology, we call the small fine details such as fine wrinkles, pores, and surface grooves the **tertiary details**. Let's add these now:

1. Select the **Draw Sharp** brush and set **Strength** to 0.5.

2. On one of the plant heads, gently start outlining one of the dome-like spore sacks that you sculpted previously. These sharper lines add an extra layer of visual detail. Without these, everything would look too smooth.

3. Continue to outline the rest of the spore sacks. The following screenshot shows how the spore sacks on the left-hand side look quite smooth, while they look sharp and defined on the right-hand side:

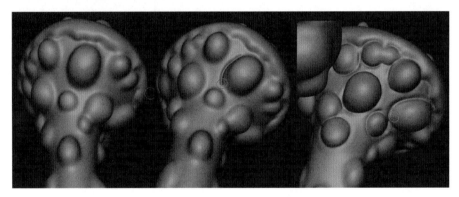

Figure 3.19 – Adding sharp creases with the Draw Sharp brush

4. Once all the spore sacks are completed, it is time to do the same thing to the spore nodules on the tops of all the plant heads. The result should resemble the model on the right in the following screenshot:

Figure 3.20 – Adding sharp creases with the Draw Sharp brush to the spore nodules

5. The last step is to add some more lines to the trunk and branches. These lines will balance all the details and create visual cohesion. Use the **Draw Sharp** brush (with the same settings you used previously) and sculpt some fine lines of varying depth and lengths that follow the direction of the trunk and branches, as shown in the following screenshot:

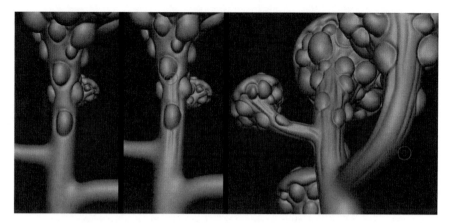

Figure 3.21 – Adding sharp creases to the trunk and branches with the Draw Sharp brush

You have just completed your first sculpture in Blender! Your model should now resemble the Alien Plant shown in the following screenshot:

Figure 3.22 – The Alien Plant sculpt completed

Save the Alien Plant model in Blender file format (.blend). You also need to export this high-poly Alien Plant model so that you can use it in the tutorial in *Chapter 4, UV Maps and Texture Baking*. Navigate to **File | Export | Wavefront (.obj)** and use the settings shown in *Figure 3.20.*

In the **File Name** entry box, choose a suitable filename for the exported file. Export this high-poly model and use the .obj model format:

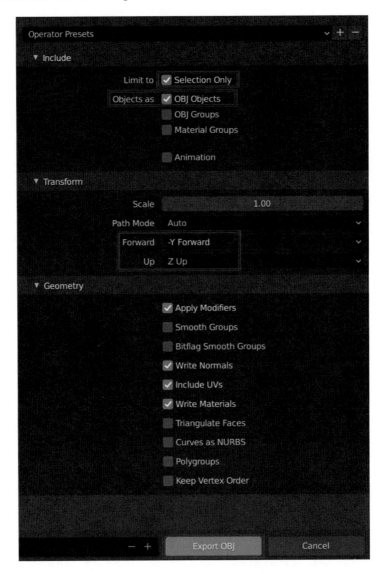

Figure 3.23 – Exporting your model using the Wavefront (.obj) settings

In this section, you learned how to add the finishing touches to the model by using the versatile **Draw Sharp** brush.

Congratulations! By completing all the practical 3D sculpting sections in this chapter, you have acquired a clear understanding of the entire sculpting pipeline: you know which brushes to use for different tasks and how to fix problem areas if they occur.

Now that the sculpt of the Alien Plant has been completed, we need to convert this model into a mesh that UE can use.

At this stage, the sculpt is too high-resolution to be used as an animated model in UE. This is because the denser the geometry is in a mesh, the more of your computer's computational power (CPU) it needs to deform that mesh (at the time of writing, a regular desktop PC's CPU is not powerful enough to deform a very dense mesh in real time). That is why we need to create a low-resolution mesh for animation purposes.

I will take you through the steps to convert our model into a lower-resolution mesh in the next section.

Generating the low-resolution mesh

To prepare the sculpted mesh for UE, we need to create a new mesh that has the same shape as the high-resolution mesh. However, the new mesh should be low-resolution in geometric density (also called a low-polygon mesh). The process of creating a low-resolution mesh is called **retopology**.

There are many ways to do retopology in Blender. The most accurate methods are all done by hand (manual retopology). They provide superior results, but these techniques are beyond the scope of this book.

I will show you how to perform retopology using a method called **auto-retopology** (automatically generated by a software algorithm). It is one of the simplest ways you can automatically generate a new low-resolution mesh. It is not as accurate, but the main benefits are simplicity and great savings in terms of production time.

We will use the free standalone software known as Instant Meshes (the download link has been provided in the *Technical requirements* section). In my experience, it has superior results compared to the built-in auto-retopology tools that are included in Blender.

The first step is to reduce our current mesh's geometric density with a modifier in Blender since Instant Meshes work better when the source mesh is low resolution.

In the next section, we will learn how to use the **Decimate** modifier in Blender.

Decimating the mesh in Blender

The Decimate modifier uses a function that decimates a mesh. Decimation reduces the mesh's geometry by converting the surface into triangular faces that are of lower resolution than the original mesh.

You may be wondering, why not just use this function to create a low-resolution mesh for UE? The answer is that the topology (the layout of the faces and edges) of the surface is not suited for a model that needs to be animated, plus there could be many smoothing artifacts on the mesh.

Let's decimate the mesh in Blender:

1. Switch to **Object Mode** and go to **Layout Workspace**.

2. Look under your **Modifiers** list and find the **Decimate** modifier.

3. When you look at this modifier in the **Properties** panel, you will see that the mesh still looks the same. This is because the ratio figure needs to be adjusted.

4. Change the default **Ratio** to 0.03. You will notice that the mesh's geometric density is greatly reduced (decimated), as shown in the following screenshot:

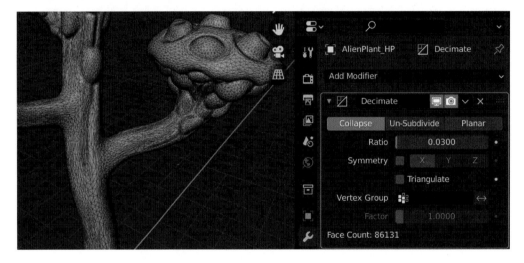

Figure 3.24 – Using the Decimate modifier to reduce mesh density for instant meshes

5. Navigate to **File | Export | Wavefront (.obj)**. This will export the model as a .obj model. The reason we're using the .obj file format is that the Instant Meshes software can only load .obj and .ply types of model formats.

6. Use the settings shown in *Figure 3.23*. In the **File Name** entry box, choose a suitable filename for the exported file. This *decimated* version of the model will only be used in Instant Meshes.

In this section, you learned how to use the **Decimate** modifier to reduce the mesh's geometric density for exporting to Instant Meshes.

In the next section, you will learn how to use Instant Meshes for auto-retopology.

Using Instant Meshes for auto-retopology

Instant meshes is a free software tool that can be used to generate auto-retopology meshes from your source mesh. You can guide this auto-retopology algorithm by drawing guidelines (called **Orientation Comb Lines** in Instant Meshes).

> **Note**
>
> The controls for Instant Meshes are **rotate:** *left mouse button,* **pan:** *right mouse button,* and **zoom:** use the mouse wheel.

Let's use the Alien Plant model in Instant Meshes:

1. Launch the Instant Meshes software.

2. Click on the **Open mesh** button and load the *decimated* version of your Alien Plant model that you've just exported (the .obj mesh).

3. Change **Target Vertex Count** to approximately 18K.

4. Position your mesh so that you can see the whole mesh at once.

5. Click on the **Orientation Comb** icon, as shown in *Figure 3.25*, part *A*. When **Orientation Comb** is active, the viewport navigation will be locked in place until you unclick the **Orientation Comb** icon. The **Orientation Comb** function creates orientation comb lines (directional guidelines) that tell the software how to direct the flow of the Edge Loops in the direction that you are *combing* over the mesh's surface.

6. Draw orientation comb lines by using your mouse cursor. First, left-click + drag a line across the surface of the mesh, as shown in *Figure 3.25*, part *A*. When you let go of the mouse button, a colored line will appear with a little **X** icon on it, as shown in *Figure 3.25*, part *B*.

    You will notice that multiple colored surface lines will appear all over your mesh's surface. These colored lines are a visual representation of the Edge Flow, as shown in *Figure 3.26*:

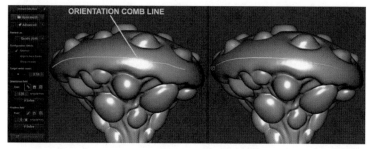

Figure 3.25 – (A) Drawing an orientation comb line across the surface of the model; (B) The orientation comb line becomes a colored line

7. We are trying to change the Edge Flow of the Edge Loops to make it easier to animate and to UV Map later. In *Figure 3.26*, part *A*, I have highlighted a part of a mesh where the default Edge Flow was not flowing correctly. In *Figure 3.26*, part *B*, I have drawn multiple orientation comb lines over the mesh's surface to adjust the Edge Flow. The following screenshot shows how much more organized the Edge Flow is now:

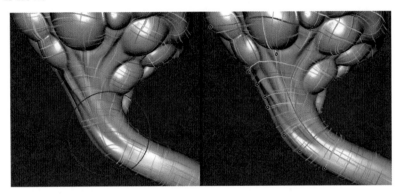

Figure 3.26 – (A) The Edge Flow was disorganized in the highlighted area;
(B) I have drawn multiple orientation comb lines to fix the Edge Flow

8. If you want to delete a line, click on the little **X** icon.

9. When you've finished drawing guidelines from your current viewing angle, unclick the **Orientation Comb** icon and rotate your view to a new angle. Re-enable **Orientation Comb** to start the guidelines again.

10. Continue this process of rotating and drawing guidelines until your guidelines look similar to what is shown in the following screenshot.

11. Press the **Solve** button under the **Orientation Field** heading. You will see colored lines appear all over your mesh:

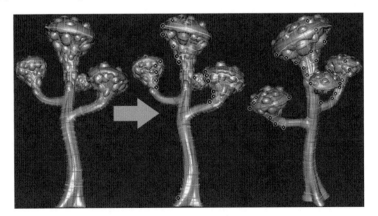

Figure 3.27 – Creating guidelines with Orientation Comb

12. Disable the **Orientation Comb** option.

13. Look for the **Solve** button under the **Position Field** heading and click it. The mesh display will turn dark blue with light blue edge lines.

14. Click on the **Export mesh** button. Another menu will appear to the right of the current menu.

15. Click on the **Extract mesh** button to see your generated mesh appear. It will have a red wireframe and blue-colored faces. Your mesh should look similar to what's shown in the following screenshot.

16. Click on **Save...** and save the new mesh to your hard disk. This will save your model in the `.obj` file format:

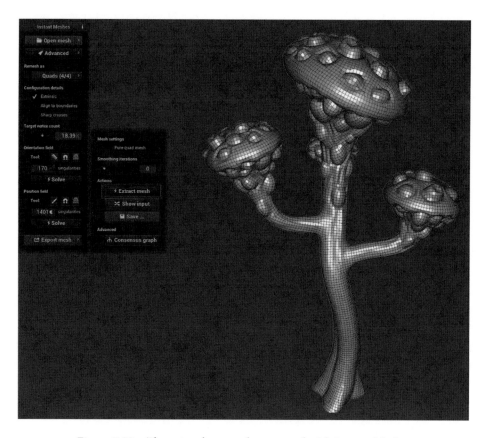

Figure 3.28 – The retopology mesh generated with Instant Meshes

You now have a thorough understanding of how to use Instant Meshes to create auto-retopology for your models.

Congratulations! You've just completed the process of sculpting a model in Blender and generating the retopology mesh!

Summary

In this chapter, you learned how to put Blender's 3D sculpting toolset to great practical use by sculpting an organic Alien Plant model to use as a set piece for our 3D movie.

You also learned how to follow the reference image to create the block-out model.

After that, you learned how to refine that shape by adding geometry and sculpting finer details. We briefly delved into fixing problem areas and how to use masking as a useful tool in 3D sculpting.

Finally, you learned how to take this sculpted model and convert it into the low-resolution mesh that we will use in UE5.

In the next chapter, we will explore how and why a model needs to be UV mapped and how to bake texture maps to use them in our texturing tutorial in a later chapter.

4
UV Maps and Texture Baking

In the practical tutorials of *Chapter 2, Having Fun with Modeling a Robot Drone Character*, and *Chapter 3, Let's Sculpt an Alien Plant!*, you created a Robot Drone model and an Alien Plant model.

So far, these gray (untextured) models look great. Unfortunately, having these plain gray models on your virtual 3D movie set would not look that realistic, would it?

In order to make them look more real, first, we need to prepare the models so that they are able to receive **textures** and **materials**.

We will start by exploring some key concepts regarding textures and materials. Then, we will move on to learn about the concept of UV mapping.

After this, we will prepare our Alien Plants' shading and then go through the step-by-step process of UV mapping the model. We will do the same process for the Robot Drone model, but with some variations to our method since it is a mechanical model made up of multiple parts.

Once both Alien Plant and Robot Drone are UV mapped, we will briefly explore a free texture map baking software, called **xNormal**. Then, we will go through the entire process of baking texture maps with xNormal, for both our Alien Plant and Robot Drone models.

Finally, at the end of this chapter, both of your models will be UV mapped and have texture maps baked. They will be ready for the final texturing stages in Blender and Quixel Mixer.

At the end of these lessons, you will have a solid understanding of the whole texturing process: model preparation, UV mapping, and texture map baking.

For those who wish to skip this chapter's practical tutorials, the UV mapped Alien Plant model, `AlienPlant_UV_Mapped.blend`, and the UV mapped Robot Drone model, `RobotDrone_UV_Mapped.blend`, along with all of their baked texture maps are all available to download from the online repository at `https://github.com/PacktPublishing/Unreal-Engine-5-Character-Creation-Animation-and-Cinematics/tree/main/Chapter04`.

In this chapter, we're going to cover the following main topics:

- Exploring the basic concept of textures and materials
- Understanding the basic concept of UV mapping and why it is needed
- Fixing shading issues on meshes
- UV mapping models in Blender
- Understanding the concept of texture baking and why it is needed
- Baking textures using xNormal

First, we will explore the core concepts of textures and materials.

Technical requirements

You will need the following hardware and software to complete this chapter:

- A computer that can run basic 3D animation software.
- You will need to install Blender from `https://www.blender.org/download/`.

  The Blender version used in this chapter is version 2.93.5. Even if your version of Blender is newer, the examples should still work without any problems.

- You will need to install the latest version of xNormal from `https://xNormal.net/`.

The files related to this chapter are placed at `https://github.com/PacktPublishing/Unreal-Engine-5-Character-Creation-Animation-and-Cinematics/tree/main/Chapter04`

What are textures and materials?

In this section, we will explore the core concepts of textures and materials. First, let's start with the concept of textures.

Textures

In 3D computer graphics, we use something called a **Texture** (or a texture map) to describe an aspect of the mesh surface's appearance.

Usually, textures (or texture maps) are made from raster images (pixels in a grid format), or the textures can be procedurally generated (this is also known as **Procedural Texturing**).

> **Note**
>
> Procedural texturing is a 3D texturing method whereby textures and materials are generated by an algorithm inside 3D software (such as xNormal, Quixel Mixer, or Substance Painter). The algorithm uses information from your texture maps and/or 3D mesh, combined with settings that you have control over to create procedural textures. We will explain procedural texturing, in more detail, in *Chapter 5, Texturing Your Models in Quixel Mixer*.

Here is a brief description of the types of texture maps that we will use for our tutorials:

- **Albedo Map**: This is the color of the surface without specular highlights or shadows. In some software, such as Unreal Engine and Blender, an albedo map is also referred to as a base color map.

- **Metalness Map**: This indicates which parts of a surface are made of metal and which parts are not. In the real world, a surface can either be metallic or non-metallic. However, because we want the creative freedom to create materials that do not need to be physically possible, we can choose a metalness value range of between 0 and 255.

- **Roughness Map**: This refers to how rough or smooth a surface is, represented as a grayscale (black to white) tonal value between 0 and 255 (where 0 = 100% smooth and 255 = 100% rough).

- **Normal Map**: These texture maps are used to give the illusion of height and depth in a material. They work by manipulating the way that light interacts with the surface of the material to fake small bumps and indentations.

- **Ambient Occlusion Map** (also known as the **AO Map**): This is a grayscale texture map that is used to create soft shadowing without a direct light source (indirect lighting), such as on an overcast day. Cracks, dents, and crevasses would receive less lighting, so these areas would get more shadows.

- **Emissive Color Map**: This is sometimes called a **Self-Illumination Map**, and it is used to create glowing areas on your mesh's surface. For example, you can use this kind of map to create interesting light effects in your material.

- **Displacement Map**: This is used to deform (displace) a mesh based on the grayscale value of the displacement texture, whereby the black areas will create deep crevices and the white areas will create peaks. In Unreal Engine, the displacement texture map works by utilizing a feature called **Tessellation**, which subdivides the mesh to give you more geometric detail to use during the displacement process.

- **Curvature Map**: This is a texture map that gives a grayscale value to sharp edges and cavities in your mesh. This information is used for procedural texturing.

- **Material ID Map**: This kind of texture map is used to assign a color value to parts of your model so that you can use that color information during procedural texturing.

Now that you understand the different types of texture maps, let's explore what materials are.

Materials

Materials are made up of one or more texture maps. Materials use these texture maps to describe the various physical aspects of a surface's appearance.

Materials can also be procedurally generated in software such as Quixel Mixer or Substance Painter.

Here is an example of how texture maps could be used inside a hypothetical rock material:

- The albedo map will describe the color of the rock material.

- The normal map will describe how bumpy the rock material should be.

- The roughness map will describe how smooth or rough the surface of the rock material is.

- The AO map describes the self-shadowed areas in the rock material.

- The rock material contains no lights or metal parts, so we do not need an emissive color map or a metalness map for the rock material.

In this section, you learned about the basic concept of textures, procedural texturing, and materials. This knowledge is an essential stepping stone for learning more about texturing as one of the main disciplines in 3D computer graphics.

In the next section, I will explain the basic concept of UV mapping and why it's needed.

Understanding UV maps

UV maps represent a 3D model's surface as a 2D representation, as shown in *Figure 4.1*.

Imagine a geographical map of the Earth; the map is 2D, but we all know that it is a flattened representation of the surface of our planet and that the map wraps around the spherical (globe) shape. Similarly, a 2D UV map represents a 3D surface.

You can download an example of an Earth Globe model (`Earth.blend`) at `https://github.com/PacktPublishing/Unreal-Engine-5-Character-Creation-Animation-and-Cinematics/tree/main/Chapter04`.

Open this Blender file and select the model named **Earth**. Then, click on the **UV Editing Workspace** tab to examine the UV map of this model.

This will give you a good understanding of the way that UV mapping works. See *Figure 4.1* to view what this Earth model looks like in the 3D Viewport window and the UV Editor window:

Figure 4.1 – The Earth model and its UV map inside the UV Editor window (on the left-hand side)

Now that you understand the basic concept of UV mapping, let's do a practical tutorial to learn how to create a UV map.

> **Note**
> UV unwrapping describes the process of UV mapping. The term UV (or UVs) also refers to a model's UV map.

UV unwrapping the Alien Plant model

We will start our journey of learning about UV maps by UV unwrapping the Alien Plant model. Before we can start, we need to prepare the mesh's shading. In the next section, we will do just that.

Fixing shading issues

Import the Alien Plant model from the directory that you used when you completed the *Using Instant Meshes for Auto-Retopology* section of *Chapter 3, Let's Sculpt an Alien Plant!*.

> **Note**
> Low-poly describes a low-resolution mesh (that is, low geometric detail).
> Similarly, the term high-poly describes a high-resolution mesh (that is, dense geometric detail).

Open the low-poly Alien Plant model in Blender and switch **to Edit Mode** with **Edge Selection** mode turned on. You will notice that parts of the mesh's edges are displayed in a turquoise color. This is because we've imported the model as a `.obj` file from Instant Meshes, and some edges are set to display as sharp. Fortunately, there is a very easy way to fix this:

1. Select all of your edges on the model and then right-click inside the 3D Viewport.

2. In the menu that pops up, select **Clear Sharp**. The edges will now turn back to how they normally appear.

3. Switch back to **Object Mode**. Select the model and right-click anywhere inside the 3D Viewport.

4. Select **Shade Smooth** from the menu.

So, you've just learned how to fix a shading issue caused by importing a model with edges that were set to display as sharp.

In the next section, I will show you how to place UV seams in your Alien Plant model.

> **Handy Tip**
> A quick way to select an edge loop (in **Edge Selection** mode) is to hold the *Alt* key while selecting an edge that is part of the edge loop. A quick way to select a range of edges (shortest path) in edge selection mode is to select the starting edge and then move your mouse pointer to the end of the range; then, hold *Ctrl* and left-click to complete the selection.

Creating UV seams

The first step of UV unwrapping the model is to place UV seams. These UV seams are a visual representation of the edges of the texture.

Take the analogy of the map of Earth. In order to flatten the Earth's shape (with no overlapping parts), it needs to be *cut* somewhere. These *cuts* are similar to UV seams.

So, now that you have a grasp of UV seams, let's create some UV seams on our Alien Plant model.

Let's start by setting UV seams on the biggest head of the Alien Plant model:

1. First, select an edge loop, as shown in *Figure 4.2*:

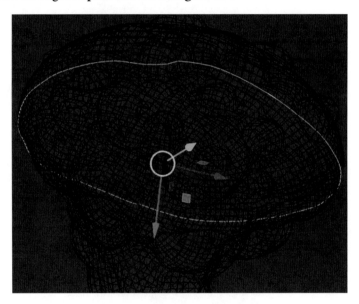

Figure 4.2 – Selecting the edges

2. If you find that your edge loops are not connecting up correctly, you can do mesh editing on some of the edges by switching to **Vertex Selection** mode and then pressing *J* to use the **Connect Vertex Path** tool.

3. Connect some of the vertices around the bases of the stems to smooth out the edge loops and make them more rounded.

4. With the edge loop still selected, right-click inside the Viewport and select **Mark Seam** from the menu. Alternatively, you can use the *U* shortcut to open the UV mapping menu and then choose **Mark Seam** from that menu:

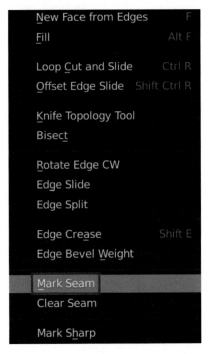

Figure 4.3 – Marking the seam

5. These selected edges will now turn red to indicate that it is a UV seam (where the edge of the UV map is), as shown in *Figure 4.4*:

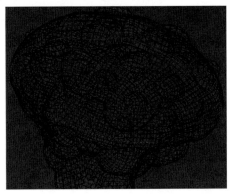

Figure 4.4 – The edges are now red

6. Continue to set UV seams for all four of the Alien Plant model heads. Use *Figure 4.5* as a guide for the creation of the remaining UV seams of the Alien Plant model. Additionally, you can load the provided Alien Plant model as an example of the UV seam placement.

If you haven't done so already, download the completed UV mapped Alien Plant model, `AlienPlant_UV_Mapped.blend`, from the online repository at `https://github.com/PacktPublishing/Unreal-Engine-5-Character-Creation-Animation-and-Cinematics/tree/main/Chapter04`.

Load this model into Blender to study the way that we have set the UV seams on the model. Switch to **Edit Mode** in the modeling workspace so that the UV seams become visible. Then, create your UV seams in the same way. The completed UV seams on the Alien Plant model can be seen in *Figure 4.5*:

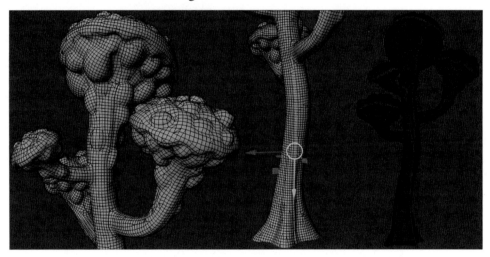

Figure 4.5 – The completed UV seams on the Alien Plant model

So, you've just learned how to set UV seams on a model. In the next section, we will learn how to do UV unwrapping.

UV unwrapping the Alien Plant model

Now, we will start on the UV unwrapping stage of the Alien Plant model. Perform the following steps:

1. Select the Alien Plant model; then, select the **UV Editing Workspace** tab from the Topbar.

2. Make sure your model is in **Edit Mode**, then enable **face selection** mode. Press *A* to select all the model's faces.

3. Press *U* for the UV mapping menu and, from there, select **Unwrap**.

4. The model will now be UV unwrapped, and you can see the result in the **UV Editor** window (the window on the left-hand side panel of your 3D Viewport).

5. In the **UV Editor** window's header bar, click on the small arrow next to the **Show Overlays** icon. Then, in the drop-down menu, use the settings shown in *Figure 4.6*:

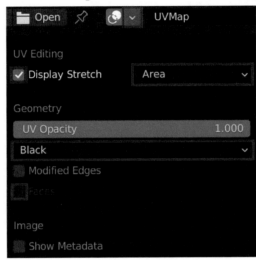

Figure 4.6 – The Show Overlays menu settings in the UV Editor window

Enabling **Stretching** and setting the **Stretching** type to **Area** (in the **Show Overlays** menu) helps you visualize any stretching of your UV map by using colors.

The **Blue** and **Green** colors mean the UVs are optimal (that is, not stretched). The **Red** and **Yellow**-colored areas mean there is stretching (or the UVs have too much texture space allocated).

6. With your model selected, switch to **Edit Mode** and then enable **face selection** mode. Press *A* to select all the model's faces.

7. In the **UV Editor** window, use the **Select Box** selection mode to drag select all the faces on the model. Then, open the UV drop-down menu in the UV Editor window's header bar.

8. Inside this UV drop-down menu, select **Minimize Stretch** to improve your UVs.

The minimize stretch function works best on organic-shaped meshes. It is best not to use the minimize stretch function on mechanical-shaped meshes (such as your Robot Drone model). The reason for this is that the algorithm that Blender uses for minimizing (UV) stretching works better on organic-shaped meshes. On mechanical-shaped meshes, it can sometimes cause unwanted distortions in your UV map.

Move and rotate the separate UV parts that you can see in *Figure 4.7* (these UV parts are called **UV islands** in UV mapping terminology) so that the UV islands can fit better into the square. If you want to scale them, make sure you scale all of the UV islands together and only use uniform scale; otherwise; your UVs won't have an even distribution of texture space.

9. Rotate the UV islands of the Alien Plant model so that they are facing the same way as the model and leave a bit of space between the UV islands, as shown in *Figure 4.7*:

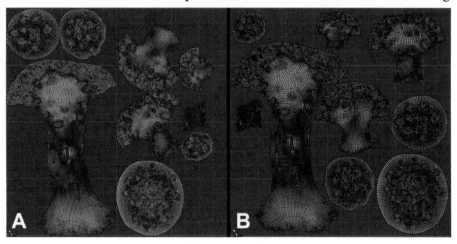

Figure 4.7 – (A) The original UV layout and (B) the modified UV layout with parts rotated to face the same direction

The UV mapping stage of the Alien Plant model is now complete. You have just learned how to UV map a model in Blender.

In the next section, we will prepare the Alien Plant model for exporting by triangulating its mesh.

Triangulating the Alien Plant model

At this point, your model is mostly made up of four-sided faces (also known as **Quads**). However, to bake the textures (and for use in Unreal Engine), we need the model to be made up of triangles (that is, triangular faces; also known as **Tris**).

Select all the faces in the model and then press *Ctrl + T* to triangulate the mesh. Save the model with the triangular faces in Blender's (.blend) file format.

You just learned how to triangulate a mesh for use in texture baking and Unreal Engine.

In the next section, I will show you how to export the Alien Plant model from Blender in .fbx file format.

Exporting the Alien Plant mesh

Now, let's take a look at the settings we will use to export the Alien Plant model from Blender in .fbx file format.

> **Important**
>
> You will use the same settings as any other model that you want to export from Blender in the .fbx file format.

Perform the following steps:

1. Select your model in **Object Mode** inside Blender.
2. Navigate to **File | Export | FBX (.fbx)**. The Blender file view window will open. Use the following settings in this window:

   - In the **Include** drop-down menu, check the **Limit to Selected Objects** checkbox.
   - In the **Transform** drop-down menu, set **Forward** to **-Y Forward**. Set **Up** to **Z Up**.
   - In the **Geometry** drop-down menu, set **Smoothing** to **Face**.
   - In the **Geometry** drop-down menu, check the **Tangent Space** checkbox.
   - In the file's **Name** entry box, choose a suitable file name for the exported file.

3. Click on the **Export FBX** button.

See *Figure 4.8* for all of the preceding export settings:

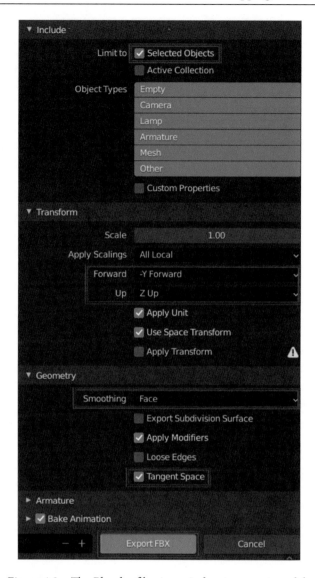

Figure 4.8 – The Blender file view window to export models

You have just learned how to export models in .fbx file format.

We will use this version of the Alien Plant model that you've just exported in .fbx format as the low-poly version of your Alien Plant model for use in xNormal for texture baking purposes in the *Baking texture maps* section. Later, we will also use this model inside UE5.

In the next section, I will show you how to create the UV maps for the Robot Drone model.

> **Handy Tip**
>
> To hide and unhide items or mesh components, use the following shortcuts: press *H* to hide the selected item or components. Press *Shift + H* to hide unselected items or components, and press *Alt + H* to unhide all items or mesh components.

UV unwrapping the Robot Drone model

In this section, you will UV unwrap each part of your Robot Drone model individually. Then, you will combine the unwrapped UV maps into a single UV map later.

We will start the lesson by loading the Robot Drone model that you created in the practical tutorial of *Chapter 2, Modeling a Robot Drone Character*. Perform the following steps:

1. Save a backup copy of the Robot Drone model that you created.

2. Delete the right-hand side of your Robot Drone's mesh parts, except for the body, as shown in *Figure 4.9*.

3. Separate all the parts of the low-poly model into individual objects. To do this, select all the faces of mesh parts that you have joined before. Press *P* to separate the model parts and choose the **By Loose** parts. Each new separated object part will also be listed in the outliner panel.

4. Use the **Hide**, **Unhide**, and **Hide Unselected** shortcuts to isolate model parts while you set your UV seams. By isolating model parts while setting UV seams, it is easier to focus on a specific model part.

5. Now create UV seams for all the Robot Drone parts. Use *Figure 4.9* as a guide to show you where to place your UV seams for the Robot Drones' model parts. You can also load my Robot Drone model to use as a guide for the UV seam placement.

   If you haven't done so already, download the completed UV mapped Robot Drone model, RobotDrone_UV_Mapped.fbx, from the online repository at https://github.com/PacktPublishing/Unreal-Engine-5-Character-Creation-Animation-and-Cinematics/tree/main/Chapter04.

6. Load this model into Blender to study the way that we have set the UV seams on the model. Switch to **Edit Mode** in the modeling workspace so that the UV seams become visible. Create the UV seams on your Robot Drone model in the same way as I did on mine:

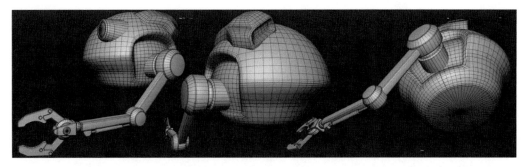

Figure 4.9 – The Robot Drone's UV seams (as indicated by the red lines)

7. Select one of the model parts of the Robot Drone model. Then, select the **UV Editing Workspace** tab from the Topbar.

8. Make sure your model part is in **Edit Mode**. Then, enable **Face selection** mode. Press *A* to select all the model part's faces.

9. Press *U* for the UV mapping menu and select **Unwrap**. This model part is now UV mapped.

10. Repeat this UV mapping process for the rest of Robot Drone's model parts.

> **Note**
>
> There should not be any significant amount of stretching in your UV map if you place your UV seams in the same way as I did on my Robot Drone model.

11. Once all your Robot Drone's model parts have been UV mapped, select all of the faces of all the model parts.

12. In the Topbar of the UV Editor window, select **UV | Average Islands Scale**. This will scale each model part's UV map to have the right proportions compared to the other model parts.

13. From the same UV menu, select **Pack Islands** to pack all the UVs into the square (with no overlapping UV parts). In *Part A* of *Figure 4.10*, you can see **Pack Islands** highlighted in the menu.

14. A minimized Operator panel will appear. Open the **Pack Islands** menu and set **Margin** to 0.015. This will move the UV Islands to have a bit of space between them. This is called **Edge Padding** in UV mapping terminology, as shown in *Part B* of *Figure 4.10*:

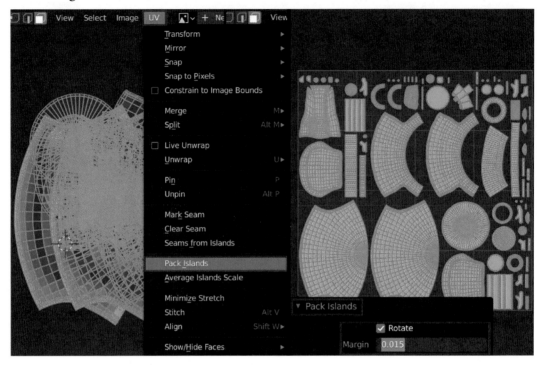

Figure 4.10 – (A) Selecting the pack islands function and (B) adjusting the margins between the packed UV islands

15. Save the model in Blender's (.blend) file format. Later in this chapter, we will return to using this saved version of the Robot Drone model.

Your UV map is now complete! The Robot Drone model should have a single UV map laid out inside the square, and this UV map contains all the individual parts of the model, as shown in *Figure 4.11*:

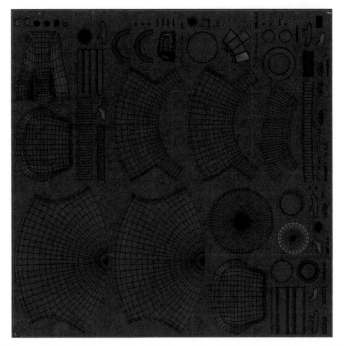

Figure 4.11 – The completed UV map for the Robot Drone model

Note

Your UV map will differ in layout from mine, but the UV islands will be similar in shape if you placed your UV seams in the same place as I did.

In this section, you learned how to do UV unwrapping for mechanical-shaped models. This will come in very useful for your own future projects.

Now that you've UV mapped both the Alien Plant and the Robot Drone models, you are ready to move on to the texture baking stage of this chapter, which we will discuss, in detail, next.

Understanding texture baking

Texture baking is a process by which the xNormal software (I will cover xNormal in the *Introduction to xNormal* section) takes certain aspects from the surface of the high-poly model and then projects those aspects onto the surface of the low-poly model, to create new texture maps. These new texture maps can be used in procedural texturing software, such as Quixel Mixer.

> **Note**
>
> We will cover the use of Quixel Mixer in *Chapter 5*, *Texturing Your Models inside Quixel Mixer*.

The end result of the texture baking process is a texture map that holds information about various aspects of the high-poly model. For example, some of these aspects include the degree of sharpness of the edges of the model or information about fine geometric details on the high-poly model.

In xNormal, we can choose which aspects from the high-poly model we want to bake into a texture map. For our tutorial, we will bake three of these texture maps. The three texture maps that we will bake are listed as follows:

- The normal map
- The AO map
- The curvature map

> **Important**
>
> In Quixel Mixer, the texture maps that we will bake in xNormal are referred to as base maps. Quixel Mixer uses these base maps to generate procedural textures and materials that we will use in Unreal Engine later on.

In this section, you learned about the concept of texture baking and why we need it for procedural texturing.

In the next section, I will introduce the software called xNormal, which we will use for texture baking later.

Introduction to xNormal

xNormal is a free, standalone 3D software that is very popular for baking texture maps.

The reason we're baking texture maps in xNormal is that the process of baking curvature maps in Blender is far too complex for the scope of this book, whereas xNormal is extremely quick and easy to use.

You now know what xNormal is used for. In the next section, we will learn how to prepare the Robot Drone model for use in xNormal.

Preparing the Robot Drone model for xNormal

Now, we need to export the Robot Drone model's high-poly and low-poly meshes so that we can bake the textures in xNormal.

There are two versions of the model to be baked: the low-poly mesh and the high-poly mesh.

Let's start by preparing the Robot Drone model's low-poly mesh first.

Preparing the low-poly mesh

In the *UV unwrapping the Robot Drone model* section, you separated all of your model parts. In other words now, the model parts are not attached to other model parts anymore.

We will now start to prepare the Robot Drone model's Low-Poly mesh for xNormal:

1. Move all of the separated mesh parts away from each other so that there are small distances between them, as shown in *Figure 4.12*:

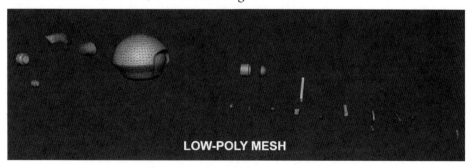

Figure 4.12 – The low-poly version of the Robot Drone's model parts are all moved away from each other and then triangulated

> **Note**
>
> The reason we're moving the mesh parts a distance away from each other is to avoid unwanted texture baking artifacts, which are caused by parts of other nearby meshes that are *projected* onto your baked mesh. The easiest solution for avoiding these texture baking artifacts is to bake your mesh parts with some distance between them. In texture baking terminology, a mesh with parts that are moved away from each other is referred to as an *exploded mesh*. You won't have the same problem when texture baking a simple (one-piece) mesh (such as the Alien Plant model), but this method is needed when you want to do texture baking on more complex mechanical model parts.

2. Save your Robot Drone file twice using a different filename for each of the two files: `RobotDrone_LowPoly` and `RobotDrone_HighPoly`.

3. In the `RobotDrone_LowPoly` file, triangulate all of the mesh parts, as shown in *Figure 4.12*.

4. After the triangulation is complete, select each model part individually. Then, right-click and select **Shade Smooth** from the menu.

5. When all the model parts have both been triangulated and shaded smooth, select all the model parts and export this file as your low-poly version. Do this export by using the `.fbx` file format in the same way that you exported the Alien Plant model previously.

The Robot Drone's low-poly mesh is now complete. Next, let's move on to prepare the high-poly mesh.

Preparing the high-poly mesh

Now we will start to prepare the Robot Drone's high-poly mesh for xNormal:

1. Load your saved `RobotDrone_HighPoly` file.

2. Apply a subdivision surface modifier to each of the following five model parts: **Body**, **Thruster_V2**, **Eye**, **Shoulder_Disk**, and **Elbow_Disk**.

3. In the **Modifier Properties** section of the **Properties** panel, set **Levels Viewport** to 2. (in *Figure 4.13*, you can see the five model parts are highlighted in orange. I've also added name tags for easy identification):

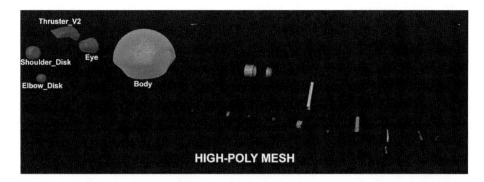

Figure 4.13 – The high-poly version of the Robot Drone model's parts

4. Now apply the modifier to these five mesh parts.

5. After you've applied all of the subdivision surface modifiers, triangulate all the model parts.

6. Apply **Shade Smooth** to the model parts that have the subdivision surface modifier on them but not the low-poly mesh parts.

7. When all the model parts are triangulated and a few selected model parts have been shaded smooth, select all the model parts and export them as the high-poly version. Do this export by using the .fbx file format in the same way that you exported previously.

Both the high-poly model and low-poly model export process are now complete. You just learned how to prepare a very complex mechanical model with many parts for texture baking in xNormal.

Now you understand the different workflows that should be used when UV mapping and exporting models to xNormal for organic-shaped models and mechanical-shaped models.

In the next section, you will learn how to use xNormal for texture baking.

Baking texture maps

In the previous section, you prepared and exported the Robot Drone model's high-poly and low-poly versions for texture baking.

In this section, we will start on the texture baking process of the Robot Drone model. Then, afterward, you will use the same method for baking the Alien Plant model.

Open xNormal. You will see a floating window with various menus:

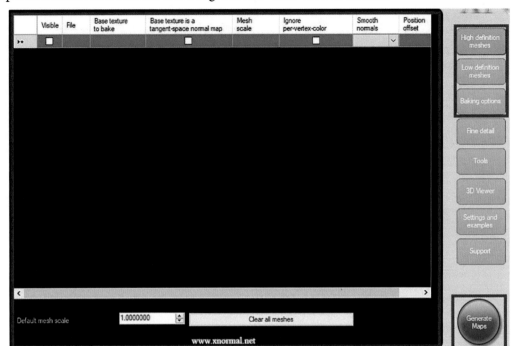

Figure 4.14 – xNormal's UI with the High definition meshes tab currently enabled

We only need a few steps of preparation before we are ready to bake our texture maps. See *Figure 4.14* for xNormal's UI:

1.   Make sure the **High definition meshes** tab has been selected.

2.   Right-click anywhere inside the xNormal's window part, as shown in *Figure 4.14*.

3.   In the menu that pops up, select **Add meshes** and select your high-poly model.

4.   Click on the **Low definition meshes** tab.

5.   Right-click anywhere inside the window part of xNormal.

6.   In the menu that pops up, select **Add meshes** and select your low-poly model.

7.   Select the **Baking** options tab, and then use the settings shown in *Figure 4.15*:

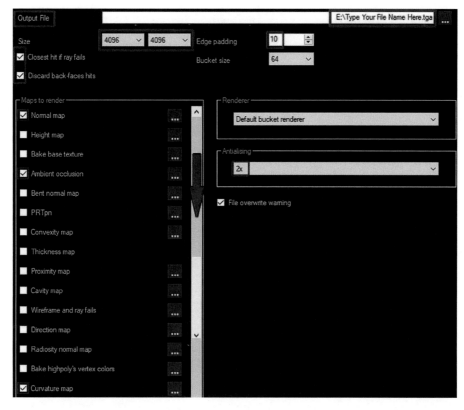

Figure 4.15 – The Baking Options tab's window

8. Change your **Normal map** settings to the settings shown in *Figure 4.16*. You can do this by clicking on the icon of a green square with three dots inside it, which is next to the name of the map, as shown in *Figure 4.15*.

Figure 4.16 – Setting your Normal map to use these settings

9. Change your AO map to the settings shown in *Figure 4.17*:

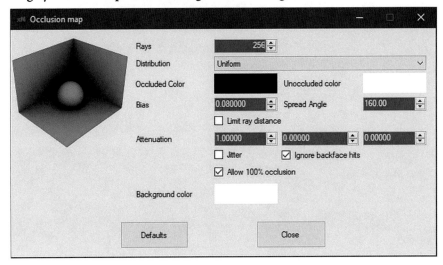

Figure 4.17 – Setting your AO map to use these settings

10. Change your curvature map to the settings shown in *Figure 4.18*:

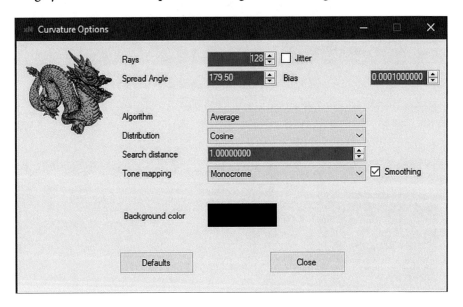

Figure 4.18 – Setting your curvature map to use these settings

11. Now that you've set up your **Render** settings for the normal map, the AO map, and the curvature map, go back to the **Baking Options** tab and click on **Generate Maps** in the bottom-right corner of the UI, as shown in *Figure 4.14*.

12. xNormal will open another window named **Preview**, which shows your texture maps as they render. Once the three texture maps are complete, the **Close** button will change states from grayed out to normal. Click on **Close** to exit xNormal.

That's it! Your texture maps are now all baked! In *Figure 4.19*, you can see the six texture maps that I have baked in xNormal for my Alien Plant model and Robot Drone model:

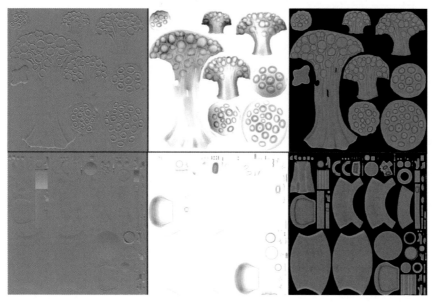

Figure 4.19 – My six baked texture maps (three for each model)

> **Note**
>
> The UV maps' layout for your Alien Plant model and your Robot Drone model will be different than mine. But, it doesn't matter if your UV layout is different than mine since the texture baking process will still work in the same way.

Now you are ready for the procedural texturing tutorial using Quixel Mixer in *Chapter 5, Texturing Your Models inside Quixel Mixer.*

Summary

In this chapter, you learned about textures and materials. You understand how to UV map 3D models that are either organic-shaped or mechanical-shaped in form.

You also gained knowledge about how to fix shading issues and triangulate and separate mesh components. Finally, you have learned how to bake texture maps in xNormal.

Going forward from here, in *Chapter 5, Texturing Your Models inside Quixel Mixer*, our learning journey will take us to the procedural texturing exercises, where we will texture both the Alien Plant and Robot Drone models.

5
Texturing Your Models inside Quixel Mixer

In *Chapter 4, UV Maps and Texture Baking*, you learned how to UV map and bake texture maps for **three-dimensional** (**3D**) assets, and you were also introduced to the concept of textures and materials.

In this chapter, we will explore the procedural-texturing process in detail.

First, you will go through a step-by-step tutorial to learn how you can utilize procedural-texturing methods to create texture maps for the Robot Drone model.

Then, afterward, you will be able to experiment by texturing the Alien Plant asset using your newfound procedural-texturing knowledge. Having this freedom to play with the various settings, instead of blindly following instructions to enter arbitrary numbers and using certain materials, helps you to really understand the software from a whole different perspective. Self-experimentation is one of the best ways to learn 3D.

But there may be those who feel more comfortable following step-by-step instructions, to understand how I got to the final result of my Alien Plant's textures.

If you fall into that category, you can download my tutorial titled *Additional Content Volume 4 - Step-by-Step Texturing of the Alien Plant.pdf*. You will find a link to this tutorial in the *Further reading* section of this chapter.

We will start this chapter by introducing you to the free procedural-texturing software called **Quixel Mixer** (also known as **Mixer**).

After your introduction to Mixer, we will start by texturing the Robot Drone and then texture the Alien Plant.

In this chapter, we're going to cover the following main topics:

- Introducing the basics of Quixel Mixer
- Texturing the Robot Drone in Mixer
- Texturing the Alien Plant in Mixer
- Exporting your materials for use in **Unreal Engine 5** (**UE5**)

To complete the texturing tutorials for the Robot Drone and the Alien Plant, you need to use the provided 3D models and texture maps (instead of using your own).

Download the Robot Drone model and the Alien Plant model along with their texture maps from the online repository here: `https://github.com/PacktPublishing/Unreal-Engine-5-Character-Creation-Animation-and-Cinematics/tree/main/Chapter05`.

After you've completed the procedural-texturing tutorials in this chapter, you should revisit this chapter... but on your second visit, use your own textures, models, materials, and settings of your own choosing. The important part of this chapter is to learn the procedural-texturing techniques to enable you to texture all your own 3D assets in the future.

At the end of this chapter, you will have practical knowledge of how to procedurally texture your own 3D models. You will also be able to create your own material variations by using different textures, materials, masks, and variations of the settings I have used.

Let's first start with an introduction to Mixer, where you will learn the basics of the **user interface** (**UI**) and the most important shortcuts that we will use.

Technical requirements

You will need the following technical skills and software to complete this chapter:

- A computer that can run basic 3D animation software.

- A basic understanding of how to navigate and manipulate meshes in Blender. This was covered in *Chapter 1, An Introduction to Blender's 3D Modeling and Sculpture Tools*.

- You need to have installed **Blender** from `https://blender.org/`. The Blender version in this chapter is version 2.93.5. Even if your version of Blender is newer, the examples should still work without any problems.

- You need to have **Quixel Mixer** installed from `https://quixel.com/mixer`.

The files related to this chapter are placed at `https://github.com/PacktPublishing/Unreal-Engine-5-Character-Creation-Animation-and-Cinematics/tree/main/Chapter05`

Introducing the basics of Quixel Mixer

Quixel Mixer is a free procedural-texturing software. You can use it to create physically accurate materials for use in UE.

The materials that Mixer exports are set up to use a **physically based rendering (PBR)** workflow. This method of rendering materials emulates how light interacts with different kinds of surfaces. We can use PBR materials in real-time renderers such as UE or in offline renderers.

You can also create non-photorealistic textures in Mixer, where physical accuracy does not matter.

Now that you have an understanding of what Mixer is, install it on your computer. During your installation process, select the option to install all the six smart material packs.

In the next section, we will set up Mixer for your first project.

Configuring your project and Mixer file

When you launch Mixer for the first time, a **Mixes** menu window will open. In the following screenshot, I have highlighted important areas you need to focus on:

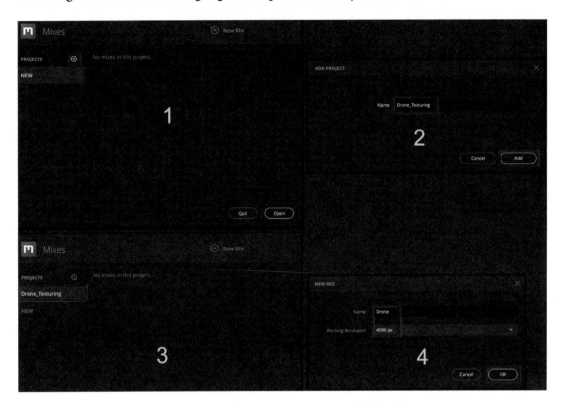

Figure 5.1 – Configuring your project and Mixer file

Execute the following steps to configure your project and Mixer file:

1.   You will see **PROJECTS**, with a + icon highlighted in red, on the left side of the window. Click on this + icon.

2.   An **ADD PROJECT** window will open up. Name the project `Drone_Texturing`. Now, click on **Add** to add this project.

3.   You will see that a `Drone_Texturing` title has been added underneath **PROJECTS**. Click on the + icon next to **NEW MIX** (a **mix** is a **Quixel Mixer** file).

4.   A **NEW MIX** window will open up. Name your mix `Drone` and set the **Working Resolution** value to `4096` px. Click on the **OK** button to open your new Mixer file.

You have successfully configured your project and Mixer file. In the next section, we will take a brief look at the UI layout of Quixel Mixer.

Quixel Mixer's UI and shortcuts

Quixel Mixer will now open, and you will see a screen like the one shown next, but without the white wording, yellow numbers, and red highlights (these were added to explain the UI).

By default, a 3D-plane model is loaded when you launch Mixer for the first time:

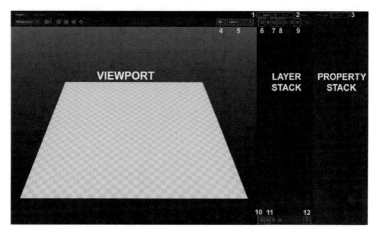

Figure 5.2 – The UI of Quixel Mixer with the 3D plane inside the Viewport

In *Figure 5.2*, you can see the UI of Mixer. I have highlighted and numbered all the items that we will use in this chapter. Let's have a look at these areas in more detail:

- **Viewport**: This is where you will view the 3D assets you are working on.
- **Layer stack**: This area will display layers of surface and smart materials.
- **Property stack**: Adjustable properties will be shown here. Also, you can add **Mask** components and **Mask** modifiers here and edit them.

The numbered icons in *Figure 5.2* correspond to the following:

1. **Layers** tab
2. **Setup** tab
3. **Export** tab
4. **3D View Mode** and **2D View Mode** drop-down menus
5. Image-based lighting drop-down menu
6. **Add Surface Layer**
7. **Add Smart Material**
8. **Add Solid Layer**

9. **Add Paint Layer**

10. **Add Mask stack on this Layer**

11. **Add Material ID on this Layer**

12. **Delete Layer/Mask**

To get started, here are the shortcuts that we will use for our tutorial:

- Mixer's Viewport navigation shortcuts are listed here:

    - **Rotate the view**: *Alt* + left mouse button

    - **Pan the view**: *Alt* + middle mouse button

    - **Zoom in/out**: *Alt* + right mouse button (or use the mouse wheel)

- Other shortcuts are listed here:

    - **Rotate the image-based lighting**: *Shift* + right mouse button

    - **Quick Eye Dropper to select Material ID map colors on your 3D model**: Press and hold *Q*.

In this section, you've learned about basic UI regions and now know the locations of icons we will use, as well as shortcuts we will use.

In the next section, we will load the Robot Drone model and start to texture it.

Texturing the Robot Drone in Mixer

Before you start on the texturing tutorial, you need to familiarize yourself with the way that lighting works in Mixer.

Try out the following shortcut in Quixel Mixer's Viewport: *Shift* + right mouse button to rotate the image-based lighting.

Also, try out different image-based lighting options in the drop-down menu (see numbers 4 and 5 in *Figure 5.2*). This step is essential since you will need to see the results of your textures/materials under different lighting angles and conditions.

Let's now get started with the practical part of our tutorial, by loading your model into Mixer.

Loading the Robot Drone model into Quixel Mixer

The first thing you want to do in Quixel Mixer is to replace the 3D-plane model shown in *Figure 5.2* with your own custom model. In the following screenshot, I have added images of the **Setup** tab's menu:

Figure 5.3 – Loading a custom model into Quixel Mixer

We will now go through all the steps to load your own custom model file, as follows:

1. Click on the **Setup** tab, as shown in *Figure 5.3*.

2. In *Figure 5.3*, you will see that **Plane** is listed as the default type of model that is loaded into Mixer.

3. Click on the **Type** drop-down menu, and select **Custom Model**.

4. Click on **Custom Model**. A **Select model file** window will open up. In this window, select the model file as RobotDrone.fbx, which you will find in the online repository here: https://github.com/PacktPublishing/Unreal-Engine-5-Character-Creation-Animation-and-Cinematics/tree/main/Chapter05.

   The 3D-plane model will now be replaced by the Robot Drone model.

5. In the **Texture Resolutions** drop-down menu, select **4096 px**.

You've just learned how to add your own custom model to Mixer. In the next section, we will see how you can add your texture maps to Mixer.

Adding texture maps

Now that you've loaded the Robot Drone model into Quixel Mixer, we can go to the next step of the preparation process, which is to add the texture maps that you've baked in xNormal into the software.

As explained before in the *Understanding texture baking* section of *Chapter 4, UV Maps and Texture Baking*, Quixel Mixer refers to these texture maps as base maps.

> **Important Note**
>
> Although I've shown you how you can bake your own texture maps in *Chapter 4, UV Maps and Texture Baking*, for this chapter's texturing tutorials, you will need to use the texture maps I have provided.

Download the following texture map files: `RobotDrone_Normals.tga`, `RobotDrone_AO.tga`, `RobotDrone_Curvature.tga`, `RobotDrone_Material_ID.png`, and `RobotDrone_Lines.png` from the online repository here: `https://github.com/PacktPublishing/Unreal-Engine-5-Character-Creation-Animation-and-Cinematics/tree/main/Chapter05`.

The reason you need to use the provided texture maps is because you are using my material ID maps for these tutorials, and in the tutorial's steps, I refer to specific colors that you need to pick. This is not possible if you are using your own material ID maps.

The way we will add base maps to Quixel Mixer is by using its **Texture Sets Editor** feature. In the following screenshot, I have highlighted the areas of **Texture Sets Editor** that are important for this section:

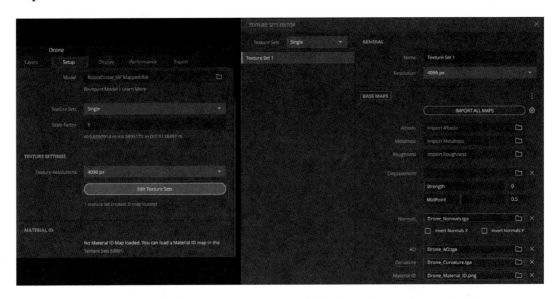

Figure 5.4 – Adding base maps to your model: (A) the Setup tab; (B) Texture Sets Editor

We will now go through the steps to set up your base maps, as follows:

1. Click on the **Setup** tab. I have highlighted this tab in *Figure 5.4.*

2. Click on the **Edit Texture Sets** button. A **TEXTURE SETS EDITOR** window will open up, as shown on the right side of *Figure 5.4.*

3. We need to load all of the base maps into their respective slots in the **TEXTURE SETS EDITOR** window. Under the **BASE MAPS** heading, assign the corresponding texture maps for the **Normals**, **AO**, **Curvature**, and **Material ID** slots by clicking on the file icon and choosing a file from your hard drive.

4. You've now set up all of your base maps. Close the **TEXTURE SETS EDITOR** window by clicking on **X**. in the top-right corner.

By default, any newly loaded model in Quixel Mixer will not have any textures or materials assigned to it, so you will notice that a checker pattern texture is currently displayed on the model's surface, as can be seen in the following screenshot:

Figure 5.5 – The Robot Drone displayed with a checker pattern texture

That's it! The base maps and the project are all set up, and you are now ready to start your texturing tutorial.

Adding paneling details

Let's add some paneling details to the model. Paneling refers to the edges of mechanical parts, where they join up. Follow these next steps:

1. We will use `Drone_Lines.png.` (the texture that you already downloaded in the previous section). This is a texture that I have painted with black lines. Mixer will use this texture to create paneling details.

2. Click on the **Layers** tab.

3. Next, click on the **Add Solid Layer** icon. I have highlighted this icon in *Figure 5.6*. You will see that the model's surface will change to a light gray color.

4. In the **Property** stack, click on **DISPLACEMENT** to open a drop-down menu, then click on **Load** and select the `Drone_Lines.png` file. The process is illustrated in the following screenshot:

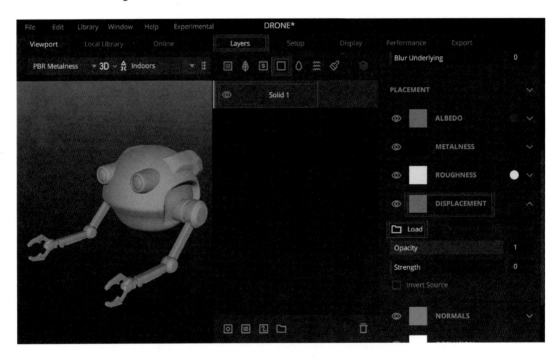

Figure 5.6 – Adding a solid layer and a displacement map

5. Still inside the **Property** stack, click on **NORMALS** (as can be seen in the bottom-right corner of *Figure 5.6*) to open a drop-down menu.

6. Check the **Generate from Displacement** checkbox to allow Mixer to use the displacement map (the texture with black lines) as a normal map, as seen in the following screenshot:

Figure 5.7 – Turning on the Generate from Displacement option

Normal mapping is a technique that is used to fake the lighting of bumps and dents inside a texture map. You will notice that as soon as you have completed this step, indented lines will appear all over the model's surface.

7. In the **Property** stack, click on **Placement** to open a drop-down menu.

8. In the **PLACEMENT** menu, click on **Box Projection**, then in the drop-down menu, select **Tiling**, as shown in the following screenshot. This will project the normal map lines to match the original hand-painted black lines texture, as seen in *Figure 5.9, Part A*:

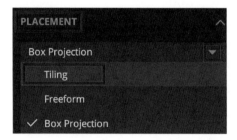

Figure 5.8 – Setting the placement to Tiling

Rotate the lighting and the model in the Viewport to observe how the indented panel lines look. The panel lines are adding visual interest to the Robot Drone (to make it look more **sci-fi**-like).

Your model should now resemble the model shown in *Part B* of the following screenshot:

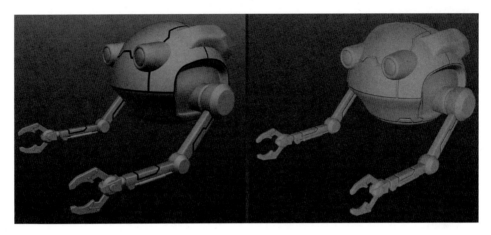

Figure 5.9 – (A) With black lines texture; (B) Black lines as a normal map for paneling

> **Note**
> Learn how to create your own paneling details by learning to paint line textures in Blender. To learn this skill, read the following document that I have created: *Additional Content Volume 3 - Painting Lines in Blender.pdf* (a link is provided in the *Further reading* section of this chapter).

Now that the normal map panel lines are set up, we can continue to work on the different layers of textures and materials.

Texturing the Robot Drone

The Robot Drone model is now ready for the procedural-texturing stage.

We will create the Procedural Textures by adding various Layers of Textures, Smart Materials, Paint Layers, Surface Layers, and Masks to the model inside of Quixel Mixer. All these various layers work together to create a final material that we will export into UE later.

Let's add the first surface layer, as follows:

1. Click on the **Add Surface Layer** icon. This will open up the **Local Library** tab that displays a variety of surface materials (I have highlighted the **Local Library** tab in *Figure 5.10, Part A*). Let's look at some terms in more detail:

- **Local library**: This is a library that shows you assets that are currently available on your own (local) hard disk drive.

- **Online library**: This is a library that shows you assets that are currently available to download from Quixel Mixer's server (on the internet).

- **Surface**: This is a type of material in Quixel Mixer and it contains multiple textures.

You can see an overview of the **Local Library** and **Online** tabs in the following screenshot:

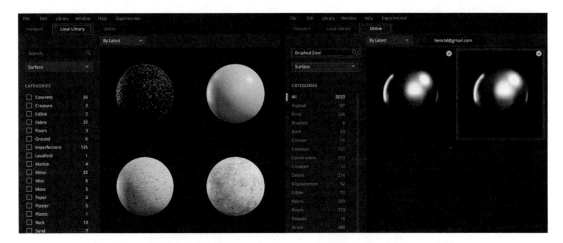

Figure 5.10 – (A) Local Library tab; (B) Online tab

2. The surface you need to use can be found in the **Online** library. Let's take a look at how to use this **Online** library. In *Figure 5.10*, *Part B*, you will see that I've highlighted the **Online** tab. This tab shows you a library of available assets (surfaces, smart materials, and so on) that are on Quixel Mixer's server.

3. In *Figure 5.10*, *Part A*, you will see a search box. In this search box, type in `Brushed Steel`. Below this search box is a drop-down menu. Set this to **Surface**, as can be seen in *Figure 5.10*, *Part B*.

4. After you've typed in your search, press *Enter*. Two surfaces (icons of metallic spheres) will appear on the right side. Select the **Brushed Steel** surface that's highlighted in *Figure 5.10*, *Part B*.

> **Note**
> The name of the surface will appear when you hover your mouse pointer over the surface icon.

5. Click on the surface icon. Another window will pop up with a button to download the surface material. Download the **Brushed Steel** surface to your local library now.

6. You've just applied your first surface material (the **Brushed Steel** surface) in a layer. In the **Property** stack, click on **PLACEMENT**, as shown in *Figure 5.11*.

7. In the **PLACEMENT** part of the **Property** stack, set the **Scale** value to 2.5 to make the brushed effect more visible to the eye, as shown in the following screenshot:

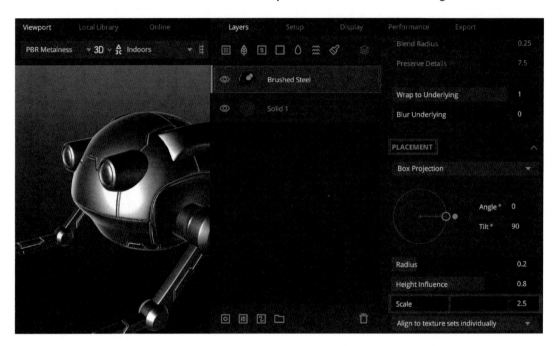

Figure 5.11 – Adjusting the scale of the Brushed Steel surface's grain

8. Still inside the **Property** stack, scroll down until you see a section that lists different material components (**ALBEDO, METALNESS, ROUGHNESS,** and so on) of the surface material. These components are shown in *Figure 5.12, Part A*. The first component is **ALBEDO**. You will see a small circle icon displayed next to each of the material components (highlighted in *Figure 5.12, Part A*). Click on the circle icon next to **ALBEDO**.

9. A **SELECT ALBEDO COLOR** menu will open up. Set the value for **Red** to 87, **Green** to 87, and **Blue** to 87, as shown in *Part B* of the following screenshot:

Figure 5.12 – (A) List of material components, with ALBEDO and the circle icon highlighted; (B) SELECT ALBEDO COLOR menu

10. Now that you know how to select colors (or black and white tones), do the same for **ROUGHNESS**. Set the value for **Red** to 98, **Green** to 98, and **Blue** to 98.

11. Let's now create a third layer for our procedural-texture material. Click on the **Add Solid Layer** icon. Set **ALBEDO** as follows: **Red** to 94, **Green** to 93, and **Blue** to 92. This layer will represent the paint that covers the metal surface on parts of the drone. At this moment, the paint covers the entire drone.

12. We will now add some edge wear around the sharp edges of the drone's surface. To do this, we will use a mask. Click on the **Add Mask Stack on this Layer** icon, or you can use the *K* shortcut key. You have just added an empty mask to your layer, as shown in the following screenshot:

Figure 5.13 – Adding a mask stack to the solid layer, then clicking the highlighted icon to add a mask component to the Property stack

13. Click on the mask in the solid layer, then in the **Property** stack, click on the **Add Mask Component** icon (the highlighted icon at the top right in *Figure 5.13*).

14. As soon as you've clicked on the **Add Mask Component** icon, a drop-down menu will appear, and in there, select **Curvature**. This will add **Curvature** settings to the **Property** stack.

> **How Do Curvature Maps Work?**
>
> Quixel Mixer uses curvature maps to calculate the convexity/concavity of a mesh. A curvature map is a texture map that assigns a grayscale value to sharp edges and cavities on your mesh. This information is used for procedural texturing. A mesh with a convex surface usually has sharper edges (peaks), while concave surfaces have cavities or indentations.
>
> Mixer uses an algorithm that determines that sharper edges on the surface will automatically get more wear and tear (and, usually, more chipped paint) while blunt edges on the surface will get less wear and tear. A curvature map is also used to determine if there are cavities or indentations that need to be filled with dirt, oil, and so on.

15. In the **Property** stack under the **Curvature** menu, click on **Default Curvature**, and in the drop-down menu, change it to **Edges & Cavities**, as shown in the following screenshot:

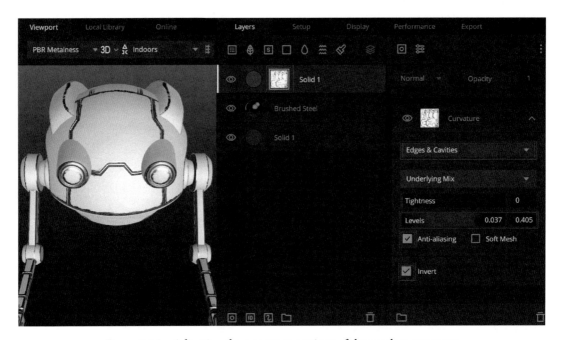

Figure 5.14 – Adjusting the curvature settings of the mask component

16. Change the **Levels** setting to 0.037 (in the first box on the left side) and to 0.405 (in the second box on the right side). This adds very smooth edge wear around all the sharp edges of the model's surface, as seen in *Figure 5.14*.

17. Check both the **Anti-aliasing** checkbox and the **Invert** checkbox. Now that the curvature mask component has been inverted, the paint is displaying the way it should. The paint is now covering the smoother and flatter areas while the paint has been masked on the sharper edges.

18. Next, we want to add some noise to break up the edge wear, since it looks too smooth at this moment. Click on the **Add Mask Component** icon that you used earlier in *Step 13* of this section, but this time, select **Noise**, and in the window that opens on the right, select **Simplex** as the **Noise** type, as shown in *Figure 5.15, Part A*.

19. In the **Property** stack, inside the **Noise** menu, there are six inputs you need to change, as follows: set the **Seed** value to -29, **Amplitude** to 1.66, **Frequency** to 7.1, **Octaves** to 5, **Lacunarity** to 3.5, and **Persistance** to 1, as shown in *Part B* of the following screenshot:

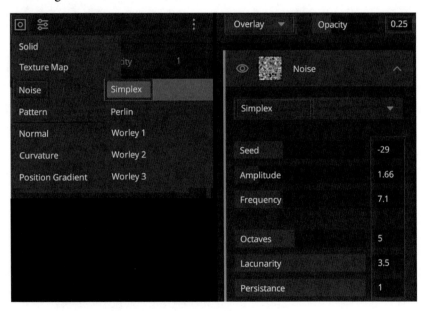

Figure 5.15 – (A) Adding a Simplex type noise mask component;
(B) Settings for noise in the Property stack

20. Directly above the **Noise** menu, you will see **Normal** (this is the blending mode) and **Opacity** (changes how much of the effect is used). Set **Opacity** to 0.25.

21. Click on **Normal**, and in the drop-down menu, set **Overlay** as the new blending mode, as shown in *Figure 5.15, Part B*.

22. Now, we will add some contrast to the noise on the edges to make it look more like chipped paint. Click on the **Add Mask Modifier** icon (I have highlighted this icon in bright green in *Figure 5.16*). In the drop-down menu that opens up, select **Brightness/Contrast**.

23. In the **Property** stack, inside the **Brightness/Contrast** menu, set **Brightness** to −1 and **Contrast** to 8. You've just completed your **Chipped Paint Edge-Wear** layer, as can be seen on the model in the following screenshot:

Figure 5.16 – Adding a Brightness/Contrast Mask modifier, and the settings used

24. Now, we will add a type of material that is known as a **smart material** in Mixer. This kind of material is usually made up of different layers, and each layer can have its own procedural masks that can act on the base maps of your model. To complete this step, click on the **Add Smart Material** icon (I have highlighted this icon in bright green in *Figure 5.17*).

25. This will open the **Local Library** tab, with the **Type** set to **Smart Material**. In the search box, search for **Brass (Oxidized)**. This smart material is included inside **Smart Materials Pack 2**. In *Figure 5.17*, you can see that I have applied this **Brass (Oxidized)** smart material to the model, and you can also see that this smart material contains four layers inside it.

The whole Robot Drone's surface will now be replaced by this smart material layer. In the **Layer** stack, click on the **Brass (Oxidized)** folder to open a drop-down menu, as illustrated in the following screenshot:

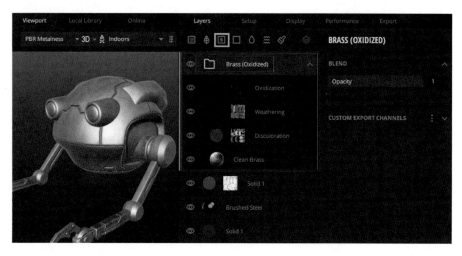

Figure 5.17 – The Add Smart Material icon highlighted in green, and the smart material with its layers highlighted in red

26. We will now change a few settings to customize this smart material. Inside the **Brass (Oxidized)** folder, you will see a flat brown circle icon in the layer named **Weathering**.

> **Note**
> A circle icon that's rendered with a flat color means it is a solid layer. Click on the circle icon to open this solid layer's properties in the **Property** stack. Change the **ALBEDO** setting as follows: **Red:** 47, **Green:** 28, and **Blue:** 4.

27. Inside the **Brass (Oxidized)** folder, click on the gray-colored circle icon in the layer named **Discoloration**. Then, in the **Property** stack, change the **ALBEDO** setting as follows: **Red:** 67, **Green:** 69, and **Blue:** 69. The gray-colored circle will now turn to a light brown color, as shown in *Figure 5.17*.

28. Inside the **Brass (Oxidized)** folder, click on the spherical icon in the layer named **Clean Brass**.

    This layer is a surface. In the **Property** stack, change the **ALBEDO** setting as follows: **Red:** 70, **Green:** 79, and **Blue:** 80. You have completed the customization of the **Brass (Oxidized)** smart material.

Your model should now resemble the one shown here:

Figure 5.18 – The result of the modified Brass (Oxidized) smart material

Let's have a quick recap of what you have learned so far in this section, as follows:

- Added surface materials, solid layers, and smart materials
- Adjusted material properties by using the **Property** stack (panel)
- Used masks and curvature maps to create edge wear in materials
- Learned how to use noise in the **Mask** component

As you can see from *Figure 5.18*, the new smart material is covering the entire Robot Drone model. This is not what we want, so in the next section, I will introduce a way that you can apply any of your materials to selected parts of your model.

Using material ID maps and masks

A **material ID** is a unique color value. You can use material ID maps to assign materials to specific areas on your mesh (these areas are defined by their unique color values in a texture map). Let's take a quick look at the terminology, as follows:

- **Material ID maps** are textures that are composed of unique colors that specify areas on a mesh.
- **Material ID masks** are masks used by **Quixel Mixer** to enable you to pick unique color areas on your **material ID map**.

- **Material ID maps** and **material ID masks** always work together. Having different materials applied to different parts of your model makes it look much more visually interesting.

> **Note**
>
> Learn how to paint your own material ID map textures in Blender by completing *Additional Content Volume 2 - Creating Material ID Maps.pdf* (a link is provided in the *Further reading* section).

In the previous section, you applied a **Brass (Oxidixed)** smart material all over your entire Robot Drone model. This is not what we want, of course. So, in this section, I will show you how you can assign a smart material or surface to a specific part of your model.

The way we will do this is by using a material ID mask.

Let's go through the steps to apply a material ID mask to your **Brass (Oxidized)** smart material, as follows:

1. Select the **Brass (Oxidized)** folder. Click on the **Add Material ID on this Layer** icon. This adds a blank material ID mask to the **Brass (Oxidized)** layer.

2. Click on **Material ID Mask** in the **Layer**. This will open the material ID mask color selector in the **Property** stack, with checkboxes for each color. Select the same colors that I selected in *Figure 5.19*.

   An alternative way to select material ID colors is to click and hold the *Q* shortcut key, which will temporarily change the Viewport to display the material ID color areas on the 3D model, as seen in the following screenshot. Left-click on a color part of the mesh that you want to assign your material to:

Figure 5.19 – Holding the Q button to select a material ID color on the model

In *Figure 5.20, Part A*, you can see how the model looked with the smart material applied all over it. In *Part B* of the following screenshot, you can see the result of using a material ID mask. As you can see, the smart material is now only applied to specific areas on the model:

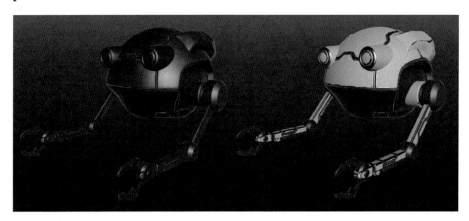

Figure 5.20 – (A) The model with the smart material over all its surface; (B) The model using a material ID mask to limit the smart material to certain areas on its surface

Next, let's add some rust inside the grooves of the paneling lines, to make it look as if the Robot Drone has been subjected to rainy weather for many years.

3. Click the **Add Surface Layer** icon. Switch to the **Online Library** tab and select **Surface** as the type of asset, then search for `Rusted Metal Sheet`. Download this surface and click on its icon. This will apply a rust coat material over the entire model.

4. With the **Rusted Metal Sheet** layer selected, look under **Placement** in the **Property** stack and change the **Scale** value to `0.69`, as seen in the following screenshot:

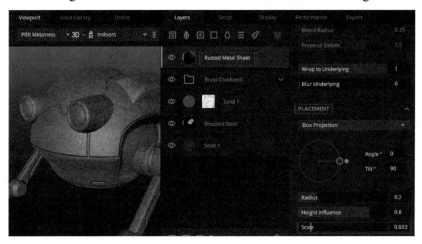

Figure 5.21 – Changing the scale of the surface material

5. With the **Rusted Metal Sheet** layer still selected, look under **Blend** in the **Property** stack and change the **Opacity** value to 0.85.

6. With the **Rusted Metal Sheet** layer selected, click on the **Add Mask Stack on this Layer** icon.

7. Select the mask you have just added. In the **Property** stack, click on the **Add Mask component** icon, and in the menu that opens up, choose **Curvature**.

8. In the **Curvature** menu, set the **Edges & Cavities** setting's **Levels** values to 0.27 and 0.825 and check the **Anti-aliasing** checkbox, as illustrated in the following screenshot. This has added some rust inside the paneling lines:

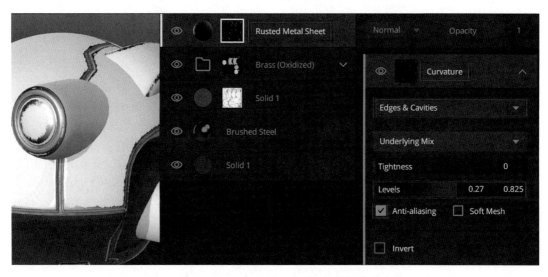

Figure 5.22 – Curvature settings for the Rusted Metal Sheet surface

9. We're now ready to add some dirt to the model since it looks far too clean at this moment. Click on the **Add Solid Layer** icon. This solid layer can be seen in *Figure 5.23*.

10. Change this solid layer's **ALBEDO** settings as follows: **Red**: 20, **Green**: 7, and **Blue**: 2. Set **Roughness** to **Pure White**. Under **Blend**, change the **Opacity** value to 0.438.

11. Press the *K* shortcut key to add a mask stack to this layer, and then click on the mask that you've just added, which can be seen in *Figure 5.23*.

12. With the mask selected, in the **Property** stack, click on the **Add Mask Component** icon and choose **Texture Map** as the option. The **Texture Map** properties can be seen in *Figure 5.23*.

13. In the **Texture Map** menu, change **Custom Map** to **Library Asset** in the drop-down menu, as illustrated in the following screenshot:

Figure 5.23 – Adding a library asset to the mask

14. Click on the **Folder** icon (highlighted in green in *Figure 5.24*) to load an asset. A **Local Library** tab will open up. Set the asset type to **Imperfection**. Search for and add `Scratched Metal`.

15. Download this **Imperfection** material and click on its icon. This **Imperfection** material will be used inside the mask, and its effect is to break up the dirt layer, making the dirt look more realistic, as illustrated in the following screenshot:

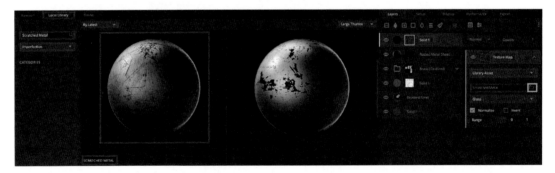

Figure 5.24 – Adding the Scratched Metal imperfection material to the layer mask

16. Click on the **Add Mask Modifier** icon and add a **Brightness/Contrast** modifier to the selected mask.

17. In the **Property** stack, find the **Brightness/Contrast** menu and set **Brightness** to `0.5` and **Contrast** to `3.42`. This will make the dirt more noticeable on the model.

18. Let's add some fine scratches to the model. Click on the **Add Surface Layer** icon, then in the **Online** surface library, search for `Scratched Painted Iron`. Download this surface material and click on its icon.

This applied the **Scratched Painted Iron** surface material (with fine scratches) all over the model. At this time, this surface is still covering the entire model, but we will fix this soon, as seen in *Figure 5.25*.

19. Change the **ALBEDO** setting as follows: **Red**: 30, **Green**: 30, and **Blue**: 30. Change the **ROUGHNESS** setting as follows: **Red**: 106, **Green**: 106, and **Blue**: 106. The **ALBEDO** and **ROUGHNESS** settings are shown in the following screenshot:

Figure 5.25 – Adding a Scratched Painted Iron surface to the model and changing its ALBEDO and ROUGHNESS settings

20. Press the *K* shortcut key to add a mask stack to this layer, and then click on the mask.

21. With the mask selected, in the **Property** stack, click on the **Add Mask Component** icon, and then choose **Texture Map**.

22. In the **Texture Map** menu, change **Custom Map** to **Library Asset** in the drop-down menu (as you did earlier in *Step 13*).

23. Click on the **Folder** icon to load an asset from the library. Switch to the **Online** library tab. Set the type to **Imperfection**, and search for Scratched Painted Metal.

24. Still in the same **Texture Map** menu of the **Mask** component, set **Range** to 0.85.

25. Click on the **Add Mask Modifier** icon and add a **Brightness/Contrast** modifier.

26. In the **Brightness/Contrast** menu, set **Brightness** to -1 and **Contrast** to 3. This changes the effect of the **Scratched Painted Iron** surface to look like fine scratches in the white paint, as can be seen in *Figure 5.26*.

27. Now, for the last step, we will texture the camera eyes of the Robot Drone. Click on the **Add Solid Layer** icon. Set **ALBEDO** as follows: **Red**: 0, **Green**: 34, and **Blue**: 255. This has added a bright blue color layer over your entire model.

28. Change **Metalness** to **Pure White color** and change **Roughness** to **Pure Black color**. This changed the blue layer, to look like a blue metallic-looking material. At this time, this **Solid** layer is covering the entire model, but we will fix this soon.

29. Select the **Solid** Layer (the blue one you just created). Click on the **Add Material ID on this Layer** icon. This creates a material ID mask in your blue metallic layer.

30. Now, we will pick the material ID color of the camera eyes. Press *Q* + left-click on **Camera Lens** inside the Viewport (the bright blue material ID color). Your blue metallic color will now be limited to the camera eyes, as seen in *Figure 5.26*.

Congratulations! You've just completed your first procedural-texturing tutorial! Your model should now resemble the model shown here:

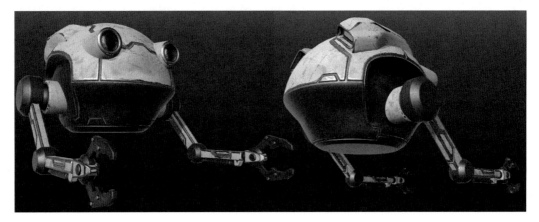

Figure 5.26 – The procedural textures are now done for the Robot Drone model

In this section, you learned a procedural-texturing workflow for mechanical types of models, by using features such as masking to create edge wear and to add dirt inside grooves.

You learned to apply surfaces, solid layers, and smart materials, and now know how to apply these to specific areas of your model by using the material ID mask feature.

In the next section, we will use procedural-texturing methods to texture the Alien Plant. This workflow will be slightly different since it is an organic-shaped model.

Texturing the Alien Plant in Mixer

In the previous section, you learned how to use procedural-texturing methods to texture the Robot Drone by following the step-by-step tutorial. This experience is invaluable since you've learned so many things while going through the steps to get to complete the Robot Drone's textures (the end result can be seen in the model in *Figure 5.26*).

But for this section, you will do something completely different. Now, you have free rein to experiment with procedural texturing on the (provided) Alien Plant model. You can apply any smart material or surface texture and use any setting that you choose. This section will provide you with a chance to put your newfound knowledge of procedural texturing to good use.

As previously mentioned, if you prefer to follow along with another step-by-step tutorial, I've created this tutorial: *Additional Content Volume 4 - Step-by-Step Texturing of the Alien-Plant.pdf*. A link to this is provided in the *Further reading* section.

Let's get started with the texturing of the Alien Plant, as follows:

1. Download the `AlienPlant.fbx` model from the online repository here: `https://github.com/PacktPublishing/Unreal-Engine-5-Character-Creation-Animation-and-Cinematics/tree/main/Chapter05`.

2. Download the following five texture files: `AlienPlant_Normals.tga`, `AlienPlant_AO.tga`, `AlienPlant_Curvature.tga`, `AlienPlant_Material_ID.png`, and `AlienPlant_Cavity.tga` from the online repository at `https://github.com/PacktPublishing/Unreal-Engine-5-Character-Creation-Animation-and-Cinematics/tree/main/Chapter05`.

3. Load the Alien Plant model into Mixer in the same way that you used to load the Robot Drone model.

4. Assign the Alien Plant's **Normals**, **AO**, **Curvature**, and **Material ID Base Maps** (in the same way that you did for the Robot Drone model).

5. Your Alien Plant model is now ready for your procedural-texture experimentation.

6. Go ahead and texture the Alien Plant model in any way that you want to. When you've finished this task, return to this point in the chapter.

Let's take a look at the way I have procedurally textured my own Alien Plant model. My model is shown in *Figure 5.27*.

> **Note**
> Your Alien Plant model will look completely different than mine if you've been experimenting with procedural textures as was suggested for this section. Remember: there is no right or wrong end result for this section. The important part of this lesson is to learn by experimentation and to have fun doing so!

Figure 5.27 – My completed Alien Plant model

In this section, you learned how to experiment with procedural-texturing methods to texture the Alien Plant model.

In the next section, I will show you how to export your textures for use in UE5.

Exporting your materials for use in UE

So, you have completed both procedural-texturing tutorials and you have some great-looking materials made up of multiple layers.

But you might be wondering how to use these materials in **UE5**. This is actually a very simple step, so let's dive right in, as follows:

1. Click on the **Export** tab shown by the number *3* in *Figure 5.2*.

2. In the **Export Target** menu, next to **Export Location**, choose a folder on your hard drive.

3. Next to **Asset Name**, type a name for your file.

4. Next to **Texture Preset**, select **Metalness Maps** as the type. For the texture maps to export, check the checkboxes that are shown in the following screenshot:

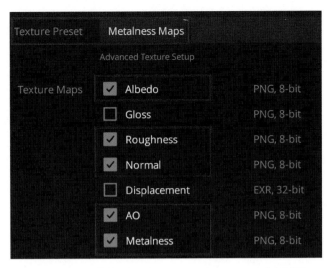

Figure 5.28 – Selecting texture maps to export for UE5

5. Now for the very last step! Click the **Export to Disk** button.

You've just learned how to export materials from Quixel Mixer. In *Chapter 7, Setting up Materials in UE5*, I will show you how to use these texture maps to create materials in UE5.

This concludes all of this chapter's tutorials!

Summary

You have successfully completed two procedural-texturing tutorials, and in the process of doing so, you've learned a great deal about different procedural-texturing workflows. In this case, you learned the difference between texturing mechanical-shaped and organic-shaped models.

You should now be able to procedurally texture your own 3D assets for your 3D movies.

Your 3D movie's Robot Drone and Alien Plant 3D assets are now 100% complete and ready to be exported to UE5. In the next chapter, we will move our focus to the basics of UE5: the UI, basic menus, and navigation controls.

See you in the next chapter!

Further reading

I have created three additional tutorials for this chapter, as follows:

- *Additional Content Volume 2 - Creating Material ID Maps.pdf*

- *Additional Content Volume 3 - Painting Lines in Blender.pdf*

- *Additional Content Volume 4 - Step-by-Step Texturing of the Alien-Plant.pdf*

You can download these three files from the online repository here:

```
https://github.com/PacktPublishing/Unreal-Engine-5-Character-
Creation-Animation-and-Cinematics/tree/main/Chapter05
```

Part 2
Building Your Virtual Movie Set in Unreal Engine 5

In this part of the book, you will learn how to use MetaHuman to create a photorealistic 3D human and build a virtual 3D movie set for Unreal Engine 5.

We will cover the following chapters in this section:

- *Chapter 6, Exploring Unreal Engine 5*
- *Chapter 7, Setting up Materials in UE5*
- *Chapter 8, Use MetaHuman to Create a Photorealistic Human for UE5*
- *Chapter 9, Building a Virtual 3D Movie Set in UE5*
- *Chapter 10, Adding Lighting and Atmospheric Visual Effects in UE5*

6
Exploring Unreal Engine 5

In the previous chapters, you learned how to create 3D assets. You now have the practical and theoretical knowledge to create mechanical and organic models. You also know how to UV map and texture these 3D assets.

You are now ready to take both of the 3D assets that you've made and use them as 3D movie set pieces (the Alien Plant) and actors (the Robot Drone) for your virtual 3D movie production.

We will begin with the basic functions of **Unreal Engine 5** (**UE5**) that we will use for our tutorials in *Chapter 7, Setting Up Materials in UE5, Chapter 8, Using MetaHuman to Create a Photo-Realistic Human for UE5, Chapter 9, Building a Virtual 3D Movie Set in UE5*, and *Chapter 10, Adding Lighting and Atmospheric Visual Effects in UE5*. This chapter will not attempt to explain every detail of UE5 since that is beyond the scope of this book.

Once you have a solid understanding of what **UE5** is and know how you can use it to create your 3D movie, we will start exploring the UI, navigation controls, and the most useful shortcuts.

In this chapter, we're going to cover the following main topics:

- Introduction to UE5
- Setting up your project using UE5's templates
- Navigating in UE5's 3D Viewport
- Learning the most useful shortcuts in UE5
- Getting to know the UI of UE5

By the end of this chapter, you will have a solid understanding of the basics of UE5 and how you can use it to create a 3D movie, and understand its UI layout, navigation, and commonly used shortcuts.

In the next section, we'll provide an introduction to UE5.

Technical requirements

For this chapter, you need to have UE5 installed. Even if your version of UE is newer, the examples should still work without any problems. You will need the following to complete this chapter:

- A computer that can run basic 3D animation software.
- UE 5.0.1. You can download it from `https://www.unrealengine.com/en-US/download`.
- Epic Games Launcher. You can download it from `https://store.epicgames.com/en-US/download`.
- UE5's hardware requirements: `https://docs.unrealengine.com/5.0/en-US/hardware-and-software-specifications-for-unreal-engine/`.

Introducing UE5

What is **UE5** and why would you want to use it to create 3D movies?

UE5 is a state-of-the-art, real-time 3D game engine and editor that can be used to create games and digital media, such as 3D movies.

While other 3D software such as Blender, Maya, and 3ds Max are true content creators where you can model, UV map, and texture from scratch, UE uses pre-made 3D assets instead of creating them.

For example, you could use UE5 to take 3D assets that you have made in Blender and then build a game or 3D movie set, animate them, and render a 3D movie's frames by using Unreal Engine's **Sequencer**.

Before you delve deeper into our introduction, take a quick look at the official UE5 information page: `https://www.unrealengine.com/en-US/unreal-engine-5`.

> **Note**
>
> **Rendering** describes the process during which 3D software generates an image by using a mesh, its materials. and the lighting in the scene for its calculation. In films and animations, a frame is one still image. When a movie is played, each frame is displayed for a very short time and immediately replaced by the next frame. This creates the illusion of movement. For every second of a movie, there are between 24 and 30 frames. This measurement is called **frames per second** (**FPS**).

The main advantage that **UE** offers compared to other digital content creation tools (such as Blender, Maya, 3ds Max, and Cinema 4D) is that it uses a method called **real-time rendering** (or near-real-time) for the output of the animation's frames.

Other digital content creation tools must render each frame using a method called **offline rendering**. This is an extremely slow method of rendering.

Real time refers to a rendering method. The 3D software renders each frame so fast that it appears to be created on the fly. This rendering speed is the most important reason why you would want to be making your 3D movie in UE.

This is because you can render the animations for your movie in (near) real time in UE. You can also edit things such as atmospheric effects, materials, and lights in your 3D scene and get near-instant feedback. This is an incredible time-saver compared to the traditional offline rendering methods.

UE is capable of producing photo-realistic renders that are close to the fidelity of renders that are made using offline rendering methods.

What can you do with UE?

UE originally started off as a game engine, but its use cases outside of the games industry have drastically increased in recent years.

Now, UE5 is used across a wide range of industries. This includes work in interactive games, films, VFX and TV productions, visualization work (architectural, transport, scientific, and medical industries), motion graphics, and mixed reality, to name a few.

Regarding 3D movies, you can use UE5 to create Control Rigs for characters, animate these characters with the Control Rigs, build scenes (3D movie sets), add atmospheric effects and VFX particles, add lighting, render these scenes, and use Unreal Engine's Sequencer to edit your movie.

You can also create interactive experiences such as mixed/virtual reality, games, and simulations.

As you have just learned, you can use UE5 for any digital media production. Let's take a look at some of the latest features in UE5.

New features in UE5

Here are some of the most exciting new features in UE5:

- **Lumen**: This is a dynamic, real-time **global illumination (GI)** system. GI is a rendering technology that calculates how light bounces off surfaces onto other surfaces (or meshes) in your scene. By doing this, it simulates indirect lighting. This helps with realism since this is the way light particles (photons) behave in the real world. In *Chapter 10, Adding Lighting and Atmospheric Visual Effectsin UE5*, you will learn how to use Lumen's GI system to light your Alien Plant 3D movie set. You can read more about Lumen in the official UE5 documentation here: `https://docs.unrealengine.com/5.0/en-US/lumen-global-illumination-and-reflections-in-unreal-engine/`.

- **Nanite**: This is a virtualized micropolygon geometry system that allows you to add massive amounts of geometric detail to (non-deforming) 3D assets. This system works great for environmental assets such as rocks, cliffs, statues, ground, and so on. We can't use the Nanite function to deform characters and foliage.

  Hard surface parts of characters are the exception to this rule since we can use Nanite on things such as a suit of armor, a robot's outer shell parts, or a stone golem's skin. In *Chapter 9, Building a Virtual 3D Movie Set in UE5*, we will learn how to use Nanite during the creation of the Alien Planet's surface. You can read more about Nanite in the official UE5 documentation here: `https://docs.unrealengine.com/5.0/en-US/nanite-virtualized-geometry-in-unreal-engine/`.

- **MetaHumans**: This cloud-based app is used to create photorealistic virtual humans. You can use it to customize the gender, age, facial features, and hairstyles of your digital human. In *Chapter 8, Using MetaHuman to Create a Photorealistic Human for UE5*, we will take you through a step-by-step tutorial to show you how to create your very own metahuman for your 3D movie. You can read more about MetaHuman in the official UE5 documentation here: `https://docs.metahuman.unrealengine.com/en-US/overview/`.

- **World Partition System**: UE5 has introduced a new world partition system that automatically divides the world into a grid system and then streams these cells as they are viewed. You can read more about the World Partitioning system in the official UE5 documentation here: `https://docs.unrealengine.com/5.0/en-US/world-partition-in-unreal-engine/`.

- **Control Rig**: This tool lets you quickly create a Control Rig for your character and share it across multiple characters, pose them in the Sequencer, and use them in the pose browser. They also use the new full-body **inverse kinematics** (**IK**) system. All of these features will be covered in the Control Rig tutorial, later in this book. You can read more about Control Rigs in the official UE5 documentation here: `https://docs.unrealengine.com/5.0/en-US/control-rig-in-unreal-engine/`.

- **Metasounds**: This feature lets you use procedural content creation methods in sound production. It gives you complete control over the audio DSPGraph generation of sound sources. You can read more about the Metasounds system in the official UE5 documentation here: `https://docs.unrealengine.com/5.0/en-US/metasounds-the-next-generation-sound-sources-in-unreal-engine/`.

You have just learned about some of the most important new features that are available in UE5. In the next section, you will learn how to download some free sample assets and projects.

Free sample projects

One of the best ways to get into UE5 is by downloading some of the (100% free) sample projects and assets.

You can play around with these assets and practice navigating around the project's scenes. It may simply serve to inspire you but it will also show you what you can achieve with UE5.

Follow these steps to get started:

1. Launch Epic Games Launcher and sign in to your account. Create an account if you haven't done so already.

2. Once the Epic Games app is open, you will see that there are two places you can download free content from. I will talk about both of these options now.

3. First, you can click on the **Samples** tab at the top of the screen, as shown in the following screenshot. Links to various **UE Feature Samples** are present on this page:

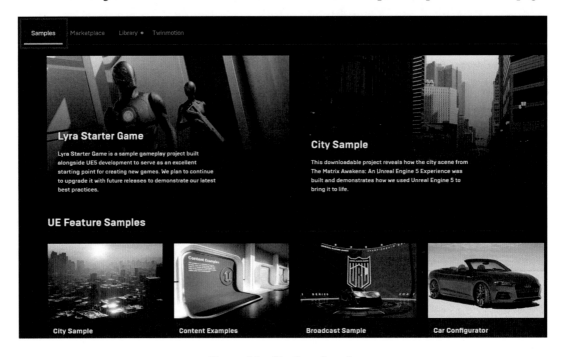

Figure 6.1 – The Samples tab

4. The next place you can look for free content is in the **Marketplace** tab, as shown in the following screenshot. Here, there are links to free content from **Epic Games** and the **Marketplace** collection. You can add any of this free content to your library by clicking on **Add to Cart**.

    There is also paid content in this window, but you can filter it by using the **Free** tag on the **Filter Results** panel:

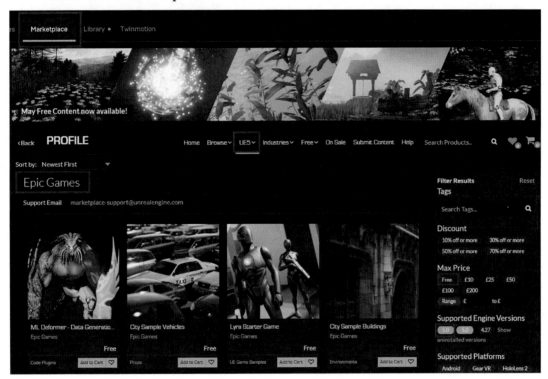

Figure 6.2 – The Marketplace tab

5. Once you've clicked on the **Add to Cart** button, your new content will be available for you in your vault. You can find your **vault** by opening the **Library** tab. The following screenshot shows these options highlighted in red. Your vault will look different from mine since the following screenshot shows the content of my vault:

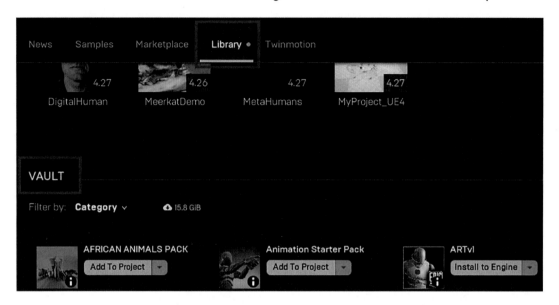

Figure 6.3 – VAULT inside the Library tab

You now know how to find and add free content (and, optionally, paid content) to UE. I recommend trying some of these assets and projects in UE5 before moving on to the tutorial.

In the next section, I will show you some interesting 3D film and TV productions that were made using UE5.

Examples of animation projects that were made in UE5

Here are a few links from UE's website:

-   An animation news feed showing many different UE projects that are in the spotlight: https://www.unrealengine.com/en-US/feed/all/animation.

-   The visually stunning animated feature called *Allahyar and the Legend of Markhor* was the first to be produced entirely in UE: https://www.unrealengine.com/en-US/developer-interviews/visually-stunning-animated-feature-allahyar-and-the-legend-of-markhor-is-the-first-produced-entirely-in-unreal-engine.

- Blue Zoo used real-time technology to create the distinctive animated short *Ada*: `https://www.unrealengine.com/en-US/spotlights/blue-zoo-uses-real-time-technology-to-create-distinctive-animated-short-ada.`

- A behind-the-scenes look at the making of Weta Digital's *Meerkat* short film: `https://www.unrealengine.com/en-US/spotlights/behind-the-scenes-on-weta-digital-s-real-time-hair-and-fur-short-meerkat.`

- Behind the lens of *The Short Film Challenge Australia*: `https://www.unrealengine.com/en-US/spotlights/behind-the-lens-of-the-short-film-challenge-australia.`

Now that you know what UE5 is and what it can do, you're ready to get started with the tutorial section. We will start by going through some common terminologies that we will use during our tutorials.

UE terminologies

There are many unique concepts and terminologies in UE, but for our tutorials, we will just go over those that you will encounter in *Chapter 7*, *Setting Up Materials in UE5*, *Chapter 8*, *Using MetaHuman to Create a Photo-Realistic Human for UE5*, *Chapter 9*, *Building a Virtual 3D Movie Set in UE5*, and *Chapter 10*, *Adding Lighting and Atmospheric Visual Effects in UE5*:

- **Actor**: Any item that can be placed inside the scene is classified as an actor. Some examples of actors are meshes, cameras, and lights.

- **Static Mesh actor**: As the name suggests, this is a kind of actor that doesn't deform.

- **Skeletal Mesh actor**: This actor type has a skeleton (known as an **armature** in Blender) that enables it to deform for animation. You can read more about actors in the official UE5 documentation here: `https://docs.unrealengine.com/5.0/en-US/unreal-engine-actors/.`

- **Post-process volume**: This is a square volume area that you can add to your scene to apply post-process effects to the area inside the defined volume space. For example, you could adjust the exposure amount inside the volume, while outside the volume, the exposure remains unchanged.

Some other post-process effects include lens effects, color grading controls, Lumen's GI settings, reflection settings, and much more. This is a very important function for 3D movie making. You can read more about post-process volumes in the official UE5 documentation here: `https://docs.unrealengine.com/5.0/en-US/ post-process-effects-in-unreal-engine/`.

Now that you know about some of the terminologies that we will be using, it's time for you to create your first project in UE5.

Setting up your project

When you launch UE for the first time, the **Unreal Project Browser** window will open. This browser lets you choose a template file that will act as the starting point for your project.

Follow these steps to get started:

1. Since we are making a 3D movie, select the **FILM / VIDEO & LIVE EVENTS** tab.

2. Inside that menu, select **Blank** as the template.

3. Under the **Project Defaults** heading, uncheck **Starter Content**.

4. Choose a project location and project name – this will be saved on your local hard disk.

5. Once you have set up your project template, you are ready to start working in UE5. Click on **CREATE** to close this menu and launch the UE5 Editor.

The following screenshot shows the UE Project Browser window with the important parts highlighted in red:

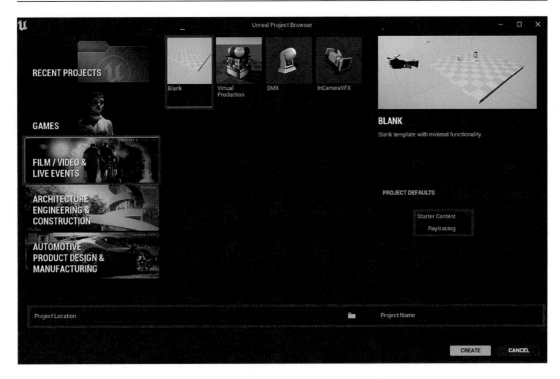

Figure 6.4 – The UE Project Browser window

> **Note**
>
> Unreal asset file is the file format that UE uses for assets. It converts other assets (meshes, textures, sound files, and so on) into `.uasset` files. These files are stored inside the content folder of the current project.

In this section, you learned how to use a UE5 template for your project.

Now that your project has been set up and the UE5 Editor has been launched, you will need to know how to navigate inside the Viewport and about some of the most useful shortcuts. We'll explore this next.

Viewport navigation

Use the following shortcuts to navigate inside the Viewport:

- **Move the view**: Click the left mouse button and drag. Moving the mouse up will move the view forward while moving the mouse down will move the view backward. Moving the mouse from side to side will rotate the view to the left or right.

- **Rotate the view**: *Alt* + left mouse button + drag the mouse.

- **Pan the view**: Middle mouse button + drag the mouse.

- **Zoom the view**: Scroll the mouse wheel up or down. Alternatively, you could use the *Alt* + right mouse button + drag the mouse shortcut.

In this section, you learned about the most useful Viewport navigation controls. You are now able to rotate, zoom, pan, and move your view to navigate around your 3D scene.

Most useful shortcuts

There are many shortcuts in UE5, but the most essential of these are as follows:

- **Move**: *W*.

- **Rotate**: *E*.

- **Scale**: *R*.

- **Focus**: *F*. This function will zoom your view to the selected item.

- **Game View (Toggle)**: *G*. This mode hides the icons and the grid in the Viewport.

- **Immersive Mode (Toggle)**: *F11*. This mode will maximize your Viewport to full-screen mode.

- **Content Drawer (Toggle)**: *Ctrl + Spacebar*.

- **Select Object Mode**: *Q*.

In this section, you learned about the most useful shortcuts in UE5. In the next section, we will explore the UI of UE5.

UE's UI

When UE5 is launched, you will see a screen that looks like what's shown in the following screenshot.

Some menus are not visible by default, so we will have a look at them soon. But first, let's explore the six main UI regions:

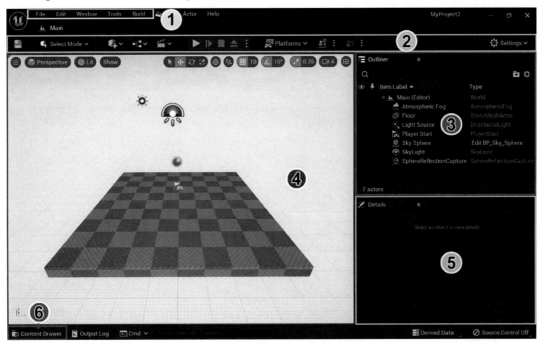

Figure 6.5 – UE5's UI regions

To explain the UI, I have highlighted and numbered the six main UI regions in the default startup screen:

1. **Menu bar**: Here, you will find drop-down menus for **File**, **Edit**, **Window**, **Tools**, **Build**, and **Help**.

2. **Toolbar**: This menu has quick access to commonly used functions and allows you to switch to different modes. For the tutorials in this book, you will need the **Create** icon and the **Cinematics** icon. Inside the **Select Mode** drop-down menu, there is an **Animation** mode. For your projects, you may also need **Landscape** mode and **Foliage** mode, which can be found inside this drop-down menu.

3. **World Outliner**: This panel displays a list of all the items (including actors) in your 3D scene. This is where you can create folders to help organize your assets.

Inside the default template project that you've loaded, you will see the **Atmospheric Fog, Floor, Light Source, Player Start, Sky Sphere, SkyLight,** and **SphereReflectionCapture** items listed in the World Outliner. We will discuss these in more detail in *Chapter 9, Building a Virtual 3D Movie Set in UE5,* when we build our virtual 3D movie set.

4. **Viewport**: This is where you view what is happening in your 3D world. The Viewport menu bar is at the top of the Viewport; we will discuss it in more detail later.

5. **Details panel**: Any item that is selected in the World Outliner will immediately have its details displayed in the **Details** panel. Some of these details are editable while some are not.

6. **Content Drawer**: This is an icon that opens the **Content Drawer** panel. **Content Drawer** becomes **Content Browser** once it is docked into the bottom of the Viewport. These panels show you all the assets in the world. Here, you can edit assets, import assets, and organize, search for, tag, and filter project assets.

Docking the Content Browser panel

The **Content Drawer** panel only stays open temporarily while you are using it, but as soon as you click outside this panel, it will close automatically.

If you want this panel to stay open, click the **Dock in Layout** icon on the top right-hand side of the **Content Drawer** panel, as shown in the following screenshot:

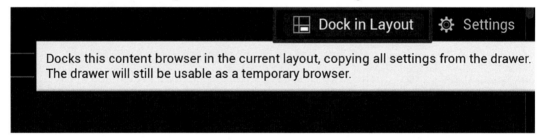

Figure 6.6 – Docking the Content Drawer so that it becomes the Content Browser

This will dock the panel at the bottom of the Viewport so that it stays open. The following screenshot shows the docked **Content Browser** panel:

Figure 6.7 – The docked Content Browser panel

In the next section, we will look at one more region in the Viewport that is of importance: the Viewport menu bar area.

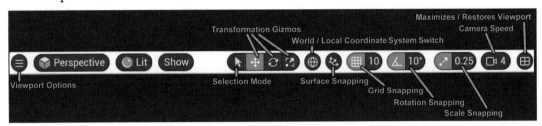

Figure 6.8 – The Viewport menu bar

To explain these icons, we will start with the icons on the left, and finish with the icons on the right:

- **Viewport Options**: This is a drop-down menu that contains basic rendering settings for your Viewport. For example, here, you can choose the **Field of View** angle, show various stats that are overlaid in your Viewport, or take high-resolution screenshots, to name but a few of the options that are available in this menu.

- **Perspective**: This icon has a drop-down menu that lets you choose a Viewport layout method. For example, the default layout is set to **Perspective**, but you can also choose between **Top**, **Bottom**, **Left**, **Right**, **Front**, **Back**, or **Cinematic**.

- **Lit**: This drop-down menu shows rendering methods for the current scene that is displayed in the Viewport. For example, the default rendering method is **Lit**, but there are other options you can choose from – **Unlit**, **Wireframe**, **Detail Lighting**, **Reflections**, and other visualization modes and/or view modes.

- **Show**: This drop-down menu contains flags for toggling how items are displayed – such as actors, volumes, meshes, and a lot more – in your Viewport. For example, you can uncheck the checkbox for **Grid** to hide the grid in your Viewport.

- **Selection Mode**: This sets **Select Object mode** to on.

- **Transform Controls/Transformation Gizmos**: These are gizmos for moving, rotating, and scaling. There's no need to explain how these work since they work in basically the same way as the Object Gizmos in Blender (see *Chapter 1, An Introduction to Blender's 3D Modeling and Sculpting Tools*).

- **Transform Gizmo Coordinate System Switch**: This icon (an icon of a globe or cube with three lines) toggles between the world and the local coordinate system. This only works on the move and rotate transform gizmos.

- **Surface Snapping**: This makes actors align to the surface of another actor or the floor grid.

- **Grid Snapping settings**: When enabled, an actor will move in increments of a specific value. For example, if you set it to `10 Units`, you can only move the actor in `10 Unit` increments. You can change this value by clicking on the number inside the icon. This will open a drop-down menu where you can select a value. (**Note**: `1 Unit = 1 cm`.)

- **Rotation Snapping settings**: When the icon of two blue angled lines is enabled, an actor will rotate in increments of a specific value.

- **Scale Snapping settings**: When the icon of a small cube with an arrow is enabled, an actor will scale in increments of a specific value.

- **Camera Speed setting**: Click on the number inside this icon to open a drop-down menu where you can choose the speed for your Viewport camera.

- **Maximizes / Restores Viewport toggle**: This icon will toggle between different Viewport layouts. If you click on it once, it will open a four-view Viewport layout (**Perspective**, **Right**, **Front**, and **Top**). If you click on the same icon inside any of these four views, it will maximize the current view.

You've just learned about all the options that are available in the Viewport menu bar. This concludes this tutorial on the basic UI, navigation, and shortcuts in UE5.

Summary

Congratulations – you have completed your introduction to UE5! In this chapter, you learned about the basics of the UI, Viewport navigation, and shortcuts in UE5. You now know how UE5 can be used in your 3D movie production pipeline.

In the next chapter, we will continue with your learning journey in UE5. You will use the 3D assets that you created in the previous chapters and learn how to import them into UE5.

After that, you will learn how to set up materials for these 3D assets by using the materials that you exported from Quixel Mixer in *Chapter 5*, *Texturing Your Models inside Quixel Mixer*.

See you in the next chapter!

7
Setting Up Materials in UE 5

In the previous chapter, you learned the basics of **Unreal Engine 5's (UE5's)** UI, basic navigation, and shortcuts.

In this chapter, you will learn the process of importing models and textures and creating materials for 3D assets.

The materials that you will create will use the textures that you exported in *Chapter 5, Texturing Your Models inside Quixel Mixer*.

In this chapter, we're going to cover the following main topics:

- Importing models into UE5

- Learning the basic UI of the Material, Texture, and Static Mesh Editors

- Importing textures into UE5

- Creating materials in UE5

- Previewing your models with basic lighting

By the end of this chapter, you will have completed both the Robot Drone and Alien Plant's UE materials setup, making them ready to be animated and placed into your virtual 3D movie set.

In the next section, we will take you through the model import process in UE5.

Technical requirements

The following are the technical skills and software you will need to complete this chapter:

- A computer that can run basic 3D animation software.

- You need to have installed UE 5.0.1. You can download it from `https://www.unrealengine.com/en-US/download`.

- Have a basic understanding of how to navigate in UE5. If you skipped ahead, this was covered in *Chapter 6*, *Exploring Unreal Engine 5*.

The files related to this chapter are placed at `https://github.com/PacktPublishing/Unreal-Engine-5-Character-Creation-Animation-and-Cinematics/tree/main/Chapter07`

Importing your 3D assets

Let's start by importing the Robot Drone and Alien Plant models into UE5.

If you prefer to use the provided models instead of your own models for this tutorial, download the `RobotDrone.fbx` and `AlienPlant.fbx` model files from the online repository here:

`https://github.com/PacktPublishing/Unreal-Engine-5-Character-Creation-Animation-and-Cinematics/tree/main/Chapter07`

These are Static Mesh versions of the models. We will only use these models for the material creation process:

1. Create a new folder in the **Content Browser** panel by right-clicking on the sources view area and in the menu that pops up, selecting **New folder**. Name this folder `RobotDrone` and then open this newly created folder.

2. Create another new folder inside the `RobotDrone` folder and name it `Model`. Open the `Model` folder.

3. Drag and drop the `RobotDrone.fbx` model from the file's location on your computer into the asset view area of the **Content Browser** panel. The asset view area is shown in *Figure 7.1*:

Figure 7.1 – Dragging and dropping your model file onto the asset view area of Content Browser

4. Once you have dropped your model file in the asset view area of the **Content Browser** panel, the **FBX Import Options** window will open up. Match your settings to the settings that are shown in *Figure 7.2*:

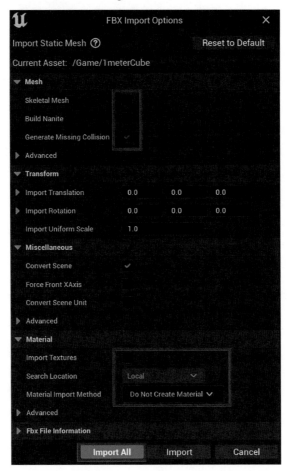

Figure 7.2 – The import settings for your Static Meshes

5.   Once you have matched the settings shown in *Figure 7.2*, click on **Import All** to complete the import of the model, as highlighted in *Figure 7.2*. Your `RobotDrone` model will now be imported into the `Model` folder.

6.   Repeat the same import process for the Alien Plant. Create a new folder for the Alien Plant in the sources view area named `AlienPlant`.

7.   Create another new folder inside the `AlienPlant` folder, name it `Model`, and open it.

8.   Drag and drop the `AlienPlant.fbx` model into the asset view area. Use the settings shown in *Figure 7.2*. Your `AlienPlant` model will now be imported into the `Model` folder.

Now, both models will be visible in their respective `Model` folders in the sources view area. You will also see the icons of the untextured models that are displayed in the asset view area. When an asset is untextured, it will display a checker pattern on its surface.

You've successfully completed the model importing stage of this chapter. In the next section, we will import the textures that you've exported from **Quixel Mixer**.

> **Tip**
> A good practice when working in UE is to save your work regularly. To save all levels and assets to your hard disk, just click on **File | Save All**. Alternatively, you can use the *Ctrl + Shift + S* shortcut. The *Ctrl + S* shortcut will save the current level only.

Importing textures

Importing textures into UE 5 is a really simple process. Let's start with the Robot Drone's textures first:

1.   Create two new folders inside the `RobotDrone` folder in the sources view area of the **Content Browser** panel. Name the first folder `Textures` and the second folder `Materials`. Open the `Textures` folder.

2.   Select all the Robot Drone's exported textures in their location on your hard drive. These are the textures that you exported from Quixel Mixer at the end of *Chapter 5*, *Texturing Your Models inside Quixel Mixer*. These textures are the following: `RobotDrone_Albedo.png`, `RobotDrone_AO.png`, `RobotDrone_Metalness.png`, `RobotDrone_Roughness.png`, and `RobotDrone_Normal.png`.

> **Note**
>
> If you prefer to use the provided textures instead of using your own exported textures, you can download all of these textures (for the Robot Drone and Alien Plant) from the online repository here: `https://github.com/PacktPublishing/Unreal-Engine-5-Character-Creation-Animation-and-Cinematics/tree/main/Chapter07`.

3. Drag and drop all five of the Robot Drone's exported textures from your hard drive's location into the asset view area of the **Content Browser** panel. This will add the textures to the `Textures` folder. You will notice that each texture has an asterisk symbol in the bottom-left corner of its icon. This asterisk indicates that the textures have not been saved yet, as shown in *Figure 7.3*:

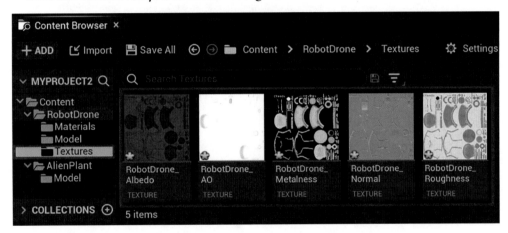

Figure 7.3 – The Robot Drone's textures are now added to Content Browser

4. Repeat the same process for the Alien Plant's exported textures. Create two new folders inside the `AlienPlant` folder. Name the first folder `Textures` and the second folder `Materials`.

5. Select the AlienPlant's `Textures` folder and then drag and drop the Alien Plant's exported textures (`AlienPlant_Albedo.png`, `AlienPlant _AO.png`, `AlienPlant_Roughness.png`, and `AlienPlant_Normal.png`) into the asset view area of the **Content Browser** panel.

You have just learned how to create new folders and import textures into **Content Browser**.

In the next section, we will see how to change the settings for each texture by using the Texture Editor in UE5.

The Texture Editor

The **Texture Editor** is used to change the settings of textures in UE5. In *Figure 7.4*, you can see a screenshot of the Texture Editor (without a texture loaded).

Instead of explaining every part of this Editor, we will focus on the parts that you need for this tutorial. This is to prepare you for setting up your own textures. There are more advanced options in this editor, but that is beyond the scope of this book:

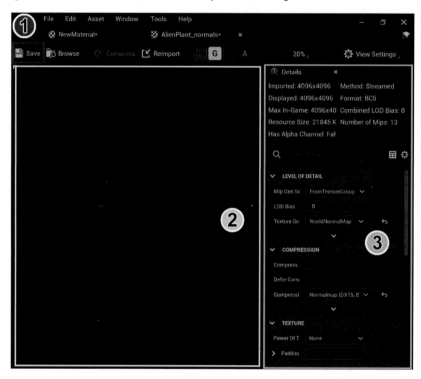

Figure 7.4 – The three areas of the Texture Editor's UI that we will focus on

The three areas of the Texture Editor's UI that we will focus on are listed as follows and correspond to the numbers of the UI regions in *Figure 7.4*:

1. **Toolbar**: Here, you will find the **Save** icon.

2. **Viewport**: This is your view of the texture that you are editing.

3. **Details panel**: You can change the settings and view details of your texture here.

Let's start by editing the RobotDrone_Albedo texture first:

1. Double-click on the RobotDrone_Albedo texture in the asset view area. This will open up the Texture Editor window. The selected texture is automatically preloaded into the Texture Editor.

2. With the `RobotDrone_Albedo` texture loaded into the Texture Editor window, set the settings in the Editor's **Details** panel to the following:

    - Under the **LEVEL OF DETAIL** drop-down menu, set **Mip Gen Settings** to **NoMipMaps**.

    - Check that under the **COMPRESSION** drop-down menu, **Compression Settings** is set to **Default (DXT1/5, BC1/3 on DX11)**.

    - Under the **Texture** drop-down menu, check the **sRGB** checkbox. Save the texture and close this window.

You have prepared your first texture successfully. I have highlighted all of the settings from this step, including the **Save** button, in *Figure 7.5*:

Figure 7.5 – Setting up an Albedo texture in the Texture Editor

3. Double-click on the `RobotDrone_AO` texture to load it into the Texture Editor. Apply the same settings that you have just used for the Albedo texture in the previous step, except this time, uncheck the **sRGB** checkbox in the **Texture** drop-down menu, to disable sRGB (only Albedo textures should have the **sRGB** option enabled).

4. Repeat *Step 3* for both the `RobotDrone_Metalness` texture and the `RobotDrone_Roughness` texture.

5. Double-click on the `RobotDrone_Normal` texture to load it into the Texture Editor and do the following:

    ▪ Under the **LEVEL OF DETAIL** drop-down menu, set **Mip Gen Settings** to **NoMipMaps**.

    ▪ Check that under the **COMPRESSION** drop-down menu, **Compression Settings** is set to **Normalmap (DXT5, BC5 on DX11)**.

    ▪ Under the **Texture** drop-down menu, make sure the **sRGB** checkbox is unchecked.

    ▪ Still under the **Texture** drop-down menu, click on the small downward-pointing arrow before the heading named **Advanced** to open the drop-down menu, then check on the checkbox for **Flip Green Channel**, as shown in *Figure 7.6*:

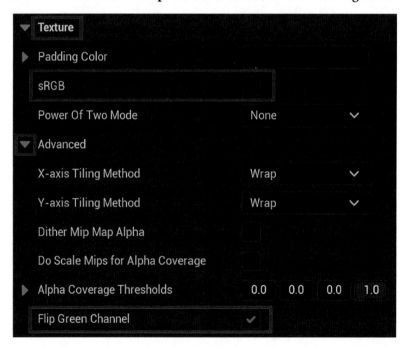

Figure 7.6 – Check the Flip Green Channel checkbox for Normal Maps that are exported from Quixel Mixer

> **Note**
>
> Quixel Mixer uses a Normal Map system with its green channel (**Y**) set in the positive direction: (**X**: +, **Y**: +, **Z**: +).
>
> UE uses a Normal Map system with its green channel (**Y**) set to the negative direction: (**X**: +, **Y**: -, **Z**: +).
>
> The **X**, **Y**, **Z** coordinates correlate to the R, G, B color channels. The reason we're flipping the green color channel of the Normal Map textures inside UE is to correct the way that light bounces off a mesh's surface. If the green color channel is flipped, it will invert the direction of bumps to look like they are indentations, and vice versa.

6. You will now repeat the texture preparation process for the Alien Plant. For the `AlienPlant_Albedo` texture, use *Step 2*. For the `AlienPlant_AO` texture and the `AlienPlant_Roughness` texture, use *Step 3*. For the `AlienPlant_Normal` texture, use *Step 5*.

> **Note**
>
> The Alien Plant does not have a Metalness texture map.

You've just learned how to set up all the textures for the Robot Drone and the Alien Plant. In the next section, I will take you through the process of setting up materials.

Creating materials

Let's now use the textures that you prepared in the previous section to create materials for your Robot Drone and Alien Plant.

> **Note**
>
> For those of you who wish to skip the materials setup part of this tutorial, you can download the completed materials from the online repository at `https://github.com/PacktPublishing/Unreal-Engine-5-Character-Creation-Animation-and-Cinematics/tree/main/Chapter07/AlienPlant/Materials`
>
> and from here: `https://github.com/PacktPublishing/Unreal-Engine-5-Character-Creation-Animation-and-Cinematics/tree/main/Chapter07/RobotDrone/Materials`.

Let's create your first material in **Content Browser** by following these simple steps:

1. Open `RobotDrone`'s `Materials` folder in the sources view area of the **Content Browser** panel.

2. Right-click in the asset view area of the **Content Browser** panel. This will open a menu. In the **CREATE BASIC ASSET** section of this menu, select **Material**, as shown in *Figure 7.7*:

Figure 7.7 – Creating a new material

3. This will create a new material in the asset browser that doesn't have any textures connected to it yet. Name this material `M_RobotDrone`. You can see your new material in *Figure 7.8*:

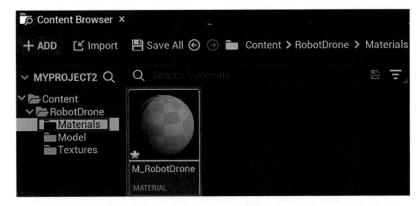

Figure 7.8 – Your new material in the asset view area of Content Browser

4. Repeat this process (*Step 1* and *Step 2*) for the Alien Plant. Create a new material in
    `AlienPlant`'s `Materials` folder and name this material `M_AlienPlant`.

5. Double-click on the newly created `M_RobotDrone` material. This will open the
    Material Editor window with the currently selected material preloaded in the
    Material Editor. In *Figure 7.9*, you can see a screenshot of the Material Editor. I have
    numbered and highlighted the parts we will focus on.

You have just learned how to create a new material in UE5. In the next section, we will
explore the Material Editor window.

The Material Editor

The **Material Editor** is used to connect textures to a Base Material node. The Base
Material node is a visual representation of your material. For each texture that you
connect to this node, you are describing a specific property of your material.

For example, if you connect your Roughness map to the node, you are describing how
rough or smooth areas of your material will be. You can have multiple textures that can
describe multiple aspects of the same material. For example, a model of a cube can have
areas on its material that are smooth described by the Roughness map and also metallic
described by the Metalness map.

Let's now explore the UI regions of the Material Editor that opened up automatically when
you double-clicked on a material in **Content Browser**'s asset view area.

In *Figure 7.9*, you will see a screenshot of the Material Editor window. I have added numbers and highlights to indicate the different UI regions for explanation purposes:

Figure 7.9 – The Material Editor's regions

The following are the UI regions that are shown in *Figure 7.9*:

1. **Toolbar**: Here, you will find the **Save** icon.

2. **Viewport panel**: View of your material.

3. **Details panel**: Displays details and changeable settings for your material.

4. **Graph panel**: Where you connect textures to the **Base Material** node.

Let's start by setting up the material for the Robot Drone:

1. Reduce the size of the Material Editor window by clicking on the Restore Down icon (the icon with two squares, on the top-right side of the window). Drag and drop all five of the Robot Drone's textures from **Content Browser** into the Material Editor's **Graph** panel.

> **Tip**
> Inside the Material Editor's **Graph** panel, use the mouse wheel to zoom in or out. Click and drag the right mouse button to pan.

2. Move the textures to the same positions that are shown in *Figure 7.10*.

3. Note that the **Base Material** node is already inside the **Graph** panel when you open it, so just move the five textures to the left of it. The **Details** panel will display the texture name when you click on a texture.

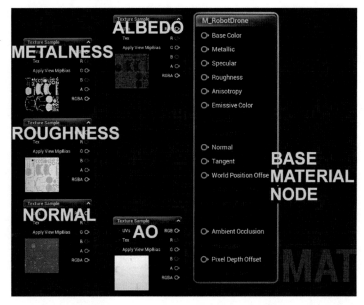

Figure 7.10 – The Graph panel with your Robot Drone's textures and the Base Material node

Next, we will start connecting the textures to the **Base Material** node.

4. Let's start with the **Albedo** texture. Left-click on the **RGB** output, as shown in *Figure 7.11*, *Part A*. Then, drag the connection and connect the line to the **Base Color** input in the **Base Material** node and then release the mouse button. As seen in *Figure 7.11*, *Part B*, (**Base Color** is the same as Albedo).

You have just learned how to connect a texture to a **Base Material** node.

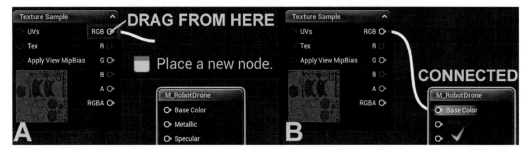

Figure 7.11 – Connecting a texture to the Material node: (A) Dragging the connection from the RGB output (B) Connecting it to the Base Color input

5. Connect the **Metalness** output to the **Metallic** input, the **Roughness** output to the **Roughness** input, the **Normal** output to the **Normal** input, and the **AO** output to the **Ambient Occlusion** input of the **Base Material** node, as shown in *Figure 7.12*:

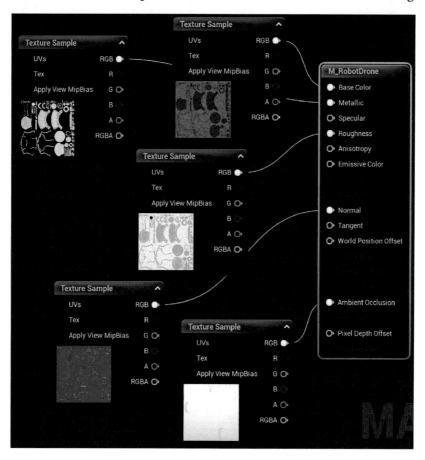

Figure 7.12 – Connecting the rest of the textures to the Base Material node

6. For the last step, just click on the **Save** icon. This will save the changes you've made to the material. Now, close the Material Editor window.

7. Repeat the same process (*Step 1* to *Step 5*) for the M_AlienPlant material but use the four textures of the Alien Plant to create this material, then save it.

You've successfully completed the materials for the Robot Drone and the Alien Plant.

In this section, you've just learned how to create new materials in UE5. You have also learned how to connect the textures that you've exported from Quixel Mixer to create UE-compatible materials.

In the next section, we will see how we can now apply these materials to the models.

The Static Mesh Editor

The Static Mesh Editor is used to change the settings of Static Meshes in UE5. We can also use it to assign a particular material to your Static Mesh.

You've completed all your texture imports for both the Robot Drone and Alien Plant and edited their individual texture settings. After this, you created new materials for these models. Finally, you are now ready to apply these materials to your models.

We will apply the materials by using the Static Mesh Editor. But first, we need to go over the basic UI regions we will use for this tutorial. In *Figure 7.13*, you can see a screenshot of the **Static Mesh Editor** window. I have added numbers and highlights to indicate the different UI regions for explanation purposes:

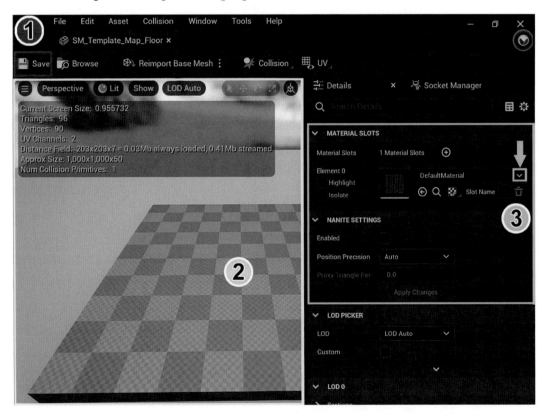

Figure 7.13 – The Static Mesh Editor's UI and the highlighted parts that we will focus on

The following numbers correspond to the UI regions that are shown in *Figure 7.13*:

1. **Toolbar**: Here, you will find the **Save** icon.

2. **Viewport panel**: This is your view of the model that you are editing.

3. **Details panel**: You can change settings, view details, and assign materials to your models here. The **Material Slot** drop-down selection menu is indicated by the green arrow.

Let's get started by assigning the Robot Drone's material first, then we will move on to the Alien Plant's material:

1. Open the `RobotDrone` folder.

2. Inside the asset view area, double-click on the **RobotDrone** model (**Static Mesh**). This will open the Static Mesh Editor, as shown in *Figure 7.13*. The **RobotDrone** Static Mesh will be preloaded and displayed in the Viewport panel.

> **Note**
> The model will still have a checker pattern applied at this point.

3. In the **Details** panel, click on the **Material Slot** drop-down selection menu, which is indicated by the green arrow in *Figure 7.13*.

4. In this drop-down menu, you will see the two materials that you created earlier. Select the `M_RobotDrone` material. This will replace the checker pattern on the Robot Drone's surface with the material you created for it.

5. Click on the **Save** icon to save the changes you've made to the Static Mesh.

6. Repeat the same process (*Steps 1–5*) for the Alien Plant model (**Static Mesh**) by applying the `M_AlienPlant` material to it.

In this section, you have learned how to use the Static Mesh Editor to assign a material to a Static Mesh. You will essentially use the same process for the Skeletal Mesh versions of the Robot Drone and Alien Plant later on by using the Skeletal Mesh Editor. In later chapters, we will take you through all the steps to assign a material to a **Skeletal Mesh**.

Now that you have materials assigned to both the Robot Drone and Alien Plant, it is time to see how they look in the Viewport.

In the next section, I will show you how to adjust the lighting in the scene so that you can see the materials better, since the default lighting has very dark shadows.

Previewing your models with lighting

The purpose of this section is to show you some very basic lighting methods to use for previewing your 3D assets. In *Chapter 10, Adding Lighting and Atmospheric Visual Effects in UE5*, you will have an in-depth exploration of the subject of **lighting**.

To get started, let's add `RobotDrone` and `AlienPlant` Static Mesh models to the scene (World) to see how they look with the materials you've made. Then, we will adjust the lighting to achieve a more pleasing look:

> **Note**
>
> This part of the process will not be used in your final 3D movie set, since we are using this step to preview what the materials look like on your models.

1. Left-click and drag the **RobotDrone** model (**Static Mesh**) from the asset view area of **Content Browser** into the Viewport. Let go of the left mouse button when you are happy with the position of the model in the World.

2. With the Robot Drone still selected, look inside the **Details** panel. Under the **Transform** heading, change the Z-axis (blue tab) location to 40, as shown in *Figure 7.14*. This will move the Robot Drone model so that it floats above the ground, instead of intersecting with it (sci-fi Robot Drones are supposed to fly above the ground):

Figure 7.14 – Adjusting the Z-axis location of the Robot Drone

3. Now, it is time to place the Alien Plant. Left-click and drag the **AlienPlant** model (**Static Mesh**) from the asset view area of **Content Browser** into the Viewport. Let go of the left mouse button when you are happy with the position of the model in the World. The Alien Plant model does not need any adjustment, because its base is already resting on the ground level.

4. Left-click inside the Viewport in an empty space, then press G on your keyboard. This shortcut will toggle the display of the icons and grid in your Viewport so you can see the models better.

5. Now that both models are in the Viewport, we will adjust the lighting. In the World **Outliner**, click on **SkyLight**. Inside the **Details** panel, under the Light (heading), set **Intensity Scale** to 6, as shown in *Figure 7.15*:

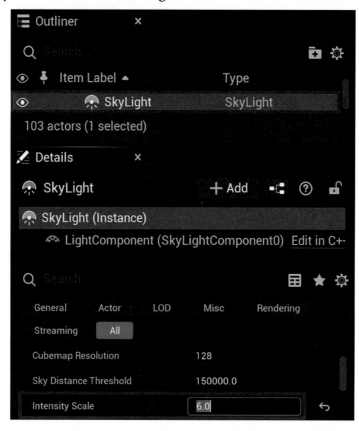

Figure 7.15 – Adjusting SkyLight's Intensity Scale

6. In the World **Outliner**, click on **Light Source**. Inside the **Details** panel, under the Light (heading), set **Intensity** to 10.0 lux, as shown in *Figure 7.16*:

Figure 7.16 – Adjusting Light Source's Intensity

7. Let's interactively adjust the angle of the sunlight in the Viewport. Left-click inside the Viewport in an empty space, then use the *Ctrl + L* shortcut while moving your mouse, to interactively adjust the angle of the sunlight.

8. When you are satisfied with the angle of the sunlight, just release the shortcut keys. In *Figure 7.17*, I have adjusted the sunlight that is used to light the Alien Plant and Robot Drone, to look more pleasing:

Figure 7.17 – Testing the models with a variety of lighting angles

Testing your models with different types and angles of lighting helps to give you a better idea of what your models will look like once they are placed inside the 3D movie set that we will build later in *Chapter 9, Building a Virtual 3D Movie Set in UE5*.

In this section, you've just learned how to place your models in the World.

You've also learned how to adjust the properties of the lights in UE5, plus how to interactively adjust the angle of the sunlight.

Summary

You have successfully completed the practical tutorials in this chapter to import your assets, create materials, connect textures to materials, and apply these materials to a 3D asset.

Finally, you've learned how to place your models in the World and how to do some basic adjustments to the lighting for previewing purposes.

In the next chapter, we will explore MetaHuman Creator, which is used to create photo-realistic human characters for use in UE 5. We will go through the step-by-step process to create a sci-fi-style female character.

See you in the next chapter!

8

Using MetaHuman to Create a Photorealistic Human for UE5

In the previous chapter, you learned how to import your assets into UE5. Then, you learned how to create materials and assign them to your assets.

In this chapter, you will learn how to create a photorealistic human character for UE5 by using the free cloud-based app from Epic called **MetaHuman Creator**.

MetaHumans are essentially digital humans (photorealistic 3D models of humans). The MetaHuman Creator app allows you to customize the facial features of the digital human you are creating. Furthermore, you can choose from a selection of body shapes, facial textures, and hairstyles and select between three sets of clothing and accessories.

Note that, at the time of writing, the MetaHuman Creator app is still in development.

I expect that when the full release version of MetaHuman becomes available, it will have a lot more outfits, accessories, and hairstyles to choose from. This will allow you to create even more variety in your characters.

In this chapter, we will explore the MetaHuman app's UI, as well as its basic navigation and functions, before moving on to a practical step-by-step tutorial to show you how to create a female sci-fi-style character that would play the role of the main character in your 3D movie.

I will show you how to import your newly created sci-fi character into UE5, assign materials to it, and assign sci-fi armor to her body.

In this chapter, we're going to cover the following main topics:

- What is MetaHuman Creator?

- Creating a photorealistic female sci-fi character

- Adding your MetaHuman to Unreal Engine 5

- Customizing your character's clothing

By the end of this chapter, you will be able to create a photorealistic human character for use in UE. You will also know how to customize the character's clothes so that they match the theme of your 3D movie.

In the next section, we will take a more in-depth look at what the MetaHuman Creator app is.

Technical requirements

You will need the following technical skills and software to complete this chapter:

- A computer that can run basic 3D animation software.

- You need to have installed Unreal Engine 5.0.1. You can download it from `https://www.unrealengine.com/en-US/download`.

- For the MetaHuman Creator app, you will need an internet connection with a Chrome, Edge, Firefox, or Safari-based web browser. You will also need a computer with Windows 10 (or higher) that supports DirectX 12 or a macOS operating system and a ray-tracing capable NVIDIA graphics card to access the MetaHuman Creator cloud-based app.

- You must have a basic understanding of how to navigate the Unreal Engine 3D user interface. If you skipped ahead, then don't worry – this was covered in *Chapter 6, Exploring Unreal Engine 5*.

The files related to this chapter are placed at `https://github.com/PacktPublishing/Unreal-Engine-5-Character-Creation-Animation-and-Cinematics/tree/main/Chapter08`

What is MetaHuman Creator?

MetaHuman Creator is a free cloud-based app that's used for creating photorealistic human characters.

At the time of writing, this app does not allow you to create young people yet, but you might be able to create young people in the full release version.

This app is made by Epic, the creator of UE. All the MetaHuman characters that the app creates are fully compatible with UE5. The MetaHuman app runs in your internet browser window.

The app gives you fine controls to customize your MetaHuman's face. At the time of writing, a small number of options are available for the body shapes, hairstyles, and clothes. For the clothes and accessories, we currently only have a choice between three varieties of tops, bottoms (pants/trousers), and shoes.

Despite the current minor limitations, this app is the best tool that's available for creating photorealistic adult humans.

With that, you've learned what MetaHuman Creator is. In the next section, we will learn how to gain access to the MetaHuman Creator app.

For more information about MetaHumans, please take a look at the official UE5 documentation: `https://docs.metahuman.unrealengine.com/en-US/overview/`.

Getting access to MetaHuman Creator

Since MetaHuman Creator is in early access at the time of writing, you need to request access from Epic. Follow these steps to do so:

1. Go to `https://www.unrealengine.com/en-US/metahuman-creator`. On the page that opens, scroll down a bit and click on the link/button that says **Request Early Access**.

2. When you click on the link, it will take you to a page where you can log into your **Epic Games Account**.

3. You will be notified by email as soon as you've been granted access to the MetaHuman Creator app.

4. Once you've been granted access, simply go to the following website to start using the MetaHuman Creator app: `https://metahuman.unrealengine.com/`.

In this section, you learned how to gain access to the MetaHuman Creator cloud-based app.

In the next section, we will launch the MetaHuman Creator app and explore the MetaHuman **Preset Selection** screen.

Launching MetaHuman Creator

It will take a few minutes to launch the MetaHuman Creator cloud-based app and open your session.

At the time of writing, MetaHuman allows users to access the app for a maximum session time of 1 hour. Once this session time has expired, you can request as many new sessions as you want. The time limit (of 1 hour per session) will still apply for any new sessions.

When the MetaHuman app finally launches, it will open the MetaHuman **Preset Screen** in your browser window. You will see something similar to the following:

Figure 8.1 – The MetaHuman preset screen

Using the preceding screenshot as a reference, you will see that there are two headings below the **MetaHuman** tile, as follows:

- **CREATE METAHUMAN**: This option gives you a selection of MetaHuman presets that you can choose from to use as a starting point for creating your own MetaHuman. On the left-hand side of the screen, you will see the **Character Preset** pane, which contains many MetaHuman portraits, and a scrollbar on the right-hand side.

- **MY METAHUMANS**: This option will show you any MetaHumans that you've created previously.

Let's get started with our tutorial:

1. Select the **CREATE METAHUMAN** option, as shown in the preceding screenshot.

2. Use the scrollbar to scroll down the selection of MetaHuman portraits. Then, click on the portrait of the female named **Pia**, who is shown in the highlighted portrait in the preceding screenshot. She will serve as the starting point for the female sci-fi character for your 3D movie.

3. Click on the **Next** button. When you click on this button, it will launch MetaHuman Creator in **Edit Mode** so that you can customize the preset character that you selected in *Step 2*.

Note

If you wish to experiment with some of the MetaHumans, you can select any of the other MetaHuman preset characters by clicking on a character portrait in the character preset pane, as shown in the preceding screenshot. Once you are in **Edit Mode**, you are free to tweak and navigate the character model to get a better idea of how this app works. Then, select the **Pia** female character (as your starting point for this tutorial) and return to this point.

You have just learned how to launch the MetaHuman Creator app and select a preset character that will serve as your starting point for your own MetaHuman.

In the next section, we will look at the user interface and basic controls of MetaHuman Creator.

MetaHuman's UI

Now that the MetaHuman Creator app has been launched with your preset character in **Edit Mode**, you will see a screen that looks similar to the following:

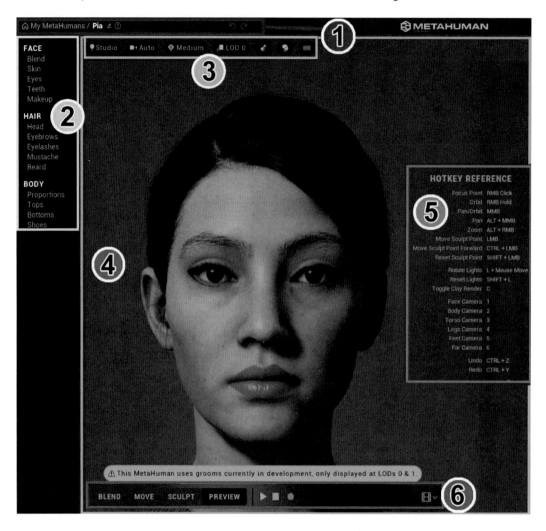

Figure 8.2 – MetaHuman Creator's user interface regions

Here, you can see that the UI regions are highlighted and numbered for explanation purposes. Let's go over these numbered regions now:

1. **Title bar:** This UI region contains a link to return to the **My MetaHumans** gallery. On the right of this link, there is the option to edit your character's name. Then, there are icons for **Help**, **Undo**, and **Redo**.

2. **Attributes and Properties selection**: Here, you will find all the customizable attributes for your MetaHuman. These attributes are divided into three groups – **Face**, **Hair**, and **Body**. Each of these attributes can be customized by changing its properties.

3. **Viewport Environment and Quality toolbar**: This menu bar contains various controls. Starting from the left-hand side, the options are as follows:

   - **Studio** (**Lightbulb icon**): This allows you to choose between various image-based environment lighting options.

   - **Auto** (**Camera icon**): This allows you to change the camera focus to view a specific part of the character.

   - **Medium** (**Diamond icon**): This provides options to choose between rendering quality settings.

   - **LOD 0**: This is the **level of detail** (**LOD**) controls – you do not need to change anything here, but make sure it stays on **LOD 0**.

   - **Toggle Clay Material icon**: This will toggle the display of your MetaHuman in gray.

   - **Head icon**: This toggle will hide or unhide the hair.

   - **Keyboard icon**: This toggles whether the hotkey reference (keyboard shortcut list) is displayed (see *Region 5*).

4. **Render preview of your MetaHuman**: This is the viewport where you can see what your MetaHuman looks like as you make changes to it and preview it in real time.

5. **Hotkey Reference panel**: This displays a list of keyboard and mouse shortcuts for easy reference. The keyboard icon (in the menu bar of *Region 3*) will toggle the display of this list.

6. **Viewport Sculpting and Animation toolbar**: This menu bar has toggle buttons for three different Viewport sculpting tools. These tools allow you to edit facial geometry. These tools are **Blend**, **Move**, and **Sculpt**. We will go over these in more detail in the next section.

The **Preview** button allows you to preview your Viewport sculpting edits in real time with animations. There are buttons to **Play**, **Stop**, and **Scrub** through animations. At the end of this menu bar is a **Film Frame** icon, which allows you to select different preview animations for the face and body.

You have just learned about the UI and the keyboard shortcuts for MetaHuman Creator.

In the next section, I will take you through the step-by-step process of customizing your MetaHuman preset character so that your new character will become unique.

Creating a photorealistic female sci-fi character

Now that you have the MetaHuman Creator app open, and **Pia** has been loaded as your preset character, we can start the editing (customization) part of this tutorial:

1. You will notice that, by default, your character is moving around. In the **Viewport Sculpting and Animation** toolbar (*Region 6* of *Figure 8.2*), click on the **Stop** icon (square) to stop the animation.

2. The first thing we want to do is establish the proportions of the female sci-fi character that we will create for your 3D movie. In *Region 2* of *Figure 8.2*, you will see a list of all the adjustable attributes and properties that you can edit for your MetaHuman. In the **Body** section of this list, click on **Proportions** to open the **Proportions** menu.

3. The default **Pia** preset character has her proportions set to **Short** (height) and her body weight set to **Normal**. Let's change her proportions so that she's Average height, while still keeping her body weight set to **Normal**, as shown in the following screenshot:

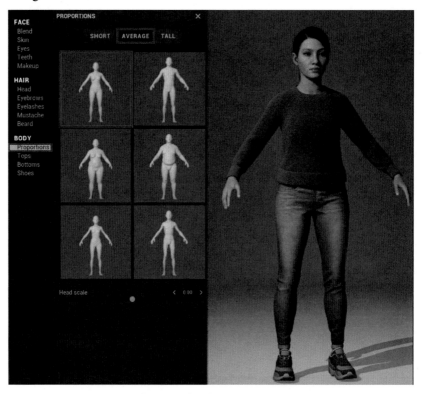

Figure 8.3 – Changing the character's body proportions

4. In *Region 2* of *Figure 8.2*, under the **Body** section, click on **Shoes**. This will open a menu with four kinds of shoes to choose from. Select **Boots** from this menu.

5. Let's change the color of the boots. Still inside the **Shoes** section, look for the **Primary Color** heading in the menu. Click on the color bar to change the color to a medium-light gray.

   We will keep her current top and bottom as-is since these are the closest in appearance to sci-fi-style clothes that are available in MetaHuman Creator at the time of writing. However, we can change the color of the clothes to appear more sci-fi-looking. To do this, click on **Tops** (*Region 2*, under the **Body** section) and change **Primary Color** from the default red to a medium-dark gray.

6. Click on **Bottoms** (*Region 2*, under the **Body** section) and change the **Primary Color** setting of the pants/trousers to dark gray.

7. Next, let's change her hairstyle. In *Region 2*, under the **Hair** section, click on **Head**. This will open the **Hairstyles** presets menu. Scroll a bit down in this menu to near the bottom. Here, you will find a female hairstyle named **Side Swept Fringe**. Click on this hairstyle to apply it to your character:

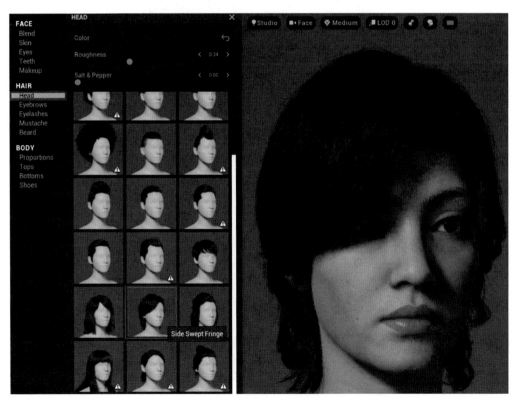

Figure 8.4 – Selecting a new hairstyle

8. Now that your character has a great new hairstyle, let's customize her hair color. Click on the color tab next to **Color**, which is shown near the top of the preceding screenshot. The hair color menu will open. Inside this menu, check the checkbox for **Enable Hair Dye** and choose a custom color (use the values that are shown in the following screenshot to change her hair color to a dark red tone):

Figure 8.5 – Customizing the hair color

9. Next, let's change her eye color and iris pattern. In the **Eyes** menu (*Region 2*, under the **Face** section) select **Preset 010,** then click on the **Iris** tab at the top of the menu. Select the iris in the middle of the selection, as shown in the following screenshot:

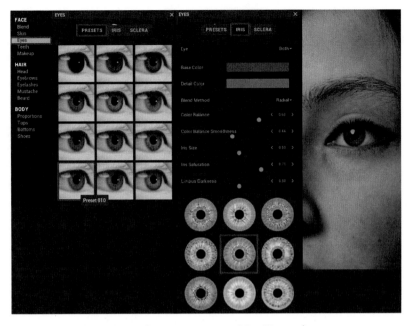

Figure 8.6 – Customizing your MetaHuman's eyes

10. You'll notice that her lipstick has a hard edge. Let's change her lips so that they have no lipstick on them, making them look more natural. Click on **Makeup** (*Region 2*, under the **Face** section) and, from the menu, select the icon of the lips with no makeup on, as highlighted in the following screenshot. Your MetaHuman's face should now look as follows:

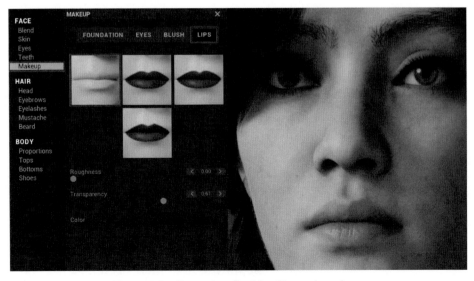

Figure 8.7 – Removing the MetaHuman's makeup

11. In the **Teeth** menu (*Region 2*, under the **Face** section) change **Variation** to 0.26. This will add a bit of random variation deformation to the teeth to make them look more realistic.

12. In the **Skin** menu (*Region 2*, under the **Face** section), click on the **Freckles** tab and choose the second freckled face image (from the selection of four). Set **Density** to 0.18, **Strength** to 0.20, **Saturation** to 0.34, and **Tone shift** to 0.5.

13. The last feature we need to change on your MetaHuman's face is her eyebrows. Click on **Eyebrows** (*Region 2*, under the **Hair** section) and, in the menu that opens, select **Medium Thick Eyebrows** (the fifth eyebrow image from the selection of 11).

14. Rename your character SciFiGirl in the **Title** bar (*Region 1*, as shown in *Figure 8.2*).

You've now made some basic changes to your MetaHuman character.

What remains now is perhaps the most important step – to customize the features of your MetaHuman's face (their facial geometry).

In the next section, I will show you the tools that you can use to customize the shape of your character's face.

Customizing the shape of your character's face

We are now ready to start customizing your character's facial shape. There are three different tools that we can use for this task. These three tools are called the **Viewport Sculpting tools**, and they are as follows:

- **Blend tool**: This tool blends the features of different characters' faces.
- **Move tool**: This tool lets you use guidelines to move parts of the face.
- **Sculpt tool**: This tool lets you push and pull control points on the face.

The goal of using these three tools is to customize the shape of your character's face. This helps to make your character unique-looking since nobody else would modify their character's face in the same way.

You can use any of these three tools to change the shape of the face or even use all three tools together – the choice is yours.

By learning how to use the three Viewport Sculpting tools, you can modify any character's face as you like.

Now, let's explore these three Viewport Sculpting tools in more depth, starting with the Blend tool.

The Blend tool

The **Blend** tool allows you to edit facial geometry, and it works by blending (also known as **morphing**) between the facial features of three preset characters in predefined areas.

First, we need to tell the MetaHuman Creator app which characters we want to blend between. We can do this by placing the preset character's portrait icon into a slot on the Blend Circle. Once you've placed all three preset characters into their slots, we can begin blending.

Let's use the **Blend** tool to customize the shape of your MetaHuman's face:

1. Click on **Blend** (*Region 2*, under the **Face** section). **Blend** is also highlighted in the following screenshot.

2. A menu will open with a portrait of **Pia** (your original present character) inside the Blend Circle. This circle is surrounded by three slots (these slots are placeholders for characters that you need to pick from the **Presets Selection** panel, as shown in the following screenshot).

3. Drag and drop the **Zhen** preset character into the bottom left-hand side slot on the Blend Circle, as shown in the following screenshot. Here, I have indicated the **Zhen** preset character with a red circular highlight. You can also see the white arrow that indicates into which slot you have to drag and drop **Zhen**. With that, you've placed your first preset character into a slot:

Figure 8.8 – Dragging and dropping the preset character into a slot on the Blend Circle

4. Drop **Valerie** into the bottom right-hand side slot, as shown in the following screenshot.

5. Then, drop **Irene** into the top slot, as shown in the following screenshot:

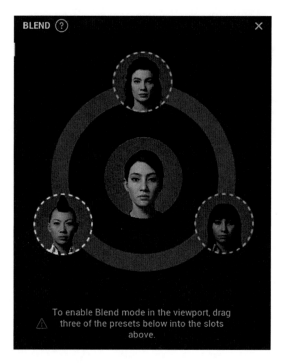

Figure 8.9 – All three preset characters are now in the slots on the Blend Circle. Now, we can start blending their features with the Blend tool

I used these three preset characters for my sci-fi tutorial, but when you are creating MetaHumans for future projects, you can select any preset characters that you want.

6. Click on the **Blend** button in the **Viewport Sculpting and Animation** toolbar (*Region 6* of *Figure 8.2*). Once you have clicked this button, small white circles will appear over different parts of the character's face. These white circles show you the areas on the face where can use the **Blend** tool.

7. Rotate the camera so that you are viewing the face from a ¾ angle. This camera angle is better because you can see when you make changes to the face in three dimensions. When you view from the front, you can only notice changes in two dimensions.

8. Left-click and hold your cursor on the white circle in the center of the lips and drag the white circle to a position between the top and the right gray circles. These gray circles are shown in the following screenshot, and they represent the slots (these slots are shown in *Figure 8.8*). This will blend the lips to the geometric shape that is the middle ground between Valerie's and Irene's lips:

Figure 8.10 – Blending the lips to the geometric shape of the other character's lips

Great! You've made your first blend between two of the other character's facial features.

Now, let's make a similar modification to her cheekbones. The **Zhen** character that you have placed in the bottom-left slot has very pronounced cheekbones. We will use the **Blend** tool to add this cheekbone shape to your female sci-fi character.

9. Left-click and hold your cursor on the white circle in the center of one of the cheekbones and drag the white circle to a position where Zhen's character slot is positioned (bottom-left slot).

This will tell the MetaHuman app that you want to blend your character's cheekbones to the shape of Zhen's cheekbones, as shown in the following screenshot:

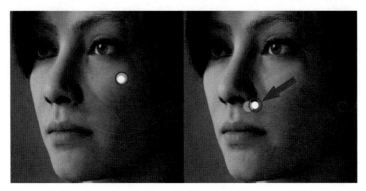

Figure 8.11 – Blending the cheekbones to the shape of another character's cheekbones

In this section, you learned how to use the **Blend** tool to blend between different characters' facial features that you would like to apply to your character.

The examples I have used here are quite subtle, but you can make bolder changes to facial features by selecting characters who have a greater difference in facial features than your character.

In the next section, we will learn how to use the **Move** tool to change the facial features of your female sci-fi character.

The Move tool

The **Move** tool has a very direct approach to changing your character's facial features. Let's have a look:

1. Click on the **Move** button in the **Viewport Sculpting and Animation** toolbar (*Region 6* of *Figure 8.2*). White guidelines will appear over different parts of your character's face. Let's see how we can use these white guidelines to modify the nose shape of the character's face.

2. Rotate the character to a profile (side) view and left-click and hold the cursor on the guideline at the tip of the nose, as shown in *Figure 8.12*, part *A*. The guidelines will disappear when you click on a guideline. In the region where you've selected the guideline, white dots and dotted blue lines will appear to indicate parts of the geometry that can be modified, as shown in *Figure 8.12*, part *B*:

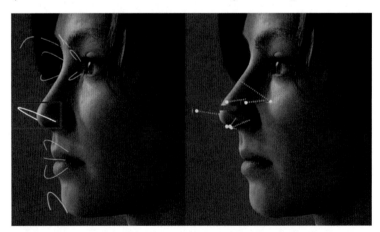

Figure 8.12 – (A) Clicking on the white guideline on the nose tip; (B) Dragging the mouse cursor forward to modify the shape of the nose

3. With the left mouse button still pressed down, slowly drag your mouse cursor forward so that you increase the nose bridge size and the shape of the nose protrudes slightly forward.

You've just learned how to use the **Move** tool to directly edit the shape of your character's facial features. This is a very useful tool to make big facial feature changes very quickly.

In the next section, we will explore the last of the three **Viewport Sculpting** tools. We will use the **Sculpt** tool in a practical exercise to learn how to use it.

The Sculpt tool

The **Sculpt** tool has similarities to the **Move** tool, in the sense that they both allow you to directly manipulate the shape of the facial features.

Let's look at a practical example by using the **Sculpt** tool to change the shape of your character's jawline, chin line, and chin shape:

1. We will start by rotating the face to the front view. Click on the **Sculpt** button in the **Viewport Sculpting and Animation** toolbar (*Region 6* of *Figure 8.2*). You will see that small gray circles will appear all over your character's face, as shown in *Figure 8.13*, part *A*.

2. Left-click and hold on to the small gray circle on one side of the jawline. When you click on a small gray circle, a gray dotted line with a white dot will appear to indicate that you can sculpt that facial feature area.

3. With the left mouse button still pressed down, slowly drag your mouse cursor slightly to the top left-hand side, as shown in *Figure 8.13*, part *B*. This will interactively change the jawline's geometric shape as you drag your mouse. When you edit one side of the face, the other side of the face will automatically be modified at the same time. This is because **Symmetry** is enabled by default. Let's keep the **Symmetry** setting in its default state:

Figure 8.13 – (A) Clicking on the gray dot on the jawline; (B) Dragging your mouse cursor to modify the shape of the jawline

Let's do the same with the chin line area of the face:

1. Left-click and hold on to the small gray circle on one side of the chin line, as shown in *Figure 8.14*, part *A*. When you've selected this gray circle, the rest of the gray circles will disappear, and you will see a gray dotted line with a white dot to indicate which sculpt area is currently active, as shown in *Figure 8.14*, part *B*.

2. With the left mouse button still pressed down, slowly drag your mouse cursor slightly down and to the side. You have now modified the chin line shape so that it's a bit sharper, as shown in *Figure 8.14*, part *C*:

Figure 8.14 – (A) Selecting the small gray circle on the chin line; (B) The gray dotted line and white dot indicate which area is currently active; (C) Adjusting the shape of the chin line by dragging the mouse cursor

The last part of the character's face that we want to modify is her chin. Currently, her chin is quite weak, so we want to push it forward by using the **Sculpt** tool. Follow these steps:

1. Rotate the face to the profile (side) view. Left-click and hold on to the small gray circle on the chin, as shown in *Figure 8.15*, part *A*.

2. With the left mouse button still pressed down, slowly drag your mouse cursor slightly down and forward. You have now modified the chin's shape so that it protrudes more forward, as shown in *Figure 8.15*, part *B*:

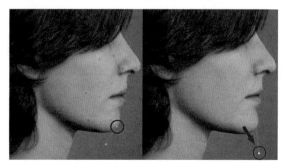

Figure 8.15 – (A) Selecting the small gray circle on the front of the chin; (B) Adjusting the shape of the chin by dragging the mouse cursor

You have just learned how to use the **Sculpt** tool to directly modify parts of your character's facial features.

The following is a close-up of the completed female sci-fi character's head:

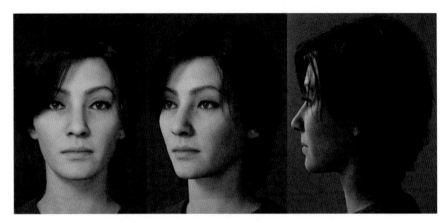

Figure 8.16 – Close-up of the completed female sci-fi character's head

This concludes the customization we can do in MetaHuman Creator to create a female sci-fi character. For the rest of the customization, we will use UE5.

The last step before we go back to UE5 is to preview the character with various animations. When you preview a character with animations, you can get a better idea of what the character will look like for your 3D movie than if you were just looking at the character in the default static pose (this static pose is known as the **A-Pose**):

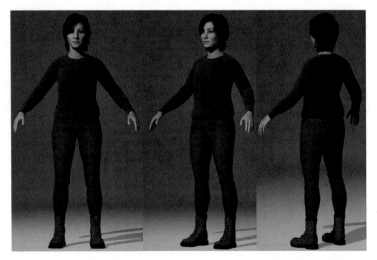

Figure 8.17 – The female sci-fi character's full-body preview in "A-Pose"

In the next section, we will explore the animation previews in MetaHuman Creator.

Previewing your character with animations

To preview your character with animations, you can use the **Viewport Sculpting and Animation** toolbar (*Region 6* of *Figure 8.2*).

The **Preview** button is selected by default. When you click on the **Blend, Move,** or **Sculpt** tool in the **Viewport Sculpting and Animation** toolbar, the animation controls will be hidden automatically. To re-enable the animation controls, simply click on the **Preview** button again.

When the animation controls are visible, you can use standard video player controls to play, stop, or scrub through the animation timeline by using the **Play** icon, the **Stop** icon, and the **Timeline** area, respectively.

On the right-hand side end of the **Viewport Sculpting and Animation** toolbar is a **Film Frame** icon. When you click on this **Film Frame** icon, a pop-up menu with options for different kinds of animations will appear, as follows:

- **Idle**: This option will play through a typical **idle** animation. This is an animation in which the character stands, looks around, and moves slightly.

- **FaceROM**: This animation file will play through a range of facial animations. (**ROM** stands for **Range of Motion**).

The following screenshot shows the ROM animations that are currently active on your character's face:

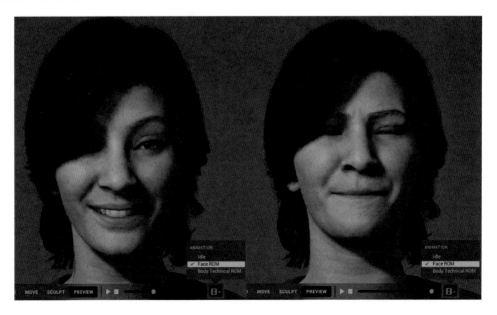

Figure 8.18 – Testing the facial animations

- **Body Technical ROM**: This animation file will play through a range of body movement animations. This is used to preview the character with a greater range of poses and motions.

The following screenshot shows the range of body movement animations (**Body Technical ROM**) that are currently active on your character's body:

Figure 8.19 – Previewing the character with a range of body motions

With that, you've learned how to preview your MetaHuman character with animations for its body and face.

In the next section, we will return to UE5. We will go through the step-by-step process of adding your newly created MetaHuman to UE5.

Adding your MetaHuman to Unreal Engine 5

In this section, you will add your newly created MetaHuman female sci-fi character to UE5.

Before we start, make sure that you have the Quixel Bridge plugin enabled in UE5. The Quixel Bridge plugin is included in the default installation of UE5. To check if this plugin is enabled, follow these steps:

1. Launch UE5. Navigate to the **Menu** bar and click on **Edit | Plugins**.
2. Type `bridge` into the **Search** bar and tick the checkbox to enable it (if it is not already enabled). Then, close this menu and close UE5.

3. Relaunch UE5. Use the project file that you created for *Chapter 7, Setting Up Materials in UE 5.*.

4. In the toolbar, click on the **Create** icon. This will open a drop-down menu. Select **Quixel Bridge** from that menu to open the Quixel Bridge app.

5. The Quixel Bridge app window will open, as shown in the following screenshot. Maximize this window. On the top right-hand side of this window, there is a **portrait** icon. Click on this **portrait** icon and then, from the drop-down menu, click on **Sign In**. This will open another window containing a menu. Click on **Sign in with Epic Games**:

Figure 8.20 – The Quixel Bridge app window with "My MetaHumans" selected

6. Once you've logged into your Quixel Bridge account, you will see **MetaHumans** in the menu on the left-hand side. Click on **MetaHumans** to open a drop-down menu. Inside this drop-down menu, select **My MetaHumans**, as shown in the preceding screenshot.

    In the central area, you will find portraits of all the MetaHumans that you've created. If **SciFiGirl** is your first character, then you will see only one character.

7. At the bottom right-hand side, you will see a menu with options to **Download** your MetaHuman at either **Low Quality**, **Medium Quality**, or **High Quality**. The quality setting refers to the texture size that you want to download for your character. Let's take a look at these texture sizes:

- **Low Quality:** `1024 x 1024 pixels`

- **Medium Quality:** `2048 x 2048 pixels`

- **High Quality:** `8192 x 8192 pixels`

8. The bigger the texture size that you want to download, the longer it will take to export your character. You will also need a more powerful computer when you want to use **High Quality** textures. For the purposes of this tutorial, I have selected **Medium Quality**.

9. Once you've chosen the quality level (texture size) that you require, click on the **Download** button. Once you've done this, you will see a progress animation, as shown in the following screenshot:

Figure 8.21 – (A) The download progress bar animation; (B) When the download is complete, the "Add" button will be enabled

10. In *Figure 8.21*, part *A*, you will see your download progression represented by the animated download circle. It will take a while time for the download to complete. Once it is completed, simply click on the blue **Add** button, as shown in *Figure 8.21*, part *B*. This will start the process of automatically exporting your selected character from Quixel Bridge and importing this character into UE5.

11. Once you've clicked on the **Add** button, you will see various message windows appear, displaying a variety of import messages. Minimize Quixel Bridge and return to UE5. Wait for all the import messages to come through. Message windows will open in UE5 telling you about missing project settings. Click on the **Enable Missing** button for each of these message windows. Once all the plugins and project settings have been updated, restart UE5.

12. When you restart UE5, you will get a message stating **Changes to source content files have been detected. Would you like to import them?**. Click on **Import**.

13. In your **Content Browser** window, under **Content**, you will see a new directory named `MetaHumans`. Open this `File` directory and click on the folder named `SciFiGirl`. You will see some folders displayed in the asset view area of your **Content Browser**. There will also be a file with an icon named `BP_SciFiGirl` (I have highlighted this file icon in *Figure 8.23*).

14. Left-click and drag `BP_SciFiGirl` (the blueprint file) onto the floor of your Viewport. This will add your MetaHuman to your UE5 Viewport.

15. Select `BP_SciFiGirl` in the **World Outliner** panel. In the **Details** panel, change her **Transform** settings, as shown in the following screenshot. Here, we are moving her slightly upwards on the *Z*-axis because her boots are currently intersecting with the floor. Then, rotate her so that you have better lighting on her:

Figure 8.22 – Changing BP_SciFiGirl's Transform values

You have just learned how to import your custom MetaHuman into UE5 using the Quixel Bridge plugin (that's built into UE5).

In the next section, you will learn how to add modified clothing materials and some sci-fi armor to your project file.

Customizing your character's clothing

You have just added your custom MetaHuman, named SciFiGirl, to your project file and she looks amazing!

To make her fit better with the sci-fi theme of an Alien-Planet movie set, let's add some custom-made sci-fi armor to her and modify her clothing materials.

Download the `Armor` and `Materials` files (including all their content) from this book's GitHub repository: `https://github.com/PacktPublishing/Unreal-Engine-5-Character-Creation-Animation-and-Cinematics/tree/main/Chapter08/SciFiGirl`.

> **Important**
> When you download these files, keep their folder structure and the file's contents as-is.

The `Armor` folder contains 16 sci-fi armor pieces, their textures, and the materials that I have created for this chapter.

The `Materials` folder contains the updated clothing materials for the boots, jeans, and sweater of your character.

If you want to create some sci-fi armor of your own, then you can use the techniques that you have learned about earlier in this book. This will be a good learning exercise to put what you have learned so far to the test.

Follow these steps to update your project with the custom sci-fi armor and the modified clothing materials:

1. Close UE5. Place the `Armor` and `Materials` folders (including all the sub-folders containing their files) inside your project's `Content\MetaHumans\SciFiGirl\` directory. I have highlighted this directory structure in the following screenshot.

2. Launch UE5. Your **Content Browser** window will now look as follows:

Figure 8.23 – The Content Browser window with the SciFiGirl folder added

3. A message window will open, stating that the project and shaders are updating. After this update process is complete, you will notice that the SciFiGirl character's clothing materials have changed slightly.

4. In the **Content Browser** window, open the Armor folder. Then, inside this directory, open the Armor_models folder. All 16 of the armor pieces will be displayed in the asset view area of the **Content Browser** window. Hold *Shift* and select all 16 armor pieces at the same time. Now, drag and drop all 16 armor pieces into the Viewport. You will see that all the armor pieces are now displayed in the **World Outliner** panel.

5. While the armor pieces are still selected, click on the folder icon with a plus (+) sign on top of the **World Outliner** panel to automatically add all the armor pieces to a new folder. Rename this new folder Armor. Now, all the armor pieces are neatly organized in a folder inside the **World Outliner** panel.

6. Open the Armor folder in the **World Outliner** panel. Press *Shift* and select all 16 armor pieces so that they are all selected at the same time. Go to the **Details** panel and set the **Transform** settings to the same ones that you used for BP_SciFiGirl, as shown in *Figure 8.22*. This will instantly move and rotate all the armor pieces together so that they match the character's position and rotation.

Great! She now has her sci-fi armor on!

> **Note**
>
> This is just temporary for us to see our progress since the sci-fi armor will be attached to the skeleton in *Chapter 20, Using Sequencer to Construct Your Final Scene*.

Your female sci-fi character should now look like the character shown in *Figures 8.24* and *8.25*:

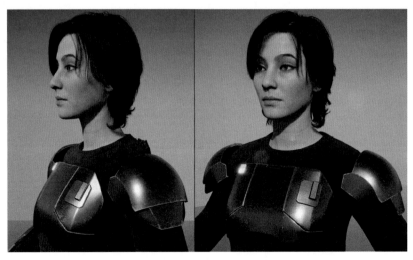

Figure 8.24 – Closeup of the sci-fi character with her sci-fi armor

The only difference is that your character's sci-fi armor won't have a glowing effect on its lights yet. You will learn how to add a glowing effect to the armor's lights in *Chapter 10, Adding Lighting and Atmospheric Visual Effects in UE5*:

Figure 8.25 – Full figure view of the female sci-fi MetaHuman with her sci-fi armor

With that, you have learned how to add new assets to your UE5 project file. You also learned how to organize assets in the **World Outliner** panel by grouping them inside a folder.

Summary

In this chapter, you completed the MetaHuman character creation tutorial. You learned how to create a character, how to export them, and how to add them to UE5.

Finally, you learned how to add custom assets to your project that will help your character match the sci-fi theme of your 3D animated movie.

In the next chapter, you will learn how to bring all your assets together in UE5 and build a virtual 3D movie set.

You will learn how to import a landscape mesh and rock assets from Quixel Bridge to build an alien landscape. After this, you will populate your alien landscape with your alien plants.

See you in the next chapter!

9
Building a Virtual 3D Movie Set in UE5

In the previous chapter, you learned how to create a custom MetaHuman and then added your character to your UE5 project.

So far, we've focused on creating actors (the female sci-fi character and the Robot Drone) and environment props (the Alien Plant) for your 3D movie. In this chapter, we will change our focus to the 3D environment that forms the basis of your virtual 3D movie set.

First, we will go through the step-by-step process of importing meshes for the ground and adding more assets to the 3D movie set. Then, we will jump into the Quixel Bridge plugin that is integrated into UE5. In Quixel Bridge, we will collect free 3D rock assets and some material assets for your 3D movie set.

I will show you how to send these assets to UE5, as well as how to customize them for use in your 3D movie set of an Alien Planet's surface.

This tutorial is aimed at beginner-level UE users. I will focus on creating a 3D movie set by using the most basic settings and techniques. While it is certainly possible to create much more detailed and realistic 3D movie sets in UE5, that is beyond the scope of this chapter's tutorial.

In this chapter, we're going to cover the following main topics:

- Setting up the basic elements of your 3D movie set

- Customizing your Material Instances

- Building the 3D movie set

By the end of this chapter, you will know how to create your own custom 3D movie sets.

Technical requirements

To complete this chapter, you must have UE5 installed. Even if your version of UE is newer, the examples should still work without any problems. You will need the following to complete this chapter:

- A computer that can run basic 3D animation software.

- Unreal Engine 5.0.1. You can download it from `https://www.unrealengine.com/en-US/download`.

- You should have read *Chapter 6*, *Exploring Unreal Engine 5*, to understand the basics of UE5's UI.

Let's start this chapter's tutorial by preparing the scene. This scene will form the basis for your 3D movie set.

The files related to this chapter are placed at `https://github.com/PacktPublishing/Unreal-Engine-5-Character-Creation-Animation-and-Cinematics/tree/main/Chapter09`

Setting up the basic elements of your 3D movie set

Your 3D movie set is the scene where all your actors, background elements, and props are placed.

In this tutorial, we will build a 3D movie set of an Alien Planet's surface. The landscape will be made up of the ground layer (base ground meshes) populated with rock formations and Alien Plants. In the sky, you will place a Sun and an Alien Planet.

I have prepared three models for you to download from this book's GitHub repository that you will need to use in this tutorial:

- The first two models are the foreground and background base ground meshes. I created these two meshes by using Blender's 3D sculpting tools. In the future, you can create base ground models by using the 3D sculpting techniques that you learned in *Chapter 3, Let's Sculpt an Alien Plant!*. For now, download the `ForeGround.fbx` and `BackGround.fbx` files from GitHub: `https://github.com/PacktPublishing/Unreal-Engine-5-Character-Creation-Animation-and-Cinematics/tree/main/Chapter09`.

- The third model I have provided for this tutorial is the Alien Planet model. This model is in UE's `.uasset` format. Download the `Planet.zip` file and extract the contents of `Planet.zip` to a folder named `Planet` on your hard drive. You can download the Alien Planet model from GitHub: `https://github.com/PacktPublishing/Unreal-Engine-5-Character-Creation-Animation-and-Cinematics/tree/main/Chapter09`.

Now that you've downloaded these three assets and extracted `Planet.zip`, you are ready to start creating the 3D movie set:

1. Launch UE and create a new **Film/Video Live Events** project, as you did in the *Setting up your project* section of *Chapter 6, Exploring Unreal Engine 5*.

2. In the **World Outliner** panel, select **Floor**, **Player Start**, and **SphereReflectionCapture**. Press the *Delete* key to delete these items since we won't be using them in our tutorial.

3. Go to your **Content Browser** window's sources view area and click on the `Content` folder. Create a new folder and name it `Terrain_models`.

4. Open the `Terrain_models` folder, then drag and drop the `ForeGround.fbx` and `BackGround.fbx` static meshes into the asset view area of the **Content Browser** window. The **FBX Import Options** window will appear. Use the same static mesh **Import** settings that you used in the previous UE chapters, but this time, tick the checkbox for **Build Nanite** under the **mesh** section. This will enable Nanite during import so that you don't have to enable it manually later. This will add the two base landscape meshes to the `Terrain_models` folder.

5. Copy and paste the `MetaHumans`, `AlienPlant`, and `RobotDrone` folders from your previous UE project's `Content` folder to this new project's `Content` folder.

6. Copy and paste the `Planet` folder (including its three sub-folders) inside your project's `Content` folder.

7. Because we copied these folders into the `Content` folder of your new project, UE will give you a message stating **Changes to source content files have been detected. Would you like to import them?**. Click on **Import** to have UE process all these source file changes.

8. You will see that the `AlienPlant`, `MetaHumans`, `Planet`, and `RobotDrone` folders are in the **Content Browser**'s sources view area:

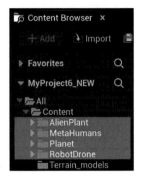

Figure 9.1 – The Content Browser window will now show the folders that you've placed in your project's Content directory

9. Now, simply drag and drop **ForeGround** (static mesh) and **BackGround** (static mesh) from the `Terrain_models` folder into the Viewport. This will place them inside the scene.

> **Note**
> The following screenshot serves as a reference to show which axes are where in the **Transform** section (the number values shown are the default values and are not part of this tutorial).

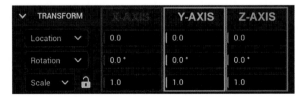

Figure 9.2 – The Transform section in the Details panel

10. Now that these static meshes are in the scene, we need to adjust their positions by using the **Transform** section in the **Details** panel. The axes mentioned in the following steps are shown in the preceding screenshot. In the **Transform** section, set **ForeGround** (static mesh) **Location** to **X-Axis:** 0, **Y-Axis:** 0, and **Z-Axis:** 20. Leave **Rotation** and **Scale** as-is.

11. In the **Transform** section, set **BackGround** (static mesh) **Location** to **X-Axis**: 0, **Y-Axis**: 0, and **Z-Axis**: 22. Leave **Rotation** and **Scale** as-is.

12. We want to add the female sci-fi character to the scene to serve as a scale and position reference. In the sources view area of the **Content Browser** window, navigate to **MetaHumans | SciFiGirl**. In the asset view area of **Content Browser**, find the BP_SciFiGirl Blueprint file and double-click it. This will open the blueprint in a new Editor window. A message with a progress bar will pop up saying that UE is compiling shaders. Wait for this process to finish.

13. More message windows will pop up to inform you about missing plugins and missing project settings. Just click on **Enable Missing** in all these message windows. Once all the missing plugins and project settings have finished updating, a message will appear saying **Restart required to apply new settings**. Click on the **Restart Now** button to restart UE5.

14. Drag and drop BP_SciFiGirl (the Blueprint file) into the Viewport. In the **Transform** section, set **Location** to **X-Axis**: 0, **Y-Axis**: 0, and **Z-Axis**: 22. Leave **Rotation** and **Scale** as-is.

15. Navigate to **MetaHumans | SciFiGirl | Armor | Armor_models**, hold down *Shift*, and select all 16 armor pieces.

16. Drag and drop all 16 of the sci-fi armor pieces from the Armor_models folder into the Viewport. In the **Transform** section, set their **Location** to **X-Axis**: 0, **Y-Axis**: 0, and **Z-Axis**: 22. Leave their **Rotation** and **Scale** as-is. This will make sure that the armor pieces are in the female sci-fi character's current location.

17. Right-click on an empty spot in the **World Outliner** panel and select the **Create Folder** option. Name this folder Armor.

18. Drag and drop the 16 armor pieces into the Viewport and add them to the Armor folder. Select all 16 armor pieces and match their **Location** with the **Location** setting of **SciFiGirl**.

19. Drag and drop **Planet1** into the Viewport. In the **Transform** section, set its **Location** to **X-Axis**: 96656, **Y-Axis**: -12354, and **Z-Axis**: 14629. Leave **Rotation** as-is. Set its **Scale** to **X-Axis**: 600, **Y-Axis**: 600, and **Z-Axis**: 600. This will place the rocky Alien Planet in the sky to make a good scene composition.

> **Note**
>
> This Alien Planet is not physically correct, so it lacks proper parallax perspective. If you ensure that the camera won't move around too much, it works well enough. Don't worry if the Alien Planet doesn't look very realistic at this stage – in *Chapter 10, Adding Lighting and Atmospheric Visual Effects in UE5*, the Alien Planet will be modified and it will look great for your 3D movie set.

20. Now, let's add the Robot Drone character to the scene. Drag and drop **RobotDrone** (static mesh) into the Viewport. In the **Transform** section, set its **Location** to **X-Axis**: 3.32, **Y-Axis**: 348.73, and **Z-Axis**: 180. Set its **Rotation** to **X-Axis**: 9.3, **Y-Axis**: 1.78, **Z-Axis**: 150. Leave **Scale** as-is.

21. Drag and drop **AlienPlant** (static mesh) into the Viewport. Then, in the **Transform** section, set its **Location** to **X-Axis**: 82.68, **Y-Axis**: -164.24, and **Z-Axis**: 37.22. Set its **Rotation** to **X-Axis**: 0, **Y-Axis**: 0, and **Z-Axis**: -71. Leave **Scale** as-is.

With that, you have placed the first seven 3D assets of your 3D movie set: **SciFiGirl**, **Armor**, **ForeGround**, **Background**, **RobotDrone**, **AlienPlant**, and **Planet**.

The following screenshot shows what your scene should look like at this point.

> **Note**
> The **ForeGround** and **BackGround** static meshes are currently untextured, which is why they are displayed with a noisy checker pattern.

The view shown in the following screenshot is the camera angle that we will use in *Chapter 20, Using Sequencer to Construct Your Final Scene*, when we set up the **Cine Camera Actor** in UE5:

Figure 9.3 – The basic elements of your 3D movie set in their correct positions

You have just learned how to place the first seven 3D assets in your 3D movie set and how to use the **Transform** section of the **Details** panel to adjust their **Location, Rotation,** and **Scale**.

In the next section, we will go over some basic settings that we need to set for our scene. The first of these settings is the exposure of your Viewport display.

Adjusting the scene's exposure

UE has a feature called **Auto Exposure** that is enabled by default. This automatically adjusts the exposure of the current scene view so that it becomes brighter or darker as your view changes.

While this feature adds a lot of realism to video games, it is not a feature that you want to have enabled when you are making a 3D movie. It is far better to have manual control over your scene's exposure.

Let's change the default setting of **Auto Exposure** to **Manual Exposure**:

1. In the toolbar, click on the **Create** icon and navigate to **Visual Effects |
    PostProcessVolume,** as shown in the following screenshot. This will create an item called **PostProcessVolume** inside your scene. You will see a wireframe box inside your scene that represents **PostProcessVolume**:

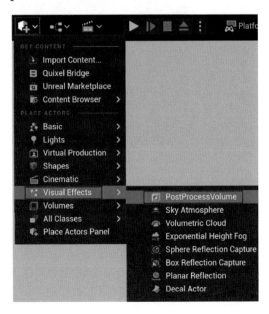

Figure 9.4 – Adding a PostProcessVolume to the scene

2. In the **World Outliner** panel, click on **PostProcessVolume**. Now, go to the **Details** panel. Find the **Global Illumination** section and make sure that you tick the **Method** checkbox and set it to **Lumen**.

3. Next, go to the **Post Process Volume** section's setting and tick the **Infinite Extent (Unbound)** checkbox. This setting tells UE that **Post Process Volume** affects the whole scene, not just the area defined by the wireframe box.

4. Go to the **Lens** section. Here, you will see another sub-section named **Exposure**. Tick the **Metering Mode** checkbox. In the drop-down list next to it, change it to **Manual**. This tells UE that you are manually controlling the exposure of your scene:

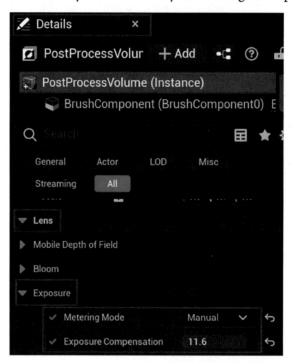

Figure 9.5 – Changing Exposure to Manual and adjusting the Exposure Compensation setting

5. Still inside the **Exposure** section, tick the **Exposure Compensation** checkbox and set it to 11.6, as shown in the preceding screenshot.

> **Note**
>
> In *Chapter 10, Adding Lighting and Atmospheric Visual Effects in UE5*, you will adjust the **Exposure Compensation** setting again when you create the lighting for your scene.

You've just learned how to set **Exposure** to **Manual Mode,** how to adjust the amount of **Exposure Compensation**, and how to set the **Post Process Volume** size to **Infinite** so that it affects the entire scene.

In the next section, we will look at the **Field of View** of your Viewport and why it is important to adjust this setting while we are building our 3D movie set.

Adjusting the Viewport's Field of View

When you start to build your 3D movie set, you need to have your Viewport's **Field of View** (FOV) set so that it matches a typical real-world camera's lens FOV.

> **Note**
>
> **FOV** is the extent of the observable view and is typically measured as an angle. A typical 35 mm camera lens has a FOV of 63 degrees, while a 50 mm camera lens has a FOV of 46 degrees.

UE's Viewport has a default FOV of 90 degrees, which is good for games where you want to see more of your surroundings. However, this is not good for 3D movies because it distorts the edges of your view.

An appropriate FOV (without distortion around the edges) will help you place your 3D assets in your 3D movie set more accurately.

Let's adjust your Viewport's FOV. In the Viewport menu bar, click on the **Viewport Options** icon (I have highlighted this icon in the following screenshot). This will open a drop-down menu. In this menu, change **Field of View (H)** to 50:

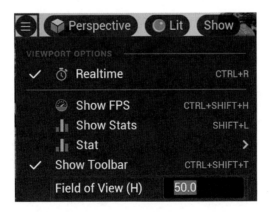

Figure 9.6 – Adjusting your Viewport's Field of View (H)

You've just learned how to adjust your Viewport's FOV so that it's closer to a real-world camera lens' FOV angle. This will help a lot when you start to populate your 3D movie set with 3D assets.

In the next section, we will explore how to use the Quixel Bridge plugin to acquire free 3D-scanned assets for your 3D movie.

Using Quixel Bridge to acquire free 3D assets

In this section, we will utilize UE5's built-in Quixel Bridge plugin to add 3D assets to our scene. In the case of this tutorial, you will find free 3D-scanned rock assets. These rocks have been scanned by using **photogrammetry** techniques so that they are photorealistic. Follow these steps:

1. In the toolbar, click on the **Create** icon. This will open a drop-down menu. From this menu, select **Quixel Bridge**, as shown in the following screenshot:

Figure 9.7 – Selecting the built-in Quixel Bridge plugin in UE5

2. The Quixel Bridge app will open automatically once you've clicked on the **Quixel Bridge** button mentioned in *step 1*.

3. At the top right of the Quixel Bridge app's window, click on the little portrait icon to open the drop-down menu. From this menu, select **Sign In** and select **SIGN IN WITH EPIC GAMES**:

Figure 9.8 – (1) Clicking on the portrait icon; (2) Selecting Sign In; (3) Signing in with your Epic Games account

4. Now, we are ready to browse for free 3D assets that we can use in UE5. Go to **Collections | Environment | Natural | Canyons of Utah**, as shown in the following screenshot:

Figure 9.9 – Browsing the "Canyons of Utah" asset gallery in the Quixel Bridge app

5. In the **Canyons of Utah** asset gallery, you will see a scrolling page full of icons of 3D rock environmental assets. But first, let's learn how to download these assets to your local hard drive. The following screenshot shows the three steps that you should perform to download an asset:

Figure 9.10 – (1) Select an asset; (2) In the panel that opens on the right-hand side, select Medium Quality; (3) Click on the downward pointing arrow to download it

6. For this tutorial, download all the 3D assets shown in the following screenshot. All the filenames of these assets to download are also shown in *Figure 9.14*. Download all of these assets at a **Medium Quality** setting.

7. On the left-hand side menu of the Quixel Bridge app window, you will see a small icon of a computer monitor named **Local**. Click on **Local | Megascans** to open a gallery displaying all the 3D assets you've downloaded to your local hard drive:

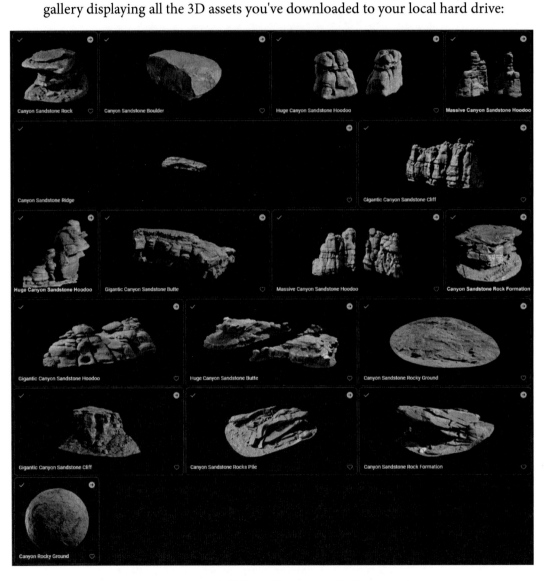

Figure 9.11 – Download all these 3D assets in the Quixel Bridge app

8. When a 3D asset has been downloaded, the **Download** icon (the downward-pointing arrow in the green circle, as shown in *Figure 9.10, step 1*) will change to an **Export** icon (a right-pointing arrow in a blue circle). There will also be a green tick symbol on the left of the 3D asset's **Gallery** icon. The preceding screenshot shows that all the 3D assets now have green tick symbols and **Export** icons.

9. Once you have downloaded all the 3D assets shown in the preceding screenshot, simply click once on the **Export** icon, as shown in the following screenshot, for each of the downloaded 3D assets in your local library. This will export your 3D asset at the quality setting that you have selected, as shown in *Figure 9.10, step 2*:

Figure 9.12 – Exporting a 3D asset from Quixel Bridge. The green tick symbol is highlighted on the left, while the Export icon is highlighted on the right

10. Once all the 3D assets have been added, you can close the Quixel Bridge app window. Go back to UE5 – you will see that two new folders have automatically been created inside UE5 named `Megascans` and `MSPreSets`. (I have highlighted these folders in the following screenshot).

These folders contain your exported 3D assets. Your **Content Browser** view area should now look as follows:

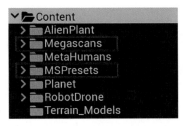

Figure 9.13 – Your Content Browser's view area should now contain these folders

You've just learned how to find and download 3D assets from the Quixel Bridge app.

In the next section, I will show you how to customize your 3D-scanned rock assets so that you can blend them with the colors of the Alien Planet's surface.

Customizing your material instances

Now that you're back in UE5, let's take a look at all the 3D assets that you've exported from the Quixel Bridge app and have automatically been imported into UE5.

Click on the little arrow next to **Megascans** in your **Content Browser** view area to expand the folder structure. The list of all the imported 3D assets is shown in the following screenshot:

Figure 9.14 – Viewing the folders of the imported 3D assets

Note

A **Material Instance** is a material copy that is linked to the original material (called an **instance** in 3D graphics). This Material Instance is created from an existing material and is used to make material variations without them affecting the original. A Material Instance has an exposed set of parameters and does not have a node graph (node tree) like the original material.

Some of the benefits of using Material Instances in your 3D movies are as follows:

Material Instances allow you to make simple edits to selected parameters instead of dealing with a complicated node graph.

They allow you to make as many variations of your original material as you want by editing the Material Instance's parameters.

The Viewport update speed is much faster since Material Instances do not have to be recompiled every time you make changes to them in the Material Instance Editor.

Let's start by assigning a Material Instance to the **ForeGround** and **BackGround** landscape meshes:

1. Hold down *Shift* and select both **ForeGround** and **BackGround** (static meshes) in the **World Outliner** panel so that they are both selected together.

2. In the sources view area of the **Content Browser** window, navigate to **Megascans | Surfaces | Canyon_Rocky_Ground_ulmiecglw**. Inside this folder, you will see a **Material Instance** named **MI_Canyon_Rocky_Ground_ulmiecglw_2K**, as shown in the following screenshot.

3. Drag and drop this **Material Instance** onto the **Material Slot** areas of **ForeGround** and **BackGround** in the **Details** panel. I have highlighted the slot with a dashed green outline in the following screenshot. This will apply the Material Instance to all the selected static meshes. This method of applying materials works with meshes that are in your **Viewport/World Outliner**:

Figure 9.15 – Dragging and dropping the material into the ForeGround and BackGround's Material Slot areas

4. The **ForeGround** and **BackGround** static meshes that are in your Viewport will now have a light brown rock material applied to them.

You have just learned how to assign a material/Material Instance to multiple meshes at once. In the next section, we will explore the UI of the Material Instance Editor.

The Material Instance Editor's UI

In this section, we'll look at the basic UI regions of the Material Instance Editor. The following screenshot shows the Material Instance Editor window:

Figure 9.16 – The Material Instance Editor's basic UI regions

I have added numbers and highlights to indicate the different UI regions for explanation purposes:

1. **Toolbar**: Here, you will find the **Save** icon.
2. **Viewport**: This is your view of the Material Instance that you are editing.
3. **Details panel**: This is where you can change the parameters and view details of your Material Instance.

You've just learned about the three basic UI regions of the Material Instance Editor that we will use for this tutorial.

In the next section, you will use this knowledge to start editing your Material Instances.

Editing your Material Instances

Let's get started by customizing the Material Instance that you've applied to the **ForeGround** and **BackGround** static meshes:

1. In the **Content Browser** window, navigate to the `Canyon_Rocky_Ground_ulmiecglw` folder.

2. Double-click on the **MI_Canyon_Rocky_Ground_ulmiecglw_2K** Material Instance. This Material Instance is also highlighted in *Figure 9.15*. The Material Instance Editor will now open.

3. In the **Details** panel of the Material Instance Editor, navigate to **Parameter Groups | 00 – Global | Tiling/Offset**. Now, click on the downward pointing arrow that's highlighted in the following screenshot. This will open the **Tiling/Offset** drop-down menu so that you can increase the tiling amount. First, tick the checkbox next to **Tiling/Offset** and set **Tiling X** to `10` and **Tiling Y** to `10`. This will make the rock material look like it has finer details in your **ForeGround** and **BackGround** static meshes:

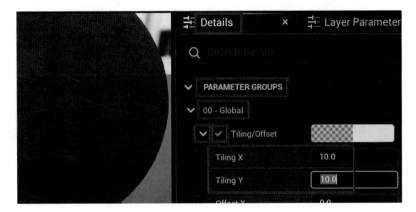

Figure 9.17 – Editing the Tiling properties of the Material Instance

4. Next, we will adjust the color of the Material Instance. This is because we want to customize this material so that it fits the sci-fi theme better. In the **Details** panel, navigate to **Parameter Groups | 01 - Albedo | Albedo Tint** and tick the **Albedo Tint** checkbox. This will allow you to edit the tint color for this **Material Instance**. Click on the color selection bar next to **Albedo Tint**, as highlighted in the following screenshot. This will open the **Color Picker** panel. Use the color settings shown in the following screenshot. Save the Material Instance before you close the Editor window:

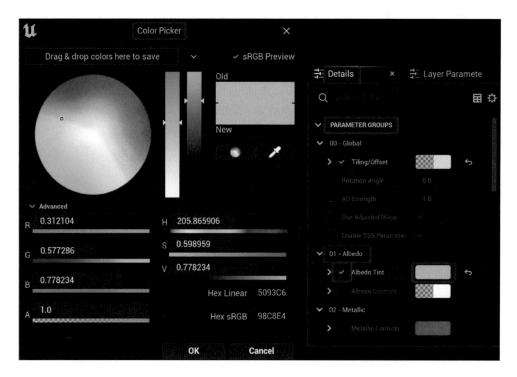

Figure 9.18 – Adjusting the Albedo Tint setting

5. Now, let's enhance the fine details (bump details) of the rock material. To do this, increase the strength of **Normal Map**. In the **Details** panel, navigate to **Parameter Groups | 05 – Normal | Normal Strength**. Tick the **Normal Strength** checkbox and set it to 3.5.

You've just learned how to edit a Material Instance by changing its tiling amount and color, as well as how to enhance the details in the **Normal Map**.

In the next section, you will make color (**Albedo Tint**) changes to all the Rock assets that you've imported from Quixel Bridge. This will make them fit better with **ForeGround** and **BackGround** static meshes' material and their new subtle blue theme will help them fit better in your Alien Planet 3D movie set.

Using Albedo Tint for the Rock assets

Now that the **ForeGround** and **BackGround** static meshes have a slight blue tint, let's adjust all the Rock assets so that they match the theme:

1. In the **Content Browser** content view area, navigate to **Megascans | 3D_assets**. Inside this folder, you will see all 16 folders of the Rock assets that you've imported from Quixel Bridge.

   In each of these 16 folders, there is a static mesh, a Material Instance, and various texture maps. For us to match the colors (**Albedo Tint**), we need to temporarily drag and drop every static mesh (rock asset) from their folder's asset view area into the Viewport. Place them close together so that it is easier to match their colors by eye.

2. Now that all 16 of the Rock assets (static meshes) are in your Viewport and resting on the **ForeGround** static mesh, we will use the View Modes in the Viewport menu bar to change the default **Lit** view mode to **Unlit** view mode, as shown in the following screenshot:

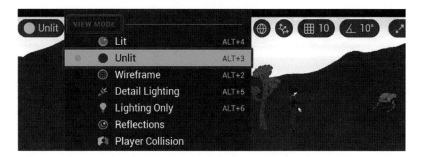

Figure 9.19 – Switch to the "Unlit" View Mode

3. It is much easier to match colors (using **Albedo Tint**) when the View Mode is set to **Unlit**. You will notice that every rock asset (static mesh) has a different shade of light brown. To change a static mesh's color (**Albedo Tint**), you need to edit its Material Instance.

> **Handy Tip**
>
> The easiest way to find a static mesh's Material Instance is to select the static mesh and then right-click inside the Viewport. A menu will open. In this menu, click on **Browse to asset**. This will open the selected asset's folder in the **Content Browser** window. In this folder, you will find its Material Instance.

4. Double-click on the selected static mesh asset's Material Instance to open the Material Instance Editor.

5. Now that the Material Instance Editor is open with your selected Material Instance loaded inside, change its **Albedo Tint** in the same way as you did earlier in *step 4* of the *Editing your Material Instances* section. Change the **Albedo Tint** property of the Rock asset to a slightly blue tone. The exact blue tone of the color you wish to use is up to you. Save the Material Instance before you close the Editor window.

6. Do the same for all 16 Rock assets. All the rock assets will now have a slightly blue tone and they will match each other better. This will make them consistent with the blue color theme of the 3D movie set. In the Viewport menu bar, change the View Mode back to **Lit**.

7. Delete the (temporary) rock assets from the Viewport by pressing *Shift* and selecting them all, then pressing the *Delete* key to delete them.

> **Note**
>
> When you delete assets in the Viewport or the **World Outliner** panel, it does not delete those assets from the **Content Browser** window.

You have just learned how to customize the color of a Material Instance by adjusting its **Albedo Tint** value.

In the next section, you will learn how to use UE5's new Nanite system on your rock assets.

Using Nanite on your rock assets

In this section, you will apply UE5's new Nanite system to your rock assets.

You will need to enable **Nanite Support** for each of the 16 rock assets (static meshes) separately. Follow these steps:

1. First, simply double-click on a rock asset's static mesh in the **Content Browser** window. This will open the **Static Mesh Editor** area.

2. Inside the **Static Mesh Editor** area, tick the **Enable Nanite Support** checkbox under the **Nanite settings** heading, as shown in the following screenshot. Make sure you click on **Save** in the toolbar panel after you make a change to an asset in the Editor:

Figure 9.20 – Enabling Nanite for each rock asset in the Static Mesh Editor

Once you have enabled Nanite for every rock asset, UE5's performance speed will be increased drastically. UE5's Nanite system is so efficient that the engine can easily handle billions of faces (triangles) and still render your scene in the Viewport in near real time.

If you do not enable Nanite on the Rock assets, your Viewport and render performance will suffer.

You've just learned how to enable the Nanite system for your static mesh assets. In the next section, you will learn how to utilize content filters in the **Content Browser** window to speed up your workflow.

Using asset filters in the Content Browser window

Before you start placing your assets in the 3D movie set, I will quickly show you a very useful function of the **Content Browser** window. This involves using asset filters to view all your rock assets (in gallery view mode) in the asset view area of the **Content Browser** panel:

1. In the **Content Browser** view area, navigate to **Content | Megascans** and click on the Megascans folder.

2. In the asset view area of the **Content Browser** window, you will see an icon consisting of three stripes. This is the asset filter, which you can use to filter your view in the asset view area of the **Content Browser** window. Click on this icon now:

Figure 9.21 – Adding an asset filter to the asset view area of the Content Browser window

3. A menu will pop up containing a list of different kinds of asset filters. Since all your rock assets are static meshes, select the **Static Mesh** filter. All the Rock asset static meshes will now be displayed next to each other in the asset view area of the **Content Browser** window, as shown in the following screenshot.

By using the asset filter feature in the **Content Browser** asset view area, it is very easy to choose an asset from a gallery list of available assets.

This saves you time by not having to browse through lots of folders to find assets. Keep this asset filter enabled so that you can use it in the next section:

Figure 9.22 – All of your rock assets are now displayed in the Content Browser's asset view area

> **Note**
> If you want to remove an asset filter, just right-click on the filter's name and select **Remove**.

Now that all your assets are within easy reach, you can visually decide what asset you want to place in your 3D movie set.

You've just learned how to use the content filters in the **Content Browser** window. In the next section, you will place your first 3D asset in your 3D movie set.

Building the 3D movie set

Now, you are finally ready to start building your 3D movie set.

The first rock asset that you will want to place in your 3D movie set is a very important one. This particular rock asset must be positioned in exactly the right place. This is because your female sci-fi character is going to be sitting on this rock asset later in this book. Let's get started:

1. Select the `Megascans` folder. All of your Rock assets will be displayed in the asset view area of the **Content Browser** window since you still have the asset filter enabled. Select the Rock asset named `S_Canyon_Sandstone_Boulder_uk4paev`.

2. Drag and drop this rock asset into your Viewport. I have highlighted this rock in the following screenshot.

3. In the **Transform** section of the **Details** panel, copy the **Location**, **Rotation**, and **Scale** values that are shown in the following screenshot:

Figure 9.23 – Placing your first rock asset in your 3D movie set

4. Now that the first Rock asset has been placed into your 3D movie set, you can start placing the rest of the Rock assets (static meshes) from your `Megascans` folder by dragging and dropping them from the asset view area of the **Content Browser** window into your Viewport. Place some Alien Plant models in the 3D movie set too. The placement and number of rock assets and Alien Plant models you put in your 3D movie set are up to you.

The following screenshot shows a map of what your current 3D movie set should look like:

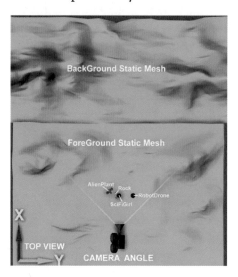

Figure 9.24 – Your current 3D movie set layout from a top view (the map has been rotated to match the camera angle)

Use your creativity with this step; however, there is only one rule when it comes to placing your assets and that is to keep an area clear from any rock and Alien Plant assets near **SciFiGirl, AlienPlant, S_Canyon_Sandstone_Boulder_uk4paev** (rock asset), and **RobotDrone,** as shown in the following screenshot.

You can place as many rock and Alien Plant assets as you want outside the red outline. This is because, later in this book, we will need an area that remains clear of any obstacles for the female sci-fi character to walk in and for the Robot Drone to fly in:

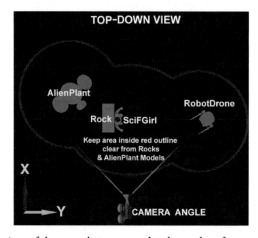

Figure 9.25 – Top-down view of the area that you need to keep clear from rock assets and Alien Plant models (the map has been rotated to match the camera angle)

Handy Tip

An easy way to clone (copy) an asset in the Viewport is to hold *Alt + drag with the mouse*. After you've cloned an asset, you can place it wherever you want to in your 3D movie set.

The following screenshot shows a map of how I've placed my assets (as an example only). You have total freedom to be creative with the placement of the assets in your 3D movie set:

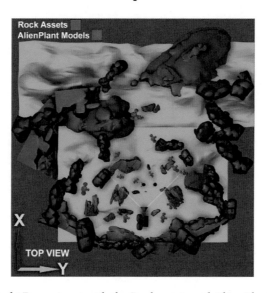

Figure 9.26 – My completed 3D movie set with the Rock assets and Alien Plant models added (the map has been rotated to match the camera angle)

The following screenshot shows another view of my completed 3D movie set:

Figure 9.27 – An alternative view of my completed 3D movie set, populated with rock assets and Alien Plant models

Now, let's take a look at my 3D movie scene through the **Camera View Angle** that we will use later in this book:

Figure 9.28 – My completed 3D movie set, viewed through the camera's viewing angle

Your 3D movie set is now complete and ready for the next stage – that is, adding lighting and atmospheric visual effects. In this section, you learned how to place 3D assets in the scene and how to clone (copy) these 3D assets directly in the Viewport. You've also gained valuable practical experience by using your creativity to place the 3D assets.

This concludes this chapter's tutorial.

Summary

Congratulations! You've completed this chapter's tutorial to build your own virtual 3D movie set.

You've also learned how to acquire free resources and modify them to suit the style that you are aiming to achieve in your 3D set. Finally, you learned how to populate your movie set with various props and environmental assets.

In the next chapter, you will take the 3D movie set that you've just created and learn how to light your scene. Then, you will add the final polish by adding atmospheric visual effects such as fog, lens flares, light bloom, and light shafts and add a glowing effect for the sci-fi armor.

See you in the next chapter!

10
Adding Lighting and Atmospheric Visual Effects in UE5

In the previous chapter, you learned how to build your own virtual 3D movie set of an alien planet's surface.

In this chapter, we will take the 3D movie set that you made in *Chapter 9, Building a Virtual 3D Movie Set in UE5*, and go through the step-by-step process of lighting and adding various atmospheric visual effects to it.

Lighting is a really important aspect of any scene. It can make or break a 3D movie set since lighting contributes so much in terms of the overall atmosphere and the viewer's emotional response to the environment.

Atmospheric effects such as **Fog**, **Lens Flares**, **Light Bloom**, and **Light Shafts** can also help to add a lot of mood to a 3D movie set, similar to how weather can influence your emotions in a traditional movie scene.

This tutorial is aimed at beginner-level UE users. I will focus on lighting and atmospheric visual effect for the 3D movie set by using the most basic settings and techniques. While it is certainly possible to create much more detailed and realistic lighting and atmospheric effects in UE5 (using more advanced features), that is beyond the scope of this tutorial.

In this chapter, we're going to cover the following main topics:

- The fundamentals of lighting in 3D graphics
- Using Lumen in your UE5 projects
- Lighting your 3D movie set
- Adding atmospheric visual effects

By the end of this chapter, you will know how to light and add atmospheric effects to your own custom 3D movie sets. Let's get started!

Technical requirements

To complete this chapter, you must have UE5 installed. Even if your version of UE is newer, the examples should still work without any problems. You will need the following to complete this chapter:

- A computer that can run basic 3D animation software.
- Unreal Engine 5.0.1. You can download it from `https://www.unrealengine.com/en-US/download`.
- You must have completed *Chapter 6*, *Exploring Unreal Engine 5*, to understand the basics of UE5's UI.

We will start this chapter's tutorial with an introduction to lighting fundamentals in 3D graphics. Then, we will go over five of the light types that are available in UE5.

The fundamentals of lighting in 3D graphics

To begin, let's start with the fundamentals of what lighting is in 3D computer graphics.

What is lighting in 3D graphics? It is the use of computer graphic techniques to simulate real-world lights inside a virtual 3D world.

What do we mean when we say we are lighting a scene? **Lighting** is the act of creating, placing, and editing lights in your scene to create the mood or visual style that you are after.

Lighting helps to convey a story in an image or movie. Lighting can be used to separate your subject, foreground, and background elements in a scene. The lighting in 3D movies can also be animated, which opens up new possibilities. For example, you could use animated lights to change the focus from one subject to another in a 3D movie.

Realistic and stylized lighting

Lighting can be realistic or stylized. Think of all the stylized lighting examples in the 3D animated movies from Pixar or DreamWorks, where style and mood are much more important than simply adhering to what real-world lighting looks like. This method of lighting is widely used in the 3D movie, film, and TV show production industry.

When the aim is realistic lighting, we can use new features in UE5, such as **Lumen**, for real-time **Global Illumination** (**GI**), to achieve this goal. We will cover Lumen in the next section.

Even when your scene is supposed to be photorealistic, you can still use additional custom lights to achieve the look that you are after.

You can mix GI and custom lighting whenever you want to. For example, just think of all the Hollywood movies or photography studio photoshoots where they use custom lighting for their real-world sets and actors.

The following screenshot shows an example of how I have used lighting and atmospheric visual effects to add mood to the scene. This helps to convey the story of an alien world.

In the following screenshot, in the top image, the scene has been lit by the default lighting, but it looks very plain, while in the bottom image, the same scene has been lit with custom lighting and I have added atmospheric visual effects to it:

Figure 10.1 – (Top) The scene with the default lighting and no effects; (Bottom) The scene with custom lighting and atmospheric visual effects added

You've just learned about the fundamentals of lighting and how it is used in 3D graphics. In the next section, we will explore the three traditional lighting techniques.

The three traditional lighting techniques

Three traditional lighting techniques are commonly used in 3D animated movies, films, TV, photography, fine art paintings, and stage performances. These are **Key light**, **Fill light**, and **Rim light**.

When you want to use any of these three lighting techniques, you need to create custom lights in your scene. You can use any of the following light types in UE5 for your lighting techniques: Directional light, Point light, Spot light, and Rect light. We will cover these light types in the next section.

You can use these traditional lighting techniques in combination with realistic lighting methods, such as Lumen, or you can use them by themselves.

Let's go over these three traditional lighting techniques now.

Key light

The **Key light** is your main light source. All the other lights are complementary to the Key light. Generally, this light will be pointing at your subject. The following screenshot shows a model of a monkey head (this model is the Suzanne Monkey head model that is available inside Blender). The model is lit with a single Key light (the light type is a Directional light):

Figure 10.2 – Using a Key light

Fill light

The **Fill light** is a light that fills in or brightens up shadowed areas. It represents the bounced (indirect) light in your scene. It is used to soften the contrast of the Key light. If your Key light is colored, then the Fill light will usually also be colored (with a complementary color to the Key light).

Another type of Fill light is ambient light. This is a natural light that fills the scene from all angles, such as the lighting of an overcast sky. In *Figure 10.3*, part *B*, you can see the Suzanne Monkey head model that is lit with a Fill light, plus a Key light (the light types that are being used here are Directional lights):

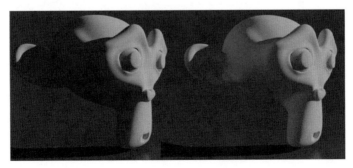

Figure 10.3 – (A) The model is lit with a Key light; (B) The model is lit with a Fill light plus a Key light

Let's move one to the next lighting technique, Rim light.

Rim light

Rim lights are used to separate the subject from the background. Rim lights are usually more intense than your Key or Fill lights, and they create sharper transitions from the lit to the unlit areas on the model's surfaces.

In *Figure 10.4*, part *A*, you can see the model that is lit with a Key light plus a Fill light. In *Figure 10.4*, part *B*, the model is lit with a Key light, a Fill light, and a Rim light:

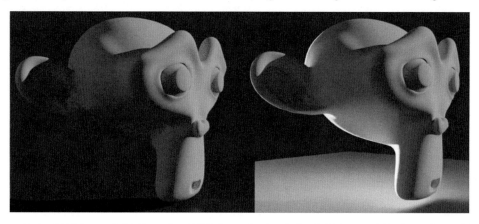

Figure 10.4 – (A) The model is lit with a Fill light and a Key light; (B) The model is lit with a Fill light, a Key light, and a Rim light

You've just learned about the three basic lighting techniques that are used in 3D graphics to add custom lighting to your scene.

In the next section, we will go over the light types (light sources) that can be used in UE5.

Types of light sources in UE5

There are a few light types that are available in UE5. In *Figure 10.5*, you can see that I have highlighted the five light types that we will discuss in this section.

To add any of these light types to your scene, in the toolbar, click on the **create** icon (the icon of a cube with a + sign). This icon is highlighted near the top of *Figure 10.5*.

In the drop-down menu that opens, navigate to **Lights** and then select any of the light types that you want to add:

Figure 10.5 – The light types that are available in the Lights menu highlighted on the right-hand side

Now that you know how to find the **Lights** menu, I will go through the five types of lights that are highlighted in the preceding screenshot:

- **Directional light**: This kind of light source simulates light that is being emitted from infinitely far away. The light rays from this light source are parallel to each other. The Sun is an example of this kind of light. You can read more about Directional lights by going to the official UE5 documentation, here: https://docs.unrealengine.com/4.27/en-US/BuildingWorlds/LightingAndShadows/LightTypes/Directional/.

- **Point light**: This is a light source that emits light rays in all directions. An electric light bulb is an example of this kind of light. You can read more about Point lights by going to the official UE5 documentation, here: https://docs.unrealengine.com/4.27/en-US/BuildingWorlds/LightingAndShadows/LightTypes/Point/.

- **Spot light**: This is a light source with light rays being emitted from a single point. The light forms a cone shape. This kind of light has two cone angles – an inner cone angle and an outer cone angle. The inner cone angle has full brightness. The brightness of the light falls off toward the edge of the outer cone angle. A handheld torch is an example of this kind of light. You can read more about Spot lights by going to the official UE5 documentation, here: `https://docs.unrealengine.com/4.27/en-US/BuildingWorlds/LightingAndShadows/LightTypes/Spot/`.

- **Rect light** (short for **rectangular light**): This kind of light is emitted from a rectangular plane. The Rect light has a source width and a source height setting (*Y* and *Z* axes). Computer monitors and television screens are examples of this kind of light. You can read more about Rect Lights by going to the official UE5 documentation, here: `https://docs.unrealengine.com/4.27/en-US/BuildingWorlds/LightingAndShadows/LightTypes/RectLights/`.

- **Sky light**: This light captures distant parts of your scene and then uses that captured result as a light source. When real-time capture is enabled for this light, the Sky light will update automatically as you move lights in your scene. You can read more about Sky Lights by going to the official UE5 documentation, here: `https://docs.unrealengine.com/4.27/en-US/BuildingWorlds/LightingAndShadows/LightTypes/SkyLight/`.

You've just learned about the five types of lights that you can use to light your 3D movie sets. You've also learned how to add any of these lights to your scene in UE5.

In the next section, we will briefly explore **Lumen**, a lighting system that will help you to create amazing lighting in UE5.

Using Lumen in your UE5 projects

Lumen is a **Global Illumination** (**GI**) lighting system that's built into UE5. Lumen is already activated for all new UE5 projects.

Lumen provides realistic and dynamic real-time indirect lighting (bounced lighting) in your scene. It does all of these GI lighting calculations without the need for lots of tweaking to get great results. Most of the heavy lifting of the GI calculations is done under the hood, so to speak.

But if you need manual control over the final gather and reflection quality, you can increase the sample counts of these by visiting the **Post Process Volume** settings in the **Details** panel.

Lumen uses software ray tracing by default but can achieve higher quality when hardware ray tracing is enabled.

> **Note**
> For hardware ray tracing, you will need a supported video card (such as an Nvidia RTX Series video card).

Things to keep in mind when using Lumen

You need to keep the following in mind while using Lumen:

- Lumen's software ray tracing currently only works on static meshes, instanced static meshes, hierarchical instanced static meshes, and landscape terrain. If you want to use Lumen with skeletal meshes, you will need to have **Hardware Ray Tracing** enabled.

- Avoid an Albedo value of pure white or pure black. This is because Lumen uses GI to calculate how much light will bounce off a material. In the real world, there are no pure white or pure black materials, so it will cause unrealistic results if your materials are using an Albedo value of pure white or black.

- Transparent materials are ignored in Lumen while masked materials are treated as opaque.

- Emissive materials on surfaces contribute to the GI calculation. Keep the size of the emissive surfaces large and relatively dim. Small and very bright emissive surfaces are problematic.

- The maximum range of the Lumen's GI solution is up to 200 meters away from the camera.

- Lumen works much faster with Nanite-enabled meshes. Change all your static meshes so that they use the Nanite system.

You can read more about Lumen here: `https://docs.unrealengine.com/5.0/en-US/lumen-global-illumination-and-reflections-in-unreal-engine/`.

You can read about Lumen's technical details and limitations here: `https://docs.unrealengine.com/5.0/en-US/lumen-technical-details-in-unreal-engine/`.

For this tutorial, we will be using Lumen (Lumen's settings have been set to their defaults).

Because we want to have creative control of the lighting in our scene, we will combine our realistic Lumen GI lighting with some of the traditional lighting techniques.

You've just learned about Lumen, its limitations, and some useful tips to remember when using Lumen in your projects. You also know that it's already being used in your project without you needing to change anything.

In the next section, we will start this chapter's practical tutorial. The first thing you need to do is prepare your project. Let's get started.

Preparing your project

To start this tutorial, load the project you created in *Chapter 9, Building a Virtual 3D Movie Set in UE5*. We will continue this chapter's tutorial by using this project.

Select **Atmospheric Fog** and **Sky Sphere** in the **World Outliner** panel and then press the *Delete* key to delete these two items from your scene. As soon as they are deleted, the sky in your 3D movie set will turn completely dark (since we deleted the **Sky Sphere** asset). Don't worry – this is all part of the steps in this tutorial.

The reason we've deleted the **Atmospheric Fog** asset is that, later, we will replace it with a more advanced type of fog: **Exponential Height Fog**.

The reason we've deleted the **Sky Sphere** is that we will use the Sky Atmosphere system instead.

Your **World Outliner** panel should now only list the following assets: multiple **Rock** assets, **ForeGround**, **BackGround**, multiple **AlienPlant** static meshes, **Planet1**, **SciFiGirl**, 16 armor pieces, **RobotDrone**, **Light Source**, **PostProcessVolume**, and **SkyLight**.

You've just completed the initial preparation stage for this tutorial by deleting the items from the scene that you won't need.

In the next section, we will learn how to add and adjust the Sky Atmosphere system for your 3D movie set.

Adding a Sky Atmosphere system

The **Sky Atmosphere** system is a physically-based sky and atmosphere-rendering technique inside of UE5.

With this system, you can create realistic Earth-like or alien-like atmospheres with adjustable time-of-day settings. This allows you to create many different lighting scenarios, such as midday, sunset, or sunrise. One of the unique features of the Sky Atmosphere system is that it approximates the scattering of light through the atmosphere to simulate atmospheric density.

You can read more about the Sky Atmosphere system here: `https://docs.`
`unrealengine.com/5.0/en-US/sky-atmosphere-component-in-unreal-`
`engine/`.

Let's add a Sky Atmosphere system to your scene:

1. In the toolbar, click on the **Create** icon. Then, navigate to **Visual Effects | Sky Atmosphere**. Click on **Sky Atmosphere** to add it to your scene, as shown in the following screenshot:

Figure 10.6 – Adding a Sky Atmosphere to your scene

2. Take a look inside your Viewport – you will see that your scene now has a clear blue sky with a horizon level. In the **World Outliner** panel, you will now see that **Sky Atmosphere** has been added to it. Now, let's go through the process of customizing the **Sky Atmosphere** system for your 3D movie set.

3. Select **Sky Atmosphere** in the **World Outliner** panel. In the **Details** panel, navigate to **Planet | Ground Radius**. Change **Ground Radius** to 1. This will move the horizon line downwards. The sky will now be a more uniform blue color.

4. In the **Details** panel, navigate to **Atmosphere | MultiScattering** and change **MultiScattering** to 2.

5. In the **Details** panel, navigate to **Atmosphere - Rayleigh | Rayleigh Scattering** and click on the color bar. In the **Color Picker** menu that opens, set **R**: 0.045, **G**: 0.41, and **B**: 0.43. Then, click on **OK** to close the **Color Picker** menu. This will change the color of your sky from a typical bluish sky color to a more alien-like turquoise color.

You have just learned how to add a **Sky Atmosphere** system to your scene, adjust the horizon level, and change the color of your sky.

In the next section, you will learn how to adjust the lighting that you currently have in your scene.

Lighting your 3D movie set

You are now ready to start the lighting process for your 3D movie set. You will begin by adjusting the light named **Light Source** that is already in your scene.

Here are some notes regarding **Light Source**:

*   **Light Source** is included in every new UE5 project.

*   This light type is a Directional light.

*   The **Sky Atmosphere** system uses **Light Source** as the Sun in your scene.

*   **Light Source** is the Key light in this tutorial.

Before we start creating and placing the lights, I want to give you a quick overview of how the lights will be placed in your 3D movie set.

Take a look at *Figure 10.7*. This diagram represents a top-down view of your 3D movie set and it acts as a reference guide for the light's placement in your scene. All the necessary steps to place these lights will be covered later in this tutorial.

Here, you can see how I've positioned two lights in the scene – **Light Source** (the Sun) and a Directional light:

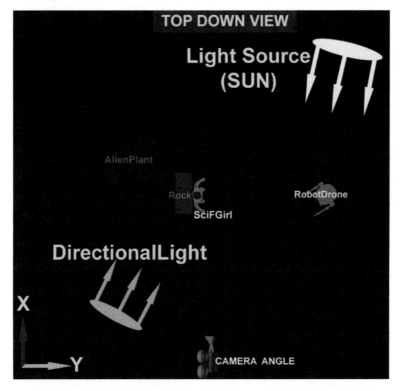

Figure 10.7 – Top-down view of the lighting placement in the 3D movie set

> **Note**
> The preceding diagram doesn't show you the placement of SkyLight (because the light from SkyLight represents the sky surrounding your 3D movie set).

You've just had an overview of the planned placement of your lights in the scene. In the next section, you will start to adjust your Key light – that is, **Light Source**.

Adjusting your Key light (Light Source)

Follow these steps to adjust Light Source:

1. In the **World Outliner** panel, select **Light Source**. In the **Details** panel, navigate to the **Transform** section. (Use the axes shown in *Figure 9.2* of *Chapter 9, Building a Virtual 3D Movie Set in UE5,* as a reference.)

2. Set the **Transform** value for **Light Source** to the following:

    -   **Location**:

        -   **X-Axis**: 100,
        -   **Y-Axis**: -225
        -   **Z-Axis**: 600

    -   **Rotation**:

        -   **X-Axis**: 56
        -   **Y-Axis**: -21
        -   **Z-Axis**: -174

3. Set all three axes of **Scale** to 2.5. This setting will change the angle of your Sun so that it is now placed just above the rocks in your 3D movie set.

4. In the **Details** panel, navigate to **Transform | Mobility** and make sure that **Mobility** is set to **Movable**.

5. Now, let's adjust the brightness of **Light Source**. In the **Details** panel, navigate to **Light | Intensity** and set it to 5 lux.

6. Let's change the size of the Sun (**Light Source**). This will help make the 3D movie set look more alien-like since the Sun will appear much larger than our Sun in the real world. In the **World Outliner** panel, select **Light Source**.

7. In the **Details** panel, navigate to **Light | Source Angle** and set it to 3. By increasing the **Source Angle** value of **Light Source**, you have changed two important things in your scene:

    -   It scaled up your Sun (**Light Source**) to appear much larger in the sky.

    -   By scaling up the **Source Angle** view, your shadows now have soft edges. The shadows will be softer the further away they are from the shadow-casting object and shadows will be harder-edged the closer they are to the shadow-casting object.

8. Now, let's adjust the Sun's (**Light Source**) light's color temperature, which is measured in **Kelvin** (**K**). In the **Details** panel, navigate to **Light | Use Temperature** and tick the checkbox to enable this feature.

9. In the **Details** panel, navigate to **Light | Temperature** and set it to 5500. This number controls the light's color temperature. A lower number will give the light a warmer color, while a higher number will give it a cooler color.

10. Now, let's adjust the indirect light (bounced light) in your scene. In the **Details** panel, navigate to **Light | Indirect Lighting Intensity** and set it to 12. This setting will brighten up the shadowed areas on the landscape and rock assets since this number makes the indirect lighting more intense.

11. In the **Details** panel, navigate to **Light | Volumetric Scattering Intensity** and set it to 10000.

You've just learned how to adjust various settings to customize the look and light qualities of your Sun (**Light Source**). In the next section, you will learn how to adjust the SkyLight to lighten the shadows in your scene.

Adjusting your first Fill light (SkyLight)

You will notice that the shadowed areas in your scene are still quite dark at the moment, even though we increased the indirect lighting in the previous section.

One of the ways to lighten the shadow areas in your scene is to use the SkyLight. The SkyLight emits lighting from multiple directions, so your shadowed areas will receive more lighting (and thus appear brighter). The SkyLight is one of the two Fill lights that you will use in this tutorial.

Let's make some adjustments to this SkyLight:

1. In the **World Outliner** panel, select **SkyLight**.

2. In the **Details** panel, navigate to **Transform | Mobility** and make sure that **Mobility** is set to **Movable**.

3. In the **Details** panel, navigate to **Light | Real Time Capture** and tick this checkbox to enable this feature. As soon as you've enabled **Real Time Capture**, your scene's shadow areas will become a bit lighter.

4. In the **Details** panel, navigate to **Light | Intensity Scale** and set it to 6. You will now notice that all your previously dark shadowed areas have been lightened considerably. By adjusting the **Intensity Scale** value, you have increased the amount of light that your scene receives from the sky, and this lightened your shadows.

You've just learned how to use the SkyLight to lighten your shadow areas, and also know how to change this light so that it updates dynamically when the lighting in your scene is changed.

In the next section, you will learn how to add a new custom light source to your scene. This new light will be your second Fill light.

Adding a second Fill light (DirectionalLight)

Let's add a second Fill light to your scene. The light type to use for the Fill light is a Directional light.

> **Note**
>
> This new Directional light is not linked to your **Sky Atmosphere** system.

We will use this new Fill light to add a low intensity of blue light to the shadowed side of your scene. This light will be positioned on the opposite side of the Key light, as shown on the top-down map shown in *Figure 10.7*.

Let's create this new Fill light now:

1. In the toolbar, click on the **Create** icon and navigate to **Lights | Directional light**. Click on **Directional light** to add this light to your scene, as shown in the following screenshot. The light from this **Directional Light** will immediately lighten your scene with intense white light:

Figure 10.8 – Adding another Directional Light to your scene

2. In the **Details** panel, navigate to **Light | Intensity** and set it to 0.8. You will notice that your Fill light (DirectionalLight) has been dimmed.

3. Let's adjust the settings for this **Directional light**. In the **World Outliner** panel, select **DirectionalLight**. In the **Details** panel, navigate to the **Transform** section and change the **Rotation** value of **Y-Axis** to -18 and the **Rotation** value of **Z-Axis** to 25. Leave **Location** and **Scale** as-is.

4. In the **Details** panel, navigate to **Transform | Mobility** and make sure that **Mobility** is set to **Movable**.

5. In the **Details** panel, navigate to **Light | Light Color** and click on the white color bar to open the **Color Picker** menu. In this menu, change the following values: **R:** 0.25, **G:** 0.5, and **B:** 0.5. This will change your Fill light's color to a dark turquoise color. I chose this color because it fits better with the blue theme of your scene.

6. In the **Details** panel, navigate to **Light | Cast Shadow** and uncheck the checkbox. We are removing the shadow casting function of this light because it is not a light that is supposed to be physically correct, since we are just using it to fill in the dark shadowed areas of your scene. *Figure 10.9*, part *A* shows the scene with the Fill light tuned off, while *Figure 10.9*, part *B*, shows the scene with the Fill light turned on:

Figure 10.9 – (A) Without the Fill light; (B) With the Fill light turned on

The following screenshot shows the Key light and Fill light on the main subject (**SciFiGirl**):

Figure 10.10 – Close up of SciFiGirl showing the Key light and Fill light on your subject

You have just learned how to add a new custom Fill light to your scene. The Light type for your additional Fill light is a Directional light, but you can use any of UE5's light types as a Fill light.

This concludes the lighting part of this tutorial. In the next section, we will explore the various atmospheric visual effects that you can utilize in your 3D movie set to give it that extra bit of atmosphere, mood, and polish.

Adding atmospheric visual effects

We will start this section by going through the process of adding fog to your scene.

Adding Fog

Fog in the world of 3D graphics is based on how fog appears to us in the real world. The most basic type of fog can be applied everywhere in the scene, but for this tutorial, I want to show you how to use a type of fog with a layered density, which is called **Exponential Height Fog** in UE5.

This is a type of fog that gets denser the closer it is to ground level, and gradually becomes less dense the further the fog is from ground level. This helps with the realism of the fog and also makes it look much more interesting.

You can read more about the individual settings inside **Exponential Height Fog** here: `https://docs.unrealengine.com/5.0/en-US/exponential-height-fog-in-unreal-engine/`.

Let's add **Exponential Height Fog** to your scene now:

1. In the toolbar, click on the **Create** icon. Then, navigate to **Visual Effects | Exponential Height Fog**.

2. Click on **Exponential Height Fog** to add it to your scene, as shown in the following screenshot. You will notice that your sky has suddenly turned very bright near the horizon level and that the landscape is also appearing lighter. This is because of the fog that has just been added to your scene:

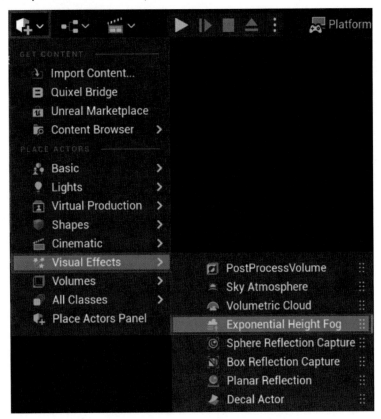

Figure 10.11 – Adding Exponential Height Fog to your scene

3. In the **World Outliner** panel, select **ExponentialHeightFog**.

4. In the **Details** panel, navigate to **Transform | Mobility** and make sure that **Mobility** is set to **Stationary**.

5. In the **Details** panel, navigate to **Exponential Height Fog Component | Fog Density** and change it to 0.012. This will change the fog's density so it is slightly less dense. Your sky will also be slightly darker now.

6. In the **Details** panel, navigate to **Exponential Height Fog Component | Fog Height Falloff** and change it to 2. This will change the **Falloff** range of the fog. The result of changing the **Falloff** range is that the fog will be denser around the horizon level, but gradually become thinner the further it is from the horizon level.

7. In the **Details** panel, navigate to **Directional Inscattering | Directional Inscattering Start Distance** and change it to 5000.

You've now finished setting up **Exponential Height Fog** in your scene. We used a low-density setting for the fog so that the effect of the fog is very subtle.

This fog effect adds some atmospheric perspective to your scene to make it look more atmospheric.

> Note
>
> **Atmospheric perspective** is when faraway objects take on some of the colors of the atmospheric haze since you are seeing them through a volume of the atmosphere. Closer objects will have less atmospheric perspective. An example of atmospheric perspective in the real world is when you look at mountains that are far away in a landscape – these mountains will take on some light blue color from the sky.

In *Figure 10.12*, part *A*, you can see a view of the 3D movie set with **Exponential Height Fog** set to **disabled**.

In *Figure 10.12*, part *B*, you can see the same view, but this time **Exponential Height Fog** is **enabled**.

This is a good example of how fog can add atmospheric perspective to your scene:

Figure10.12 – (A) Fog is disabled; (B) Fog is enabled

You've just learned how to add **Exponential Height Fog** and customize it. This fog helps build the overall mood of your 3D movie set.

In the next section, we will use a function that is inside **Exponential Height Fog** that allows you to create Light Shafts that will be shining through your fog.

Light Shafts

The **Light Shafts** are also commonly referred to as **volumetric lights** or **God rays** in 3D graphics, and they are created when rays of light are shining through a volume of fog. In *Figure 10.13*, you can see an example of Light Shafts that are visible in my scene.

To create Light Shafts, you need to use the **Volume Fog** function that is inside **Exponential Height Fog**. This will cause your Directional lights to create Light Shafts that will shine through the fog.

You can read more about Light Shafts here: https://docs.unrealengine.com/5.0/en-US/using-light-shafts-in-unreal-engine/.

Let's add Light Shafts to your 3D movie set:

1. Select **Exponential Height Fog**. Then, in the **Details** panel, navigate to **Volumetric Fog | Volumetric Fog** and tick the checkbox to enable this feature. Your whole scene will now turn white but don't worry – we will fix this now.

2. In the **Details** panel, navigate to **Volumetric Fog | Scattering Distribution** and change it to 0.22.

3. In the **Details** panel, navigate to **Volumetric Fog | Albedo** and click on the white color bar to open the **Color Picker** menu. In this menu, change the following values: **R:** 0.168 **G:** 0.558, and **B:** 1. This will change the fog so that it's slightly blue, although you won't be able to notice this yet.

4. In the **Details** panel, navigate to **Volumetric Fog | Extinction Scale** and change it to 0.065. This will make the fog a lot less dense. Now, you will notice the blue tint in the fog's color that you assigned in the preceding step.

5. In the **Details** panel, navigate to **Volumetric Fog | View Distance** and change it to 1000. Now, your fog will look much more realistic because it is less dense the closer it is to your point of view.

6. Now, let's add a function called **Light Shaft Occlusion** that creates volumetric shadows inside the volumetric fog. **Light Shaft Occlusion** adds shadows that are created when objects occlude Directional lights inside a volume of fog.

7. In the **World Outliner** panel, select **Light Source** (the Sun).

8. In the **Details** panel, navigate to **Light Shafts | Light Shaft Occlusion**. Tick the checkbox for **Light Shaft Occlusion**. You will notice that there are now shadow areas (volumetric shadows) behind objects that occlude the Sun's light. This effect is very subtle, so to notice it, you need to pan your view from side to side. The following screenshot shows that there is a volumetric shadow behind the Alien Plant:

Figure 10.13 – Light Shafts with Light Shaft Occlusion are now visible in your scene

You have just learned how to add Light Shafts and Light Shaft Occlusion to your scene by changing the settings in **Exponential Height Fog** and **Light Source**.

In the next section, you will add the final polish to your 3D movie set, which will be to add Light Bloom, Lens Flare, and a glowing effect for the female sci-fi character's armor.

Lens Flare and Light Bloom

Now that your lighting is complete and you've added **Exponential Height Fog**, Light Shafts, and a **Sky Atmosphere** system, we can continue by adding the final polish to your scene.

Let's start by making the Sun's light appear more realistic. To achieve this, you will use a **Light Bloom** effect so that your Sun will have a glowing effect around it. The **Light Bloom** effect will also cause the illuminated buttons on the sci-fi armor to glow.

Light Bloom (also known as **Light Glow**) is the light that extends from the borders of bright lights.

You can read more about the **Light Bloom** effect here: https://docs. unrealengine.com/5.0/en-US/bloom-in-unreal-engine/.

Follow these steps:

1. In the **World Outliner** panel, select **PostProcessVolume**.
2. In the **Details** panel, navigate to **Lens | Bloom | Method**. Tick the checkbox for **Method**. In the drop-down menu, select **Standard**.
3. In the **Details** panel, navigate to **Lens | Bloom | Intensity**. Tick the checkbox for **Intensity**. Change the amount to 0.03.

    You will notice that your Sun (Light Source) now has a Light Bloom effect (glowing effect) around it, as well as a Lens Flare that is emanating from the Sun's direction toward the bottom of the screen, as shown in *Figure 10.14*.

4. At the moment, the Lens Flare effect is a bit too intense. Let's scale the intensity down a bit. In the **Details** panel, navigate to **Lens | Lens Flares | Intensity**. Tick the checkbox for **Intensity** and change the amount to 0.2. You will notice that the Lens Flare that's emanating from the Sun is much subtler now. The following screenshot shows the Lens Flare:

Figure 10.14 – Lens Flare added to the Sun

5. Let's modify the Sun's Bloom effect to make it look more interesting. In the **World Outliner** panel, select **Light Source** (the Sun).

6. In the **Details** panel, navigate to **Light Shafts | Light Shaft Bloom**. Tick the checkbox for **Light Shaft Bloom**. Your Sun's Bloom effect will be far too intense when you've enabled this option. We will fix this in the next few steps.

7. In the **Details** panel, navigate to **Light Shafts | Bloom Scale**. Change this to 0.04. The Bloom effect will be slightly dimmer now.

8. In the **Details** panel, navigate to **Light Shafts | Bloom Threshold**. Change this to 0.9.

9. Let's add a red-orange color tint to the Sun's Bloom effect. This will make it look more interesting and alien-like. In the **Details** panel, navigate to **Light Shafts | Bloom Tint**. Click on the white color bar to open the **Color Picker** menu. In this menu, change the following values: **R:** 0.5, **G:** 0.05, and **B:** 0. This will change your Sun's Bloom color to a red-orange color tone.

In the following screenshot, you can see what the Sun looks like with **Lens Flare** and **Light Shaft Bloom** enabled:

Figure 10.15 – (A) The Sun with no Bloom effect and no Lens Flare; (B) The Sun with a Bloom effect and Lens Flare enabled

Adjusting the Bloom inside **PostProcessVolume** in *Step 2* and *Step 3* of this section caused the illuminated buttons on the sci-fi armor to glow, as shown in the following screenshot. In the top left, I have added a close-up of the forearm armor with its glowing buttons:

Figure 10.16 – The button lights on the armor are now glowing

Your 3D movie set is now complete and should look similar to the scene shown in the following screenshot, although your scene will be laid out differently than mine:

Figure 10.17 – The final 3D movie set

You have now completed the entire lighting process and learned how to use Fog, Light Shafts, Lens Flares, and Light Bloom to add atmospheric visual effects to your 3D movie set.

This concludes the practical lighting and atmospheric visual effect tutorial.

Summary

In this chapter's tutorial, you learned how to light and add atmospheric visual effects to your 3D movie sets. You can use this knowledge for your own future 3D movie productions.

Throughout the past 10 chapters, we've focused on the process of 3D asset creation, as well as how to use these assets in UE5.

In the next chapter, we will explore the rigging process for the Alien Plant model. You will learn how to add a skeleton to a mesh so that you can create some animation to bring the Alien Plant to life.

Further reading

To learn more about the topics that were covered in this chapter, take a look at the following resources:

- *Post Process Effects in Unreal Engine*: https://docs.unrealengine.com/5.0/en-US/post-process-effects-in-unreal-engine/

- Complete the Post Processing Essentials (free) course for UE5: https://dev.epicgames.com/community/learning/courses/GKm/post-processing-essentials/dZL/introduction-to-post-processing-essentials

- Lumen: Complete the Lumen Essentials (free) course for UE5: https://dev.epicgames.com/community/learning/courses/2Wo/lumen-essentials/dL16/introduction-to-lumen-essentials

- Watch this overview of Lumen from Unreal Engine's YouTube channel: https://youtu.be/Dc1PPYl2uxA

Part 3
Character Rigging
for Animation in UE5
with Control Rig

This part of the book will cover how to make a skeleton and Control Rig for your assets to be able to animate them easily.

We will cover the following chapters in this section:

11
Alien Plant Joint Setup in Blender

In *Chapter 3, Let's Sculpt an Alien Plant,* you learned how to model and texture the Alien Plant. Now it's time for us to prepare it for animation and to finally give it some *life*. Most 3D software offers many different ways to animate models. Among these, two are the most common.

The first way to animate a 3D model is by directly moving, rotating, and/or scaling it. This method is best suited for simple animations involving a rigid model. The second method uses a **skeleton** (sometimes called an **armature**) that is linked to the structure of the model.

Unless it's a very simple animation, the animation is normally better done using skeletons. The skeletons of 3D models are made up of bones. Just as bones in a real skeleton define the overall shape and mobility of a person, the bones of a 3D model skeleton correspond to the underlying structure, therefore defining which parts of the model can move in animations.

You will notice that some 3D software refers to bones as **joints**. This may seem confusing at first but think of them as joints in a real skeleton; by the end of this chapter, you will see that it is just another way of looking at the same thing.

In this chapter, we will cover the following:

- Preparing our model for the skeleton
- Parent/child hierarchies in 3D software
- Creating a skeleton for the Alien Plant

Technical requirements

You need to have Blender installed for free from `https://www.blender.org/` (at the time of writing). The Blender version in this chapter is *3.1.2*, but some older and newer versions will also work.

You also need to have a basic understanding of how to navigate the 3D user interface. If you skipped ahead, this was covered in *Chapter 1, An Introduction to Blender's 3D Modeling and Sculpting Tools.* If you want further in-depth tutorials on how to use Blender, `https://www.blender.org/support/tutorials/` is a great resource.

The files related to this chapter are placed at `https://github.com/PacktPublishing/Unreal-Engine-5-Character-Creation-Animation-and-Cinematics/tree/main/Chapter11`

Preparing our 3D model for the skeleton

Like many things in life, it's all about preparation. Before we can do anything, we need to prepare our 3D model to set us up for success. Here, we will learn how to import and prepare our model for the best results. This is also the *best practice* way if you were to work in a team or a studio with other artists.

Importing the Alien Plant into Blender

The model of the Alien Plant can be imported into Blender via the **FBX format**. This is a universal file format used by most 3D software packages, including UE5, Blender, Maya, and 3D Studio Max. FBX has limitations and will not contain some program-specific things. It is mainly used to transfer 3D assets from one 3D program to another for further work.

To import your Alien Plant model, simply follow these steps:

1. Open Blender and go to the top-left corner and click on **File | Import | FBX (.fbx)**, as shown in *Figure 11.1*:

Figure 11.1 – Importing an FBX file into Blender

2. After clicking on **FBX (.fbx)**, the following dialog box will appear, as shown in *Figure 11.2*. Use it to navigate to your previously saved FBX model file for your Alien Plant or the one included with the book files. The FBX file can also be downloaded here: https://github.com/PacktPublishing/Unreal-Engine-5-Character-Creation-Animation-and-Cinematics/blob/main/Chapter11/AlienPlant.fbx. Once you locate the file, click **Import FBX** in the bottom-right corner:

Figure 11.2 – Importing an FBX file into Blender file navigation

3.   The Alien Plant should now be in Blender, as shown in *Figure 11.3*:

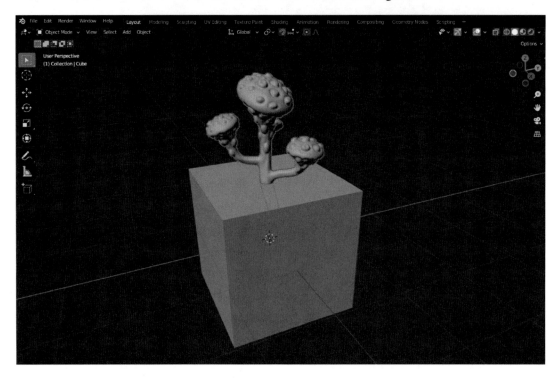

Figure 11.3 – The Alien Plant FBX 3D model imported into Blender

Best practice when importing your model

Before moving on to the next step, and as a general note, it is best practice to make sure that whatever the model is you want to create a skeleton for, the model is positioned as perfectly as possible in the middle of the 3D scene, also commonly referred to as the **origin** of the scene.

It's also better if the 3D model is facing straight as perfectly as possible in one of the 3D scene axes (*X*, *Y*, and *Z* directions) while the bottom of the model is on the ground. For example, the Unreal Engine Mannequin model would be positioned as shown in *Figure 11.4*. His feet are on the ground, perfectly at the origin, and he is facing directly on the *Y* axis:

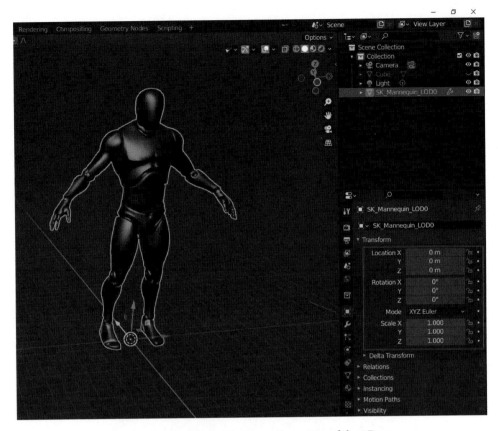

Figure 11.4 – Model positioning at the origin of the 3D scene

You will notice that in Blender, the feet of the character are on the floor (0 height) and where the green and red lines cross is the origin of the scene (0, 0, 0 coordinates). Left-clicking on any model, in this case, the Mannequin model, on the right side of the screen, you can see the **Transform** tab. If you don't see it, click on the **Object Properties** icon indicated by the red arrow. Notice that **Location** and **Rotation** are set to 0, 0, and 0, and **Scale** is set to 1, 1, and 1. You can change those numbers by clicking on them and changing them.

It's best practice (and recommended) that you set those values as such to move your model's local pivot to the world origin. However, if your model is then sticking through the floor, or has the wrong orientation or wrong scale, you can fix that easily. Your model's scale should also be correct before you create a skeleton for it.

Positioning and scaling the Alien Plant

Before moving on to the creation of the skeleton, let's look at the Alien plant again. Let's examine whether it is positioned and scaled correctly. The model is on the floor and since it has irregular branches, it is facing the best it can in a flat forward direction. However, how about the scale? Let's check. This can be done in several ways.

A less accurate way is to import a human character (such as the UE Mannequin) into the scene and scale the other 3D objects to match the relative human scale visually. I often do this just to double-check that things look in proportion to my correctly-scaled player characters.

The easiest and most accurate way to check the scale of an object in Blender is with the **Measure Tool**, as shown in *Figure 11.5*:

1. Place the viewport in the **Right Orthographic** view so the Alien Plant model can be measured more easily from the flat side view.

2. On the toolbar on the left, select the Measure Tool, marked with **X**.

3. Left-click and hold the mouse button at the base of the Alien Plant model (**A**) and drag it to the top of the Plant. Release the mouse button at **B** to complete the Measure Tool guide:

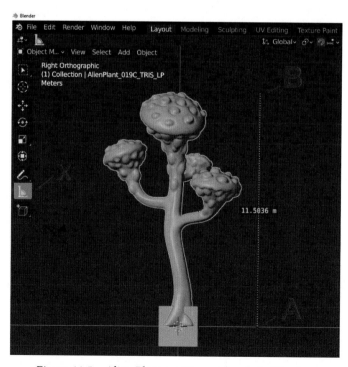

Figure 11.5 – Alien Plant position and scale in Blender

You can now see that this particular Alien Plant model is about 11.5 meters tall. Your custom-created plant might be of a different scale, so this is just for illustration. For our final scene, we want it to be just a bit taller than a human, so about 2.2 meters to 2.4 meters, as shown in *Figure 11.6*.

4. Repeat the previous steps to create another **Measure Object**, but this time drag it so it's about 2.4 meters tall as a guide.

5. Use the Scale tool to scale the Alien Plant to that guide height. The Measure Tool will disappear while using the scaling tool, but you can switch between the Scale tool and the Measure Tool for reference:

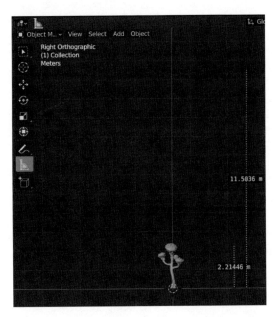

Figure 11.6 – Scaling the Alien Plant with the Scale tool

Tool Note

If you still have the cube in the scene that opens with a standard Blender scene, you can delete it at this point, since it's not needed and will most probably only get in the way.

---

6. You can then reframe your scene to focus on the newly resized plant by using **View | Frame Selected** or the period (.) key on the number pad (depending on your keyboard shortcut setup), as shown in *Figure 11.7*:

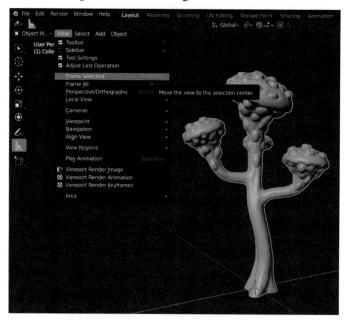

Figure 11.7 – Framing the selected Alien Plant in the Blender viewport

7. Finally, in the top-right corner, click on **Object | Apply | All Transforms**. This should reset all the transform values of the 3D model to the default 0, 0, 0 and 1, 1, 1 for **Scale**, without affecting the actual size of the 3D model, as shown in *Figure 11.8*:

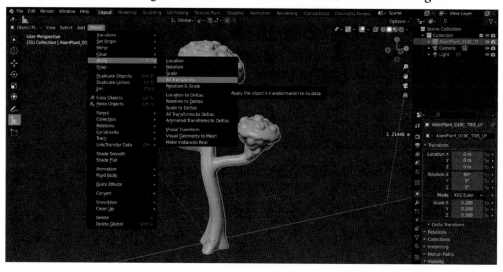

Figure 11.8 – Applying transforms to reset to the default values

> **Important Note**
>
> The reason we do this is that it makes the creation of the skeleton, skinning, and rigging much easier. It keeps things nice and tidy and is generally just good practice if you work with other artists in a team. Having a skinned model with non-default scale and transform values might be confusing later.
>
> Also, once a character is skinned, it becomes very hard to scale the model afterward in some 3D packages. In Unreal Engine, it's not such a big problem, but it's still better to have the correct scale before skinning in case you need to use other 3D packages in your pipeline later.

You've learned how to import a `.fbx` model and check the world position and scale. After making sure your self-modeled Alien Plant is positioned optimally in the 3D scene, it's time to move on to the next step. Alternatively, import the Alien Plant model provided in the book materials: `https://github.com/PacktPublishing/Unreal-Engine-5-Character-Creation-Animation-and-Cinematics/blob/main/Chapter11/AlienPlant.fbx`.

Next, we will learn about parent/child relationships in 3D software.

Parent/child hierarchies in 3D software

Before we start creating the skeleton itself, I just want to take a moment to explain the **parent** and **child** concepts, also called the **hierarchy** in 3D programs.

Parent/child hierarchies in 3D software are explained with the simple concept that a child always follows the parent as they walk around when the parent is holding the hand of the child.

However, if the child pulls away, the parent doesn't follow the child. Now, imagine a family: the *parent* and four children, *Child A*, *Child B*, *Child C*, and *Child D*. They are connected in the following way, as shown in *Figure 11.9*:

- If we now select the *parent*, all the children will move with the *parent* since it is at the top of the hierarchy, as shown in *Figure 11.9*.

- In the same way that *Child A* and *Child B* are the children of the *parent*, *Child B* is the parent of *Child C* and *Child D*. If we only select and move *Child B*, then *Child C* and *Child D* would follow and the rest would stay where they are, as shown in *Figure 11.9*.

- *Child A*, *Child C*, and *Child D* are at the end of the parent/child hierarchy chain, and if you select and move them, the *parent* and *Child B* will stay in the same place, as shown in *Figure 11.9*:

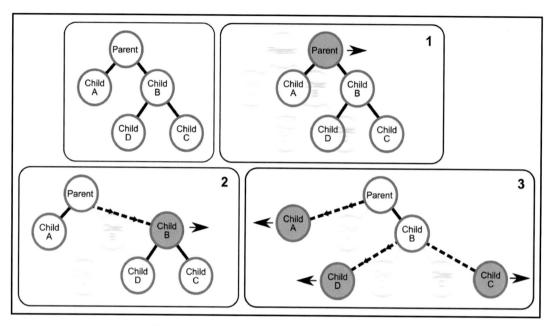

Figure 11.9 – How parent/child hierarchies work

Skeleton hierarchies work in the same way as these parent/child relationships. *Figure 11.10* shows an example of the standard UE Mannequin hand skeleton in Maya. I chose to show it in Maya because it is visually a bit easier to understand the relationship between the joints.

The little circles are the actual joint pivots. The elongated triangular lines are the parent/child linkages, with the thicker part of the triangle on the parent side and getting thinner as it points to the child. Most 3D software displays it in a similar way:

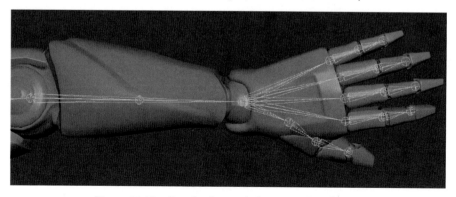

Figure 11.10 – Standard arm skeleton in 3D software

They work the same way in Blender, but Blender displays the parenting a bit differently at times and it can be visually a bit more confusing at first glance when a custom parenting is created. However, it's nothing to worry about, as you will see in the rest of the chapter as we make our skeleton.

Now that you understand child/parent hierarchies, we can move on to making the skeleton.

Creating a skeleton for the Alien Plant

Blender is just one of the many 3D software packages that can be used to create skeletons and joints for your models or characters. Most use roughly the same kind of workflow, with some small differences. In Blender, skeletons and their bones are created under a grouping called **Armature**, named after the wire supports used for stop motion animation and inside some sculptures. Blender might not refer to them as skeletons but in the industry, more generally, people just call them skeletons.

Everything is now ready to create our Alien Plant skeleton. Blender has some oddities in how it displays the hierarchy in the viewport with parenting, but in reality, it is the same as most 3D packages in structure.

Creating the skeleton

As we mentioned earlier in the chapter, in Blender, skeletons are grouped under the name of **Armature**. Now, let's learn how to make one for our plant:

1. At the top left of the standard Blender interface, click on **Add | Armature**, as shown in *Figure 11.11*:

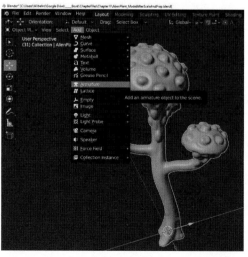

Figure 11.11 – Adding an armature in Blender

At the bottom left of the screen, an **Add Armature** menu will appear. Here, we can check the unit scale. If needed, change this to 1 m so the bones are bigger and more visible on the screen, as shown in *Figure 11.12*:

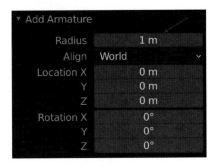

Figure 11.12 – Setting the bone size in Blender

2. With the newly created armature still selected, on the bottom right of the screen, click on the green stick figure tab on the **Properties** tab (**Object Data Properties**), expand **Viewport Display**, then click the checkbox to toggle **In Front** and **Axes** on, as shown in *Figure 11.13*:

Figure 11.13 – Bone Viewport Display settings

This will display the skeleton bones over the 3D models so it's easier to work with. **Axes** will display the axes (local orientation) of the bones. In some cases, this is very helpful to see this in the viewport, so it's a good habit to switch them on.

You can see your **Armature** group and **Scene Collection** in the viewport, as shown in *Figure 11.14*.

> **Note**
>
> If the armature doesn't appear at the origin of the scene, you probably need to reset the 3D cursor back to the world origin. The armature will be created on the cursor like other objects. You do this by using the drop-down menu at the top left of the screen: **Object | Snap | Cursor To World Origin**.

Figure 11.14 – Bone Viewport Display in Blender

3. If you expand the hierarchy by clicking on the little triangle, you will see that our armature currently only has one bone, as shown in *Figure 11.15*. This is also a good place to check on your parent/child hierarchy, as we will see later:

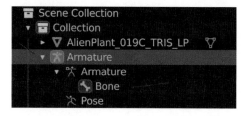

Figure 11.15 – Bone hierarchy display in Blender Scene Collection

Next, I like to keep the first bone, or what we call the **root bone**, at the origin of the scene. This bone will be a good overall parent for our entire skeleton at the origin of the 3D scene later in UE, but the bone is visually a bit too big, so let's scale it down.

4. Put Blender in **Edit Mode**. Now, all the regular editing tools are available to use on the bones, as shown in *Figure 11.16*:

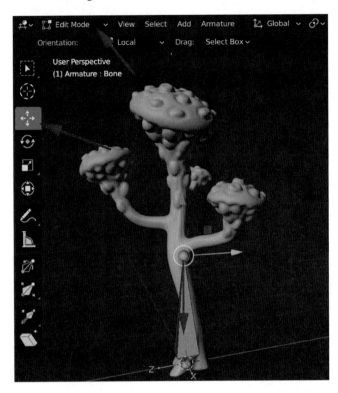

Figure 11.16 – Editing bones in Blender with Edit Mode and the Scale tool

5. Select the Move tool, then select the small sphere at the end of the bone in the viewport. Move it downward on the *Z* axis. You will see that the bone will scale down as you move the little sphere down. Move it till it's not visually so much in the way, as shown in *Figure 11.17*:

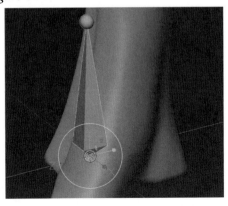

Figure 11.17 – Editing bones scale in Blender result

6. Now, select the bone itself, and click on **Armature | Duplicate** to create another copy of the bone, as shown in *Figure 11.18*. The new bone will move with the mouse till you click again. Don't worry if it's in the wrong location after this step:

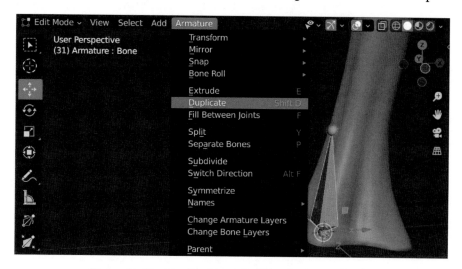

Figure 11.18 – Duplicating and editing bones in Blender

7. You can position it afterward, as shown in *Figure 11.19*, above the previous bone, but roughly in the middle of the plant's stem. You will also notice that we now have one extra bone in the **Scene Collection** hierarchy:

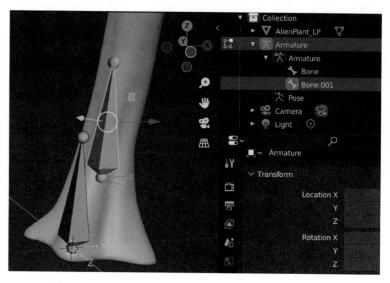

Figure 11.19 – Moving and editing the duplicated bone

8. By double-clicking on the name of the bones in the Scene Collection, rename them as `RootBone` and `StemBone01`, as shown in *Figure 11.20*:

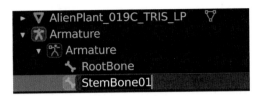

Figure 11.20 – Renaming bones in Blender

Creating a parent/child relationship

However, there's a problem. We want **RootBone** to be the overall parent of our entire skeleton so all the other bones follow **RootBone**. At the moment, the bone hierarchy itself is what we call **flat**. Both **RootBone** and **StemBone01** are on the same level in the hierarchy, so neither will follow the other. Let's fix that:

1. While still in **Edit Mode**, select **StemBone01** first in the viewport. Hold *Shift* on the keyboard and then select **RootBone** second. The order of selection is important since the last selected object will be given the role of the parent. In the top-left corner, select **Armature | Parent | Make**, as shown in *Figure 11.21*:

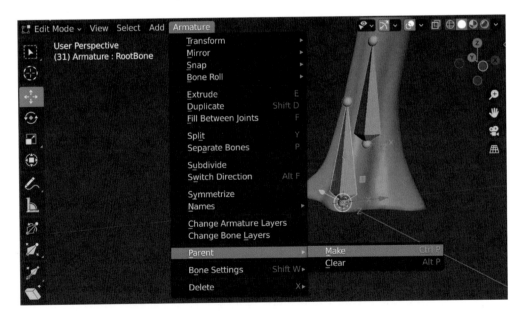

Figure 11.21 – Editing the bones parenting in Blender

2. A second menu will appear. Choose **Keep Offset**, as shown in *Figure 11.22*:

Figure 11.22 – Keep Offset menu in bones parenting

3. If you look at **Scene Collection** again, it might seem like **StemBone01** disappeared, but if you click on the little triangle, the hierarchy will expand and, as you can see, **StemBone01** is now the child of **RootBone**, as shown in *Figure 11.23*:

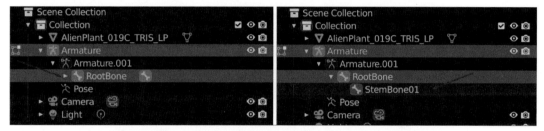

Figure 11.23 – Bones hierarchy displayed in Scene Collection

In the viewport, the parenting is indicated with a dotted line, as shown in *Figure 11.24*:

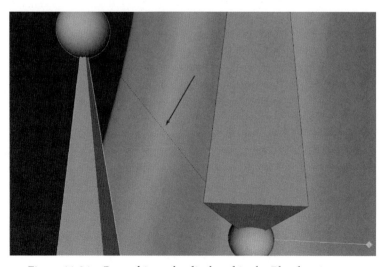

Figure 11.24 – Bones hierarchy displayed in the Blender viewport

We have now learned how to do custom parenting if needed. Now, let's learn a way to make a longer joint chain quickly.

Making a long joint chain for the main stem

We now need a longer skeleton parent/child chain to do the main stem of the Alien Plant. Instead of repeating the previous steps one by one till we have a long enough chain from the bottom of the main stem to the top, we will use the special **Extrude** function for bones:

1. The next step is better done in the **Right Orthographic** view instead of in perspective. Simply select the little sphere at the top of the bone of **StemBone01** and then click **Armature | Extrude**. The bone will extrude till we click the mouse again. There's also a keyboard shortcut in the default Blender settings by just pressing *E*, as shown in *Figure 11.25*:

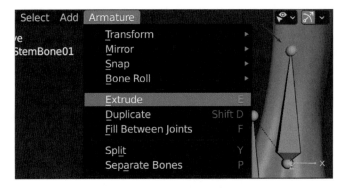

Figure 11.25 – Creating more bones by extruding them

2. Repeat this step until your armature resembles that of *Figure 11.26*. Notice that I created a bone on each split of the branches to link their bone chains up in the later steps. I marked these with arrows in *Figure 11.26*:

Figure 11.26 – Extruded bones result and bones for forked branches

3. Now, switch to the **Back Orthographic** view. Because we extruded in the **Right Orthographic** view, it created the extrude on a flat plane relative to that view. This is what we wanted; now, we just need to adjust it from the back (the side of the Alien Plant) view.

The easiest way to do this is to select and move the little spheres at the top of the bones. You can also select the main bone and move it if needed, but it behaves differently. Feel free to experiment as shown in *Figure 11.27*:

Figure 11.27 – Adjusting the bone positions

Important Note

The aim of creating this kind of skeleton is for the bones to run down the middle of the main stem at regular enough intervals so we get nice deformations once it's skinned. Once you have done a few, you will start to get a feel of where the best places are to place the bones in future projects.

After moving the bones according to the stem profile, it should look something like *Figure 11.28*:

Figure 11.28 – Results after moving the bones, back and side view

Make sure to navigate around the 3D model to check that the bones are well-positioned inside the main stem. If not, make small adjustments till you're happy with the placement.

We now have a full bone chain for the main stem of our Alien Plant. Next, we will explore how to create additional bones for the branches as part of the same skeleton.

Making the skeleton for the branches

To make the branches, we're going to use **Extrude** and **Subdivide**. The latter is another one of the techniques available and is very useful to make quick joint chains:

1. First, select one of the little spheres where a branch would fork off and extrude it like before. This time, you can see that it forks the joint, as shown in *Figure 11.29*:

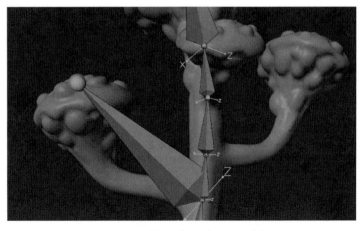

Figure 11.29 – Extruding the branch bone

2. Position the end of the bone to the top and middle of the bulb, as shown in *Figure 11.30*. Make sure to navigate around the plant in your perspective view to check that it's in the right position before the next step:

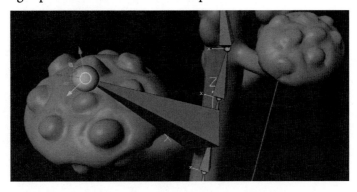

Figure 11.30 – Checking the bone position

3. Use the **Scene Collection** menu to select the branching base bone again so that it's highlighted, and then click **Armature | Subdivide**, as shown in *Figure 11.31*:

Figure 11.31 – Subdividing a bone

This will subdivide the bone into two equal pieces, as shown in *Figure 11.32*:

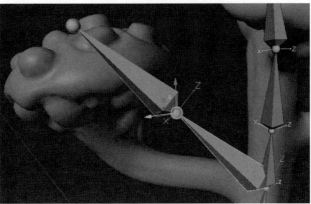

Figure 11.32 – Subdividing a bone results

4. Position this new joint (little sphere) at the base of the bulb while making sure to navigate around the object to check that the position is correct from all angles like before, as shown in *Figure 11.33*:

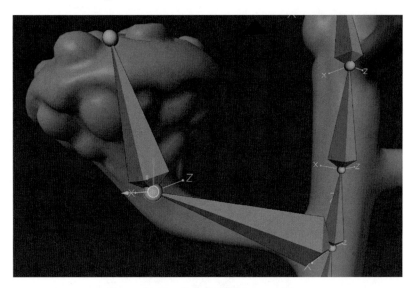

Figure 11.33 – Subdivide bone position

5. Select the base joint again and repeat the process following the branch arc, as shown in *Figure 11.34*:

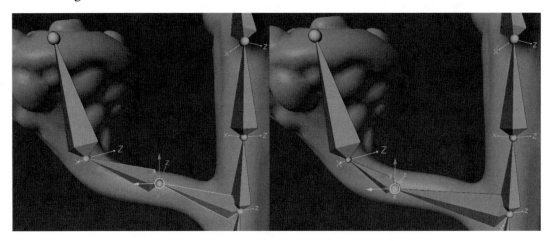

Figure 11.34 – Subdividing bones again and editing position

6. Repeat this one final time so that you have a separate joint at the base of the branch too, as shown in *Figure 11.35*:

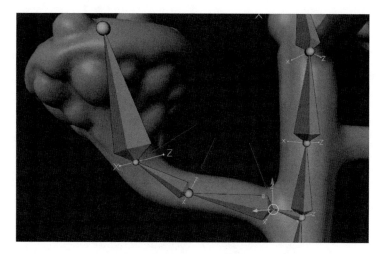

Figure 11.35 – Subdivide bone edit result

7. Repeat this process for the other two branches so you end up with something like *Figure 11.36*:

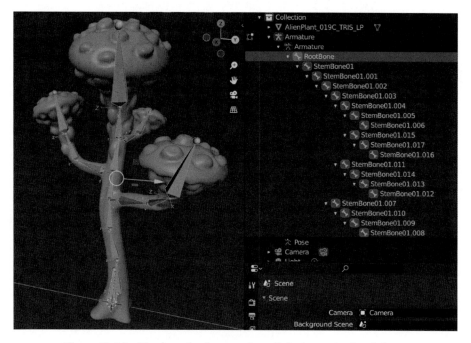

Figure 11.36 – Final result after creating all the bones in the skeleton

8. Finally, it's best to rename your bones to something that will make sense. It's a good habit to get into since if you do more complex rigging and skinning, good bone names can make the job much easier, as shown in *Figure 11.37*:

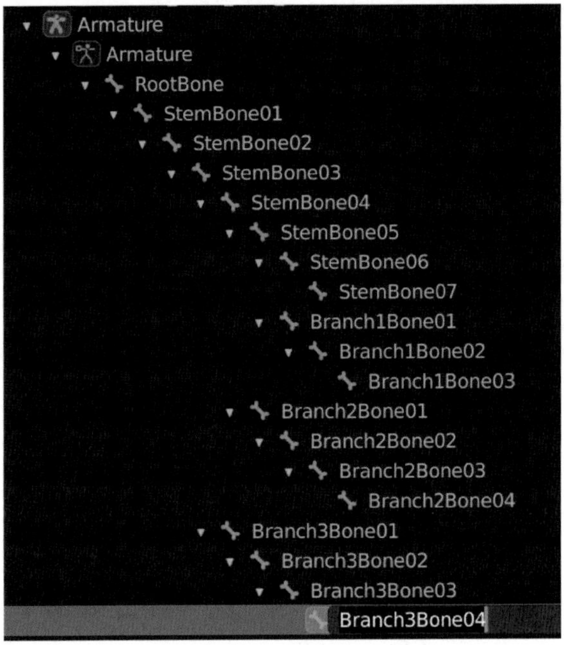

Figure 11.37 – Editing bones by renaming them

9. Save this Alien Plant Blender file with a descriptive name in a convenient location to use later in this book.

We have now built a skeleton for our Alien Plant and we are ready to move on to learning about skinning in the next chapter.

Summary

In this chapter, you've learned how to prepare 3D models before you create skeletons for them with some industry best practices. You've created a skeleton for your Alien Plant and got a deeper insight into how it works. You are well on your way to creating custom animatable characters.

In the next chapter, we will learn all about **skinning** and how it works.

12
Alien Plant Skinning in Blender

In the preceding chapter, we created a skeleton armature for our Alien Plant. Using a skeleton with a 3D model, you need to tell the 3D software what part of the model needs to follow which joints. You also need to tell the 3D software how much it influences that part of the model, particularly the blend between different joints. This process is called **skinning**. It is much like the way your forearm skin follows your forearm bone and the elbow skin is a blend between your forearm and upper arm bones. Skinning is also commonly called **skin deformation**.

All this might sound very complicated to do. Indeed, to do the skinning of a full human or animal character, for example, can be very challenging and time-consuming. However, in this lesson, we will start with the very basics, which are easy to master and will enable you to achieve a lot in your 3D scenes. In this chapter, we will cover the following:

- Introduction to skinning in Blender
- Skinning the Alien Plant mesh to its skeleton

Technical requirements

You need to have Blender installed, which can be installed for free from `https://www.blender.org/` (at the time of writing). The Blender version in this chapter is *3.1.2*, but some older and newer versions will also work.

You will also need a basic understanding of how to navigate the 3D user interface. If you skipped ahead, this was covered in *Chapter 1, An Introduction to Blender's 3D Modeling and Sculpting Tools*. If you want further in-depth tutorials on how to use Blender, `https://www.blender.org/support/tutorials/` is a great resource.

The files related to this chapter are placed at `https://github.com/PacktPublishing/Unreal-Engine-5-Character-Creation-Animation-and-Cinematics/tree/main/Chapter12`

Introduction to skinning in Blender

As I explained in the introduction to this chapter, **skinning** is where we tell the 3D model how to deform and follow the bones. We need a way to tell the 3D software what part of the 3D model we want to follow, which bones, how much, and how to blend between them. We call this **skin deformation**, generally. Skinning is applied to the vertices of the 3D model. Editing the amount a vertex is deformed by a bone is called editing its **weights**.

There are mainly two kinds of skin deformations:

- **Rigid**, where the vertices follow the bone at 100%.
- **Blended**, in which two main areas of the 3D model meet and are deformed by two different bones. The blend is to have a smooth transition between them, such as an elbow or a knee.

It is the blended deformations where things can get tough in certain circumstances where one vertex can be influenced by not just two, but three, four, or even five bones at the same time. A typically difficult area to skin is around the clavicle area of the human body. There, a vertex can be influenced by the clavicle, upper spine, upper arm, and sometimes, even the neck bone.

However, the basics are simple, and we will learn how to do it with some easy examples. Advanced skinning is beyond the scope of this book, but with some extra research and practice, you too can become good at skinning 3D characters.

Painting skin weights

Most 3D animation software has **skin weight editing tools**, but perhaps the most common are **skin weight painting tools**. Blender also has the ability to paint skin weights. Let's look at a basic example that will teach you how to use this tool.

Applying or parenting a 3D object to a skeleton

First, let's learn how to apply the skin modifier to our model in Blender. I pre-prepared a simple file for you that you can load from the files provided: `https://github.com/PacktPublishing/Unreal-Engine-5-Character-Creation-Animation-and-Cinematics/blob/main/Chapter12/AlienPlant_Skinning_Introduction.blend`

1. Open `AlienPlant_Skinning_Introduction.blend`, as shown in *Figure 12.1*.

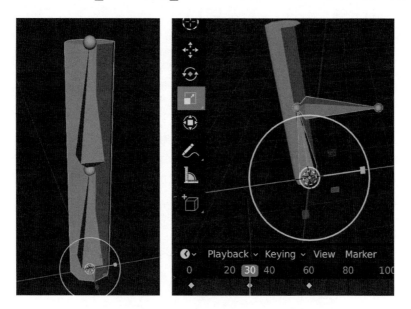

Figure 12.1 – Skinning example file

In this file, there is just a simple cylinder with a simple joint chain. Imagine it being an elbow or a knee. If you drag the blue animation timeline at the bottom, the bone also has a very simple bending animation, but the cylinder's skin doesn't follow it yet.

2. The next step is to skin it to the bones. To do this, make sure you are in **Object Mode** in Blender, select the cylinder (your skin) first, and then a bone (the parent). Hold *Shift* on the keyboard to select more than one object in the viewport. The selection order is important since the last selected will be the parent. Select **Object | Parent | With Automatic Weights** as shown in *Figure 12.2*:

Figure 12.2 – Parent skin weights

You will see that the cylinder's skin now deforms with the bone when we drag the animation timeline. Blender did most of the work for us by using automatic weights, as shown in *Figure 12.3*:

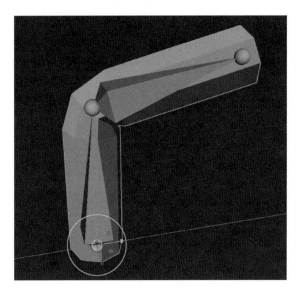

Figure 12.3 – Skinning results

However, we can edit this using weight paint if the automatic weight results are not good. Next, we will see how it works.

How does it work?

To edit the skin or see the weights in the viewport, while the cylinder is selected, switch to **Weight Paint** mode, as shown in *Figure 12.4*:

Figure 12.4 – Weight Paint mode

Now, let's explore the basic **Weight Paint** setting on the **Properties** menu; under **Active Tool**, you will see the **Weight Paint** tool settings, as shown in *Figure 12.5*:

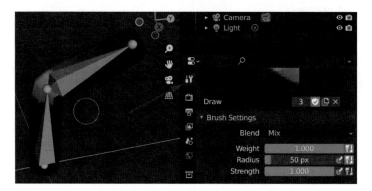

Figure 12.5 – Weight Paint settings

There are lots of **Weight Paint** settings but for the scope of this book, we will just get started on the essentials that are used the vast majority of the time.

The most important is **Brush Settings**:

- Make sure **Blend** is set to **Mix**.

- **Weight** is a more advanced setting, and you don't need to worry about it for now. You can just leave that at **1.000** for the vast majority of cases.

- **Radius** is important since that controls the size of the **Weight Paint** brush in the viewport. That is the orange circle you can see next to the bent 3D model in the viewport of *Figure 12.5*.

- **Strength** is important since that controls how much weight you're painting to the vertex from the selected bone.

If you look at the 3D model, you'll see it is rainbow-colored. The colors represent the weights of a selected bone (the amount it follows a selected bone) and its vertex group (the vertices assigned to it).

In simple terms, this is what the colors mean:

- **Red** means it's 100% weighted to the bone.
- **Green** means it's 50%/50% weighted between two bones.
- **Blue** means it's 0% weighted to the bone.
- The in-between values are a mix of those colors.

If you look at the Blender documentation, it gives you a chart, as shown in *Figure 12.6*. This is how the colors and weights are laid out:

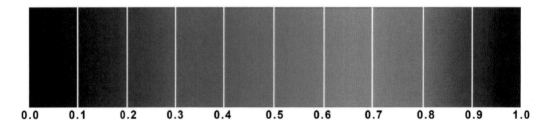

Figure 12.6 – Weight Paint colors in the Blender documentation

However, to really understand this in practice, let's do an exercise.

Painting the weights

Follow these steps to edit skin weights with painting:

1. While in **Weight Paint** mode, on the **Properties** menu, under **Active Tool**, you will see the **Weight Paint** tool settings. Open the **Options** dropdown and check **Auto Normalize** as shown in *Figure 12.7*. This will give you more predictable weight painting results.

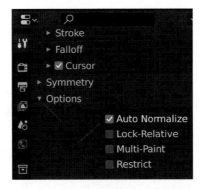

Figure 12.7 – Weight Paint settings

2. In **Scene Collection**, expand the hierarchy **Cylinder | Vertex Groups** to see your **Bone** vertex groups. You can select the bone and the weights you want to paint here, as shown in *Figure 12.8*:

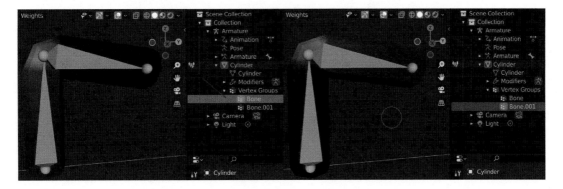

Figure 12.8 – Weight paint vertex group selection

You'll notice that when you select **Bone** (the root bone), the bottom is red, and the top is blue to reflect the weight. The root bone on the world floor is influencing the bottom part of the cylinder 100% (red) and the top of the cylinder 0% (blue).

Now, if you select **Bone.001** (the top bone), the top is red and the bottom is blue. This is the opposite of the previous. The top part of the cylinder follows the top bone 100% (red) and the bottom 0% (blue).

Notice that the middle stays green in both cases because it's a mix between the two bones.

Let's do some weight painting:

1. To make the process a bit easier, let's turn on **Wireframe** in the shaded view to see where the vertices are that we're going to paint, as shown in *Figure 12.9*:

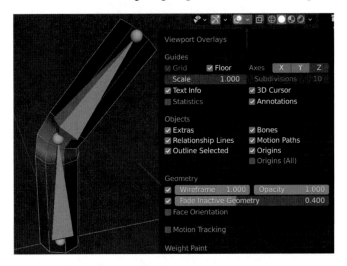

Figure 12.9 – Weight paint display wireframe

2. Drag the animation timeline to around frame **14** so the joint has about a 40-degree angle in it. This is so it's easier to see the effect of the weight painting.

3. With the first root **Bone** vertex group selected and the brush **Radius** set at **50 px** and **Strength** set at **1.000**, left-click and drag the orange brush circle across the middle part of the cylinder where it bends, repeatedly releasing the mouse button between strokes and pressing it again for the next stroke.

    You'll see the vertices move. As you do this, the vertices will become solid red as the weight you are painting builds up with every stroke of the brush. Keep doing this while navigating around the cylinder to paint all sides of the middle vertices till they're all solid red, as shown in *Figure 12.10*:

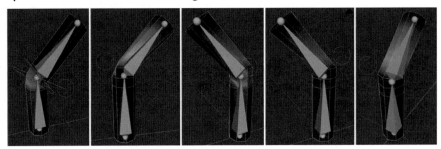

Figure 12.10 – Weight painting

4. With all the middle vertices painted red, they now stay with the **Bone** joint 100% and stop following **Bone.001**. You can see this more clearly if you scrub the Playback timeline to see the animation.

So, now we've painted the weights, the only problem is that if we drag the animation timeline to frame **30**, the bend doesn't look very good anymore because all the vertices in the middle bend part are rigidly weighted to the root bone, as shown in *Figure 12.11*:

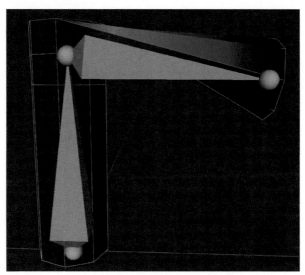

Figure 12.11 – Weight painting result

Let's paint some of the weights back to **Bone.001** for a more natural bend.

5. Set **Strength** to 0.200 and select the **Bone.001** vertex group, as shown in *Figure 12.12*:

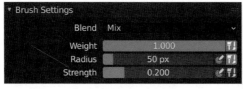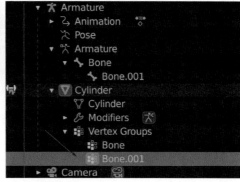

Figure 12.12 – Weight Paint settings

6. This time, paint with single left-clicks over the vertices you want to paint as you navigate around the cylinder. See whether you can end up with something like this in *Figure 12.13*. It is not great, but let's now try to make it better:

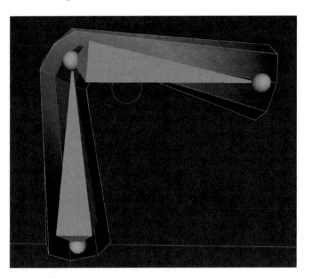

Figure 12.13 – Weight painting edit

7. In the top-left corner of the viewport, select the **Blur** tool instead of the default paintbrush. Using strokes and dabs, left clicking and releasing the mouse button between strokes, use this tool. This tool just evens out the weights for a smoother and cleaner transition. Keep doing this till the whole middle area has a nice and even bend, as shown in *Figure 12.14*:

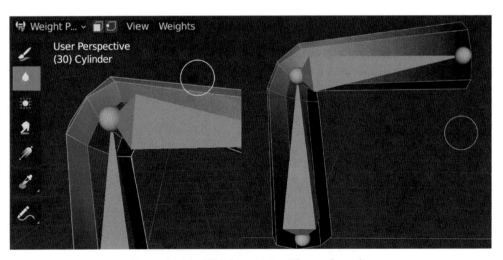

Figure 12.14 – Weight painting Blur tool results

Note

Even though the skinning is better now, you'll notice that we're losing some volume towards the bend as it narrows towards it, which we didn't get when Blender did the automatic weights originally. Losing volume on the bends is a common issue with painting skinning. The quick fix is to switch between vertex groups and paint 100% weight on the two edge loops that maintain the volume (as shown in *Figure 12.15*). This is followed by blur painting the middle edge till it's even between the two outer loops.

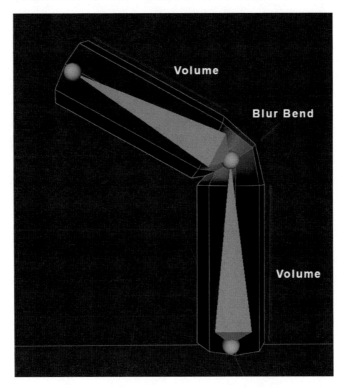

Figure 12.15 – Weight painting keeping volume

Here are some additional notes to further improve the skinning:

- It's very useful to have a temporary animation covering the extremes of the likely amount the joint will bend so you can just drag the animation timeline to see it at those extremes and everything in-between – a bit like this example we've been working on in the tutorial. Alternatively, rotate the joints often to test the skinning as you paint the weights.

- Make the brush size smaller when needed so as not to paint vertices you don't want to move, or bigger if you want to smooth over a bigger area.

- Keep switching between the vertex groups to pull the vertex weights towards the selected bone. If you weight it too much to one bone, select the other bone and paint the weight the opposite way.

- Switch between painting weights and smooth blurring regularly.

To get the skinning perfectly right is sometimes a long and laborious process on a more complex model. To experiment and practice is the best way. There are also other skinning tools available that are outside the scope of this book, but there are many resources available to learn more. However, with this basic set of skills, you can do a decent job of skinning most 3D models.

Now that you have a basic understanding of how skinning works, let's skin our Alien Plant.

Skinning the Alien Plant mesh to the skeleton

Now, for the final part of this chapter, we'll finally get to skin our alien plant. Your plant might be different from mine if you modeled it yourself in the previous chapters. Your skinning results might be different from mine and might require more editing. Since you have learned the basics of skin weight painting in this chapter, you should be able to fix any problems that come up. If not, load the file provided (`https://github.com/PacktPublishing/Unreal-Engine-5-Character-Creation-Animation-and-Cinematics/blob/main/Chapter12/EndOffChapter11_Results_AlienPlant_withSkeleton.blend`)

so you can proceed with the rest of the instructions.

Skinning the Alien Plant

We'll use the skeleton we created earlier and skin our Alien Plant to it. To do so, follow these instructions:

1. Load the file you saved earlier with the Alien Plant and the skeleton.

2. Once the file is loaded, just like in the previous section, we will parent the Alien Plant mesh to the skeleton by selecting the Alien Plant 3D model first and then the skeleton. Click **Object | Parent | With Automatic Weights**.

3. Now that the skinning is applied to the Alien Plant, let's test it and see whether there's anything that needs fixing. Place Blender in **Pose Mode**, select the bones one by one, and test the deformation by rotating them as shown in *Figure 12.16*:

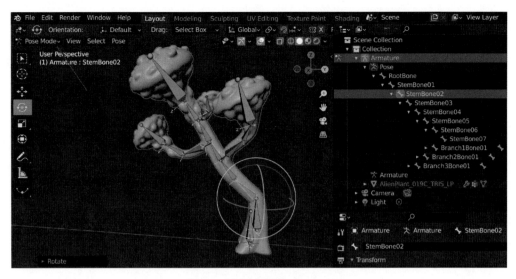

Figure 12.16 – Skinning test

4. Undo (*Ctrl + Z*) after each rotation or after testing to get the bone back to the default pose it was skinned in. Alternatively, you can achieve the same by selecting all the bones (default keyboard shortcut *A*) and then using **Pose | Clear Transform | All**, as shown in *Figure 12.17*:

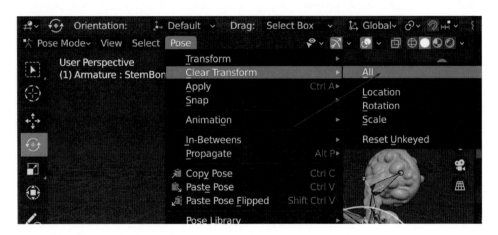

Figure 12.17 – Resetting pose after testing

5. You can also put Blender in **Object Mode**, select the plant model, and then **vertex Paint** to inspect each vertex group individually by selecting them in **Scene Collection**. Make sure to expand the hierarchy if you don't see the vertex groups at first glance as shown in *Figure 12.18*:

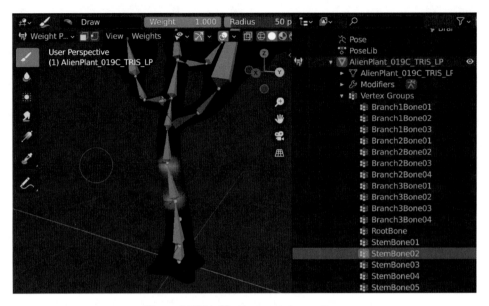

Figure 12.18 – Vertex group inspection

6. Use the **Paint Skin Weights** tools if you need to fix any problems with the skinning.

7. Save the Alien Plant Blender file for use in a later chapter with a descriptive name in a convenient location.

Congratulations, you have successfully skinned your Alien Plant! This is a big step forward in your journey through this book.

Summary

In this chapter, you've learned how to do skinning and how to edit skinning with weight painting, and finally, you have skinned your Alien Plant to your skeleton. If you enjoyed this process, this is the very first step in becoming what they call a **character rigger** in the industry, a specialized job for people who enjoy skinning and rigging characters for games and movies. Even if this process is not one of your favorites, it's important to learn how to do it if you want to create new animated content on your own as a generalist.

In the next chapter, we will use what we have learned so far and create a skeleton and skin for our robot character.

13

Robot Joint Setup and Skinning in Blender

In the previous chapter, we completed a very simple skeleton for the Alien Plant. Now, we can move on to something a bit more complex. The robot character has more independently moving parts, and it also has an arm that will need a better control system than just rotating joints when we come to the rigging and animation parts later in this book. Creating the skeleton for our robot will be very similar to what we did in the previous chapter; however, here, we need to pay a bit more attention to our **joint orientations** and **local axes** of our bones/joints. This will be explained in more detail later in this chapter.

The robot is a rigid metal body, so the way we will do the skinning will be a bit different from the previous chapter, but in some ways much simpler.

In this chapter, we will cover the following topics:

- Creating a skeleton for the robot
- Checking and editing the local joint orientations of the joints
- Skinning the robot to the skeleton in a rigid way

Technical requirements

You need to have Blender installed, which can you get for free at `https://www.blender.org/` (at the time of writing). The Blender version that's being used in this chapter is 3.1.2, but some older and newer versions will also work.

You also need to have a basic understanding of how to navigate the 3D user interface. If you've skipped ahead, then please go back to *Chapter 1, An Introduction to Blender's 3D Modeling and Sculpting Tools*. If you want further tutorials on how to use Blender, then `https://www.blender.org/support/tutorials/` is a great resource.

Finally, you should have completed *Chapter 12, Alien Plant Skinning in Blender*.

The files related to this chapter are placed at `https://github.com/PacktPublishing/Unreal-Engine-5-Character-Creation-Animation-and-Cinematics/tree/main/Chapter13`

Creating a skeleton for the robot

To create a skeleton for the robot, we will begin where we began in the previous chapter when we worked with the Alien Plant model.

Opening, positioning, and scaling the robot

Open the Blender file of the robot you created in *Chapter 2, Modeling a Robot Drone Character*. If you didn't do this, open the completed robot model file that accompanies this book: `https://github.com/PacktPublishing/Unreal-Engine-5-Character-Creation-Animation-and-Cinematics/blob/main/Chapter13/RobotDrone_Blender_File.blend`. Check that the scale and positioning of the model are correct and that the model is in the center of the scene. We want a model that is around 40-50 cm tall for our final scene, so use the **Measuring** tool to check this. If you have any trouble remembering how to do this, please refer to *Chapter 11, Alien Plant Joint Setup in Blender*, the *Positioning and scaling the Alien Plant* section, as shown in the following screenshot:

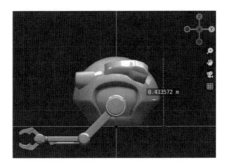

Figure 13.1 – Robot scale

To tidy things up even further, even if the robot is correctly scaled and positioned, select all the parts of the robot and use **Object | Apply | All Transforms** to reset all the pivots to the origin of the scene. This means that if you need all the separate parts to line up again after you move it, all you need to do is type in 0, 0, 0 in the **Transforms** section and 1, 1, 1 in the **Scale** section. This also makes it cleaner for skinning later, as shown in the following screenshot:

Figure 13.2 – Apply | All Transforms

Everything is now in place for the next step.

Body and left arm bones

Now, let's create the skeleton for our robot:

1. In the **Perspective** view, go to **Add | Armature**, as shown in the following screenshot:

Figure 13.3 – Armature

2. With the armature still selected (the **Add Armature** dialogue at the bottom left will disappear if you deselect it), set **Radius** to 0.2 m and make sure that, under **Viewport Display**, the **In Front** and **Axes** boxes have been checked, as shown in the following screenshot:

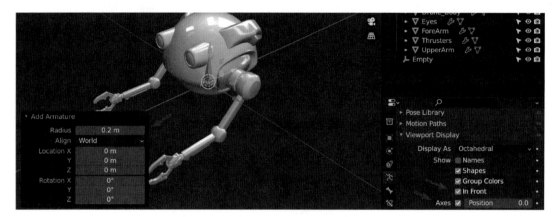

Figure 13.4 – Add Armature

> **Note**
>
> If the armature doesn't appear at the origin of the scene, you probably need to reset the 3D cursor back to the world origin. The armature will be created on the cursor just like other objects. To do this, go to **Object | Snap | Cursor To World Origin**.

3. Switch to the **Right Orthographic** view and **Edit Mode**, as shown in the following screenshot.

4. Select **Bone** and then click **Armature | Duplicate**, as shown in the following screenshot:

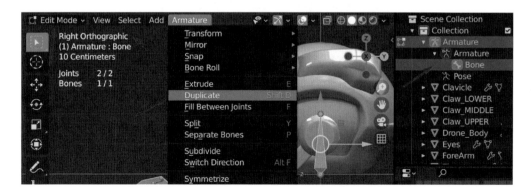

Figure 13.5 – Duplicating the Bone object

5. Place the new `Bone.001` in the middle of the mass of the body of the robot. Set **X** and **Y** in the dialogue to `0 m` – you can round off the **Z** property if you want to get the closest cm, but this isn't essential:

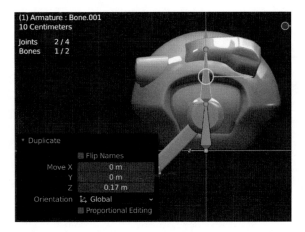

Figure 13.6 – Placing Bone.001

6. Switch to the **Front Viewport** option and while `Bone.001` is still selected, select **Armature | Duplicate** to duplicate it again. This time, position the new `Bone.002` where the shoulder joint would be and in the middle of the arm from the front view, as shown in the following screenshot:

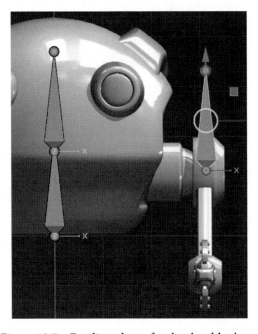

Figure 13.7 – Duplicate bone for the shoulder bone

7. Switch to the **Right Orthographic** view again.

8. Switch **Viewport Display** to **Wireframe**. Then, set **Viewport Display | In Front** to off for the bones. After that, zoom into the central point where the robot shoulder cylinder mesh edges converge to find the more accurate middle:

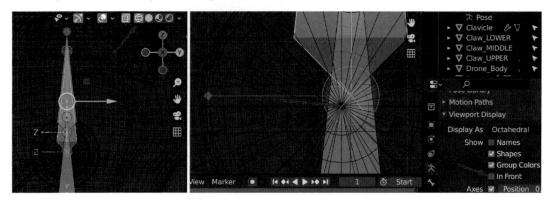

Figure 13.8 – Bone for the shoulder position

9. With Bone.002 still selected, move it so that it aligns with the center of the shoulder cylinder where the edges converge:

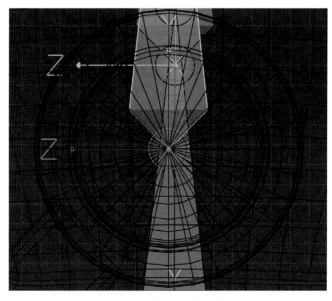

Figure 13.9 – Bone for the shoulder position

10. Zoom out while in the **Right Orthographic** view and select the little sphere at the end of Bone.002. Then, move it to the position of the robot arm's elbow, as shown here:

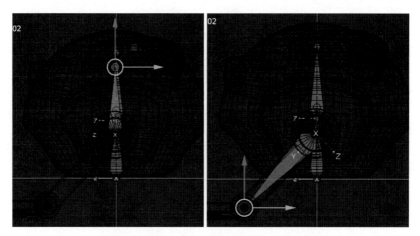

Figure 13.10 – Bone for the elbow position

11. Zoom in on the elbow and place it as accurately as visually possible in the center of the elbow cylinder, as shown here:

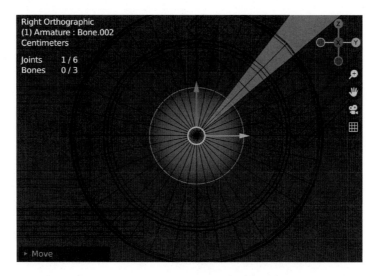

Figure 13.11 – Bone for the elbow position

12. Next, with the end of the bone still selected, select **Armature | Extrude** to create a new elbow bone to span to the wrist. Zoom in and make sure it's positioned in the center of the wrist ball joint after, as shown here:

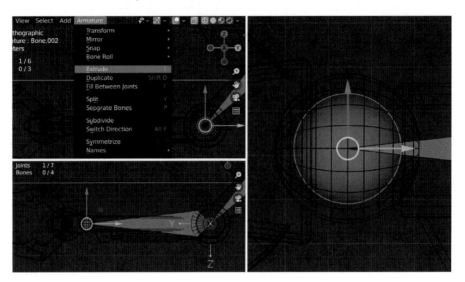

Figure 13.12 – Bone for the wrist position

Everything looks good from the **Right Orthographic** view, but let's switch to the **Top Orthographic** view to make sure. In this case, the Wireframe display of the wrist ball is a useful guide to judge if the arm joint chain is in the middle of the arm like when it's viewed from the top. You'll notice that it might be off and not visually exactly in the middle of the elbow joint from the top, as shown here:

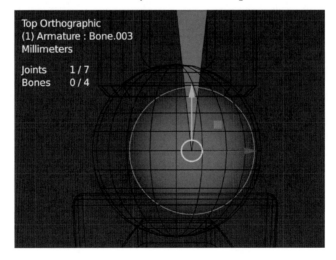

Figure 13.13 – The Top Orthographic view

13. This is why it's important to always check from different viewports while you work. To fix this, select both the new shoulder and elbow bones at the same time and move them together until they're in the visual center of the arm as much as possible. In this case, the center can easily be identified by the wrist ball joint in the Wireframe view, as shown here:

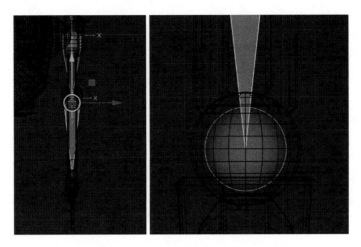

Figure 13.14 – The Top Orthographic view

14. Switch back to the **Right Orthographic** view again and select **Armature | Extrude** to create the hand bone, as shown in the following screenshot. Zoom in to make sure it's in the center of the hand:

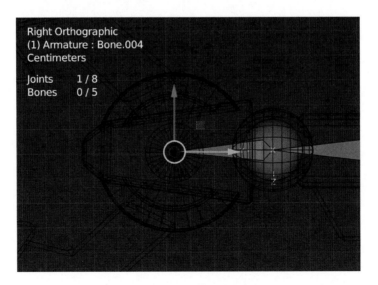

Figure 13.15 – Hand bone

15. Now, with the little ball of the hand bone still selected, select **Armature | Extrude** again to form a lower claw bone, as shown here:

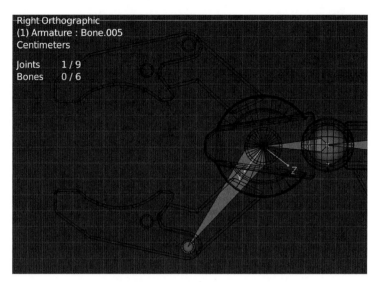

Figure 13.16 – Lower claw bone

16. Next, select the end of the hand bone again and, just like you did in *Step 15*, select **Armature | Extrude** to form an upper claw bone, as shown here:

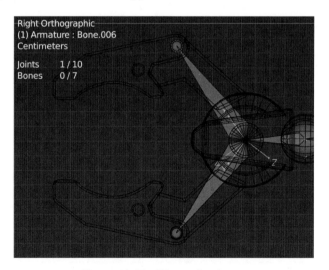

Figure 13.17 – Upper claw bone

With that, we've created our armature with bones for the body and left arm. Instead of following the same process for the right arm, we will take a shortcut by creating symmetrical bones with the **Symmetrize** tool. However, before we can do that, as always, we need to lay the groundwork. We will do that next.

Renaming and parenting the bones

Before moving on, we need to organize and edit the parenting of our skeleton. Then, we must use a naming convention for the bones so that the **Symmetrize** tool can use them to create our right arm bones quickly and easily.

If the left- and right-hand sides of our character or 3D model are the same, like most animals and creatures where the right-hand side is a mirror image of the left, we don't need to create bones for both sides. Blender and most other 3D software have something like a **Mirror bones** tool. In Blender, it is called the **Symmetrize** tool. The tool recognizes bones that should be mirrored by how they're named.

Blender is good at recognizing the most common industry standard naming formats for bones. A few working examples are as follows:

- `Left_Bone`
- `L_Bone`
- `Bone.L`
- `Bone.l`
- `Bone.right`
- `Bone_right`

I like `L_Bone` or `R_Bone` the most. They are short and since the bone name begins with `L_` or `R_`, it doesn't get lost visually when you're organizing hierarchies, skin weight painting, and performing other tasks with the skeleton.

Now, let's rename the bones by following these steps:

1. Currently, our bone names would look similar to what's shown in the following screenshot since Blender auto-named them as we created them:

Figure 13.18 – Bone names

2. Rename the bones by double-clicking on the bones' names in the **Scene Collection** area and typing in the new names. Rename them like so:

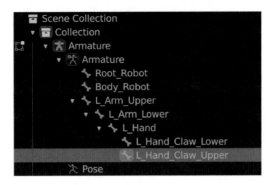

Figure 13.19 – Bone names

3. Next, we need to correct and edit the parenting. In **Edit Mode**, select the **Body_Robot** and **Root_Robot** bones by holding *Ctrl* while you left-click on one and then the other in the **Scene Collection** area (the order of selection is important since the last to be selected will be the parent).

4. Then, click **Armature | Parent | Make**. Select **Keep Offset** in the dialogue that appears:

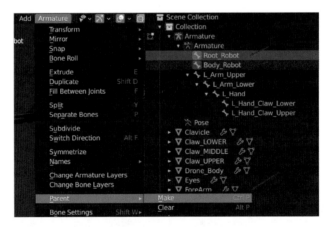

Figure 13.20 – Parent

5. Next, select **L_Arm_Upper** and then **Body_Robot**. Use **Armature | Parent | Make** once more, also with **Keep Offset** selected in the next dialogue.

Our robot armature skeleton hierarchy should now look as follows:

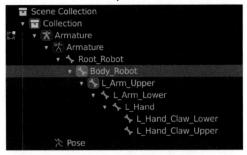

Figure 13.21 – Bones hierarchy

Our **Root_Robot** bone is the **Parent** of everything. The **Body_Robot** bone is the next one in the hierarchy, while the **L_Arm_Upper** (shoulder) bone is the child of the **Body_Robot** bone, so it flows right down to the claws on the hand.

With that, our robot skeleton and the left arm bones have been named correctly, and the hierarchy is in the right order. Next, we will create the Right Arm Bones with the Symmetrize tool.

Using the Symmetrize tool

Using the **Symmetrize** tool on armatures in Blender's **Edit Mode** could not be simpler. Follow these steps to learn how:

1. Select all the left arm bones in **Scene Collection** by first selecting **L_Arm_Upper**, holding down *Shift* on your keyboard, and then left-clicking on the last claw bone in the list – that is, **L_Hand_Claw_Upper**. This is the same as what you would do when selecting multiple files in Windows 10 Explorer.

2. Select **Armature | Symmetrize**, as shown here:

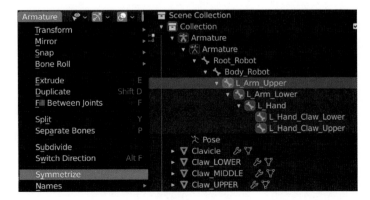

Figure 13.22 – Using the Symmetrize tool to create the right arm

If you look at the result shown in the following screenshot, you will see that Blender created the right arm bones for us. Not only that, but it also renamed the bones in the right arm **R_** instead of **L_** and did the parenting for us so that the bones are the same as the left arm bones.

At the bottom left in the **Symmetrize** dialogue, we can change the **Symmetrize Direction** option to a different axis if needed when our character or 3D model is facing another way. However, in this case, the default direction was correct:

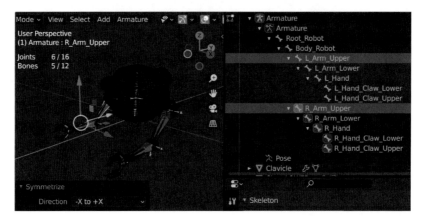

Figure 13.23 – Right arm result

With that, we have successfully created a full skeleton for our robot character. Before we skin our Robot 3D model to our skeleton, we need to check our bone **Local axes** and **Orientations** since this will be important later in this book.

Checking and editing the local joint orientations of the joints

We've completed our robot skeleton, just like we did for our Alien Plant in *Chapter 11*, *Alien Plant Joint Setup in Blender*. However, there's a difference between our Alien Plant and our robot. Later in this book, we will use an **inverse kinematics (IK)** animation controller on our robot arms. Don't worry about what exactly an IK controller is at this point. We will get to that later, in *Chapter 15*, *Creating a Control Rig with Basic IK Controls for the Robot in UE5*. All you need to know for now is that our **Bone Orientations** and **Local axes** need to be set in a certain way for our robot arm to animate correctly with an IK controller.

In general, it's good to have clean and sensible bone orientations, so this is very important to be aware of and understand. Next, we will find out what they are.

What is the local orientation of a bone?

To see the local orientation of a bone visually, we do not have to go far. We already switched them on in the Viewport earlier in this chapter, as shown in *Figure 13.4*.

As you may have noticed by now, 3D software uses *X*, *Y*, and *Z* axes to define the position of a 3D object in the software's 3D world or space. In the same way, the rotation of a 3D object or bone is divided up into *X*, *Y*, and *Z* axes. This makes it easier for us and the computer to know exactly how we want to rotate our 3D object by inputting its *X*, *Y*, and *Z* values or a combination of them, as shown here:

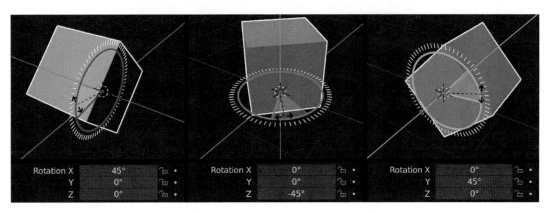

Figure 13.24 – Local rotate combination

To see the **Local Rotation Orientation** value of any 3D object or bone, select **Local** from the **Transforms Orientations** drop-down menu while the **Rotate Transform** tool is enabled, as shown in the following screenshot:

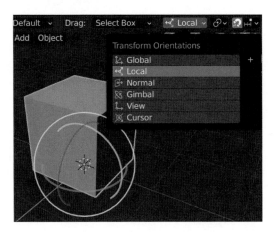

Figure 13.25 – Local rotate

This **Local Rotation Orientation** value becomes very important for things such as knees and elbows, which can and should only rotate in one direction along one axis. For example, our robot arm's elbow bone should only rotate along the X-axis, as shown here:

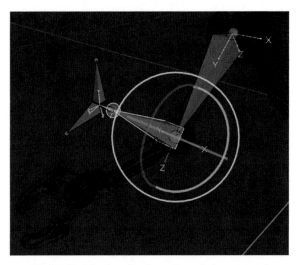

Figure 13.26 – Local robot elbow being rotated

In **Pose Mode**, if you select the **R_Arm_Lower** bone, you'll see that our **Local Bone Rotate Orientation** with the **Rotate** tool is in very good shape and that it rotates correctly directly along the X-axis if we were to rotate it. With the display axes already on, it's also easy to see visually that they're correct:

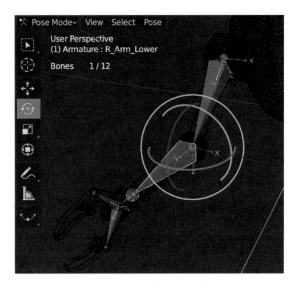

Figure 13.27 – Elbow local axis

Partly because we created and extruded these arm bones earlier in the **Right Orthographic** view, it was easy for Blender to work out how we want the local axis to be. In this case, we have good local axes in our entire skeleton if we were to check them all. However, very often in the skeleton creation process, we end up in a situation where these joints may have an undesirable **Local Orientation**. Luckily, Blender (and other 3D software) gives us a way to fix them.

Editing local bone orientations

To learn how to edit the **Local Bone Orientation** value, let's imagine we want the elbow joint on our robot to deform weirdly. Follow these steps to edit the **Local Rotation Axes** value without influencing the child bones further down the hierarchy:

1. Save the current Blender file for later use since we are about to make a correct skeleton incorrect in the process of learning how to edit bone orientations.

2. Switch back to **Edit Mode**.

3. With the **R_Arm_Lower** bone selected, left-click on the **Bone Roll** tool, as shown in *Figure 13.28*.

4. Left-click inside the yellow circle and *drag* your mouse to roll the bone. You can see the **Roll** value in degrees in the top-left corner.

5. Release your mouse button at the desired angle.

6. For exact values, you can type them in the **Bone Properties** tab, under **Roll**. For example, type in -45, as shown here:

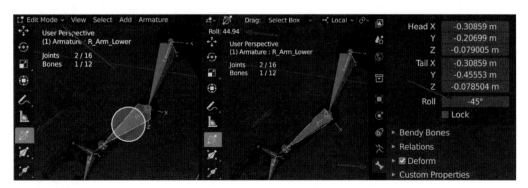

Figure 13.28 – Roll value

7. Return to **Pose Mode** and **Rotate** the bone on the *X*-axis. You will see that it behaves very differently when rotating on the new -45 degree angle that's been set:

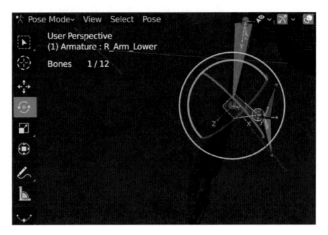

Figure 13.29 – Edited Roll value

8. Reload the file you saved in *Step 1* before we made these changes. Don't save these changes when opening the file. We want the correctly orientated skeleton back for the last part of this chapter.

With that, we have learned how to edit our local bone orientations if needed. This will come in very helpful at some point if you continue to build character rigs in the future. Next, we'll move on to the last part of this chapter and skin our robot in a rigid way.

Skinning the robot to the skeleton in a rigid way

In the previous chapter, we learned how to paint the skin weights with the **Skin Weight Painting** tool. However, there's also another more *direct* and *exact* way to assign specific skin weights to specific vertices on our 3D model. In the case of our robot, this is the perfect situation to try this method.

Our robot has rigid, solid, and unbendable separate moving parts. In this case, we know that every moving part will have to follow their bones 100%. Rather than weight painting each part at 100% after assigning **Automatic Skin Weights**, we will do so in a different way to speed up the process.

As always, let's make sure our model is ready before we skin.

Preparing the model and collapsing modifiers

If parts of the robot model have modifiers applied to them, such as **Mirror**, it may complicate how we select the vertices for our skinning process, we need to remove them. To find out if you have modifiers on any of the robot parts, in **Scene Collection**, expand the hierarchy of the object. To get rid of (or *collapse*) the modifiers, in **Object Mode**, select **Object | Apply | Visual Geometry to Mesh**, as shown in *Figure 13.30*.

Go through all your robot parts until there are no modifiers left, as shown in the following screenshot:

Figure 13.30 – Collapsing modifiers

Now that the parts of the robot are ready, let's skin them.

Skinning the robot body parts

The first part of this process is almost the same as what we laid out in the preceding chapter but with a slightly different skin parenting. Instead of using **Parenting | With Automatic Weights**, we'll use **Empty Weights** so that you can start with empty vertex groups. Because we will assign vertex weights manually, it is better to start from a clean slate instead of battling automatic skin weights that have been assigned by Blender. Follow these steps:

1. In **Object Mode**, select one of the robot body parts, such as **Drone_Body**. Then, select an armature. As we mentioned previously, selection order is important.

2. Parent **Drone_Body** to the armature by applying **Object | Parent | With Empty Groups**, as shown in the following screenshot:

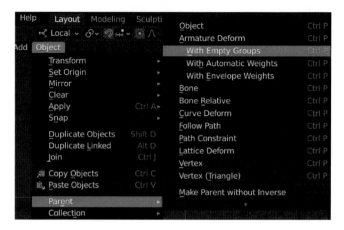

Figure 13.31 – Selecting vertices

3. Repeat this process one by one for every robot body part until they're all skinned to the armature individually.

We now have all the parts of the robot skinned to the skeleton. It will function, but if you go to **Pose Mode** and move the bones, you'll notice that it doesn't deform correctly since the vertex groups are still empty. Next, let's do the rigid skin weights.

Assigning exact skin weights to vertices

In this section, we'll learn how to assign the exact values of an individual or whole group of vertices to a specific bone. We know that we want the robot body parts to follow specific bones 100% so that the parts can stay rigid and not bend between bones like an organic or soft and bendy model would. Follow these steps:

1. Select one of the robot body part models. In my case, it will be **Drone_Body**.

2. Go to **Edit Mode** in Blender. Select **Vertex select**, as shown in *Figure 13.32*.

3. Select all the vertices in the robot body part model.

> **Note**
>
> This can be done easily by selecting one vertex from each group of linked polygons. For example, if your arm is made of a simple cylinder and a long box, select one vertex from the cylinder and one vertex from the box. Once selected, go to **Select | Select Linked | Linked** or use *Ctrl + L* (the default Blender shortcut).
>
> Also, putting Blender in X-ray mode using the top-right display options means that you'll be able to select front and back vertices by just **Select Box** dragging over the entire mesh for quick selection. By far the quickest way to select all the vertices of an active object in **Edit Mode** is using the default Blender shortcut key – that is, *A*.

4. Click on and open the **Object Data** tab and expand **Vertex Groups**, as shown in the following screenshot:

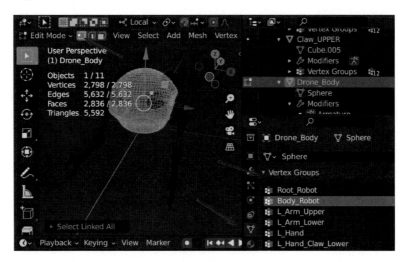

Figure 13.32 – Vertex Groups

We know we want all the **Drone_Body** vertices to follow the **Body_Robot** bone 100%.

5. In **Vertex Groups**, select the **Body_Robot** bone's **Vertex Group**, as shown in *Figure 13.33*.

6. Make sure that **Weight** is set to `1.000` (100%) and click on **Assign**:

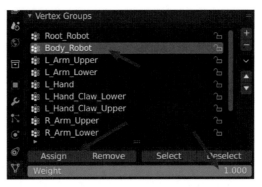

Figure 13.33 – Assigning vertex weights

Because we had *all* the vertices selected in our robot body and then assigned them to the **Body_Robot** bone at a value of `1.000`, these vertices will now follow the **Body_Robot** bone 100%. You can test this now in **Pose Mode**. Always test in-between the steps to make sure what you've done works.

> **Important Note**
>
> Depending on how your robot model is split up and constructed, you need to think through what part should follow what bone vertex group. Note that the main body of the robot is skinned to the **Body_Robot** bone, *NOT* the **Root_Robot** bone, and so should all the static attachments to the Robot body be, such as the **Thrusters, Clavicle,** and **Eyes** meshes.
>
> On my Robot model, the left upper arm and right upper arm are parts of the same 3D model. In this case, I must first select the vertices on the left upper arm, assign them to the **L_Arm_Upper** bone vertex group, and then select the vertices on the right upper arm and assign them to the **R_Arm_Upper** bone vertex group. This logic applies to the rest of the skinning. This is also why naming bones properly is important – it makes assigning them easier.

7. Repeat this process for all the other robot body part models. Match the model vertices selection with the correct bones and assign a weight. Make sure to exit **Edit Mode** and use **Object Mode** after each weight assignment to select the next robot body part object; then, enter **Edit Mode** again to do the assignment.

8. Test what you've got in **Pose Mode** by rotating each bone to see if it all works the way it is supposed to, and that the right part of the robot follows the right bone. Undo after each rotation to return to the original pose. Alternatively, with all the bones selected in **Pose Mode**, right-click in the Viewport and select **Clear User Transforms** to return the bones to their original skinned pose. This is not essential, but it keeps the scene clean when you exit **Pose Mode**, as shown in the following screenshot:

Figure 13.34 – Testing in Pose Mode

1. Save the Blender file once you've done all the skinning on the robot body parts.

> **Advanced Skinning Tip**
>
> This method can also be useful for assigning not only rigid weights but also blends when you get more advanced with skinning. If the value is set to 0.5, for example, you can assign a blend between two or more bones, such as an elbow.
>
> If you want to set a 50%/50% blend on a ring of vertices in the middle, between a parent and child bone (such as an elbow), select the ring of vertices and assign it at a **Weight** value of 1.000 to the parent bone. This will ensure you start with a clean full weight value on the selected vertices.
>
> Then, while the ring of vertices is still selected, change the weight value to 0.5 and assign it to the child bone. Now, your ring of vertices should be a perfect blend between the two bones. This can be any blend value, be it 30%/70% or 10%/90%, depending on what you're trying to do and what looks good.

With that, you've learned how to assign specific and exact vertex weights to bone vertex groups. This will be a very helpful tool in the future.

Summary

In this chapter, you learned how to create a more advanced skeleton and check its joint orientations. You learned how to edit those orientations in case you need to in the future. Finally, you learned a more exact and direct way to assign skin weights that is particularly useful for rigid skinning.

This is the last chapter of this book that we'll do in Blender. From now until the end, we will do almost everything in **Unreal Engine 5** (**UE5**). In the next chapter, we will learn how to rig our models in UE5 to make them easy to animate.

14

Making a Custom Rig for Our Alien Plant with Control Rig

In the previous chapter, we completed a more complex skeleton for the robot. Now we'll move on to the next stage of creating an **animation-friendly rig** in **Unreal Engine** (**UE**). Creating a skeleton and skinning it are the first steps toward making our 3D model or character animatable. We will learn how to add **controllers** that make it easier for animators to animate it.

With good controllers on top of a skeleton, it makes it possible for animators to edit, organize, and refine animations in a much more effective way. The general process of setting up a more complex 3D model to be animatable is called **rigging** it.

Rigging has three general steps:

1. Creating a skeleton
2. Skinning the 3D model to the skeleton
3. Creating controllers to drive or control our skeleton, otherwise called creating an animation rig

Until recently, there weren't any effective tools in UE to create and manage animation rigs and animation, but with the development of **Control Rig** and the tools around it, it has become possible to create and animate these rigs effectively natively inside UE5 itself.

There's no longer a need to do this in third-party software, such as Blender or Maya. In the following chapters, we will learn how this pipeline works in UE5 so you can create new animations or edit existing ones freely.

In this chapter, we will cover the following:

- Introduction to the Control Rig Editor
- Creating basic Control Rig controllers
- Controlling the Alien Plant skeleton with the controllers

Technical requirements

The following are the technical skills and software you need to complete this chapter:

- A computer that can run basic 3D animation software.
- You need to have Blender installed for free from `https://www.blender.org/` (at the time of writing). The Blender version used in this chapter is 3.1.2, but some older and newer versions will also work.
- A basic understanding of how to navigate the 3D user interface. If you skipped ahead, this was covered in *Chapter 1, An Introduction to Blender's 3D Modeling and Sculpting Tools*. If you want further tutorials on how to use Blender in depth, `https://www.blender.org/support/tutorials/` is a great resource.
- You need to have installed UE5.
- Have a basic understanding of how to navigate the UE 3D user interface. If you skipped ahead, this was covered in *Chapter 6, Exploring Unreal Engine 5*.

Finally, you should have completed *Chapter 12, Alien Plant Skinning in Blender*.

The files related to this chapter are placed at `https://github.com/PacktPublishing/Unreal-Engine-5-Character-Creation-Animation-and-Cinematics/tree/main/Chapter14`

Introduction to the Control Rig Editor

The **Control Rig Editor** is where you make the animation rig and its controls inside UE. At the time of writing this book, it's still very much in development, but I'm sure the capabilities will expand over time, as well as its simplicity and optimizations.

First, we need to activate and load the Control Rig plugin in UE since it's not currently loaded by default. The Control Rig Editor can be a very powerful tool, with many features that are outside the scope of this book to cover. However, the basic parts that we will learn about will enable you to rig and animate most things in UE5.

Loading the Control Rig tools in UE

Control Rig in UE5 is a plugin. Plugins are just extra functionality in the software. Sometimes, they don't load by default to make the program run lighter and load faster. With plugins, you have the ability to just load what you need. To load the Control Rig tools plugin, execute the following simple steps:

1. Load UE with a new **Blank** project under the **GAMES** tab. Also, uncheck **Starter Content** so you have a nice, clean project, as shown in *Figure 14.1*:

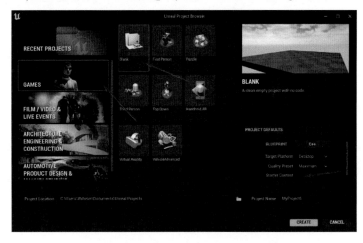

Figure 14.1 – Creating a blank UE project

2. Once loaded, select **Edit | Plugins**, as shown in *Figure 14.2*:

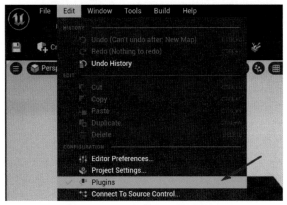

Figure 14.2 – Opening the Plugins menu

3. In the **Plugins** menu, search for `control`, click the **Enabled** checkbox, and then click the **Restart Now** button to restart UE with the Control Rig tools set to **Enabled**, as shown in *Figure 14.3*:

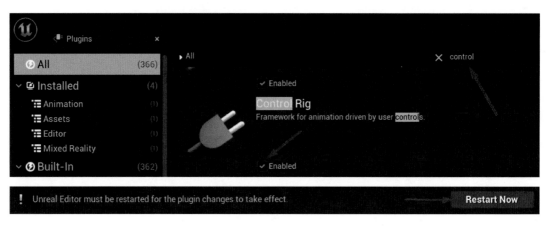

Figure 14.3 – Enabling the Control Rig plugin and restarting UE

Once UE has restarted, we will have loaded the Control Rig tools and they will be ready to use. Next, let's get our Alien Plant model into UE too.

Getting the Alien Plant and its skeleton into UE

The following is the basic process to get a skinned model FBX file into UE. We need to do this before we can work with it in UE. Once you know this process, you can import any skinned mesh into UE and then use it in your scenes or games inside UE. But first, we need to export the FBX file from Blender.

> **Important Note**
>
> Control Rig is much more sensitive to correct scale and orientation than just normally importing a model into UE. As a general rule, we want the root bone of our skeleton to be positioned at 0, 0, 0 if we can and the scale to be 1, 1, 1. This will make it much easier to work with and create a Control Rig for our skeleton.
>
> Different software packages can differ in the way they handle scale and units. In the previous chapters, you should have set up Blender to have a **Unit Scale** setting of 0.01 while set to **Meters**. With these settings in Blender, exporting FBX files from Blender and importing them into UE should give better results in older versions of Blender. In newer versions of Blender, this issue might be resolved, and you can have the default **Unit Scale** setting of 1.0 while set to **Meters**.

Exporting the Alien Plant from Blender

In order to import a skinned FBX file of our Alien Plant into UE, we first need to create an FBX file of this model. Here's how you create or export a skinned FBX model from Blender to be used in UE:

1. Open Blender and then the previously saved **Skinned Alien Plant** from *Chapter 11, Alien Plant Joint Setup in Blender*. You can also download a prepared version from here: https://github.com/PacktPublishing/Unreal-Engine-5-Character-Creation-Animation-and-Cinematics/blob/main/Chapter14/EndOffChapter12_Results_AlienPlant_Skinned.blend.

2. Put the Viewport in **Front Orthographic**. This is just to get a reference of the orientation for the **Export** settings (we want our **Export** settings to be the same as our scene).

3. In **Object Mode** in Blender, select the Alien Plant model and then hold down *Shift* and left-click to select the skeleton, so both are selected.

4. In the top left of the Blender interface, click on **File | Export | FBX (.fbx)** to bring up the Export menu.

5. Select the name and file location for your exported file and under the Export settings, we will have the following settings, as shown in *Figure 14.4*. Export the Alien Plant:

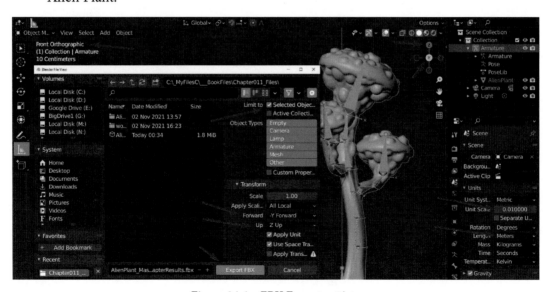

Figure 14.4 – FBX Export settings

Here's an explanation of the settings in *Figure 14.4*:

- Set **Limit to Selected Objects** in the export menu settings to only export selected objects.

- In the **Front Orthographic** view, you can see that **-Y Forward** is set. If you look at the **Viewport Orientation Gizmo** at the top right, you can also see that **Z** is set to Up. Match the **Forward** and **Up** settings in the export menu to be the same.

- Double-check that you've set **Unit Scale** to 0.01 and **Length** to **Meters**.

Additional Note

At the time of writing, the unit scaling issue between Blender and UE seems to mainly be a problem in older versions of Blender and how it exports scale units to UE. Some export tests I've done seem to suggest that from Blender version 3.1.2, the scale unit issue also works if **Unit Scale** is set to 1.0 and **Meters**. Regardless, the **Unit Scale** setting of 0.01 and **Meters** will work in any current version, so it is still the safest to use.

If your Blender scene's Unit Scale is not set to 0.01 and Meters on older versions of Blender, you may need to convert it. This can be fixed in the following way. A detailed description of this fix is beyond the scope of this book, but here's a brief description of the process:

1. Create a new Blender scene. Set the scene scale's **Unit Scale** to 0.01 and **Meters**.

2. Append the wrongly scaled model with its skeleton to this scene.

3. Scale the models and skeleton if **Scale** is incorrect (checking the model with the Measuring tool). Normally, they will be 100 times smaller or larger. Once correctly scaled, select the **Root Armature** node and **Object/Apply/All Transforms** so the native scale is reset to 1, 1, 1.

4. Do the same for the 3D model. Now, it should be ready to export to UE at the right scaling units.

Now we have a ready-to-use FBX file of our Alien Plant. Let's import it into UE.

Importing the Alien Plant into UE

Back in UE, do the following to import the Alien Plant FBX file:

1. Open **Content Drawer** at the bottom of the interface and click on **Import**, as shown in *Figure 14.5*:

Figure 14.5 – FBX import

2. In the following menu, navigate to the **Alien Plant FBX** file and select **Open**. Alternatively, download an already exported version from here: https:// github.com/PacktPublishing/Unreal-Engine-5-Character- Creation-Animation-and-Cinematics/blob/main/Chapter14/ EndOffChapter12_Results_AlienPlant_Skinned.fbx.

3. The **FBX Import Settings** window will open. For the Alien Plant, we have no animation, so you can uncheck **Import Animation**.

4. There are three additional settings that help this file import correctly – **Convert Scene, Force Front XAxis**, and **Convert Scene Units**. Check all these options, as shown in *Figure 14.6*. The **Force Front XAxis** option can be unchecked for some files to import the correct orientation. It depends on many factors:

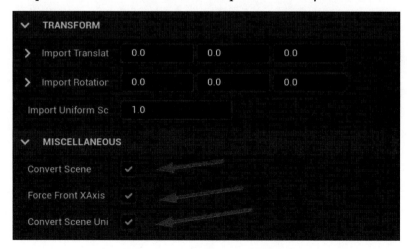

Figure 14.6 – FBX Import settings

5. Click **Import All**. You might see a warning in a log window about no vertex weights on bones, but you can ignore it and close the log window.

6. The Alien Plant asset will now be in **Content Drawer** at the bottom. It is divided into **MATERIAL** (texture), **SKELETAL MESH** (skinned model), **PHYSICS ASSET**, and **SKELETON**. Double-click the **SKELETON** asset to see the skeleton hierarchy page, as shown in *Figure 14.7*:

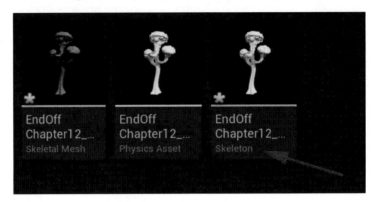

Figure 14.7 – Imported Alien Plant

7. On the skeleton hierarchy page, select **RootBone**. Double-check that the **RootBone** values are 0.0, 0.0, 0.0 for **Local Location** and **Local Rotation**. **Scale** should be 1.0, 1.0, 1.0. Of these, it is most important to set **Local Rotation** and **Scale** to be 0.0, 0.0, 0.0 and 1.0, 1.0, 1.0, respectively, as shown in *Figure 14.8*:

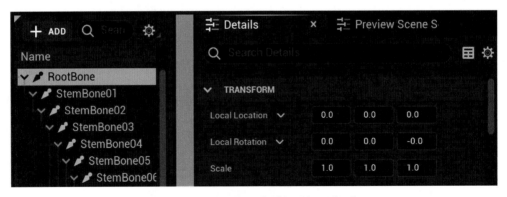

Figure 14.8 – Imported Alien Plant check

If all of this is correct, you have successfully imported your Alien Plant. We're ready to move on to the next stage, creating the Control Rig.

Creating the Control Rig node on the Alien Plant

To create the Control Rig node on top of or linked to the Alien Plant, execute the following easy steps:

1. Close the skeleton hierarchy page.

2. Back in **Content Drawer**, right-click **SKELETAL MESH**. The **SKELETAL MESH ACTIONS** context menu will appear. Left-click and select **Create | Create Control Rig**, as shown in *Figure 14.9*:

Figure 14.9 – Create Control Rig

3. Double-click the new **CONTROL RIG** asset to open the **Control Rig Editor** window, as shown in *Figure 14.10*:

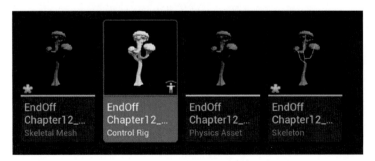

Figure 14.10 – Created Control Rig

We have now learned how to create a Control Rig node on top of our Alien Plant skeleton. Now, let's explore the main Control Rig Editor interface.

Understanding the Control Rig Editor interface layout

Let's have a look at the Control Rig Editor interface so you can navigate your way around it while working your way through this section.

Figure 14.11 – Control Rig interface

This is just a basic layout of the Control Rig Editor interface as a general reference for what we will need in this book, as shown in *Figure 14.11*:

1. **Toolbar**: This is where the basic tools are.

2. **Viewport**: This is where you navigate the 3D scene.

3. **Rig Hierarchy**: This is where we will see our skeleton and rig hierarchy.

4. **Rig Graph**: This is where UE will enable us to visually add rigging elements and tools to our rig to modify its behavior.

5. **Details** and **Preview Scene Settings**: This is where we can access more detailed settings of the selected object, plus set up our preview display setting.

When you first open the Control Rig interface, your Alien Plant might not display in the viewport. To fix this, in **Preview Scene Settings**, under **Preview Mesh**, select your Alien Plant Skeletal Mesh under the dropdown, as shown in *Figure 14.12*:

Figure 14.12 – Selecting the Skeletal Mesh

We enabled the Control Rig plugin, imported our Alien Plant, and created a Control Rig node. We are now all set up to start creating controllers for our skeleton.

Creating basic Control Rig controllers

The Alien Plant only needs a very simple **forward kinematics** (**FK**) rig setup. This sounds very complicated but FK is just basically the same parent/child setup we did with the skeleton itself. The child bone follows the parent all the way down the chain. Our FK animation rig controllers will behave in the same way.

> **Note**
>
> In animation, there are two main ways to control a joint: FK and **inverse kinematics** (**IK**). We will cover FK in this chapter and IK in *Chapter 15, Creating a Control Rig with Basic IK Controls for the Robot in UE5*.

Let's create our controllers. First, we'll create a few simple control shapes.

Creating two simple control shapes

We'll start in a very simple way and create two control shapes that will control our skeleton bones. Control shapes are the things we select in the 3D Viewport to move our character in the scene:

1. Right-click on an empty space in the **Rig Hierarchy** panel and select **New | New Control**. A new controller will appear at the bottom, as shown in *Figure 14.13*:

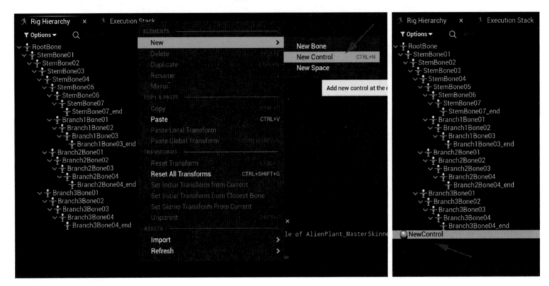

Figure 14.13 – Creating a new controller

2. With the new controller still selected, on the **Details** panel, under **Shape Properties**, from the **Shape** dropdown, select **Circle_Think**. Set **Shape Transform**'s **Scale** setting to 10.0 for all the axes, as shown in *Figure 14.14*.

    This is where you can set and edit how your controller looks purely visually. There are many options here, but for our Alien Plant, the circle-shaped controllers are one of the best options. As a rule of thumb, choose controller shapes that will make it visually easier to see what you're doing while animating.

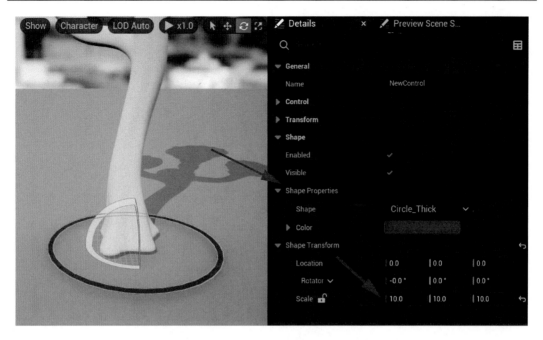

Figure 14.14 – New controller shape

3. Rename **NewControl** by double-clicking on it in the **Rig Hierarchy** panel, typing Root, and pressing *Enter*, as shown in *Figure 14.15*:

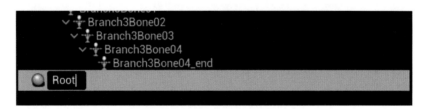

Figure 14.15 – Renaming a controller

4. Right-click on the newly renamed **Root** controller and a dialog will appear. Select **Duplicate**. This will make a copy of the controller. Rename it to `Stem01` using the same method as in *step 3*, as shown in *Figure 14.16*:

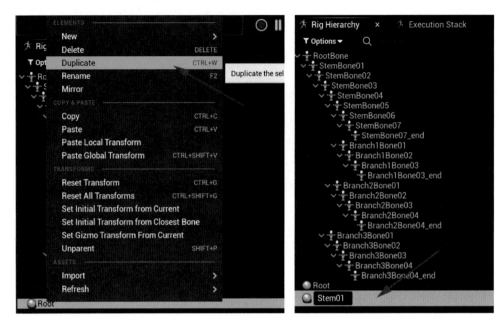

Figure 14.16 – Duplicating and renaming a controller

5. With the **Stem01** controller selected, change the *X*, *Y*, and *Z* scale to `5` instead of `10`. You can now see the smaller controller, as shown in *Figure 14.17*:

Figure 14.17 – Scaling a new controller

We have now created the two main controller shapes we need.

The bigger **Root** controller will be used to move our entire rigged object around. The smaller controller will be further duplicated and used as child controllers around the stem and branches of our Alien Plant.

Next, let's work out what controllers we need in this animation rig setup.

Deciding on the controllers we need

In order to decide what controllers we need, we need to work out what skeleton bone positions we want to be able to bend and deform on our plant.

Our Alien Plant has four main elements – the **Main** stem, **Branch 1**, **Branch 2**, and **Branch 3**. We want both the **Main** stem and the branches to be able to deform where we have our main joints.

Let's start by eliminating joints we do not need controllers for. The first bones we can eliminate, in this case, are the **_end** joints. They simply mark the end of the last joints in the branches and the **Main** stem.

In this case, on our Alien Plant skeleton, we don't need controllers for the first joint of each branch. They share the position with their **Main** stem parent joints. Two controllers in the same position, in this case, won't be needed. There are, however, some cases where you would want that. This needs to be considered on a case-by-case basis, based on your specific skeleton and how it needs to animate.

After eliminating unnecessary joints that we do not need controllers for, that leaves us with the joints where we do need controllers to move the joints.

In *Figure 14.18*, I selected these joints in the **Rig Hierarchy** panel to make them display in the viewport and marked their positions. In the **Rig Hierarchy** panel, I also marked the joints we don't need controllers for.

In conclusion, for this Alien Plant animation rig, we need the following:

- **Main Root** controller
- 7x **Main Stem** controllers
- 2x **Branch 1** controllers
- 3x **Branch 2** controllers
- 3x **Branch 3** controllers

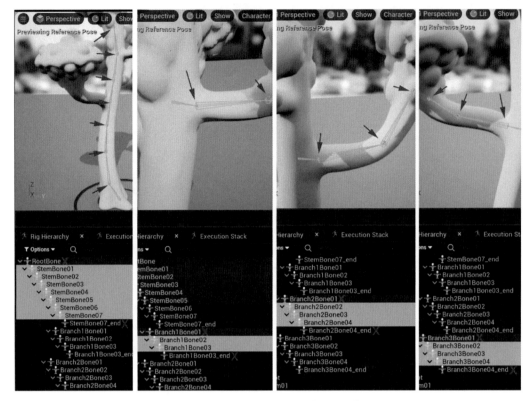

Figure 14.18 – Bones that need controllers

We have now worked out the number of controllers we need for this Alien Plant. Next, let's create them.

Creating all the controllers

In order to create our **Main** stem and branch controllers quickly, we're going to use the smaller controller, called **Stem01**:

1. Right-click on **Stem01** in the **Rig Hierarchy** panel and in the dialog, select **Duplicate**, as shown in *Figure 14.16*. You can also use *Ctrl + D* as a shortcut to duplicate. This will create another controller of the same size.

2. Repeat the previous duplication step until you have 15 controllers that are the same (7x **Main Stem** controllers + 2x **Branch 1** controllers + 3x **Branch 2** controllers + 3x **Branch 3** controllers = 15 controllers).

3. Rename those controllers to correspond to the bones/joints you want to control. Try to match the names of the controllers closely (but not exactly, so you don't have duplicate names) with the actual bone names so it is easier to link them up correctly later, as shown in *Figure 14.19*.

To the left in *Figure 14.19* are the duplicated controllers, while to the right are the bone names. In the center are the final controller names after the rename:

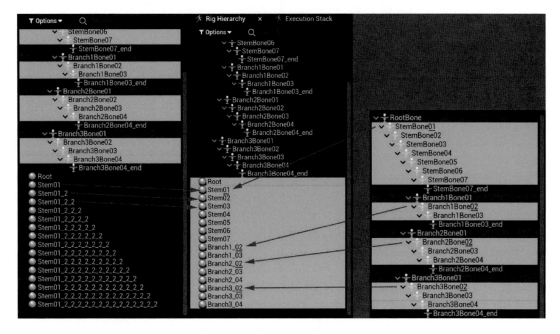

Figure 14.19 – Controller names

We have now created all the controllers we need. Next, we want to organize them in a hierarchy that makes the Alien Plant easy to animate.

Organizing the controllers in a hierarchy

As mentioned earlier in the chapter, we want to create a simple FK setup for our Alien Plant. This is remarkably similar to our current skeleton hierarchy.

> **Note**
>
> You might ask: *Why don't we just animate the bones directly, instead of going through all this trouble of creating a Control Rig animation setup?* The answer is you could, but it is not the best way to work. Having an animation rig makes everything a bit easier. When we get to IK in *Chapter 15, Creating a Control Rig with Basic IK Control for the Robot in UE5*, you absolutely need a Control Rig to make it work. Most character animation rigs have a combination of FK and IK in the same rig.

In our Alien Plant skeleton, we have four parts: the **Main** stem and the three branches. Each of these is just a simple parent/child chain, so let's create these simple hierarchies.

It is very simple to create a hierarchy in the Control Rig interface:

1. In the **Rig Hierarchy** panel, left-click to select and hold the mouse button on the child and drag it on top of the parent. In this case, left-click to select and hold the mouse button on the child, **Stem02**, and drag it on top of the parent, **Stem01**, as shown in *Figure 14.20*:

Figure 14.20 – Controller hierarchy

2. Repeat this process until the **Main** stem and the three branches are organized in separate parent/child chains, as shown in *Figure 14.21*:

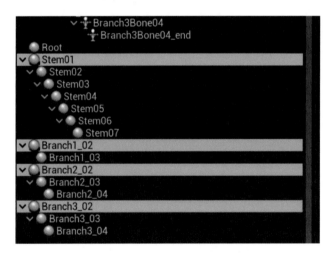

Figure 14.21 – Controller hierarchy

Finally, we need to complete the hierarchy. We need to make the branch hierarchy parent the children of the appropriate bones on the **Main** stem.

3. In this case, the **Branch1** chain should be the child of **Stem06**. Left-click to select, then hold the mouse button on the child, **Branch1_02**, and drag it on top of the parent, **Stem06**.

4. The **Branch2** chain should be the child of **Stem05**. Left-click to select, then hold the mouse button on the child, **Branch2_02**, and drag it on top of the parent, **Stem05**.

5. The **Branch3** chain should be the child of **Stem04**. Left-click to select, then hold the mouse button on the child, **Branch3_02**, and drag it on top of the parent, **Stem04**.

6. Finally, the **Stem01** chain should be the child of **Root**. Left-click to select, then hold the mouse button on the child, **Stem01**, and drag it on top of the parent, **Root**.

The final result should look like *Figure 14.22*:

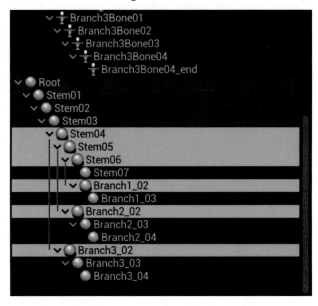

Figure 14.22 – Controller hierarchy

We have now created a hierarchy very similar to our skeleton, but since we need fewer controllers than joints, it is slightly different. Now, we need to position the controllers on the joints.

Positioning the controllers on the joints

At the moment, this setup doesn't look like much since all the controllers are on top of each other at the origin of the scene. The reason we do the hierarchy first is that if we did the positions first, the relative offset of the controllers as children would have to be constantly readjusted as we changed the hierarchy. With our hierarchy already correct, we only need to position them once.

Our bigger **Root** controller will stay at the origin of the scene.

There is a simple method to position the other controllers exactly on the joints. Right-click to select the bone/joint. In the dialog that appears, select **Copy**. Then, right-click to select the corresponding controller, and in the dialog that appears, select **Paste Global Transform**, as shown in *Figure 14.23*:

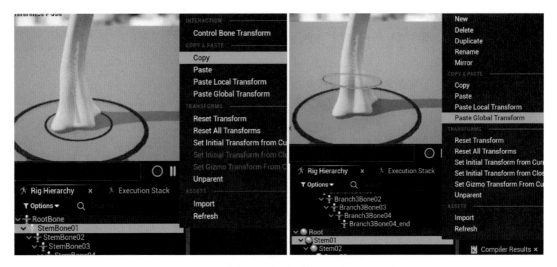

Figure 14.23 – Controller position

To make this new position on the controller permanent as far as the rig is concerned, right-click to select the controller again and then select **Set Offset Transform from Current**, as shown in *Figure 14.24*:

Figure 14.24 – Setting the controller position

Now, let's do this for **StemBone01** first:

1. Start with the **StemBone01** bone and paste the position to the **Stem01** controller, then right-click to select the controller again and then select **Set Offset Transform From Current**, then repeat these steps, working your way down the hierarchy from parent to child in the following order: **Stem01**, then **Stem02**, then **Stem03** to the end of the stem joint chain.

2. Once the **Main** stem is done, repeat this process for the branches, also working down the hierarchy, like with the **Main** stem.

3. The final result should look like *Figure 14.25*. Additionally, you can scale the controllers further by changing the **Shape** scale values, as shown in *Figure 14.17*, so visually, it's easier to make sense of it:

Figure 14.25 – Controller position results

We've now created all controllers and positioned them so they line up exactly to the bones they will control. Next, we'll get the controllers to control the bones in our skeleton.

Controlling the Alien Plant skeleton with the controllers

The final step in creating the Control Rig for our Alien Plant is to get the controllers to drive/control the skeleton. The Control Rig system can be used to create very complicated rigs that are beyond the scope of this book. The Control Rig system uses a series of *nodes* that can be linked together in a visual way to drive the behavior of our Animation rig.

For a simple FK, we just need a few basic nodes in our **Rig Graph** panel, as follows:

- **Forwards Solve:** This node simply starts the flow of the rig node logic and is at the start of any Control Rig we build.

- **Set Transform - Bone**: This is typically used to "set" or receive the transform values from the controller and apply them to the bone.

- **Get Transform - Control**: This is typically used to "get" the transform values from the controller and feed them to the bone.

If this sounds complicated, don't worry. It is simpler in practice than it sounds.

Practical setup for three basic nodes

Let's create a setup to drive **RootBone** with the **Root** controller:

1. In the **Rig Hierarchy** panel, left-click to select and hold the mouse button and drag the **RootBone** bone into the **Rig Graph** panel.

2. Let go of the mouse button and a dialog will appear. Select **Set Bone**, as shown in *Figure 14.26*:

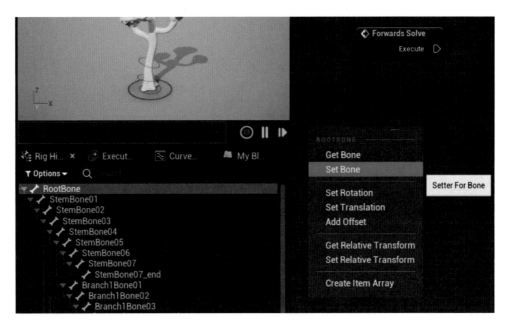

Figure 14.26 – Set Bone

A **Set Transform - Bone** node box will be created. Note that under **Type**, it's **Bone**, and under **Name**, **RootBone** has been automatically set, as shown in *Figure 14.27*.

3. On the **Forward Solve** node box, there is an **Execute** socket. Left-click on the arrow socket next to **Execute**, hold the mouse button, and drag to create a connecting line. Drag this line to the **Execute** socket on the **Set Transform - Bone** node box and release the mouse button to create the connection, as shown in *Figure 14.27*:

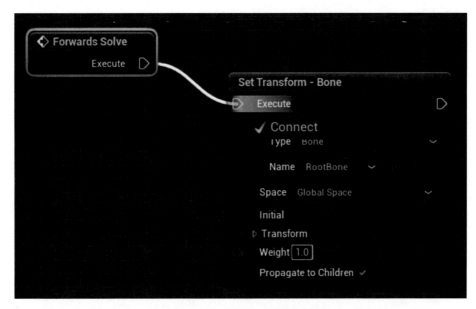

Figure 14.27 – Set Transform results

You can select the node boxes and move them around. You can use the mouse wheel to zoom in and out, and the right mouse button to pan around the **Rig Graph** panel.

4. In the **Rig Hierarchy** panel, left-click to select and drag the **Root** controller into the **Rig Graph** panel. Let go of the mouse button and a dialog will appear; select **Get Control**, as shown in *Figure 14.28*:

Figure 14.28 – Get Control

This will create a **Get Transform - Control** node box, as shown in *Figure 14.29*.

5.   On the **Get Transform - Control** node box, at the bottom is an orange **Transform** socket. Left-click on this socket, hold the mouse button, and drag to create a connecting line. Drag this line to the **Transform** socket on the **Set Transform - Bone** node box and release the mouse button to create the connection, as shown in *Figure 14.29*:

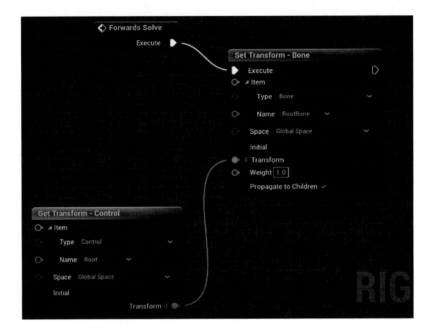

Figure 14.29 – Transform connection

The **Root** controller now feeds its transform values into **RootBone** and drives/controls it.

> **Note**
> If you make a mistake, you can use *Alt* + left-click on the connection line or socket to delete the connection.

6.   If *not* checked already, check the **Propagate to Children** checkbox and the resulting setup should look as in *Figure 14.30*:

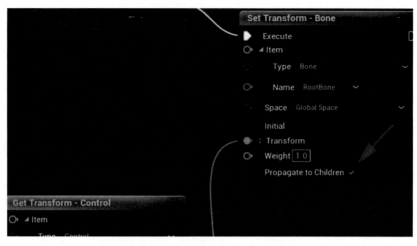

Figure 14.30 – Propagate to Children

7. You can now test this setup to make sure it's working correctly by selecting the **Root** controller, then moving it in the viewport. When you move the **Root** controller, the whole plant should follow as a result, as shown in *Figure 14.31*:

> **Important Note**
>
> Be careful not to use undo (*Ctrl + Z*) after you move or rotate controllers in the viewport in the Control Rig interface. It will undo the last things you did on the rig setup and not undo the translation on the rig itself in the viewport. Instead of undo, click **Compile** at the top left to return your rig to its original pose and translations, as shown in *Figure 14.31*.

Figure 14.31 – Test root setup

We have now set up one controller driving one bone. Now it's time to hook up the rest.

Completing the animation rig

To set up the rest of the animation Control Rig, we follow exactly the same process as the **Root** controller setup. Here's a recap:

1.   Left-click and drag **Bone** into the **Rig Graph** panel and select **Set Bone**.

2.   Reposition the resulting **Set Transform - Bone** node box.

3.   Create a new link from **Execute** on the previous **Set Transform - Bone** node box to **Execute** on the new **Set Transform - Bone** node box.

4.   Left-click and drag the corresponding controller that will drive that joint into the **Rig Graph** panel and select **Get Control**. A new **Get Transform - Control** node will be created.

5.   Link the **Transform** socket from the new **Get Transform - Control** node box to the corresponding **Set Transform - Bone** node box's **Transform** socket.

6.   Check **Propagate to Children** if needed.

7.   Repeat this process until you've done all your controllers. The bones without a corresponding controller can be ignored.

After we complete three of the controllers, it should look as in *Figure 14.32*. This flow continues until all controllers are connected:

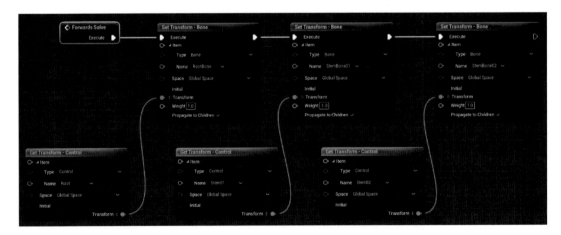

Figure 14.32 – Three controllers set up

After we have completed all of the controllers, it should look as in *Figure 14.33*:

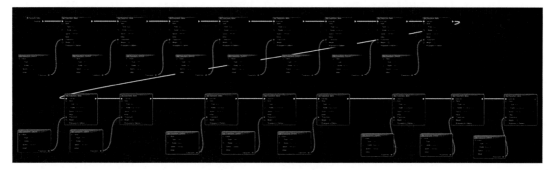

Figure 14.33 – All controllers set up

It looks complicated, but it is just the same two basic nodes repeating to cover all our controllers, linked together by **Forward Solve/Execute**. In *Figure 14.33*, the connected nodes are organized in two horizontal tiers to fit easier on the screen, but it doesn't affect the rig behavior.

You can now test your Control Rig setup by rotating your controllers and making sure the Alien Plant and its skeleton are following and deforming with the controllers, as shown in *Figure 14.34*. Remember to use **Compile** instead of **Undo** during the testing. If everything is fine, you can save your UE5 project in a safe place for later use:

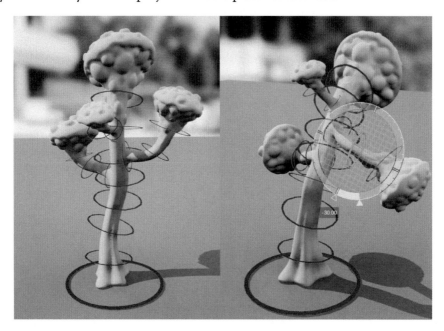

Figure 14.34 – Testing rotations

We provide the completed Control Rig in the final project file, which can be downloaded here with installation instructions: `https://github.com/PacktPublishing/Unreal-Engine-5-Character-Creation-Animation-and-Cinematics/tree/main/FullFinalUE5Project`.

The example Control Rig is under **Content/AlienPlantControlRig**.

We now have a completed Control Rig for our Alien Plant.

Summary

In this chapter, we learned how to correctly export our Alien Plant from Blender and import it into UE. We learned how to activate the Control Rig plugin and navigate its basic interface. Finally, we built a basic FK rig with the Control Rig system. With this knowledge, you can now build FK animation rigs in a UE5 Control Rig. This means you can build FK animation rigs for all kinds of different animated objects and characters for your scenes.

In the next chapter, we will build a Control Rig for our robot that will include IK.

15

Creating a Control Rig with Basic IK Controls for the Robot in UE5

In the previous chapter, we made a Control Rig for our Alien Plant. The Alien Plant Control Rig was a simple **forward kinematics (FK)** setup. Like we said in *Chapter 14, Making a Custom Rig for Our Alien Plant with Control Rig*, this is just like a basic **parent/child hierarchy** setup. In this chapter, we will set up the Control Rig for our Robot Drone. We will learn how to set up **inverse kinematics (IK)** for the arms of our Robot Drone as well as the rest of the Control Rig.

In this chapter, we will cover the following:

- What is IK?
- Creating the controllers for the robot character
- Ordering the control objects in the correct hierarchy and linking them to joints
- Creating an IK controller and testing the whole rig

Technical requirements

The following are the technical skills and software you need to complete this chapter:

- A computer that can run basic 3D animation software.

- You need to have Blender installed for free from `https://www.blender.org/` (at the time of writing). The Blender version in this chapter is 3.1.2, but some older and newer versions will also work.

- You need to have installed **Unreal Engine (UE)** 5. You can download it from `https://www.unrealengine.com/en-US/download`.

- You need to have a basic understanding of how to navigate the UE 3D user interface. If you skipped ahead, this was covered in *Chapter 6, Exploring Unreal Engine 5*.

The files related to this chapter are placed at `https://github.com/PacktPublishing/Unreal-Engine-5-Character-Creation-Animation-and-Cinematics/tree/main/Chapter15`

What is IK?

A **character Animation Rig** is normally a combination of FK and IK setups. The spine, neck, and head, plus things such as tails, are normally set up as an FK. However, things such as arms and legs are normally set up as an IK within an Animation Rig. On more advanced Animation Rigs, it is possible to set arms and legs up in such a way that they can switch between the IK and FK, but that is beyond the scope of this book. Most of the time, you want a good IK setup for your arms and legs.

Understanding IK

Imagine we had an arm and a hand. We want to move the hand from **A** to **B**. With an FK setup, we will first need to rotate the upper arm joint and then the lower arm joint for the hand to reach **B**, as shown in *Figure 15.1*:

Figure 15.1 – FK A to B

In reality, we'll have to keep switching between rotating the upper and lower arm joints until we reach **B** exactly. This is a very time-consuming process. Very early on in the history of computer animation, they invented a much more practical way to do this.

With an IK setup, we will simply have a controller (in IK setups, this is sometimes called an **end effector**) on the hand that we move from **A** to **B**. The 3D software will then *automatically* work out what the angles of the upper and lower arm joints should be, not only at the end keyframe of the animation but also on every frame in between, as shown in *Figure 15.2*:

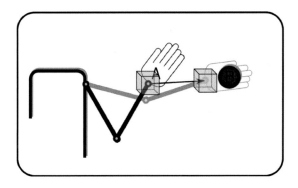

Figure 15.2 – IK A to B

Now, we just have *one* controller that needs to be animated for a hand to reach its destination. What is maybe even more useful is the fact that it also works in the *inverse*.

Imagine, for example, that we have a leg, and the foot of our character is planted on the ground while the body moves. We want our foot to stay in exactly the same spot on the ground while the body shifts weight. With an IK setup, the foot will stay with the IK controller (end effector) and lock it in place while the parent/body moves, as shown in *Figure 15.3*:

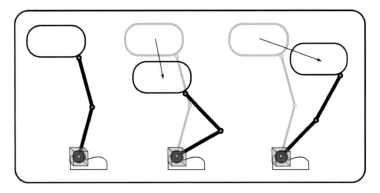

Figure 15.3 – Foot controller

There's one more feature that can be added to most standard IK setups. We can add a controller that controls in what direction the knee or elbow should face when the limb is moving. It is commonly referred to as the **pole vector**. The knee or elbow will try to point in the direction of this controller. The pole vector controller is **B** in *Figure 15.4*:

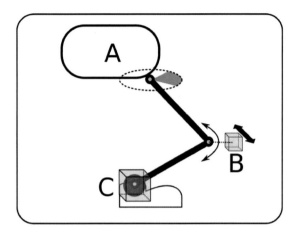

Figure 15.4 – Pole vector

The standard IK setup has three main elements, as shown in the preceding figure:

- **A**: The parent/base
- **B**: The pole vector
- **C**: The end effector

IK setup can be more than two joints, like in the case of the back leg of an animal like a horse, cat, or dog. These setups can be slightly more complex but in principle, they function in roughly the same way.

Now that we have learned what IK is, we can move on to learning how to set it up in a UE Control Rig.

Creating the controllers for the robot character

Next, we will create the Control Rig controllers as we did for the Alien Plant in *Chapter 14, Making a Custom Rig for Our Alien Plant with Control Rig*.

Exporting the robot and its skeleton from Blender

Before we can start, we need to export the skinned robot and its skeleton from Blender. The Blender file can also be downloaded from `https://github.com/PacktPublishing/Unreal-Engine-5-Character-Creation-Animation-and-Cinematics/blob/main/Chapter15/EndOffChapter13_Results_Drone_Skinned.blend`. In Blender, we need to select all the parts of the robot as well as the armature and export it as an FBX file. The export settings are the same as what we used for the Alien Plant in the *Exporting the Alien Plant from Blender* section in *Chapter 14, Making a Custom Rig for Our Alien Plant with Control Rig. Figure 15.5* provides an overview of the important robot export settings:

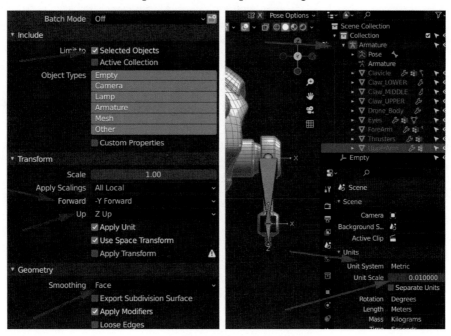

Figure 15.5 – Robot export settings

We have provided an already exported example of the Robot Drone if you want to use that instead. This exported FBX file can be downloaded here: `https://github.com/PacktPublishing/Unreal-Engine-5-Character-Creation-Animation-and-Cinematics/blob/main/Chapter15/EndOffChapter13_Results_Drone_Skinned.fbx`.

Importing the robot into a UE project

You can either import the robot into the existing UE project you created for the Alien Plant Control Rig setup covered in *Chapter 14, Making a Custom Rig for Our Alien Plant with Control Rig*, or you can create a new project. If you create a new project, remember to enable the Control Rig plugin. See *Figure 14.2* and *Figure 14.3* in *Chapter 14, Making a Custom Rig for Our Alien Plant with Control Rig*.

In the UE project in **Content Drawer**, import the exported robot FBX file with similar settings to what we used in *Chapter 14, Making a Custom Rig for Our Alien Plant with Control Rig*, for the Alien Plant, as shown in *Figure 15.6*:

Figure 15.6 – Robot import settings

To double-check whether everything has been imported correctly, double-click the Robot Drone **SKELETON** file to open it, as shown in *Figure 15.7*:

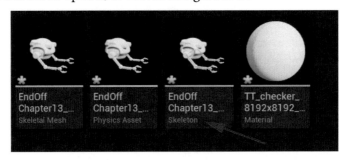

Figure 15.7 – Checking the import part 1

If everything is correct, when you select the root bone, in my case, **Root_Robot**, the position and scale transforms should be 0.0, 0.0, 0.0 and 1.0, 1.0, 1.0, respectively.

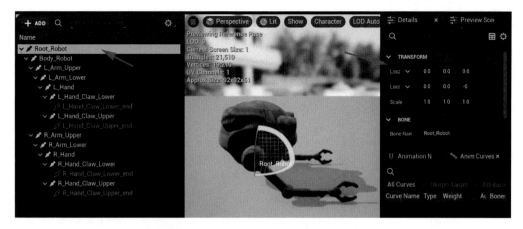

Figure 15.8 – Checking the import part 2

Our Robot Drone is now imported. Next, let's create the Control Rig.

Creating the Control Rig controllers

Just like we covered in *Creating the Control Rig node on the Alien Plant* in *Chapter 14, Making a Custom Rig for Our Alien Plant with Control Rig*, as shown in *Figure 14.9*, in **Content Drawer**, right-click on the **Skeletal Mesh** object and select **Create Control Rig**, as shown in *Figure 15.9*:

Figure 15.9 – Control Rig created

Double-click the **Control Rig** object to open up the **Control Rig** interface.

Let's think about what controllers we need for our Robot Drone. Our Robot Drone needs the following:

- A root controller that moves the entire rig
- A controller that moves the body and is the parent of the arm controllers
- IK controllers for the arms
- Controllers for controlling the two claws on each hand

Now, let's create the controllers we need to drive our Robot Drone. This is done in the same way we covered in the *Creating basic Control Rig controllers* section in *Chapter 14, Making a Custom Rig for Our Alien Plant with Control Rig*, so I'll be going through these steps in less detail here:

1. Right-click in an empty spot in the **Rig Hierarchy** panel and select **New | New Control**, as shown in *Figure 15.10*:

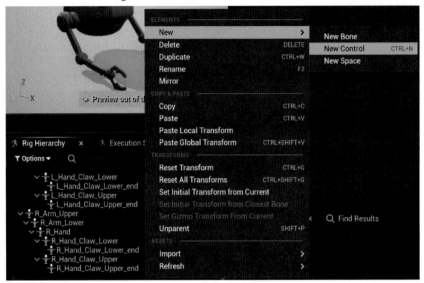

Figure 15.10 – Creating a new controller

2. In the **Details** tab, in the **Shape Properties** section, set the new controller to **Circle_Thick**. Set **Shape Transform**'s **Scale** to about 8.0. This will be the main root controller, as shown in *Figure 15.11*:

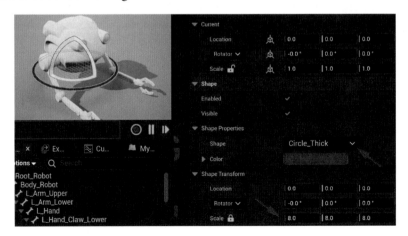

Figure 15.11 – Creating controller options

3. Right-click again in an empty spot and create a second controller, but this time set **Shape** as **Box_Thick** and **Scale** to 4 . 0. This will be the controller for the body of the robot:

Figure 15.12 – Creating a second controller

4. Now select this second controller with the **Box_Thick** shape, right-click on it, and select **Duplicate**.

5. Set **Scale** of the new **Box_Thick** controller to 1 . 0. This will be the controller for one of the hands.

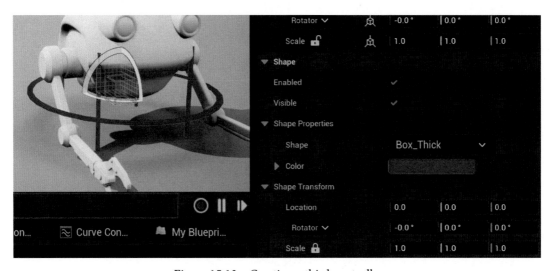

Figure 15.13 – Creating a third controller

6. Right-click and select **Duplicate** for this smaller **Box_Thick Shape** controller three more times, so you have a total of four of these. This will be one for each hand, and one for each elbow (pole vector).

7. Rename the controllers with descriptive names like the ones on the right-hand side of *Figure 15.14*:

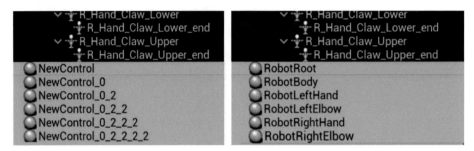

Figure 15.14 – Renaming controllers

Next, we'll create the controllers for the claws on the hands in a slightly different way so we can see what they will look like in the final position.

8. Instead of right-clicking in an empty spot in the **Rig Hierarchy** window, right-click on the **L_Hand_Claw_Lower** bone and select **New | New Control**. This will create the controller on the position (and as a child) of the bone. Now we can see what the controller will look like in its final position.

9. Change **Shape** to **QuarterCircle_Thick** and **Scale** to 2.0; rename it LeftLowerClaw.

Figure 15.15 – Claw controller

10. In the same way, right-click to create a controller on top of the **L_Hand_Claw_Upper** bone. Change **Shape** to **QuarterCircle_Thick** and **Scale** to 2 . 0, plus change the color to blue (to visually stand out from the other claw controller) by clicking on **Color** and using the color selector, as shown in *Figure 15.16*:

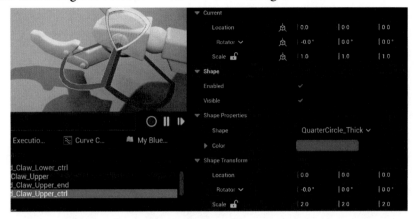

Figure 15.16 – Claw controller upper changed to blue

11. Rename this controller LeftUpperClaw.

12. Repeat this process for the claws on the right hand.

13. Once all four claw controllers have been created, press *Ctrl* + left-click to select all four of them. Right-click to select one of the claw controllers and choose **Unparent**.

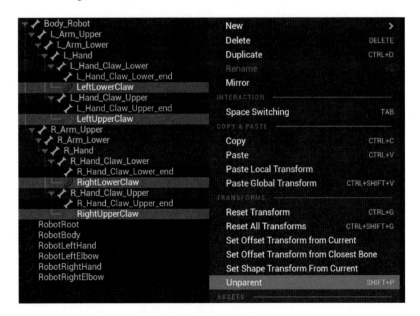

Figure 15.17 – Unparenting claw controllers from the bones

The claw controllers will be unparented from the bones and move to the bottom of the **Rig Hierarchy** window with the other controllers.

We should now have something as in *Figure 15.18*:

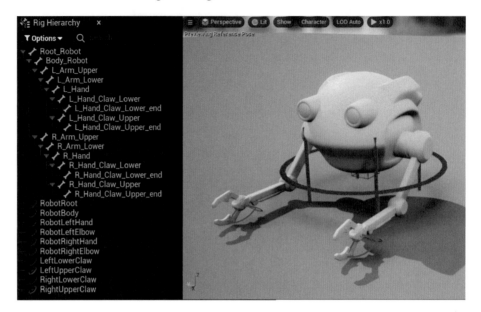

Figure 15.18 – Controllers result

We have now created all the controllers we need for our Animation Rig. Next, we'll organize them in the correct hierarchy.

Ordering the control objects in the correct hierarchy and linking them to joints

In this section, we need to organize our rig controllers in the correct hierarchy. Just like with all our parent/child hierarchies in our Animation Rigs, the hierarchy needs to be parented in the right order, so our rig works correctly.

Controller hierarchy

Like with our Alien Plant Control Rig, we need to figure out how we want our hierarchy to work.

Firstly, we want an overall *root* controller (**RobotRoot**) that can move our entire Animation Rig if we need to. That needs to be at the top of the hierarchy and the *parent* of everything in the Animation Rig.

Secondly, we want the body controller (**RobotBody**) as the child of the root controller. We just need to left-click to select and hold the mouse button to drag the **RobotBody** controller on top of the **RobotRoot** controller, as shown in *Figure 15.19*:

Figure 15.19 – Parent body controller to root controller

Following that, **RobotLeftHand**, **RobotLeftElbow**, **RobotRightHand**, and **RobotRightElbow** should be the children of the **RobotBody** controller, as shown in *Figure 15.20*:

Figure 15.20 – Parent hand controller to body controller

Finally, the claw controllers should be the children of their respective hands, as shown in *Figure 15.21*:

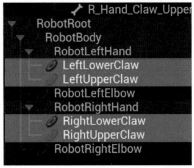

Figure 15.21 – Parent claw controller to hand controller

Our controllers are now in the right hierarchy, but they do not line up with our bones yet. Next, we'll do that like we did in the *Positioning the controllers on the joints* section in *Chapter 14, Making a Custom Rig for Our Alien Plant with Control Rig*.

Positioning the controllers to line up with the bones

To line up the controllers to the bones, we need to copy the bone transforms and paste them onto the controllers. Like with the Alien Plant, we need to start at the top of the hierarchy with the parents and work our way down. We'll leave the **RobotRoot** controller at the origin of the scene.

Let's line up the **RobotBody** controller first since it's next in the hierarchy:

1. Right-click on the **Body_Root** bone and select **Copy**.

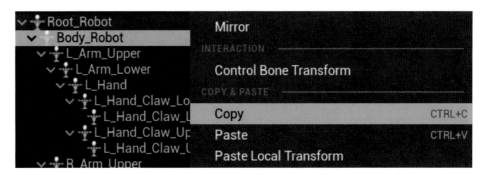

Figure 15.22 – Copy transform

2. Right-click on the **RobotBody** controller and select **Paste Global Transform**, as shown in *Figure 15.23*:

Figure 15.23 – Paste transform

3. Right-click on the **RobotBody** controller again and select **Set Offset Transform from Current,** as shown in *Figure 15.24*:

Figure 15.24 – Setting a transform

4. Now, work your way down the entire controller hierarchy until all the controllers are lined up with their respective bones. The elbow controllers should line up with lower arm bones. The end result should be something like shown in *Figure 15.25*:

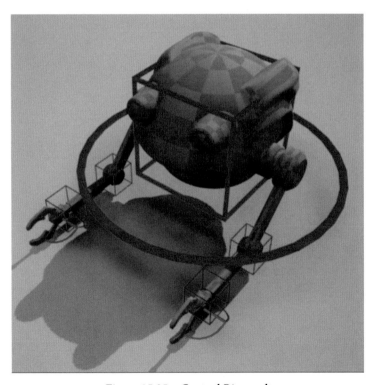

Figure 15.25 – Control Rig result

5. In the Viewport, select **RobotLeftElbow**, then hold *Ctrl* + left-click to select
    RobotRightElbow. Select the **Move** tool at the top of the Viewport and move them
    slightly down and slightly back, as shown in *Figure 15.26*:

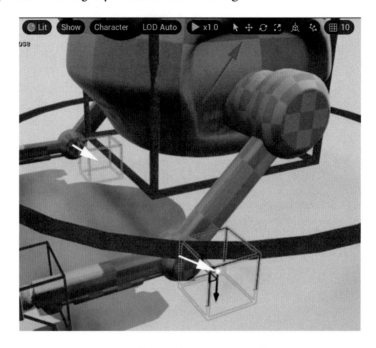

Figure 15.26 – Elbow pole vector controller position

We do this since we want the elbows to point toward them, so they need to be a bit
offset. This is how IK pole vector controllers work. Later in this chapter, you will see
this in action.

6. With both the elbow controllers still selected, right-click in the **Rig Hierarchy**
    window and select **Set Offset Transform from Current**.

We have now created and positioned all the controllers we'll need for our Robot Drone
Animation Rig. Next, we need to link the bones to the controllers in **Rig Graph**.

Linking bones to controllers in Rig Graph

This first part of the process is the same as what we did for the FK setup in the *Controlling
the Alien Plant skeleton with the controllers* section in *Chapter 14, Making a Custom Rig for
Our Alien Plant with Control Rig*:

1. Start by dragging the bone object, the **Root_Robot** bone, into the **Rig Graph**
    window and setting it to **Set Bone**.

2. Drag the **RobotRoot** controller into the **Rig Graph** window and set it to **Get Control**.

3. Connect the **Transform** socket from **RobotRoot**'s **Get Transform** to **Root_Robot**'s **Set Transform** node.

4. Now do the same for the **Body_Robot** bone and the **RobotBody** controller. Also connect the **Execute** sockets, as shown in *Figure 15.27*:

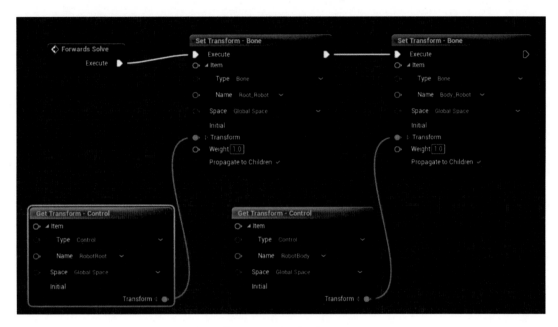

Figure 15.27 – Body rig

Now, we will do something a bit different from the Alien Plant rig. This is purely to help us organize more complex rigs visually more easily in **Rig Graph**.

5. Press *Ctrl* + left-click to select all the **Set Transform - Bone** and **Get Transform - Control** for the root and body, so four in total. Press *C* on the keyboard to create a comment. This is just a display box around those items, as shown in *Figure 15.28*.

6. Rename the **Comment** box `Body Controls`.

    We now know at a glance that these nodes in the rig control the main body of our Robot Drone.

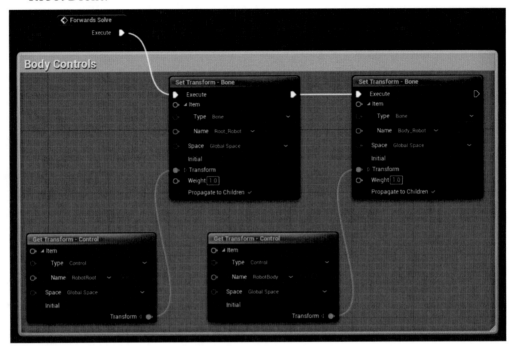

Figure 15.28 – Body rig comment

Next, we'll create the setup for the left hand and the two claws.

7. Same as with the body controls, drag the **Lhand**, **L_Hand_Claw_Lower**, and **L_Hand_Claw_Upper** bones into **Rig Graph** and set to **Set Bone**. Then, drag the **RobotLeftHand**, **LeftLowerClaw**, and **LeftUpperClaw** controllers into **Rig Graph** and set it to **Get Control**. Link up the respective **Transform** and **Execute** node sockets.

8. Select all six of these new nodes in **Rig Graph** and press *C* to add a comment. Name it `Left Hand`, as shown in *Figure 15.29*.

    Now, all the controls for the left hand of the Robot Drone are grouped together. Adding these comments does not change the functioning of the Animation Rig. It is just a visual tool to quickly make sense of a more complex rig. This rig is not complicated, but in the future, you might do much more complex setups than this.

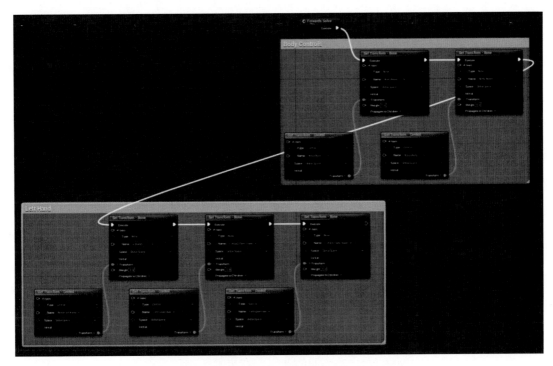

Figure 15.29 – Body rig and left-hand comments

9. Repeat this process for the right-hand controls and bones, and also comment them into a group and name it Right Hand, as shown in *Figure 15.30*:

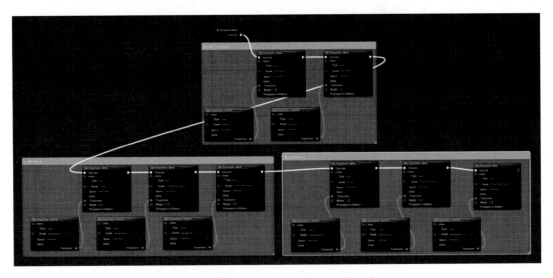

Figure 15.30 – Body rig and left- and right-hand comments

We have now set up the standard FK parts of our Animation Rig, the body and both hands with claws. Now we can set up the arms with IK.

Creating an IK controller and testing the whole rig

Before we set up the IK controls, we need to get a few bits of information from our arm skeleton. This is going to be used later to set up the orientation of our IK control.

Getting bone orientations of our arm bones

In the **Rig Hierarchy** window, right-click on the **L_Arm_Lower** bone and select **Control Bone Transform**, as shown in *Figure 15.31*:

Figure 15.31 – Control Bone Transform

This will display the local transform of the bone. Make sure it's set to **Local Space** and select **Move**, as shown in *Figure 15.32*:

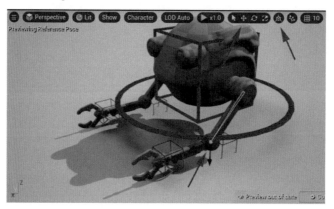

Figure 15.32 – Axes primary and secondary

Notice that the *Z* axis (blue Z arrow) is pointing directly down the arm toward the hand. Note this direction down as +Z (if the blue Z-axis arrow were pointing in the opposite direction but along the same axis to the hand, it would have been -Z).

This +Z value is what we will use later as the **primary IK axis**. Now note in what direction axes the elbow is mainly pointing (in this case, toward the ground). This would be the +X axis along the red X arrow. This +X value is what we will use later as the **secondary IK axis**. Note this down too.

These primary and secondary values we note down now will simply tell the IK controller in what direction our elbow bends when we input them later in this chapter. Now that we have these values, we can build our IK setup.

Setting up an IK controller

To set up the IK controller, there's a **Basic IK** node in Control Rig that takes care of everything. Let's create it:

1. In the **Rig Graph** window, right-click in an empty space underneath the **Left Hand** comment group. This will bring up a menu of all the possible nodes that could be added to **Rig Graph**. In the **Search** bar at the top, type in `ik`, then select **Basic IK**, as shown in *Figure 15.33*:

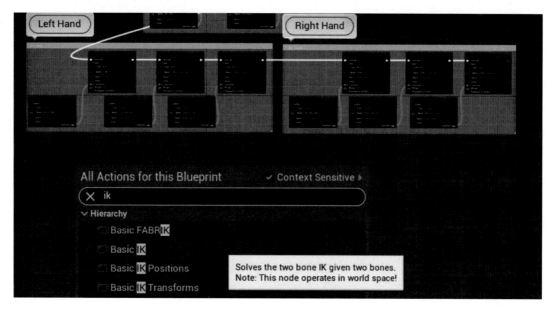

Figure 15.33 – Creating a Basic IK node

This creates the **Basic IK** node shown in *Figure 15.34*:

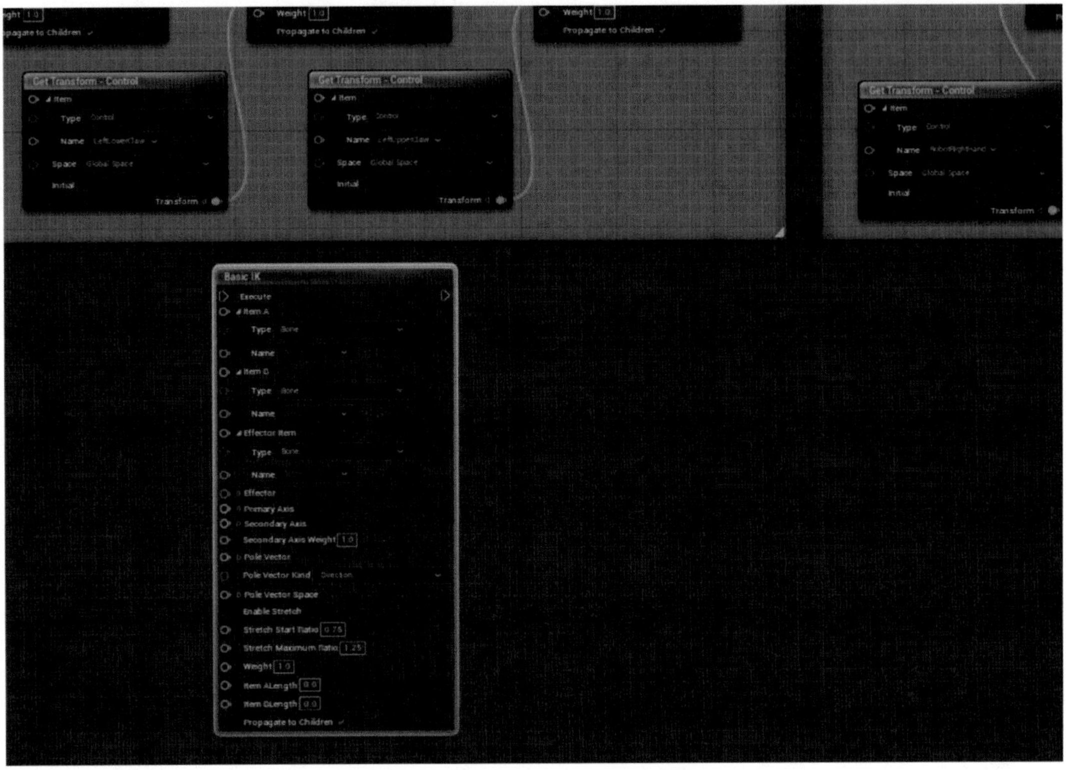

Figure 15.34 – Basic IK node

In the **Basic IK** settings, there are **Item A**, **Item B**, and **Effector Item**. These are the three bones that will be in our IK setup:

- **Item A**: Parent or beginning of the IK chain (**L_Arm_Upper**)

- **Item B**: The bone that bends like an elbow or knee (**L_Arm_Lower**)

- **Effector Item**: Where the IK ends, or in other words, where it's trying to reach (**L_hand**)

2. From the drop-down menu settings on the **Basic IK** node, make sure **Type** is set to **Bone**, and then select **L_Arm_Upper** for **Item A**, **L_Arm_Lower** for **Item B**, and **L_Hand** for **Effector Item** under the **Name** drop-down menu, as shown in *Figure 15.35*:

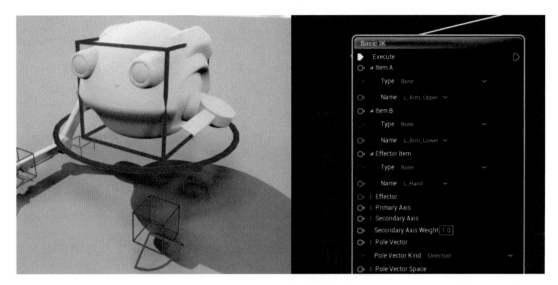

Figure 15.35 – Basic IK node bone select

Remember to connect the **Execute** socket from the last **Set Transform - Bone** to the **Basic IK Execute** socket. Otherwise, **Basic IK** won't be activated. The robot's left arm will look broken at this point. No need to worry about that since we need to set up the rest of the settings before it will function correctly.

Next, we want our **RobotLeftHand** controller to be the thing that the IK aims for. Just like it controls the **L_Hand** bone position, it can also control the **Effector** position.

3. Drag and link the **Transform** socket connection from **RobotLeftHand Get Transform - Control** to the **Effector** socket on the **Basic IK** node. Now it splits and drives both the **L_Hand** bone and **Basic IK Effector**, as shown in *Figure 15.36*:

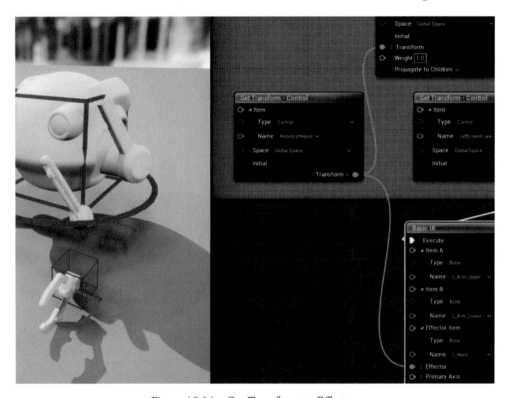

Figure 15.36 – Get Transform to Effector

Now we'll use the values we got from the *Getting bone orientations of our arm bones* section of this chapter to input the correct values under the primary and secondary axes.

Expand the **Primary Axis** and **Secondary Axis** settings by left-clicking on the small arrow in front of their names. The value we noted down for **Primary Axis** was +Z, so set **Z** to `1.0` (`1.0` = plus and `-1.0` = minus). Make the rest `0.0`.

The value we noted down for **Secondary Axis** was +*X*, so set **X** to 1.0. Make the rest 0.0, as shown in *Figure 15.37*:

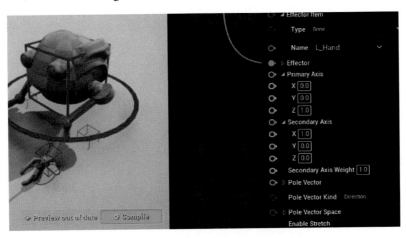

Figure 15.37 – Primary and secondary axes

The arm will still look broken, but less so. This is because the pole vector controller (the direction that the elbow points) is set to be at the origin of the scene by default. We created the **RobotLeftElbow** and **RobotRightElbow** controllers for this reason, so now, let's hook up the **RobotLeftElbow** controller to our **Basic IK** settings.

4. Drag the **RobotLeftElbow** controller into **Rig Graph** from the **Rig Hierarchy** panel, set to **Get Control**, expand the **Transform** socket with the little arrow, then connect the yellow **Translation** socket to the yellow **Pole Vector** socket, as shown in *Figure 15.38*.

This is because pole vectors are not influenced by rotation or scale. They are merely points in space that the elbow or knee can point to.

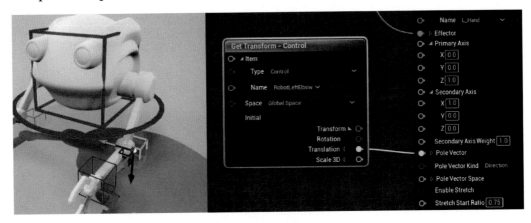

Figure 15.38 – Pole vector

The arm should not look broken anymore. The IK setup for the left arm should now be complete. Next, let's test the IK setup.

Testing the IK setup

You can now test the left arm IK by moving the **RobotLeftHand** and **RobotLeftElbow** controllers. Remember not to undo after moving the controllers in the Viewport; when wanting to return them to the original positions, press **Compile** instead. If you undo, it will undo the work you just did on your rig setup.

Particularly look how the elbow points to the **RobotLeftElbow** controller when you move it, as shown in *Figure 15.39*:

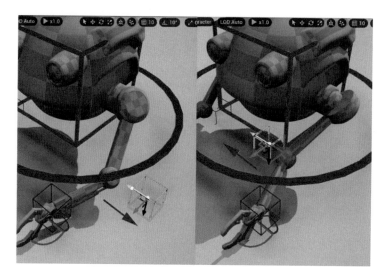

Figure 15.39 – Pole vector test

Hopefully, this will help you to understand what a pole vector is when you see it in action. Move and rotate **RobotLeftHand** and see that the arm bones automatically bend to always reach the hand. This is IK in action. You can also select the claw controllers and rotate them as a test.

If you're happy with how everything works, repeat this process to create IK controls on the right arm. Test it all, as shown in *Figure 15.40*, and save your UE project once you're done:

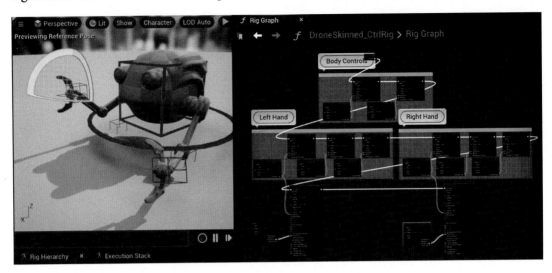

Figure 15.40 – Complete Animation Rig tested

We have provided the completed Control Rig for the Robot Drone in the final project file, which can be downloaded from here with installation instructions: `https://github.com/PacktPublishing/Unreal-Engine-5-Character-Creation-Animation-and-Cinematics/tree/main/FullFinalUE5Project`

The example Control Rig is under **Content/RobotDroneControlRig**.

Your Robot Drone Animation Rig is now complete.

Summary

In this chapter, we learned how to correctly export our Robot Drone from Blender and import it into UE. We learned what IK is. We also built a basic FK rig for the body controls and then set up IK controls for our Robot Drone arms on the same Animation Rig.

If you can set up basic FK and IK on an Animation Rig, you're well equipped to set up almost any basic character rig and can achieve a lot. Rigging can be very complicated on complex rigs, but these two basic building blocks of basic FK and IK setups are at the core of it all.

In the next chapter, we will do some animation on these Animation Rigs we created.

Part 4
Animation in UE5 Using Control Rig and Sequencer

Now comes the fun part where all your hard work pays off! In this part, you will learn how to animate your characters in Sequencer with the Control Rigs you created. You will also learn how to use Sequencer to assemble your final scene.

We will cover the following chapters in this section:

- *Chapter 16, Creating a Simple Swaying Animation Cycle in UE5 Sequencer*
- *Chapter 17, Creating Three Simple Animations for the Robot in UE5 Sequencer*
- *Chapter 18, Importing Motion Capture onto the MetaHuman Control Rig*
- *Chapter 19, Motion Capture Editing and Cleanup Using Control Rig and Sequencer*
- *Chapter 20, Use Sequencer to Construct Your Final Scene*

16

Creating a Simple Swaying Animation Cycle in UE5 Sequencer

In the previous chapter, we made a Control Rig for our Robot Drone, but in this chapter, we're going back to our Alien Plant animation rig to animate it. The Alien Plant Control Rig was a simple **forward kinematics (FK)** setup, and it would be a good starting point to learn the basics of animating in **Unreal Engine Sequencer (UE Sequencer)**. At this stage, we can start breathing life into our animatable characters and objects by making them move the way we want them to.

Animation is not simply making something move from A to B. It is a whole art form in itself and it takes a lot of practice to get really good at it. In this chapter, we will start with the basic building blocks to get you started. If you enjoy the following chapters on animation, a career as a character animator is something you might want to consider.

Going into the details and principles of character animation is beyond the scope of this book, but if you want to take it further as an animator, learning about the **12 basic principles of animation**, as outlined in the book, *Disney Animation: The Illusion of Life*, by Frank Thomas and Ollie Johnson (ISBN: 9780786860708), is always a good place to start.

However, this is not necessary for the chapters in this book, since this is more of a technical overview of how to use the animation tools in UE.

If you're an experienced animator, these chapters might help you to bring your skills to the UE pipeline directly.

In this chapter, we will cover the following:

- Overview of the Sequencer interface
- Setting keyframes for animation
- Editing keyframes and animation curves

Technical requirements

In this chapter, we will only need to work in UE5. You will need the following to complete this chapter:

- A computer that can run basic 3D animation software.
- You need to have installed UE5. You can download it from `https://www.unrealengine.com/en-US/download`.
- A basic understanding of how to navigate the UE 3D user interface. If you skipped ahead, this was covered in *Chapter 6, Exploring Unreal Engine 5*.

Overview of the Sequencer interface

In UE, we're going to use Sequencer to animate our animation rigs. The Sequencer Animation Keyframe and Animation Curve tools are very similar to the ones you find in other 3D animation software. However, you might ask what **keyframes** and **curves** are in 3D animation.

Before I teach you exactly what they are, I'm first going to show you how to open the Sequencer, add the Alien Plant rig, and give you a basic overview of the interface.

Opening the Sequencer and adding the Alien Plant animation rig

To have our Alien Plant Control Rig in Sequencer, follow these steps:

1. Open the saved project with the Alien Plant Animation Rig in it.

   We also provide the completed Alien Plant Control Rig in the final project file, which can be downloaded here with installation instructions: `https://github.com/PacktPublishing/Unreal-Engine-5-Character-Creation-Animation-and-Cinematics/tree/main/FullFinalUE5Project`. The Alien Plant Control Rig is under: **Content/AlienPlantControlRig**.

2. In the top menu bar, left-click on **Cinematics | Add Level Sequence** to open a new Level Sequence in Sequencer.

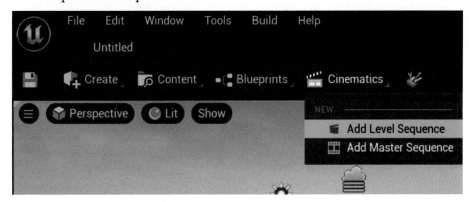

Figure 16.1 – Opening the Sequencer

Save the asset as `AlienPlantAnimation`.

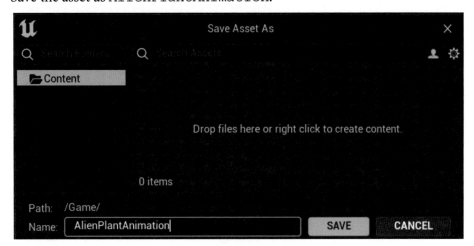

Figure 16.2 – Saving the asset

3. The **Sequencer** window should appear as default at the bottom of the screen. Open up your **Content Drawer**, then left-click and hold and drag the Alien Plant Control Rig into an empty space in the **TRACK** window on the left.

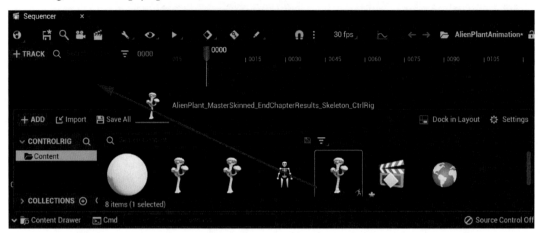

Figure 16.3 – Dragging the Control Rig into TRACK

If you have trouble with the Sequencer window being covered by the **Content Drawer** in the viewport, just drag and extend the **Sequencer** window taller than the **Content Drawer**.

We have our Alien Plant Control Rig in Sequencer now. Next, let's have a look at the interface.

Sequencer interface overview

The Sequencer interface is very similar to most video editing software. You have a window on the left for your tracks, as shown in **A** in *Figure 16.4*. This is where you place the objects, animation rigs, or elements you want to animate or adjust over time in the timeline.

The timeline window (as shown in **B** in *Figure 16.4*) is where you can view your keyframes and see what happens when. You can scrub forward and backward in time, play it back to see the results, or edit the timing of it.

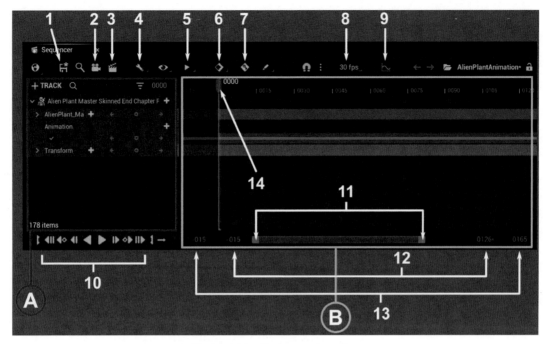

Figure 16.4 – Sequencer interface

Listed from 1-14 in *Figure 16.4* are some of the more important controls in the Sequencer interface:

1. **Save**: Save the sequence.
2. **Camera**: Create a new camera in the scene.
3. **Render**: Render as a movie.
4. **Various Tools**: We don't cover these extra helpful tools in this book, but you can explore these as you become more advanced in Sequencer. Refer to the official documentation at https://docs.unrealengine.com/5.0/en-US/cinematics-and-movie-making-in-unreal-engine/.
5. **Playback Settings**: Various playback settings, such as playback speed, which can be set to half speed.
6. **Keyframe Settings**: This is where you adjust your keyframe settings.

7. **Auto Keyframe**: If enabled, it will automatically place keyframes when there's a change as long as you set the first keyframe manually as a starting point.

8. **Set the Frame Rate**: For most digital video, 30 frames per second is good enough and pretty much the standard. For games and real-time rendering, 60 frames per second is better.

9. **Curve Editor**: This is where you open the Curve Editor.

10. **Playback Controls**: This is where you control the playback, such as play, pause, and stop.

11. By left-clicking and dragging here, you can adjust the range of the timeline workspace and you can use this to zoom in or out of a specific point of time on your timeline display window. You can also click and drag it in the middle of the bar to move the whole thing.

12. **Visible Range**: Here, you can manually type in the visible range of your timeline in the timeline workspace.

13. **Overall Range**: Here, you can manually type in the overall range of your timeline workspace.

14. You can left-click and drag this to scrub backward and forward in the timeline to a specific time or frame.

You now have a broad overview of the most important parts of the Sequencer interface.

Additionally, UE automatically puts the interface in **Animation Mode** as you add the Alien Tree (or any) Control Rig to the **Track** window. You can also access the **Animation Mode** interface with the drop-down menu at the top left. This mode makes the selection of your Control Rig controllers easier in **Anim Outliner** on the right of the interface.

You can also access things such as the **Poses Tool** and other animation tools In the **Animation** tab on the left. In the Sequencer **Track** window, you can also expand the Alien Plant Control Rig to select any of the controllers, as shown in *Figure 16.5*:

Figure 16.5 – Animation Mode

Now you can find your way around the Sequencer interface, we can move on to using it and seeing for ourselves what these different animation tools do within Sequencer.

Setting keyframes for animation

Setting keyframes and editing curves are at the core of computer animation, but what are they?

What are keyframes and curves in computer animation?

You probably already know that traditional film animation is a series of drawings with small changes, but when you play it back in sequence fast enough, it creates the illusion that the things in the series of drawings are moving/animating.

In traditional animation, the animation artists had to draw every single frame. So, if the frame rate was 24 frames per second, the artists had to draw 24 pictures for every 1 second of animation.

> **Note**
>
> Animation frames are normally talked about in **frames per second** (**fps**). If an animation is 24 fps, it just means a second is divided into exactly 24 equal parts and when played back at regular speed, each consecutive frame is displayed for 1/24th of a second before displaying the next one. This (24 fps) is very much an old film frame rate since, at 24 fps, the human eye perceives it as smooth motion, so most old films were shot at 24 fps. Standard digital HD video is about 30 fps or 60 fps. Fast-paced computer games play better at 60 fps or above.

As animation matured, the big animation studios realized that their best and most talented animators were spending too much time drawing every single frame of their animation sequences. Therefore, they came up with the plan that the main animator would only draw **keyframes**. Otherwise worded, keyframes are key moments in the timing and acting of the cartoon character in the animation sequence.

Then, the experienced animator would hand the sequence over to a junior or apprentice animator who could fill in the in-between drawings. This way, their best animators could set the tone and standard on more sequences, while junior animators did the work to fill in the rest of the drawings.

With computer animation, the computer can fill in the rest of the drawings for us when we set a few keyframes, so there's no more need for a junior animator to do all this boring work.

In computer animation, if we want to move a box from point A to point B, 80 cm in the X axis direction over 8 frames, we follow this basic process:

1.   Set a keyframe at **frame 0** to have a starting keyframe.

2.   Navigate in our timeline to **frame 8**, where we want the next keyframe.

3.   Move the box **80 cm** in the **X Axis** direction.

4.   Set our second keyframe at **frame 8**.

With just these two keyframes, the computer will fill in frames 1, 2, 3, 4, 5, 6, and 7 for us. The computer can work it out from just having the two positions in space and the number of frames in-between, as shown in *Figure 16.6*:

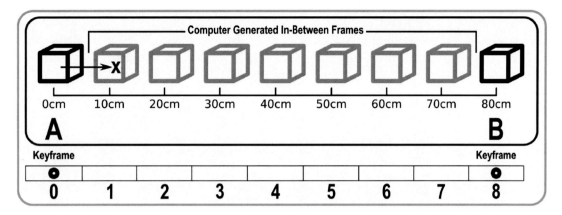

Figure 16.6 – Keyframes A to B

The simplest way for the computer to know how much the box moves on every in-between frame is to take the 80 cm distance the box moves from A to B and divide it by the number of frames (8).

80 cm/8 frames = 10 cm per frame

This is, of course, if the box moves at a perfectly constant speed from A to B. The problem with a perfectly constant speed is that it is very mechanical, and in most cases, very unrealistic. If you stop at a red traffic light while driving your car and the light turns green, when you press the accelerator, the car is not at its full speed; instead, it starts slow and accelerates over time till it gets to its full speed.

The same is also true when you get to the next red traffic light. The moment you press on the brakes, the car does not go to zero speed instantly; instead, it decelerates over time till it gets to zero speed. When you go from full speed to zero speed instantly, that is normally caused by an accident or a crash and is not generally considered to be a good idea.

How do you see this **acceleration** and **deceleration** over time in animation frames? Animation frames are equal parts of time, so the more distance the car travels between animation frames, the faster it moves. The opposite is also true: the less distance the car moves between frames, the slower it moves.

With this logic, if a car starts accelerating from standing still on frames 0 to 1, it would not have moved much in distance; on frames 1 to 2 there would be a little more distance between frames, frames 2 to 3 a bit more, and so on. If you superimpose all the drawings/frames on top of each other for the accelerating car, it will look something like *Figure 16.7*:

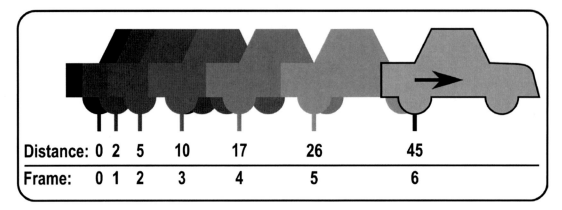

Figure 16.7 – Car acceleration

We can take the acceleration of this car and represent it in a graph, as shown in *Figure 16.8*:

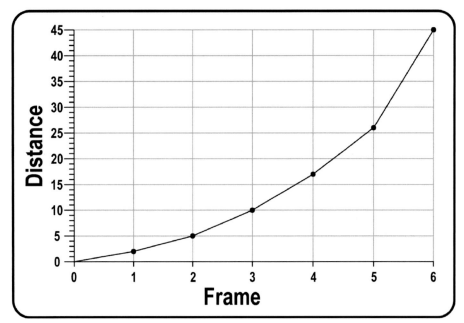

Figure 16.8 – Car acceleration graph

You can see that the acceleration follows a smooth curve that gets steeper as the car starts picking up speed.

As you can well imagine, to animate more realistically, more often than not, we need to accelerate and decelerate the objects we're animating. In the case of this car, it means that we need a keyframe for each frame where the acceleration and deceleration take place. If the computer could only do a linear calculation from keyframe A to B, as in *Figure 16.6*, it would need a keyframe on every frame, since the speed constantly changes between keyframes. Since we need to do this a lot, this would take away the labor-saving gains from just having a few keyframes.

However, as you can see from *Figure 16.8*, acceleration and deceleration can be represented as curves. Graphs or curves could be used to represent how we want animated objects to accelerate or decelerate between keyframes, thereby eliminating the need for a keyframe on every frame.

As a professional character animator, you spend most of your time setting keyframes and editing animation curves. If you don't fully understand, don't worry; once you start editing curves in **Curve Editor** in practice, I'm sure it will be easier to understand. Broadly, these curves are also sometimes called the **interpolation** between keyframes.

The *Bouncing Ball* animation is a popular first lesson taught to student animators in animation schools.

In *Figure 16.9*, you have a rubber bouncy ball falling and hitting the ground while traveling in direction X. Each time it hits the ground, it bounces again, but a bit lower each time because the loss of energy makes the upwards momentum (Y) less on each bounce. It also loses momentum in direction X as it slows down or decelerates.

Additionally, each time it bounces, it accelerates very quickly upward because the rubber springs it back up, but as it moves upward, gravity makes it decelerate to the point that it stops moving upward and starts accelerating while falling back to the ground:

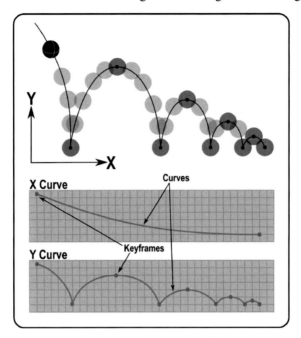

Figure 16.9 – Bouncy ball

This fairly complex animation can be animated with two keyframes on the X axis and 10 keyframes on the Y axis, using the curves in **Curve Editor** to edit the acceleration and deceleration between keyframes. In all the animation curve/graph editor interfaces I know about, frames or time are always along the horizontal axis of the graph, and the value of the translation is on the vertical axis.

We have now had an overview of what keyframes and curves are in computer animation, but these are always better understood while using them in practice. Next, let's make some keyframes for our Alien Plant Control Rig.

Setting keyframes for the Alien Plant Control Rig

Before we start animating, the first thing we want to do is clean up our workspace in the viewport a bit. I had a checkered floor object that was poking through my Alien Plant stem at the bottom, so I moved it down to its base.

I also moved the *start object* player and lights away from my Alien Plant so I see it clearly when it plays back the animations and it's also easier to select the controllers in the viewport itself, as shown in *Figure 16.10*:

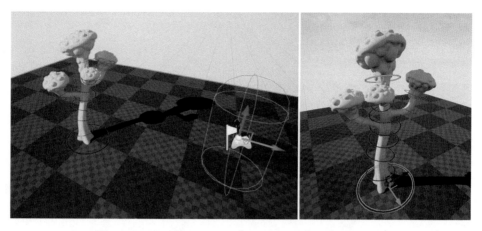

Figure 16.10 – Cleaning up the viewport for a better view

In this exercise, we will try to create a very subtle animation cycle or loop of the Alien Plant swaying in a light breeze. This is the kind of animation where the first and last frames are exactly the same, so when you play it in a loop, you can't tell where the beginning and end are.

This is often used in games with things such as walking or running cycles, so you can just keep repeating the loop for as long as the character keeps moving and it seems seamless, without a glitch when the end of the cycle flows back to the beginning.

We also don't want awkward acceleration or deceleration at the beginning or end of the cycle so it doesn't flow well.

Now, let's start animating:

1. If you have not already done so, expand the Control Rig item tree for the Alien Plant rig in the **TRACK** window to see the controllers of your Control Rig

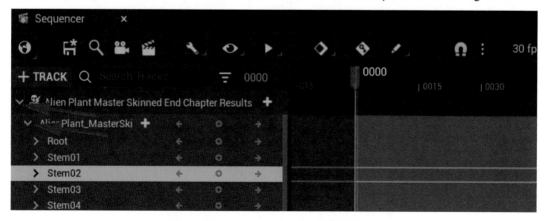

Figure 16.11 – Expanding the TRACK tree

Now, let's set the active workspace time in our timeline. For this swaying animation loop, we will need 160 frames at 30 fps.

2. Set the overall and active range of the timeline window to frame **-20** to **200**. At the bottom of the timeline window, on the left, type in -20 and -20. On the right, type in 200 and 200, as shown in *Figure 16.12*.

3. Use the red time-scrubbing control (**A** in *Figure 16.12*) and drag it to frame **0000**. Set the start of the **Active Working Range** to frame **0000** by clicking the button shown by **B** in *Figure 16.12*. The thin green line will snap to frame **0000** when you do that:

Figure 16.12 – Setting the start of the Active Working Range

> **Note**
>
> The **Active Working Range** is the time range that will play back when we click **Play**. It is also the range where it will loop while playing back, so we can set our looping keyframes at the start and end of it and see whether the cycle works when we play it back. If we export animations, this is also the time range that will export.

4. To set the end of the **Active Working Range**, scrub to frame **160** with **A** in *Figure 16.13* and set it with **B**. The thin red line will snap to that frame:

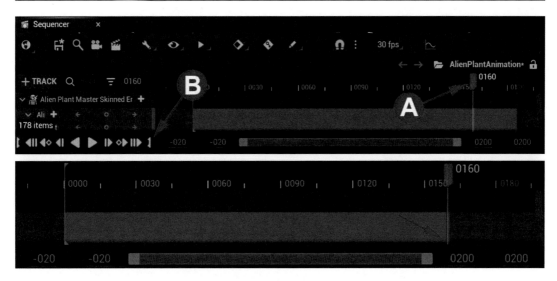

Figure 16.13 – Setting the end of the active working range

> **Note**
>
> You can also move the start and end of the Active Working Range by left-clicking and dragging them directly in the timeline window, but if you want an exact frame, it's better to do it with the method mentioned in the preceding steps.

5. In the **TRACK** window, select the Alien Plant rig parent node in the tree just above the list of controllers. Scrub the time to frame **0000**. In the middle between the two arrows is a + icon (add keyframe). Click it to create a keyframe for all the rig controllers under it in the tree. Then, navigate to frame **160** and set another keyframe for all the controllers, and then another at **80**, as shown in *Figure 16.14*. By putting keyframes on the Alien Plant rig parent node, it adds keyframes on all the Control Rig controllers:

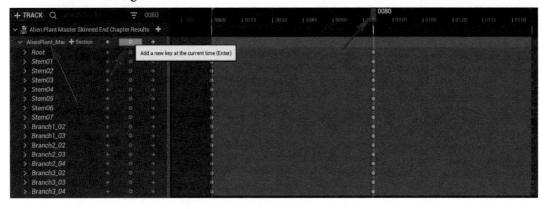

Figure 16.14 – Setting keyframes for all the controllers

> **Note**
>
> We set a keyframe on all the controllers at the beginning and end of this animation so that we know the start and end are going to be exactly the same for the animation cycle. If we don't set these keys at the beginning, we might forget and find it hard to get it back to a cycle. We also set keyframes for everything in the middle of the animation at frame **80**. The stem here is first going to sway left, then back to the middle, and then right. It's good to have an *anchor* key here to bring it back to the middle An anchor keyframe is just a normal keyframe that we set to preserve the current position of a controller..

6. In the viewport, select the **Stem02** controller and select **Rotate**. Make sure **Local Axis** is set instead of **World Axis**. This is so we only animate along a single axis for simplicity and switch **Angle Snap** off so that we can animate at smaller angles. In the Sequence editor top menu, switch **AutoKey** on so that when we rotate the controller, it will automatically create a keyframe, as shown in *Figure 16.15*:

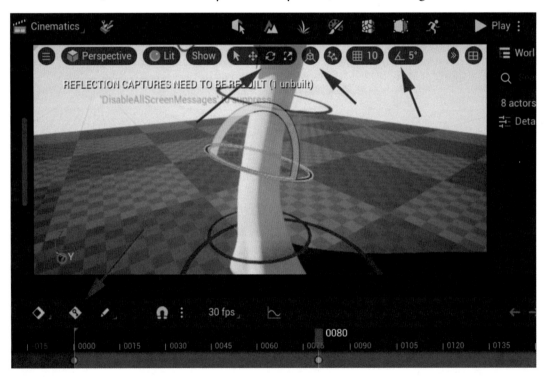

Figure 16.15 – Red arrows pointing to Rotate, Local Axis, Angle Snap off, and Autokey

7.   Scrub to frame **40** and rotate the **Stem02** controller around one degree toward the left along the main corresponding axis. It can be a little bit more or less, but around one degree so as to keep it subtle, as shown in *Figure 16.16*.

> **Note**
>
> Since this controller is at the base of the Alien Plant, even just a rotation of one degree is still very noticeable. When rotating things at the far ends of the plant, you can rotate and animate them a bit more. However, still keep it subtle to get the effect of a gentle breeze in the final animation.

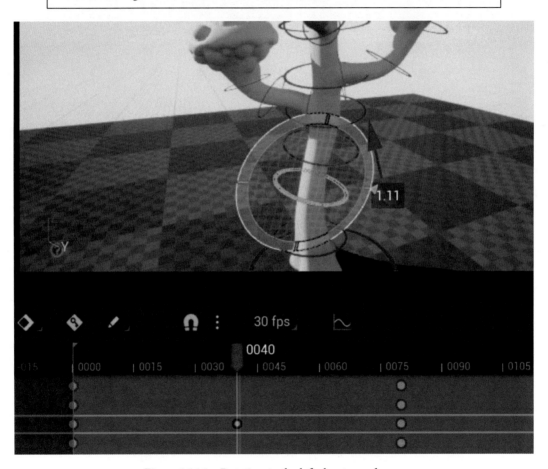

Figure 16.16 – Rotating to the left about one degree

8. Now, scrub to frame **120**. As you scrub right towards frame **120**, you'll see the subtle animation as it rotates back to the *anchor* frame at **80** that we set in the beginning. Rotate the **Stem02** controller around one degree toward the right along the main corresponding axis, as shown in *Figure 16.17*:

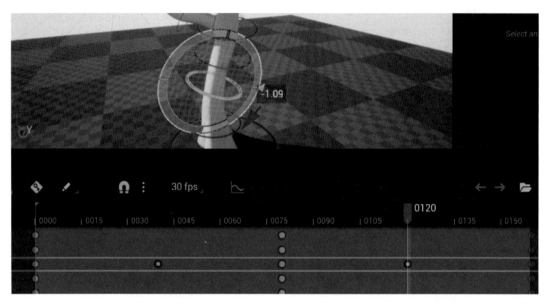

Figure 16.17 – Rotating to the right about one degree

> **Note**
>
> You'll notice that the new keyframes were automatically created at the same time in the timeline as we rotated the controller. When **Autokey** is **ON**, any change we make on the controller will automatically create a new keyframe to record the change, provided there's at least one other key created manually by us anywhere in the timeline.
>
> You can also overwrite an existing keyframe by simply making a change again at the same keyframe. If **Autokey** is **OFF**, we need to manually click + to record the change. In this case, if we make a change, and don't click + to record the key, the change will be lost when we scrub the timeline.
>
> When **Autokey** is **OFF** the process is as follows: scrub to the time you want to set a key, make the change, and then click + to record it and set the keyframe before scrubbing the timeline again or select another controller in the case of Sequencer.

9. In the **TRACK** window, expand the **Stem02** controller, and you'll see the **X**, **Y**, and **Z** channels for **Location**, **Rotation**, and **Scale**.

A keyframe for all the channels was set when we set a keyframe for the Control Rig parent in *Figure 16.14*. When we rotated it using **Autokey** along one main local axis, it only set a key on that one axis, which changed as shown in *Figure 16.18*:

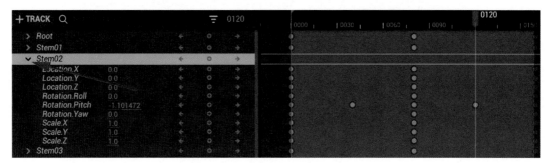

Figure 16.18 – Expanding keyed channels

> **Note**
>
> It's important to get into the habit of organizing your keyframes in such a way that you don't get random or stray results that are hard to track down. For me, for example, when I keyframe one rotation in the X, Y, or Z channel of a controller, I like to key the other two axis channels as well. The mixture of the three interdependent rotation axis channels determines the final angle in the animation. If one is just slightly off, the result could be very different. You'll also notice that in Sequencer, they changed X, Y, and Z in the **Rotation** channels to **Roll**, **Pitch**, and **Yaw**, but it's the same as X, Y, and Z in practice, just the name is different.

At frames **40** and **80**, manually add keyframes on the **Roll/X** and **Yaw/Z** channels by clicking the + keyframe. Now, we have keyframes on all the **Rotation** channels for the **Stem02** controller, as shown in *Figure 16.19*:

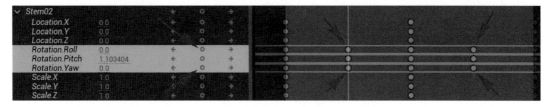

Figure 16.19 – Setting keyframes on all the Rotation channels for the controller

If we clicked the + keyframe next to **Stem02** itself, it would put a keyframe on all the transform channels (the **X**, **Y**, and **Z** channels of **Location**, **Rotation**, and **Scale**). However, we are only concerned with rotating this controller in this animation, so there is no need for the other animation channels to have a keyframe.

Now, you can play back the animation in the viewport.

10. Set it to **Looping** and click **Play**, as shown in *Figure 16.20*:

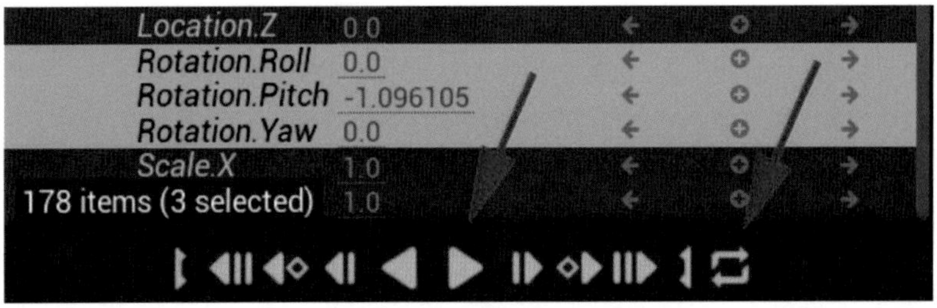

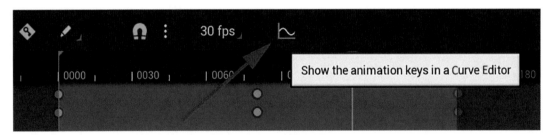

Figure 16.20 – Loop play

Congratulations! You've animated your first cycle animation! However, if you look closely, you'll see there's an awkward slow-down deceleration at the beginning and end of the animation cycle that makes the animation cycle feel a bit wobbly and less smooth.

Next, we'll edit the animation curves in **Curve Editor** to smooth them out.

Editing keyframes and animation curves

As we discussed in the *What are keyframes and curves in computer animation?* section, in-between keyframes acceleration and deceleration are controlled by animation curves. Here's how we edit them:

1. Open **Curve Editor** by clicking on the icon in the top menu bar of the Sequence editor, as shown in *Figure 16.21*:

Figure 16.21 – Opening Curve Editor

2. In the **Curve Editor** interface on the left, there is a window where you have the same items as the **TRACK** window in the main **Sequencer** interface. Select the **Rotation** channels on the **Stem02** controller, as shown in *Figure 16.22*:

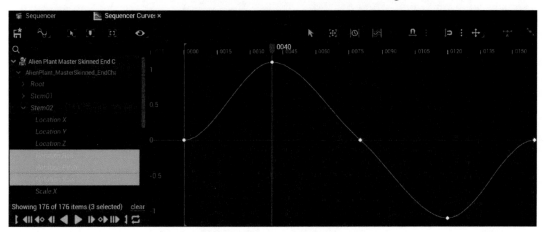

Figure 16.22 – Curve Editor

> **Note**
>
> To navigate the right-hand side curve window in **Curve Editor,** use the middle mouse wheel scroll to zoom in and out. Press *Alt + middle mouse + hold* to pan around the view. Press *F* on the keyboard to focus on a selected curve or selected keyframes. Left-click and drag in an empty spot in the curve window to box-select specific keyframes.

3. Select the specific rotation channel that you want to edit in the Curve window. If you drag and box-select all the keys of this curve, you'll see the keyframe curve handles, as shown in *Figure 16.23*:

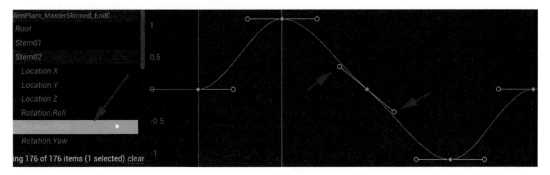

Figure 16.23 – Curve handles

4. You can left-click to select these handles and hold and drag to edit them.

5. You can also change them to different kinds of handles that behave differently in the top menu bar of the **Curve Editor** interface, as shown in *Figure 16.24*:

Figure 16.24 – Different curve handle types

Here's a basic overview of them, but feel free to experiment for yourself to get a feel for what they do. Select a keyframe in the **Curve Editor** window and change its type by clicking on the different curve handle icons shown in *Figure 16.25*:

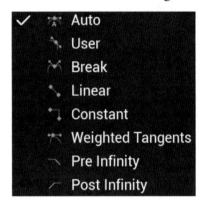

Figure 16.25 – Curve handle types

The different curve handle types in the UE **Curve Editor** are as follows:

- **Auto**: This is the default handle. It tries to make a best guess on how you want your curve to look for smooth animation, but it does not always get it right. The left and right sides of the handle are locked together in a straight line.

- **User**: Very similar to **Auto** but more user-based and may need more manual adjustment via the curve handles.

- **Break**: With this, it breaks the connection between the left and right sides of the handle so you can move them independently. You'll typically use this in cases like the bouncing ball in *Figure 16.9*, at the moment when the ball hits the ground to get that V-shaped sharp acceleration back upward in the curve.

- **Linear**: Makes the curve a perfectly straight line from one keyframe to the next so there is a perfectly constant speed between them, without any acceleration or deceleration.

- **Constant**: It will keep the same transform value till the next keyframe or, in other words, make the curve perfectly flat with no change till the next keyframe overwrites the value.

- **Weighted Tangents**: Here, you can drag the handles out further to round the curve off, or pull the handles in closer to make the curve sharper.

- **Pre Infinity/Post Infinity**: With this, you can set what happens before or after your keyframes into infinity on the timeline. For example, you can set it to **Cycle** and the keyframes and curves will cycle forever before or after your created keyframes, repeating what your keyframes do in the **Sequencer** timeline. There is also **Constant**, where in effect it does nothing before or after, basically the same as the **Constant** one above.

With these options combined, you can make your curve into any shape you want or need. For this animation, we want to make a smooth, cycled animation so it would be a good idea if we could visualize what happens in the curves as they flow from the current cycle to the next. Luckily **Pre Infinity/Post Infinity** does that for us.

With the **Rotation** channel still selected, switch **Pre Infinity/Post Infinity** to **Cycle** instead of **Constant**:

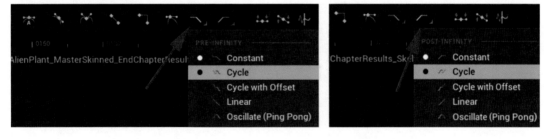

Figure 16.26 – Pre and Post Infinity cycle

If you now look at the curve with **Pre Infinity/Post Infinity** on **Cycle**, at the beginning and end of the cycle, the rotation decelerates at a time that we want it to flow better from the previous cycle to the next cycle. We want it to be more like frame **80** in the middle of the animation, as shown in *Figure 16.27*:

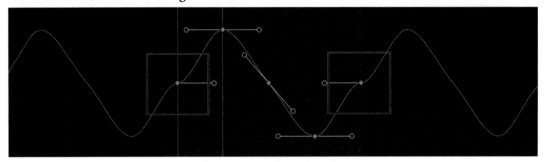

Figure 16.27 – Cycle deceleration

6. Select the curve handles and adjust them so it smooths out the start and end of the cycle. As you adjust the handle of the first keyframe, you'll see it is adjusted automatically at the beginning of the next **Post Infinity** cycle:

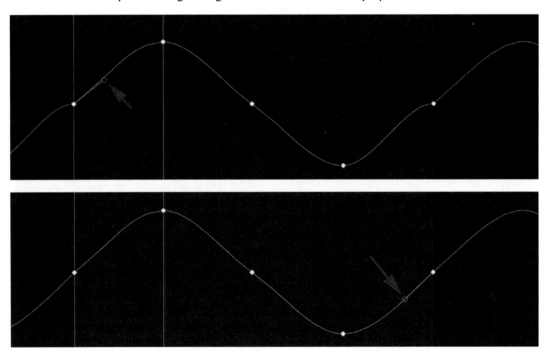

Figure 16.28 – Adjusting the start and end curve handles

However, also looking at the curve handle in frame **80**, we can see that it can also be improved.

7. Adjust the curve handle in frame **80** as shown in *Figure16.29*:

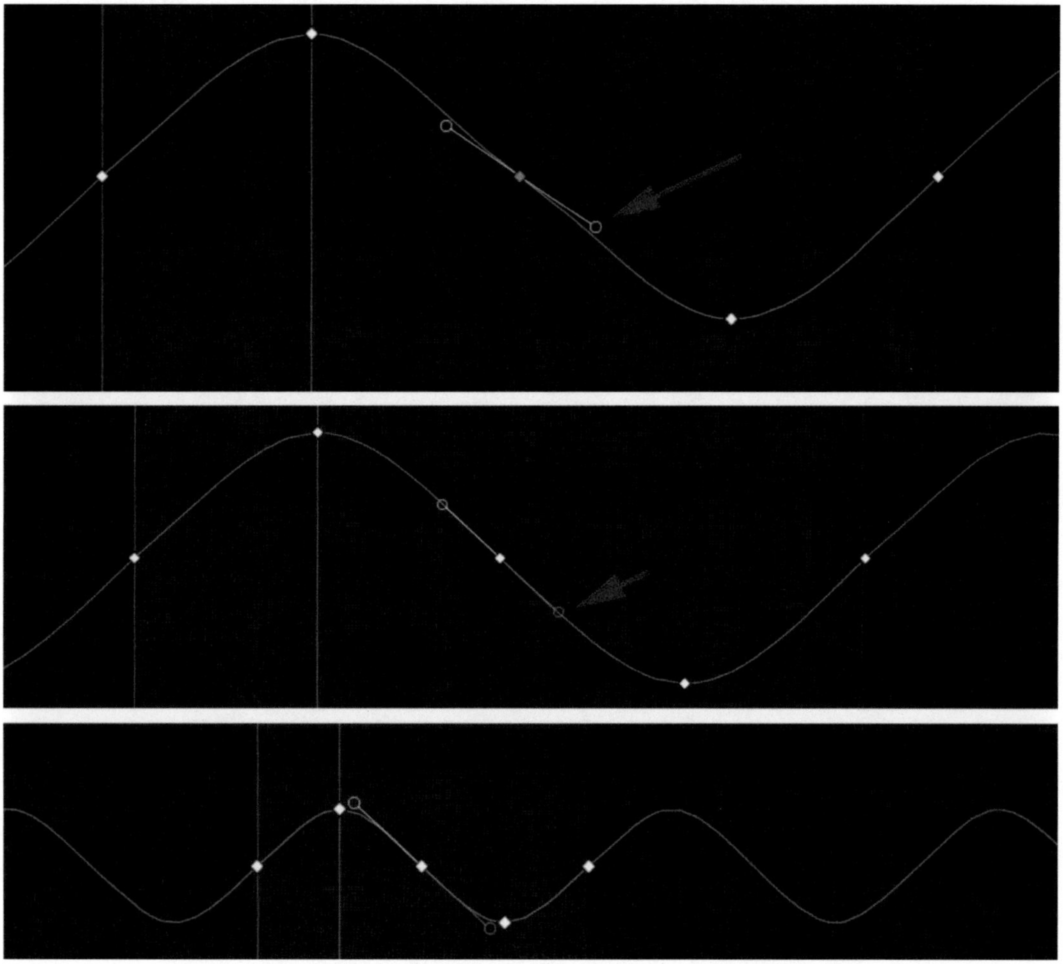

Figure 16.29 – Adjusting the curve handle at frame 80

We now have a smoothly looping curve for the rotation channel using just a few keyframes and the power of animation curves.

8. Using this same method, animate the other controllers of Alien Plant to have the same subtle sway animation and clean up their curves. Make sure to keep it subtle.

> **Note**
> You can also edit the amount of rotation on a particular keyframe in **Curve Editor** directly. Select the keyframes and drag them up or down to change the value, or if you drag the keyframes left or right, you can also change the frame/timing.

9.   After you're happy with your animation, right-click on the overall parent of the Alien Plant Control Rig in the **TRACK** window and choose **Bake Animation Sequence**:

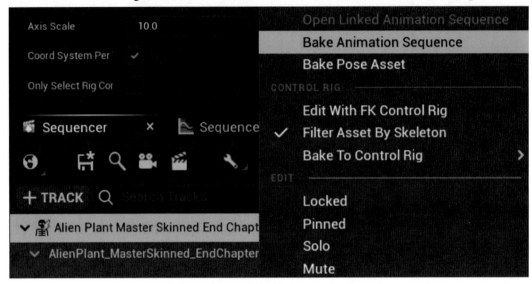

Figure 16.30 – Bake animation

10.   Give it a name, as shown in *Figure 16.31*:

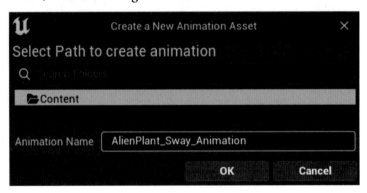

Figure 16.31 – Naming the animation

11.   You can export both the transforms and curves as default, as shown in *Figure 16.32*:

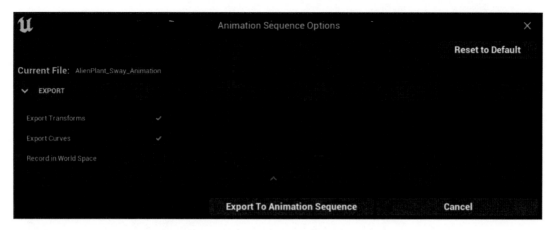

Figure 16.32 – Exporting animation sequence

Your swaying animation will be exported to your **Content Drawer** as an independent animation that could be used anytime on your Alien Plant.

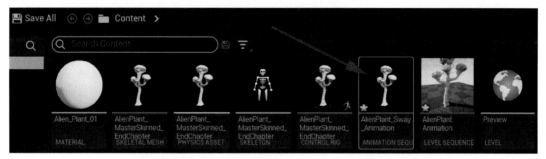

Figure 16.33 – Exported animation in Content Drawer

Advanced Animation Tip

You can make your swaying animation better by using a technique called **Overlap**. Animate the Alien Plant as explained in this chapter. Make sure **Pre and Post Infinity** are set to **Cycle** on all of the animated controllers or you'll break your seamless cycle in the following step.

Select the last controllers in the rig chain. These are the ones controlling the large bulbous ends of the branches of the Alien Plant. Select all the keyframes of just those controllers and drag them to the right so their timing is delayed by 3-4 frames. This will mean that they will cycle a little after the rest of the Alien Plant, creating an *overlap* effect in your animation and making it feel more natural. Overlap is basically when everything in your character doesn't move at the same time, but things at the extremities are a little delayed in their movement.

Congratulations on completing the first animation in this book!

Summary

In this chapter, we learned how to add our Alien Plant animation rig to Sequencer. You had an overview of the **Sequencer** interface and animated your first keyframes after learning what they are. You learned about animation curves and how to edit them in **Curve Editor**. Then, you exported your animation from Sequencer to your **Content Drawer** for later use.

You have now completed your first custom animation from scratch in UE5. Hopefully, this opens up a whole new world of possibilities to create your own animations and have fun with them.

Next, we'll animate some animation cycles for our Robot Drone and use its IK controllers in the animation also.

17

Creating Three Simple Animations for the Robot in UE5 Sequencer

In the previous chapter, we animated a subtle swaying animation cycle for our Alien Plant on the animation rig that only uses **Forward Kinematics (FK)**. In this chapter, we will animate three animation cycles for our Robot Drone. Our robot has **Inverse Kinematics (IK)** controllers on its arms. This will give us a chance to get used to animating with IK controllers. You'll see for yourself how useful this kind of controller is for your animation workflow.

We will also learn how to save and load **poses** onto our Control Rig. Poses in animation are like a snapshot recording of all the transform values on all your controllers on your Control Rig. This is useful if you want your animations to start or end at exactly the same pose so they can seamlessly play from one to another.

In this chapter, we will cover the following:

- Animation A: idle cycle
- Animation B: movement cycle
- Animation C: action animation

Technical requirements

In this chapter, we will only need to work in Unreal Engine 5. You will need the following to complete this chapter:

- A computer that can run basic 3D animation software.
- You need to have installed Unreal Engine 5. You can download it from `https://www.unrealengine.com/en-US/download`.
- A basic understanding of how to navigate the Unreal Engine 3D user interface. If you skipped ahead, this was covered in *Chapter 6, Exploring Unreal Engine 5*.
- You should have completed the tutorials in *Chapter 16, Creating a Simple Swaying Animation Cycle in UE5 Sequencer*, for basic knowledge of how to set keyframes and edit animation curves in UE5.

The files related to this chapter are placed at `https://github.com/PacktPublishing/Unreal-Engine-5-Character-Creation-Animation-and-Cinematics/tree/main/Chapter18`

Animation A: idle cycle

In computer game animation, it is very common to have an **idle cycle** for a character. This is the kind of animation where the character does almost nothing. Typically, in a computer game, this is where the player is not pressing any buttons on the gamepad or keyboard and the character is just standing there. You'll notice during these times in games that the character normally has something like just a subtle breathing animation.

This is an idle cycle. It is an animation that repeats so the character still looks alive while doing nothing. If there was no animation the character would look like a statue and not *alive*. In some games, if you leave the character standing there long enough, it might scratch its head or look around. These animations are normally called **fidget animations**.

We will only need an idle cycle animation since the final sequence we will put together at the end of this book will be short, so there's no need for fidget animations.

However, before we start to animate our idle cycle, let's learn how to use the **Poses** tool in UE5.

Using the Poses tool in UE5

In this section, we will create and save a pose for our Robot Drone as its default pose before we start animating it. This is useful since if we want to return the robot to the default pose without any transforms applied, we can do that by loading this pose.

Sometimes you start an animation and don't like the result. This way, you can reset all the controllers and start afresh. Let's get started:

1. Open the UE5 project in which you saved the Robot Drone Control Rig that we created in *Chapter 15, Creating a Control Rig with Basic IK Controls for the Robot in UE5.*

    We also provide the completed Robot Drone Control Rig in the final project file, which can be downloaded here with installation instructions: `https://github. com/PacktPublishing/Unreal-Engine-5-Character-Creation- Animation-and-Cinematics/tree/main/FullFinalUE5Project`.

    The Robot Drone Control Rig is under: **Content/RobotDroneControlRig**.

2. Select **Cinematics | Add Level Sequence** to open a new level sequence in Sequencer.

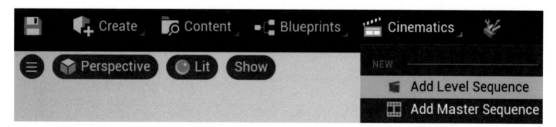

Figure 17.1 – Adding a level sequence

3. Name the sequence `RobotAnim01_IdleCycle` and click on **SAVE**.

Figure 17.2 – Saving the sequence

4. Left-click, hold, and drag the robot Control Rig from **Content Drawer** to the
    TRACK window in Sequencer to add it to the Sequencer timeline as shown in
    Figure 17.3.

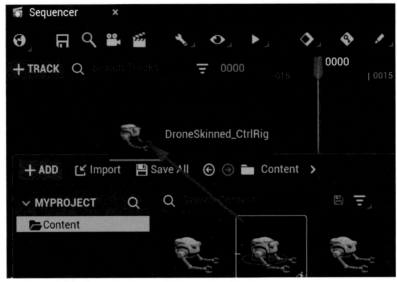

Figure 17.3 – Adding the robot Control Rig to Sequencer

5. In the main UE interface, tidy up your workspace by moving the floor if needed and
    anything obstructing your view. If the default UE grid floor is in the way, click the
    visibility eye icon on the **Outliner** tab to make it invisible in the viewport as seen in
    Figure 17.4.

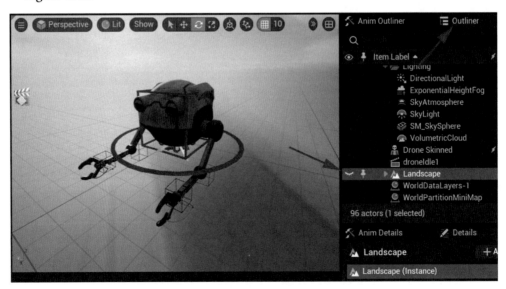

Figure 17.4 – Opening the Animation window

6. In the Sequencer timeline, set the overall and timeline workspace from -010 to 0070. Set the active range from 0000 to 0060 as seen in *Figure 17.5*. If you need a reminder on how to do this, refer to the *Setting keyframes on the Alien Plant Rig* section in *Chapter 16, Creating a Simple Swaying Animation Cycle in UE5 Sequencer*.

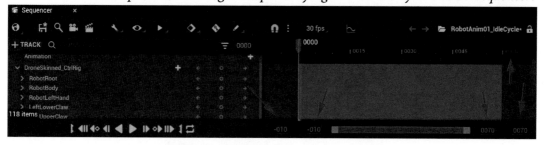

Figure 17.5 – Setting the timeline workspace

7. In the **Animation** window, select all the controllers in your Robot Drone Control Rig in **Animation Outliner**, then click on **Poses** in the **Animation** tab. Click **Create Pose** at the top left of the **Control Rig Pose** window, name it default_pose and click **Create Asset** to add this pose to your new library of poses:

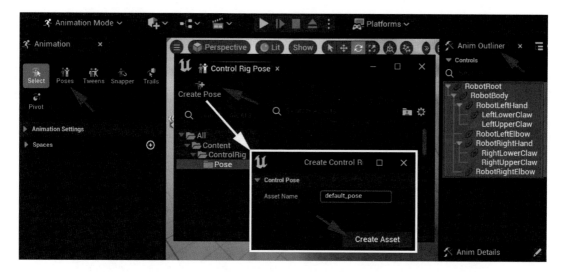

Figure 17.6 – Adding the default pose

8. Now let's test the **Poses** tool. In the main viewport, move the controller of your Robot Drone, including the controller for the main body – in my case, **RobotBody** – till it's in a random position. It does not matter what the pose is, as long as it's very different from the default pose as shown in *Figure 17.7*:

Figure 17.7 – Random pose

9. Select only the controller controlling the main body – in my case, **RobotBody** – in either the viewport, the **Animation** window, or Sequencer. In the **Control Rig Pose** window, with the **default_pose** pose item selected, click **Paste Pose** as shown in *Figure 17.8*.

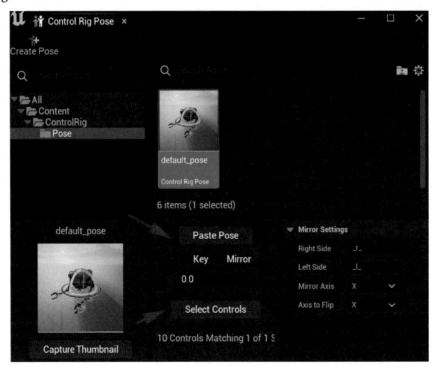

Figure 17.8 – Paste Pose

The **RobotBody** will return to its original position, but the rest of the controllers will still be offset as shown in *Figure 17.9*.

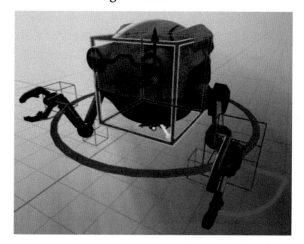

Figure 17.9 – RobotBody returning to default pose

10. Now, as shown in *Figure 17.8*, in the **Control Rig Pose** window, click on **Select Controls**. This will select all the controllers that were originally selected when creating the pose. Now select **Paste Pose**. All the selected controllers will now return to the default pose.

> **Note**
>
> With the **Poses** tool, the **Paste Pose** option will only paste the pose to the selected controllers. When creating a pose, it will only save the pose of the controllers selected at the time. This is actually very useful since we might be happy with the body and left arm pose we created, but unhappy with the pose we created for the right arm.
>
> In this case, we can just select the right arm controllers and select **Paste Pose**. This will return just the right arm controllers to the default pose without losing the work we did on the body and left arm. Additionally, when saving a pose, it creates a thumbnail screenshot for us as a visual reference to the pose. If you don't like the thumbnail, you can reposition the character on the screen to something you like and change it by clicking **Capture Thumbnail** as shown in *Figure 17.8*.

We have now learned how to save poses to the Poses library and then how to paste them back to our Control Rig. Next, we can start animating the idle cycle.

Animating the idle cycle

When animating an idle cycle, we want to make sure our main pose is interesting but neutral. Also, in character animation, generally, we want to avoid poses that are perfectly symmetrical, where the left and right sides are mirror images of each other. It just makes for very uninteresting visuals and makes it feel too mechanical.

Technically, our robot is mechanical, but we want to give it some personality, so it's better to give it a more interesting idle start pose. Typically, a lot of animations in computer games flow from the idle cycle base pose so this is also why we want something a bit more interesting here. At the same time, it is an idle pose, so it can't be too over the top.

Let's set our starting pose for our Robot Drone:

1. First, we can move the left- and right-hand controllers closer to the body and then move the right-hand controller up a bit and the left-hand controller down a bit to break the symmetry. Notice how our IK controllers in our animation rig do their job perfectly while the elbow bends as seen in *Figure 17.10*.

Figure 17.10 – Idle pose moving hand controllers

2. Select the elbow/pole vector controllers and move them back and down so the elbows can point towards them. Move the elbows outwards a bit.

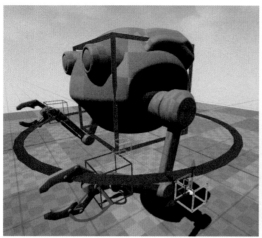

Figure 17.11 – Idle pose moving elbow/pole vectors

3. Finally, rotate to angle the hands slightly. Rotate the claw controllers to close the claws on the left hand a little and open the claws on the right hand a little as seen in *Figure 17.12*.

Figure 17.12 – Idle pose moving hands and claws

Now we have a nice pose that is not perfectly symmetrical, and the Robot Drone is starting to come to life. We can now save this pose to our pose library in the Poses tool.

4. Click on **Poses** in the **Animation** window, select **Create Pose,** and name it
    `IdleBasePose`.

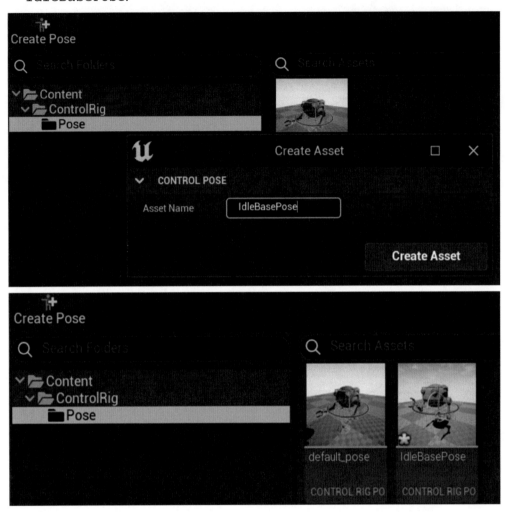

Figure 17.13 – Saving the idle pose

> **Note**
> We now have our base idle pose saved, so if we load a fresh sequence and start
> a new animation with our Robot Drone Control Rig, this pose will be accessible
> to us if we want to start or end the new animation with this pose.

5. Scrub to frame **0000** in the **Sequencer** timeline and keyframe this pose for all the
    controllers by clicking + in the **TRACK** window on the parent of the controllers.

Figure 17.14 – Setting the keyframe at frame 0000

6. Now scrub to frame **0060** in the **Sequencer** timeline and keyframe all the controllers by clicking + in the **TRACK** window on the parent of the controllers. We now have keyframes for this pose at the start and end of the animation.

7. In the **Sequencer** window, at the top, turn on the **Automatic Keyframe** by clicking on it so it creates keyframes when we make changes automatically as seen in *Figure 17.15*.

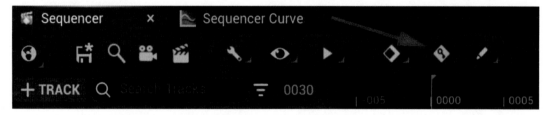

Figure 17.15 – Auto Keyframe on

8. Scrub to frame **0030** in the **Sequencer** timeline (halfway between frames **0** and **60**) and select the controller called **RobotBody**.

> **Note**
>
> At this point, you have three ways you can select the controller called **RobotBody** – in the main UE viewport itself, in the **Sequencer TRACK** window, or in the **Anim Outliner** window. It doesn't matter what method you use to select it. They all do the same thing.

9. In the viewport, using the **Move** transform tool, move the **RobotBody** controller up about 2 cm. Then rotate the **RobotBody** controller so the front angles upwards a little bit more than 2 degrees as seen in *Figure 17.16*.

10. Because we have **Automatic Keyframe** on, it will create a keyframe for the
    RobotBody controller at frame **0030** for the move and rotate channels automatically.

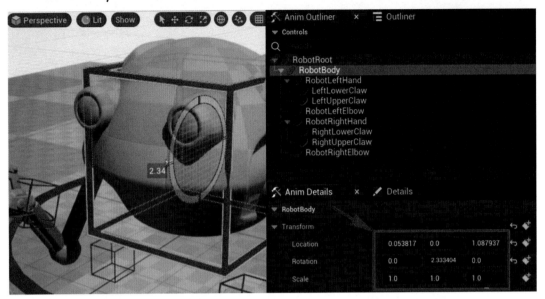

Figure 17.16 – Keyframe 0030 values

11. In the **Anim Details** window, with the **RobotBody** controller still selected, you'll
    notice that you can see the current **Location, Rotation**, and **Scale** values at frame
    30 under **Transform**. I pointed this out with the red arrow in *Figure 17.16*.

    The three boxes with the values are ordered: the **X** axis value in the first box on the
    left, then **Y** in the middle, and **Z** on the right.

    So, looking at that, at frame **30** (on mine, since yours will probably be a little
    different), **Location Z** = **0.053817** and **Rotation Y** = **1.087937**.

    I just roughly moved and rotated the **RobotBody** controller, and that is fine if the
    resulting animation looks good when you play it back, but for the purpose of this
    exercise, let us change those values.

12. Make sure you are still on frame **0030** in the **Sequencer** timeline. Double-click
    on the **Location Z** value field. That will select and highlight the value and you can
    change it to 2.0. In the same way, change **Rotation Y** to 1.5 and the rest to 0.0 as
    shown in *Figure 17.17*.

Figure 17.17 – Changing the values in CHANNELS

This will change the **Location** and **Rotation** value of the **RobotBody** controller keyframe on frame **0030**. But to be safe, let us place a keyframe on all the **RobotBody** controller channels.

In the *Setting keyframes for the Alien Plant Rig Control* section in *Chapter 16, Create Simple Swaying Animation Cycle in UE5 Sequencer*, we set keyframes in the Sequencer **TRACK** window using the + keyframe. We can also set keyframes in the **Anim Details** window and they will appear as usual in our **Sequencer** timeline, just like doing it in the **Sequencer TRACK** window.

13. With **BodyRobot** still selected, add a keyframe on all the transform channels at frame **0030** using the **Add Keyframe** button in the **Anim Details** window under **Transform**. I Indicated this button in *Figure 17.17* with the red arrow.

Now let us animate the arms of the robot.

If you look at frame **0000** and the **Idle Cycle** start pose, the right-hand controller is higher than the left-hand controller, so in the next step I'll be animating it down. I'll do the opposite and animate the left hand upwards, so they do the opposite in the animation cycle.

14. Still at frame **0030**, select the controller called **RobotRightHand**, move it down about 6 cm and rotate it a little bit upwards, maybe 3 degrees or so. Just like in *Step 13*, set a keyframe on all the channels on this controller also.

15. Still at frame **0030**, select the controller called **RobotLefttHand**, move it upwards about 4 cm and rotate it a little bit downwards, maybe 3 degrees or so. Just like in *Step 13*, set a keyframe on all the channels.

On frame **0000** in the **Idle Cycle** start pose, the claws on the right hand are more open and the claws on the left hand are more closed. Let's do the opposite during the animation cycle.

16. Still at frame **0030**, select the claw controllers on the right hand and close them a bit, but not completely closed. Select the claw controllers on the left hand and open them a bit, but not completely open by rotating the controllers as seen in *Figure 17.18*. Set a keyframe on all the channels for the claw controllers.

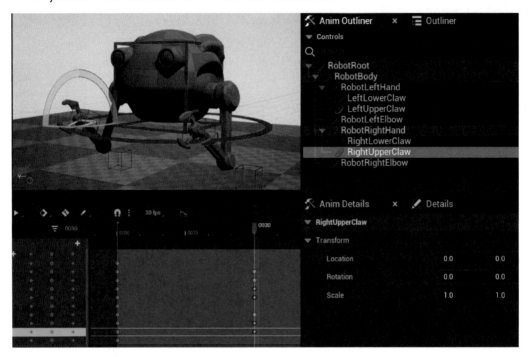

Figure 17.18 – Mid-cycle pose

We now have set the pose and keyframes for the middle of the idle cycle animation. You can now press play on the **Sequencer** timeline to see the animation cycle play. Hopefully, the cycle looks okay at this point.

If not, you can edit the animation curves as we did in the *Editing keyframes and animation curves* section in *Chapter 16, Creating a Simple Swaying Animation Cycle in UE5 Sequencer.*

However, we can improve our new idle cycle a little bit by offsetting the arm animation keyframes to create what we call an **overlap** (things not moving at the same time in the animation).

17. Select the **RobotLeftHand**, **LeftLowerClaw**, and **LeftUpperClaw** keyframes at frame **0030** in the **Sequencer** timeline together by left-clicking, holding, and dragging, to box selecting them, or holding *Shift* + clicking on them.

18. Move the keyframes for these controllers from frame **30** to frame **25** by clicking, holding, and dragging them to the left as shown in *Figure 17.19*.

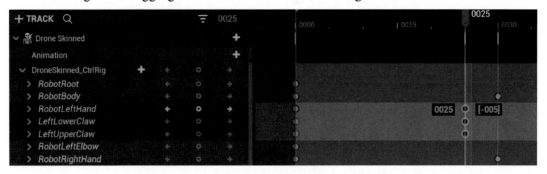

Figure 17.19 – Offset left hand and claws minus 5 frames

19. Select the **RobotRightHand**, **RightLowerClaw**, and **RightUpperClaw** keyframes at frame **0030** in the **Sequencer** timeline. Move the keyframes for these controllers from frame **30** to frame **35**.

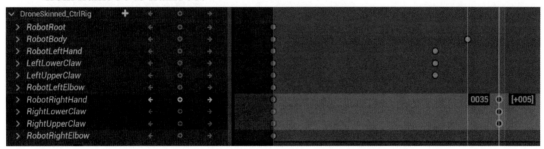

Figure 17.20 – Offset right hand and claws plus five frames

Advanced Note

This is just a simple offset in the middle of the cycle to create some overlap with the arms, but we could do a complete offset by putting pre- and post-infinity on the curve channels for the arm controllers and offsetting all the arm controller keyframes. But that would mean a longer process and having to resave the start pose. For the purposes of this exercise, what we have done by just offsetting the keys in the middle of the cycle is good enough.

If you expand **RobotLeftHand** in the **Sequencer TRACK** window to see all the transform channels, you'll see that by moving the single keyframe on the collapsed view of the **RobotLeftHand** controller in the **TRACK** window, it moved all the transform channel keyframes at that frame.

It is like the keyframe on the un-extended view of the controllers in the **TRACK** window is the **parent** of the other keyframes on the transform channels that are on the same frame as shown in *Figure 17.21*.

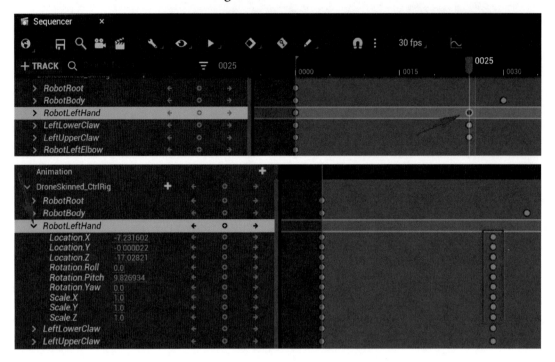

Figure 17.21 – Extended controller view

Sometimes this just makes it easier to move keys around if we have lots of controllers and we don't want to extend them all to move the keys on all the channels. Also notice that when you extend the controller to show the channels, the **parent** keyframe stops displaying in the timeline. When you collapse (un-extend) the channels, it displays again.

If you're happy with your idle cycle after playing it back, you can export it as its own UE animation to be used later together with other animations.

20. In the **Sequencer TRACK** window, right-click on the overall parent of the Control Rig. In my case, it is **Drone Skinned**. Click **Bake Animation Sequence** to export it as a regular UE animation with a keyframe on every frame.

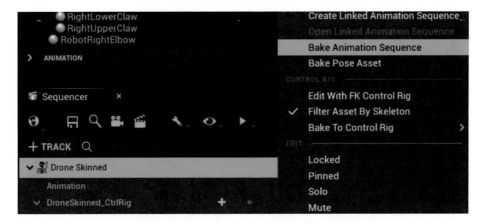

Figure 17.22 – Bake Animation Sequence

21. Save it as **Animation Name:** `Robot_Idle_Cycle` to your project:

Figure 17.23 – Naming the animation

The default export settings are good.

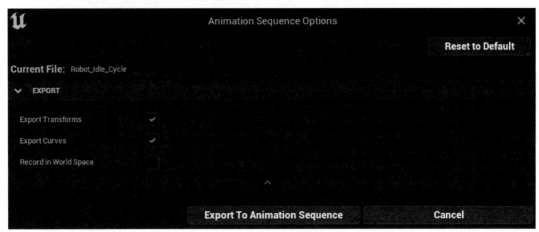

Figure 17.24 – Export settings

We have now finished our first animation idle cycle for our Robot Drone. Next, we will animate a movement cycle for the robot.

Animation B: movement cycle

During the tutorial in this section, after completing the idle cycle in the previous section, I will teach you how to repurpose the idle cycle animation and adapt it to a **movement cycle**. This is a great way to reuse what we have already done and at the same time, you can learn a few ways to edit existing animations.

I call it a movement cycle, but in reality, it will be animated on the spot and the Robot Drone won't be moving forward for now, during the creation of this animation cycle. This movement cycle is a bit like an idle cycle but looks more like the character is flying forward while doing it.

We will play this movement cycle in our final sequence when our Robot Drone is moving around the scene and will then put actual forward movement in. So, during our final scene in this book, when the robot is hovering in the same spot, we will play the idle cycle, but when it starts moving, we will play the movement cycle.

We can start by duplicating the **Idle Cycle LEVEL SEQUENCE** so we can make it into something else:

1. In the **Content Drawer**, right-click on the **RobotAnim01_IdleCycle LEVEL SEQUENCE** and select **Duplicate** as shown in *Figure 17.25*.

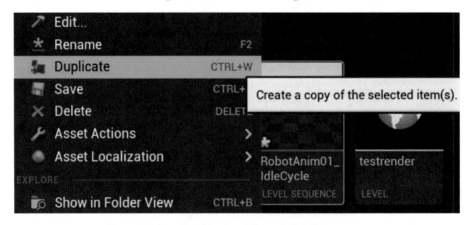

Figure 17.25 – Duplicating idle cycle level sequence

2. Name the duplicate `RobotAnim02_MovementCycle`:

Figure 17.26 – Renaming the duplicate

3. Double-click the **RobotAnim02_MovementCycle LEVEL SEQUENCE** to open it in **Sequencer**.

During the movement cycle, we want to keep the motion of the Robot Drone's body and arms, but we want it a bit faster while moving forward, so let's make it faster by reducing the length of the cycle from **60** frames to **40**.

4. Set **Active Range** (thin red and green lines) from the current 0000-0060 to 0000-0040 in the **Sequencer** timeline as shown in *Figure 17.27*.

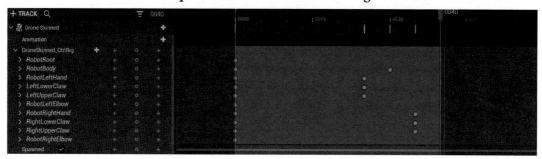

Figure 17.27 – Setting new Active Range 0-40

5. Now select and move the **RobotLeftHand, LeftLowerClaw**, and **LeftUpperClaw** keyframes from 0025 to 0015. Move the **RobotBody** keyframe from 0030 to 0020. Move the **RobotRightHand, RightLowerClaw**, and **RightUpperClaw** keyframes from 0035 to 0025. Finally, move all the keyframes that were on 0060 to 0040 as shown in *Figure 17.28*.

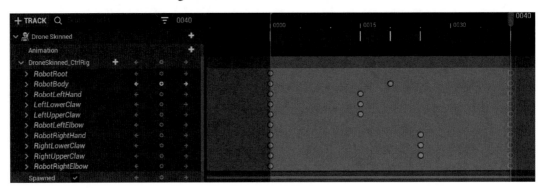

Figure 17.28 – Moving keyframes

When you now press play in **Sequencer**, you'll see it is still almost exactly like the idle cycle, only it plays about one-third faster.

Now let's adjust the animation further with an **Additive** layer of keyframes. Additive layers are simply a way in UE5 (and most good 3D animation software packages) to keep the existing underlying animation and add extra values on top of it without losing the original animation.

A practical example of this is what we will do next on our robot. We want to keep the body and arms bobbing up and down in the idle cycle, but we want everything to lean forward as it flies forward through the air.

Let's set up an additive layer for our Robot Drone Control Rig.

6. In the **Sequencer TRACK** window, click on + on the parent of all the controllers – in my case, **DroneSkinned_CtrlRig** – and select **Additive**:

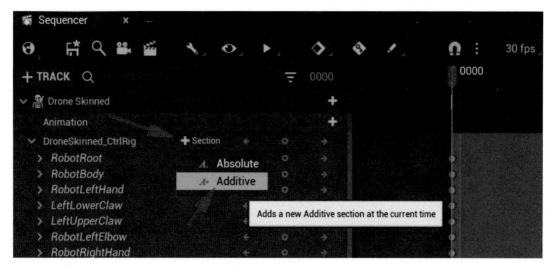

Figure 17.29 – Adding an Additive animation layer

This will seem to duplicate the Robot Drone controllers, but when you hover with the mouse over the blue bar next to them in the **Sequencer** timeline window, it will display **Additive** as shown in *Figure 17.30*.

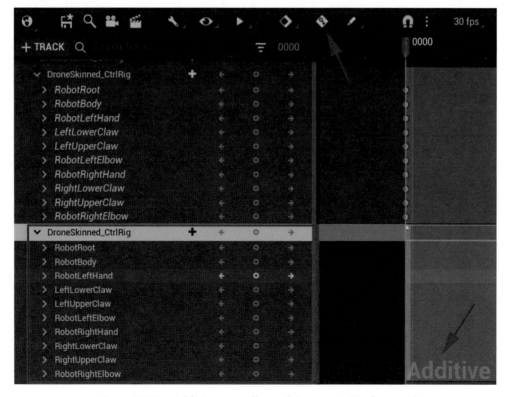

Figure 17.30 – Additive controller and Automatic Keyframe off

7. Turn off **Automatic Keyframe**.

    This is particularly important since we now want exact control over what channel we set the keyframes on. With **Automatic Keyframe** on, it will record changes on all the channels and sets of controllers as we make changes. This is not what we want. We want to only set keyframes on the new **Additive** controllers, so it needs to be off.

    As an additional tip, when working with **Additives** in Sequencer, don't select the controllers in the viewport since it will select both the regular and additive controller and it might get confusing.

8. Select them in the **Sequencer TRACK** window instead so you know the selected one is the one you should + keyframe once you have made a change. This is just until you get used to setting keyframes on the right controllers with additives.

9. Set a keyframe on all the controllers at frame 0000 with the + keyframe on the additive version of the **DroneSkinned_CtrlRig** parent of the controllers as shown in *Figure 17.31*.

Figure 17.31 – Setting a keyframe on frame 0000 of the additive layer

10. On frame `0000`, select the additive controller called **RobotBody** in the **TRACK** window and rotate it about `-16` degrees in the viewport, to angle the front of the robot downwards, and click the + keyframe in the **TRACK** window. Make sure you set a + keyframe for the **Additive** version of the controllers (see *Figure 17.32*).

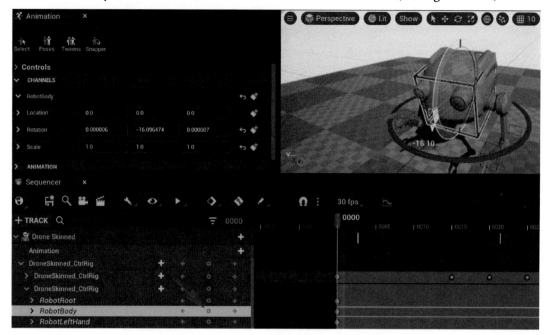

Figure 17.32 – Keyframe Additive forward leaning

Now when you click play in Sequencer, the entire animation plays leaning forward. You applied your first **Additive** animation. To make the movement animation more distinctive, let's change the arms too.

11. Sill on frame **0000**, pose your Robot Drone arms as in *Figure 17.33*. Each time you move a controller to pose it, since **Automatic Keyframe** is still off, remember to set a + **keyframe** on all the **Additive** arm controllers on frame **0000** to key the pose. Once again, remember to set it on the Additive set of controllers.

Figure 17.33 – Movement Additive arms pose

Play the animation in Sequencer, and if you're happy with the result, it's time to export it.

12. As in the *Animating the idle cycle section*, *Step 21*, *Figure 17.22*, right-click on **Drone Skinned** in the Sequencer **TRACK** window and then select **Bake Animation Sequence**. Name it `Robot_Movement_Cycle`. It should appear in the **Content Drawer** as shown in *Figure 17.34*.

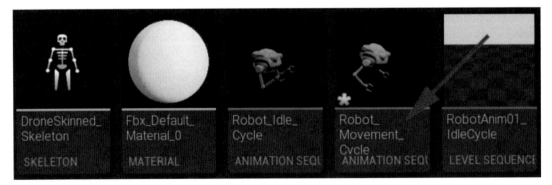

Figure 17.34 – Exported/baked movement idle

We have now completed our second animation for our Robot Drone. Now let's do our third.

Animation C: action animation

For the third animation, we will do an activation. In this activation, the robot turns on, then performs a greeting gesture, and then ends with the idle cycle pose. Here, you can let your creativity run wild and do what you want. At the end of the book, we will put together a final sequence in Sequencer where we will use all the assets we created while working through this book.

Our MetaHuman character will at some point push a button on its suit to activate the drone. The drone will activate, then acknowledge/greet them and then go to the idle cycle pose we saved before so it can blend seamlessly back into the idle cycle animation that we animated here.

How the Robot Drone activates and how it greets the character is up to you. The only thing we must do is end with the `IdleBasePose` pose (see *Figure 17.13*) that we can load from our pose library at the end frame of the animation.

Here, you will use everything you have learned so far about animating your Control Rig in Sequencer. I realize this might be a daunting assignment if you haven't done a full custom animation from scratch before. To help you, I'll briefly run you through the process I followed to complete this task.

I decided to do a salute after the Robot Drone activates. I hope it will serve as a good example of the basic process. The animated **RobotAnim03_ActionAnimation LEVEL SEQUENCE** will also be in the UE project at `https://github.com/PacktPublishing/Unreal-Engine-5-Character-Creation-Animation-and-Cinematics/tree/main/FullFinalUE5Project` accompanying this chapter so you can examine it if needed:

1. Add a new level sequence for this animation by selecting **Cinematics | Add Level Sequence**. Name it `RobotAnim03_ActionAnimation`.

2. Left-click, hold, and drag the robot Control Rig from the **Content Drawer** to the **TRACK** window in **Sequencer** (see *Figure 17.3*).

3. Activate **Automatic Keyframe** (see *Figure 17.15*).

4. Set the first pose to look like the robot is inactive at frame **0000** and set + keyframe on all the controllers (see *Figure 17.14*).

5. On frame **0010**, I set exactly the same keyframe so from frame **0000** to frame **0010**, the robot is perfectly still in the inactive position as seen in *Figure 17.35*.

    This will be helpful later if we want to export this part as an un-activated cycle to extend the playback for as long as we need in our final sequence.

6.   We then have keyframes on frames **0020** and **0032** as part of the activation process.

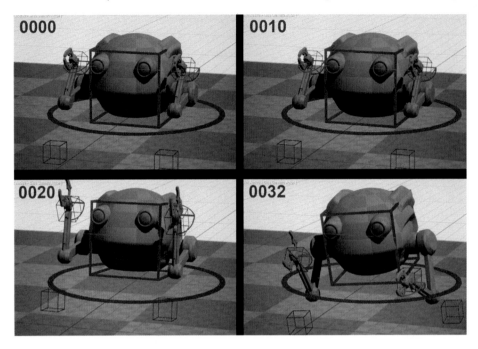

Figure 17.35 – Keyframes 0000 to 0032

7.   On frame **0046**, we will keyframe the right hand in the lower position before the salute. On frame **0057**, we will set another similar keyframe with the lowered hand position, but a bit different so there's a little movement between the two keyframes as shown in *Figure 17.36*.

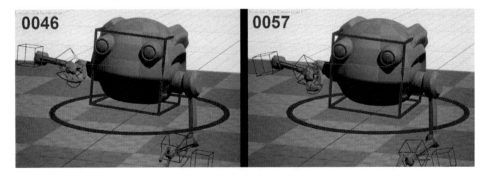

Figure 17.36 – Keyframes 0046 to 0057

8.   From keyframe **0057** to **0062**, the right hand goes to the salute position, and we then set another keyframe at **0080** that is very similar (just slightly different to keep some subtle movement in the character) to hold the salute till then.

9. From frames **0080** to **0086**, the hands come back down from the salute as shown in *Figure 17.37*.

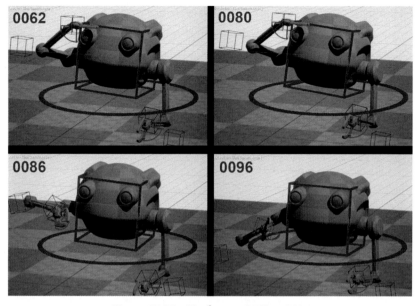

Figure 17.37 – Keyframes 0062 to 0096

10. Frame **0096** is an in-between frame before we load the idle cycle pose at frame **0110** as shown in *Figure 17.38*.

Figure 17.38 – Keyframes 0110

If you have trouble remembering how to paste a pose from the Poses tool, have a look at *Figure 17.8* in the *Using the Poses tool in UE5* section of this chapter.

11. Select the `IdleBasePose` we saved earlier in this chapter under the *How to use the Poses Tool in UE5* section. Select controllers and then select **Paste Pose** at frame **0110**. Set a keyframe on all the controllers.

12. Set your active frame range (thin green and red lines in the timeline) from frame **0000** to **0110**.

13. As in *Figure 17.22*, right-click on **Drone Skinned** and then select **Bake Animation Sequence**. Name it `Robot_Action_Animation`.

14. Set your active frame range from frame **0000** to **0010**.

15. Right-click on **Drone Skinned** and then select **Bake Animation Sequence**. Name it `Robot_Action_Unactivated`.

I hope you have great fun animating this last animation for the Robot Drone. It does take a bit of practice and experimenting to get animations to look good so don't worry if you found this difficult.

Summary

In this chapter, we learned how to use the animation tools in Sequencer and the **Animation** window better. We learned about saving specific poses in the Poses tool and pasting them back into our animations. We animated an idle cycle, then repurposed it to create a movement cycle, and finally, we animated a specific action with a few parts to it from scratch. We saw how useful and easy it is to animate with IK after the somewhat complicated process to set it up in the first place. We saved the animations we created for later use in the final scene we will construct.

In the next few chapters, we will explore how to use motion capture on our MetaHuman in UE5.

18
Importing Motion Capture onto the MetaHuman Control Rig

In the preceding chapter, we animated our Robot Drone with some **Inverse Kinematics (IK)**. In this chapter, we will work with **Motion Capture (MoCap)** on the MetaHuman we created in *Chapter 8, Using MetaHuman to Create a Photorealistic Human for UE5*.

MoCap, as it is referred to by people in the industry, is just realistic motion captured from real human actors in special MoCap suits that can record all their movements, including the subtleties in 3D animation software. It's then converted to keyframes on a skeleton, like the ones we created for our Alien Plant and Robot. The only difference in this case is that the skeleton is human-like.

MoCap normally has a keyframe on every frame because it captures the full subtlety of organic human motion. If you have a realistic-looking human, like the one we created in MetaHuman, it's good to use something like MoCap.

It's hard and very time-consuming to animate as realistically as real captured motion from real actors, so MoCap has changed the amount of quality content in games and films. I started being a professional animator before MoCap was used. When MoCap started to become accessible to studios, animators thought that they would be replaced by this new technology.

This was not the case. Studios simply started creating more content. MoCap needs a lot of editing and tweaking by people with a good eye for motion, like animators. I spent a large part of my career working with MoCap, editing it, combining different MoCap takes together, and directing cutscenes shot with actors.

In the next two chapters, I will give you an introduction to how to use and edit MoCap in UE5.

In this chapter, we will cover the following:

- Getting MoCap animations from Mixamo

- Getting MoCap animations from the UE Marketplace

- Retargeting MoCap animations to a MetaHuman skeleton

Technical requirements

In this chapter, we will need to work with UE5 and the Mixamo website. You will need the following to complete this chapter:

- A computer that can run basic 3D animation software.

- You need to have installed UE5. You can download it from `https://www.unrealengine.com/en-US/download`.

- Internet access to visit the free MoCap library at `https://www.mixamo.com/` (optional).

- A basic understanding of how to navigate the UE 3D user interface. If you skipped ahead, this was covered in *Chapter 6, Exploring Unreal Engine 5*.

You can download the complete project from the GitHub repository of this book at `https://github.com/PacktPublishing/Unreal-Engine-5-Character-Creation-Animation-and-Cinematics/tree/main/FullFinalUE5Project`.

The files related to this chapter are placed at `https://github.com/PacktPublishing/Unreal-Engine-5-Character-Creation-Animation-and-Cinematics/tree/main/Chapter18`

Getting MoCap animations from Mixamo

Mixamo is a free-to-use online MoCap tool and MoCap library. The Mixamo library is subject to change, so I included the downloaded .fbx files from Mixamo in the file source for this chapter. Mixamo is incredibly easy to use. The aim here is to get some free-to-use MoCap and there're lots of different free resources out there if you search for them. Mixamo is just one of them. I hope to teach you more generally about how to work with MoCap. For UE, we preferably want our MoCap source file to be in the .fbx format.

Before we proceed to Mixamo, let's have a think about what MoCap we need for our final sequence. Our female character is going to be in a sitting idle animation, then stand up, and maybe stand there for a moment before walking a few steps forward, stopping, pressing a button on her arm (then the Robot Drone activates), and will then go back to a standing idle animation.

What follows is an example of how I found the MoCap we will use in this chapter on Mixamo. It's probably better to use the files I provided with the chapter since many MoCap files in Mixamo have similar names and later in the chapter, we want to make sure we're using the same source files as the ones I provided. The source FBX files can be found here: https://github.com/PacktPublishing/Unreal-Engine-5-Character-Creation-Animation-and-Cinematics/blob/main/Chapter18/MixamoMocapSource.zip.

You can execute the following steps – just discard the downloaded files afterward:

1. Use your internet browser and go to https://www.mixamo.com/.

2. Click on **Sign Up**.

3. Create an account like any standard website where you need an account.

    Once you sign up for a free account, you will have access to the https://www.mixamo.com/ website and its resources.

4. Click on the **Characters** tab at the top.

5. In the search bar, search for xbot, select it, and download it by clicking the **DOWNLOAD** button on the right of the screen, as shown in *Figure 18.1*.

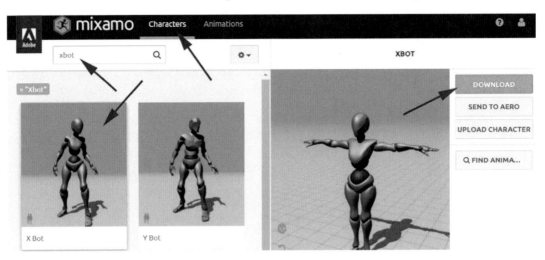

Figure 18.1 – Download standard skinned female character

This is simply their standard female character skinned to a skeleton without any animation on it. To use MoCap in UE, it's better to have a skinned character without any animation on it. This is so that you can have one skinned character file that you can play multiple animations on. It's like our Robot Drone has one skinned skeleton and animation rig but we can play multiple animations on it.

6. Click on **DOWNLOAD** to go into the **DOWNLOAD SETTINGS** pop-up window. Select **Format** as **FBX Binary(.fbx)** and **Pose** as **T-pose**. Next, click on **DOWNLOAD** as shown in *Figure 18.2*.

Figure 18.2 – DOWNLOAD SETTINGS for standard female skinned character

This will download the xbot.fbx file to your computer. We will include this same file in the files accompanying this chapter.

7. Next, look for sitting idle MoCap animations.

8. Click on the **Animations** tab at the top, and search for `sit`. Select the **Sitting Rubbing Arm** animation as shown in *Figure 18.3*:

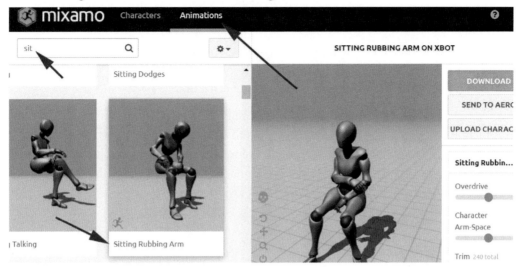

Figure 18.3 – Search and find the Sitting Rubbing Arm MoCap

9. Click on **DOWNLOAD** on the right of the screen and select the following settings:

-   **Format** as **FBX Binary(.fbx)**

-   **Skin** as **Without Skin**

-   **Frames per Second** as **30**

-   **Keyframe Reduction** as **none**

10. Click **DOWNLOAD** to download the `.fbx` as shown in *Figure 18.4*.

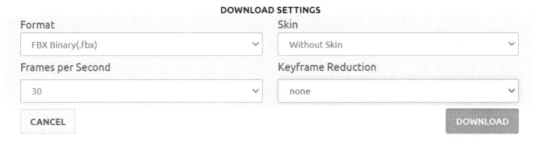

Figure 18.4 – Sitting Rubbing Arm MoCap download settings

Since we already downloaded the skinned skeleton in *Step 6*, for the animations, we don't need it again. By selecting, in the options in *Step 9*, **Skin** as **Without Skin**, it downloaded only the skeleton with the MoCap animation on it and not the skinned 3D model too.

11. Next, search for a **Stand Up** MoCap animation in Mixamo. The one I liked was on a male model. This is not a problem since Mixamo will map it intelligently to the female skeleton for preview once you select it as shown in *Figure 18.5*.

12. On the right of the Mixamo interface, under **DOWNLOAD**, there are some sliders as shown in *Figure 18.5* where you can adjust MoCap animations. Different MoCap animations in Mixamo have different sliders sometimes and it's worth playing around with them, to customize the MoCap if needed.

    For example, I changed the **Seat** slider from **50** to **40** since that lowered her sitting position, changed the **Rate** slider from **50** to **60** to make it a bit faster, changed **Overdrive** from **50** to **60** to exaggerate the movement a bit; and **Character Arm-Space** from **50** to **58** to make it a bit wider since they were clipping the legs. See the sliders in Mixamo as shown in *Figure 18.5*.

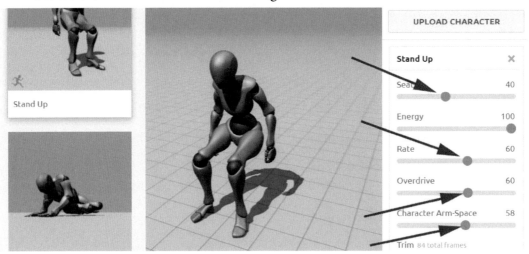

Figure 18.5 – Slider adjustment for the Stand Up MoCap in Mixamo

13. Download the Stand Up MoCap `.fbx` file using the same settings as *Step 9*.

14. Search for and select the **Standing Idle** MoCap animation and download it using the same settings as *Step 9*.

15. Search for and select the **Female Stop and Start** MoCap animation where she stands still, then starts walking forward for a few steps, and then stops again. I downloaded it using the same settings as *Step 9*.

16. Lastly, I found the **Button Pushing** MoCap animation and set **Character Arm-Space** from **50** to **62,** as shown in *Figure 18.6*, before downloading it using the same settings as *Step 9*.

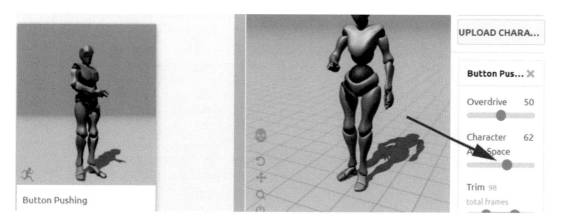

Figure 18.6 – Button Pushing MoCap

I hope this is a useful guide on how to get some free MoCap animations from Mixamo. As I said, all these files I downloaded are available in the chapter files at `https://github.com/PacktPublishing/Unreal-Engine-5-Character-Creation-Animation-and-Cinematics/blob/main/Chapter18/MixamoMocapSource.zip`.

Now that we know how to get free MoCap animations from an external source such as Mixamo, next, let's see how to get MoCap animations from the UE Marketplace itself.

Getting MoCap animations from the UE Marketplace

The UE Marketplace is a vast resource of UE-compatible content. Some of it is free, but some of it is paid for since it was created by external content creators that then sell on the UE Marketplace.

Since you have already installed UE, it will have installed the Epic Games Launcher app with it. We can find the UE Marketplace in the Epic Games Launcher software application:

1. If you're unsure how to open the Epic Games Launcher, search for it in the Microsoft Windows **Search** tab at the bottom left of the Windows desktop and open it from there by clicking on **Epic Games Launcher App** as shown in *Figure 18.7*.

Figure 18.7 – Open Epic Games Launcher from the Windows desktop

2. In the Epic Games Launcher app, on the left panel, if you select **Unreal Engine** and then **Marketplace** at the top, you can search for motion capture in the search bar. It will come up with lots of free and paid-for MoCap content. You can also search for something such as animation or any related keywords to find an animation or MoCap content as shown in *Figure 18.8*.

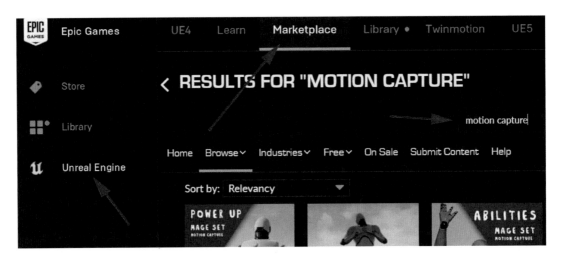

Figure 18.8 – Search for UE Marketplace MoCap animation content

3. Let's download some free MoCap/animation content from the Marketplace. As an example, in the UE Marketplace, search for `animation starter pack` and select it as shown in *Figure 18.9*.

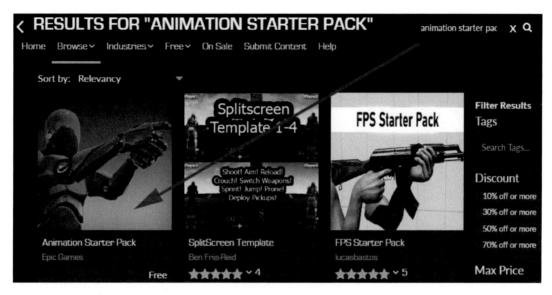

Figure 18.9 – Search for animation starter pack

4. In the next window, after selecting **Animation Starter Pack**, click on **Free** to get it and it will be added to your UE Library as shown in *Figure 18.10*.

Figure 18.10 – Get Animation Starter Pack

5. You can access this newly added **Animation Starter Pack** in the library, on the tab at the top, next to **Marketplace**, under **VAULT**. From there, you can select **Add To Project** to add these resources and files to your own project as shown in *Figure 18.11*. This will bring up the next window to select the project you want to add it to.

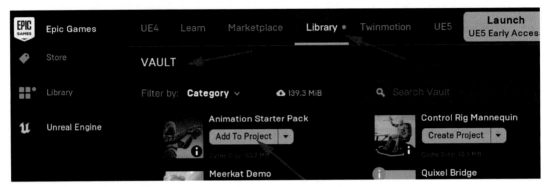

Figure 18.11 – Add Animation Starter Pack to a project

6. Select the project you want to add this content to and click on **Add To Project**.

7. Now, if you open the project you added **Animation Starter Pack** to, in the project's **Content Drawer**, you'll see an `AnimStarterPack` folder under `Content` consisting of a collection of MoCap animations as shown in *Figure 18.12*:

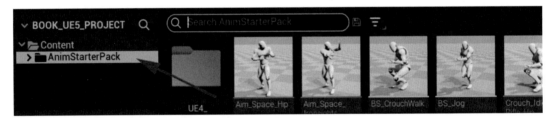

Figure 18.12 – Animation Starter Pack in the project's Content Drawer

8. If you want to find the **Skinned Skeleton character** that these animations in the pack can play on, it's in the **Content | AnimStarterPack | UE4_Mannequin | Mesh** folder in the project **Content Drawer** as shown in *Figure 18.13*.

Figure 18.13 – Skinned Skeleton character for Starter Animation Pack folder

You have now learned how to add MoCap and animation content from the UE Marketplace to your project. Next, we will learn how to use this MoCap on the MetaHuman we created in *Chapter 8, Use MetaHuman to Create a Photo-Realistic Human for UE5.*

Retargeting MoCap animations to a MetaHuman skeleton

In UE, there's a way to retarget or share animations between character skeletons. Retargeting an animation is like converting it to work and be playable from one skeleton to a different skeleton. So, for example, you can use the MoCap we downloaded from Mixamo on their standard female skeleton and retarget it to play on our MetaHuman skeleton.

These two skeletons have different bones and bone names, and even proportions and sizes, but UE has a built-in way to cleverly map (retarget) and interpret animations between them. But for UE to do that, we need to set it up first.

However, first, let's import the Mixamo MoCap .fbx files into UE.

Importing Maximo MoCap into UE

Here's the process to import Maximo MoCap FBX files into UE:

1. In the top left of the Content Drawer, while in the Content folder, click on + **ADD** | **New Folder**. Name it MoCap_From_Mixamo as shown in *Figure 18.14*.

Figure 18.14 – Add New Folder

2.   Open the new `MoCap_From_Mixamo` folder and click on **Import** on the top bar of the Content Drawer to import content into this folder as shown in *Figure 18.15*.

Figure 18.15 – Import MoCap content

3.   Select `xbot.fbx` in the next pop-up window after browsing to the location it is stored in and then click **Open**.

4.   After clicking **Open**, the **FBX Import Options** dialogue window will appear. Make sure **Import Mesh** is checked and **Import Animations** is unchecked as shown in *Figure 18.16*.

We want to make sure there's no animation on this import since this will be the clean Skinned Skeleton Mesh that the MoCap animations can play on.

5.   Click on **Import All** at the bottom of the **FBX Import Options** to import.

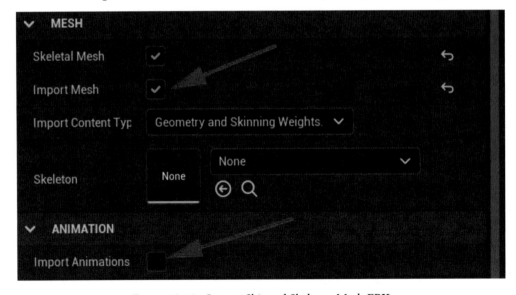

Figure 18.16 – Import Skinned Skeleton Mesh FBX

If there is a **Message Log** window that appears after the import with some warnings, most of the time you can ignore this. It is normally minor things UE could not resolve in the FBX file from an external source. Most of the time, it has no bearing on the visual result of the import.

6. Now, inside the `MoCap_From_Mixamo` folder, add another folder called `MoCap` as shown in *Figure 18.17*.

Figure 18.17 – Add MoCap folder

This is just to keep the animations organized in their own folder, so they're easier to find later.

7. While inside the `MoCap` folder, on the top bar, click **Import** to import the animations into this folder. In the next pop-up window, browse to their location folder and select all the Mixamo MoCap `.fbx` files to import them all at the same time.

After clicking **Open**, the **FBX Import Options** dialogue window will again appear, but this time, the settings look slightly different because UE can detect that there's no skinned mesh included with the skeleton. UE detects that these are probably animations on the skeleton only. We need to define what skinned mesh we want these animations to play on in UE. We need to select the Mixamo `xbot` skeleton we imported in *Step 2* and *Step 3*.

8. In the **FBX Import Options** dialogue window, under **MESH**, next to **Skeleton**, click on **None**. From there, you can select `xbot_Skeleton` as shown in *Figure 18.18*. Click **Import All** at the bottom of the **FBX Import Options** to import.

Figure 18.18 – MoCap animation FBX import settings

The imported animations will appear in the `MoCap` folder, and they will be represented on the skinned `xbot_Skeleton` mesh as shown in *Figure 18.19*.

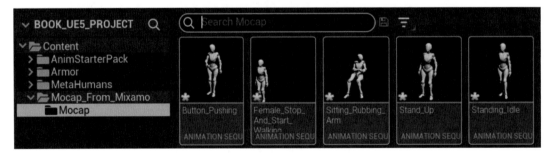

Figure 18.19 – Imported MoCap in Content Drawer

Now, with our Mixamo xbot Skinned Skeleton Mesh and MoCap imported, we can move on to setting up the retargeting setting for the Mixamo skeleton.

Setting up retargeting on the Mixamo skeleton

In the next steps, we will set up the retargeting settings on the Mixamo skeleton. The biggest part of this is to confirm to UE which skeleton bone is which body part. UE can then do its clever calculations in the background to map the motion from one skeleton to another.

In the full UE5 release, the way retargeting works has changed significantly from previous versions of UE. Two new **Animation Node** types are used to achieve retargeting and they are the **IK Rig** node and the **IK Retargeter** node.

Let's set up our first **IK Rig** node on our Mixamo xbot skeleton:

1. In UE, add a new folder under the **Content** folder and name it `Mocap_Retarget`.

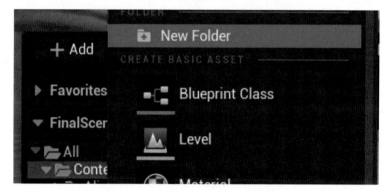

Figure 18.20 – Create a new folder

2. Open the new **Mocap_Retarget** folder in the Content Drawer and right-click on an empty spot in the folder to bring up the right-click menu. Then, under **Animation**, select **IK Rig** as shown in *Figure 18.21.*

Figure 18.21 – Create an IK Rig node

3.   Select **xbot Skeletal Mesh** from the list as shown in *Figure 18.22*.

Figure 18.22 – Select xbot Skeletal Mesh

4.   Name the new **IK Rig** node NewIKRig_xbot as shown in *Figure 18.23*.

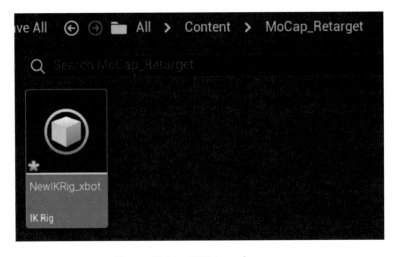

Figure 18.23 – IK Rig node name

5. Double-click the **NewIKRig_xbot** node to open the IK Rig interface.

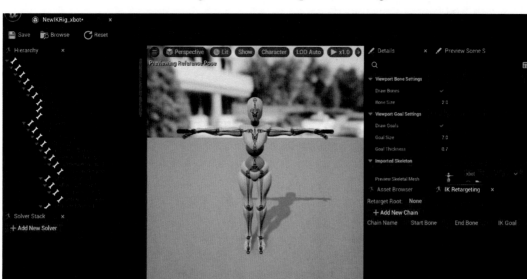

Figure 18.24 – IK Rig interface

In the IK Rig interface, you can define different body parts by their bone chains. This is a very open system compared to the old way of doing retargeting in UE where it only really worked well on humanoid characters. With this new system, it is much more open and much more powerful, but the user has to use much more of their own common sense to get good results.

Since we're retargeting MoCap from one humanoid character to another, we need to define the main separate body parts that we want to retarget. On a humanoid character, this will typically be **Head**, **Neck**, **Spine**, **LeftArm**, **RightArm**, **LeftLeg**, **RightLeg**, and **Hips**.

Now, let's define these body parts by starting with **Head**.

6. Select the **Head** bone, then right-click and select **New Retarget Chain from Selected Bones** as seen in *Figure 18.25*.

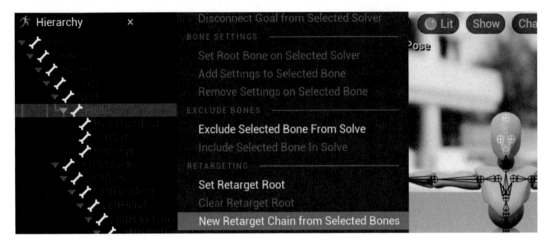

Figure 18.25 – New Retarget Chain from Selected Bones

7. In this case, we can keep **Chain Name** as Head as shown in *Figure 18.26*. Click **OK** to complete.

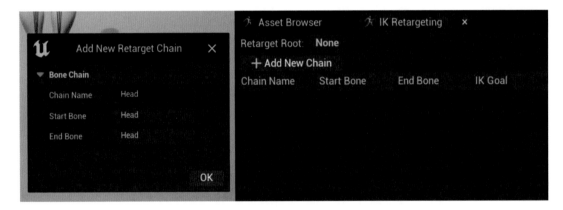

Figure 18.26 – Add New Retarget Chain

The new chain will appear in the **IK Retargeting** list tab as seen in *Figure 18.27*.

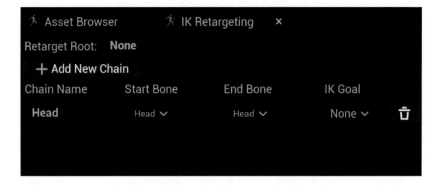

Figure 18.27 – New IK Retargeting chain

8. Select the **Neck** bone, then right-click and select **New Retarget Chain from Selected Bones** as seen in *Figure 18.28*. Also, keep **Chain Name** as Neck and click **OK**. The **Neck** bone chain will appear in the **IK Retargeting** list.

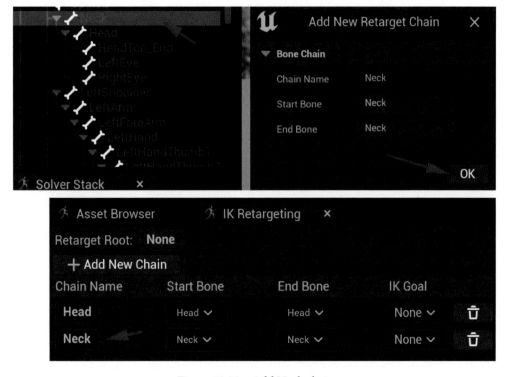

Figure 18.28 – Add Neck chain

9. Next, for the spine, select the following bones in this order: **Spine, Spine1**, and then **Spine2** as seen in *Figure 18.29*. Then, right-click and select **New Retarget Chain from Selected Bones**. Keep **Chain Name** as `Spine` and click **OK**.

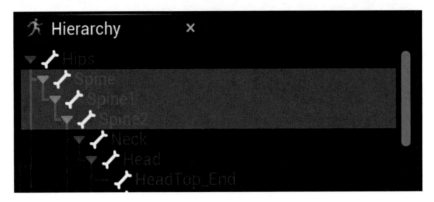

Figure 18.29 – Spine chain

10. For the left arm, select **LeftShoulder, LeftArm, LeftForeArm**, and **LeftHand** as shown in *Figure 18.30*. Then, right-click and select **New Retarget Chain from Selected Bones**.

Figure 18.30 – Left arm chain

11. However, in this case, change **Chain Name** to `Left_Arm` as shown in *Figure 18.31*. This is so the name is more descriptive and consistent.

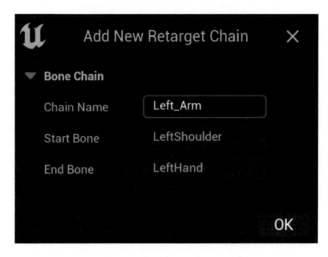

Figure 18.31 – Chain Name Left_Arm

12. Repeat this process on the corresponding right arm bones and change **Chain Name** to `Right_Arm`.

13. For the left leg, we select the **LeftUpLeg**, **LeftLeg**, and **LeftFoot** bones, then right-click and select **New Retarget Chain from Selected Bones** and set **Chain Name** as `Left_Leg` as seen in *Figure 18.32*.

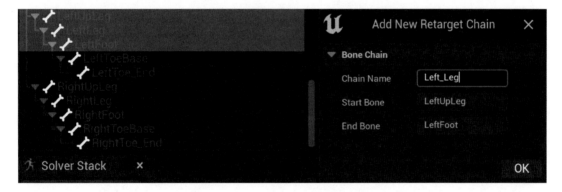

Figure 18.32 – Left_Leg Chain Name

14. Repeat this process on the corresponding right leg bones and set **Chain Name** to `Right_Leg`.

15. Finally, select the **Hips** bone and right-click, then select **Set Retarget Root** as shown in *Figure 18.33*.

Hierarchy
Hips
Spine
Spine1
Spine2
Neck
Head
HeadTop_End
LeftEye
EXCLUDE BONES
Exclude Selected Bone From Solve
Include Selected Bone In Solve
RETARGETING
Set Retarget Root
Clear Retarget Root
New Retarget Chain from Selected Bones

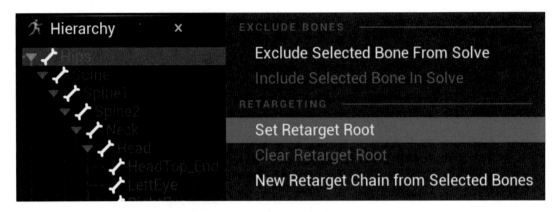

Figure 18.33 – Set Retarget Root

The resulting **IK Retargeting** list should look as in *Figure 18.34*.

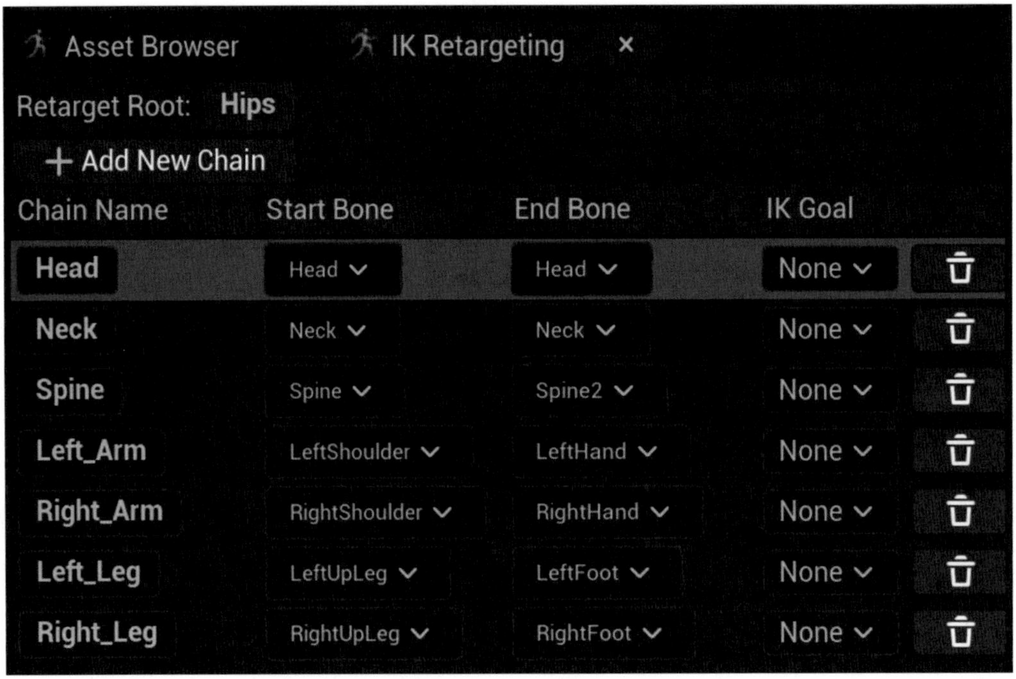

Asset Browser
IK Retargeting
Retarget Root: Hips
Add New Chain
Chain Name
Start Bone
End Bone
IK Goal
Head Head Head None
Neck Neck Neck None
Spine Spine Spine2 None
Left_Arm LeftShoulder LeftHand None
Right_Arm RightShoulder RightHand None
Left_Leg LeftUpLeg LeftFoot None
Right_Leg RightUpLeg RightFoot None

Figure 18.34 – IK Retargeting list final result

16. Save this IK Rig node setup by clicking **Save** at the top left of the interface.

Congratulations! You've set up your first IK Rig node.

You have probably noticed that we only selected the main bones of every chain. This is roughly in line with the main universal IK or FK chains in these kinds of body parts.

For the arms, we left out things such as fingers, but we included what would be the clavicle joint. The clavicle joint is not normally included in an IK chain, but it has a big influence on the arm in general, so it is better to include it. For the legs, we left out the ball and toe joints since things such as toes and fingers might just complicate things for a simple retarget like this.

Next, we will set the IK Rig node up for the MetaHuman skeleton.

Setting up retargeting on the MetaHuman skeleton

To set up the **IK Rig** node on the MetaHuman skeleton, the basic process is almost the same as the Mixamo xbot setup. However, because the MetaHuman rig is a far more complex rig with multiple skeletons linked via complex rigging, we just need to make sure we set the retargeting up on the correct asset in the first place.

If the **MetaHumans** and **SciFiGirl** assets you created in *Chapter 8, Use MetaHuman to Create a Photo-Realistic Human for UE5*, are not already in your project file, you can migrate them into your current project using the instructions in *Chapter 20, Using Sequencer to Construct Your Final Scene*, in the *Migrating UE content between projects section*. Alternatively, you can download the final example project and get it from within that at `https://github.com/PacktPublishing/Unreal-Engine-5-Character-Creation-Animation-and-Cinematics/tree/main/FullFinalUE5Project`.

To find the correct skeleton asset, do the following:

1. In the **Content Drawer**, **Content | MetaHuman | SciFiGirl** folder where our female MetaHuman is saved, find the **BP_SciFiGirl** blueprint and drag it into the viewport as shown in *Figure 18.35*.

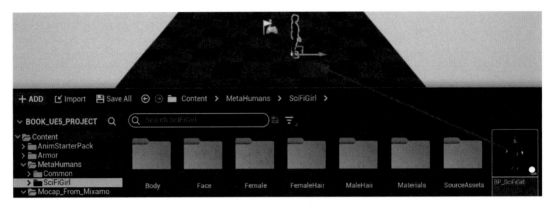

Figure 18.35 – Drag the MetaHuman blueprint into the level

2. Select it in the viewport so that there's an orange selection line around it. In the **Details** panel on the right, select **Body (Inherited)**. Then, under **MESH | Skeletal Mesh**, double-click on the box to the right of it. That will open the asset in UE as shown in *Figure 18.36*.

Figure 18.36 – Find the MetaHuman skeleton asset

Once open, this may visually look weird and broken with just some polygons showing. Don't worry about this, we're still not at the skeleton asset itself. This is the f_med_nrw_body (female med) skinned model. This might be different depending on the style of MetaHuman we created.

3. To get to the skeleton asset itself, click on the skeleton asset icon in the top bar as shown in *Figure 18.37*.

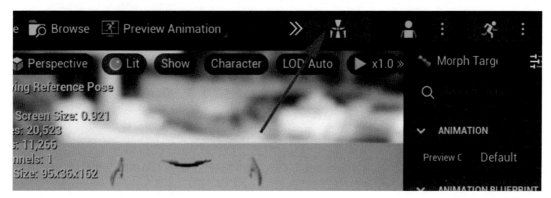

Figure 18.37 – Open the MetaHuman skeleton asset

Next, we want to make sure we apply **Preview Mesh** to our skeleton, so we can see our animations clearly when we retarget them.

4. In the **Preview Scene Settings** tab on the right, under **MESH**, set **Preview Mesh** to f_med_nrw_preview. Make sure to click **Apply To Asset** as shown in *Figure 18.38*.

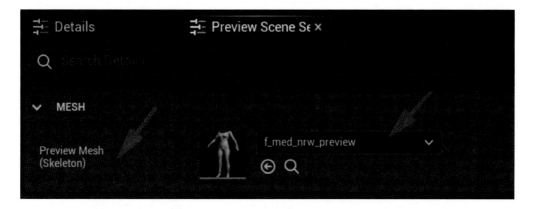

Figure 18.38 – Apply the preview asset to the MetaHuman skeleton

She will unfortunately have no head. This is normal since, on the MetaHuman, the facial skeleton is separate.

Now, let us set up the IK Rig node on the MetaHuman skeleton.

5. In the **Mocap_Retarget** folder, right-click on an empty spot in the folder to bring up the right-click menu. Then, under **Animation**, select **IK Rig**. Select f_med_nrw_preview as shown in *Figure 18.39*.

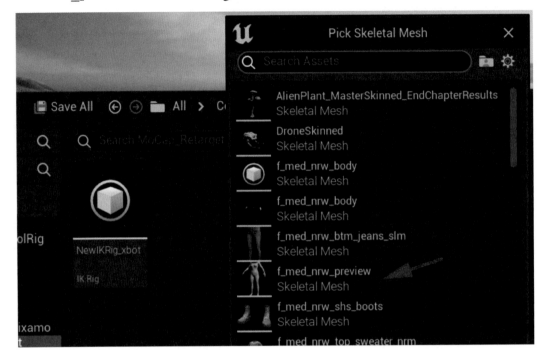

Figure 18.39 – Select the MetaHuman skeleton

6. Name the new **IK Rig** node NewIKRig_meta as shown in *Figure 18.40*.

Figure 18.40 – NewIKRig_meta node

7. Double-click the **NewIKRig_meta** node to open the interface.

    Just like we did in the *Setting up retargeting on the Mixamo skeleton* section, we will define the body parts of this skeleton. We will use the same naming convention so it's easier for UE to match up the different limbs.

8. Select the **head** bone, then right-click and select **New Retarget Chain from Selected Bones** and change **Chain Name** to Head with a capital letter, just like the previous setup for the **NewIKRig_xbot** node.

9. Next, select the **neck_01** and **neck_02** bones, then right-click and select **New Retarget Chain from Selected Bones** and change **Chain Name** to Neck, just like the previous setup for the **NewIKRig_xbot** node.

10. Select the **spine_01**, **spine_02**, **spine_03**, **spine_04**, and **spine_05** bones, then right-click and select **New Retarget Chain from Selected Bones** and change **Chain Name** to Spine.

> **Note**
>
> You will notice that in this skeleton, the number of neck and spine bones is different from the **NewIKRig_xbot** IK Rig node. This doesn't matter; UE can still interpret this and retarget the animations.

11. On the left arm, we select the **clavicle_l**, **upperarm_l**, **lowerarm_l**, and **hand_l** bones as seen in *Figure 18.41*, then right-click and select **New Retarget Chain from Selected Bones** and change **Chain Name** to Left_Arm.

Figure 18.41 – Left arm bone selection

You will notice that I ignore all the extra bones in the arm chain and only select the main arm bones.

12. Repeat this process for the corresponding right arm bones and change **Chain Name** to `Right_Arm`.
13. Next, for the left leg, select the **thigh_l**, **calf_l**, and **foot_l** bones, then right-click and select **New Retarget Chain from Selected Bones** and change **Chain Name** to `Left_Leg`.
14. Repeat this process for the corresponding right leg bones and change **Chain Name** to `Right_Leg`.
15. Select the **pelvis** bone, right-click, and select **Set Retarget Root**.

    The result should look like *Figure 18.42*:

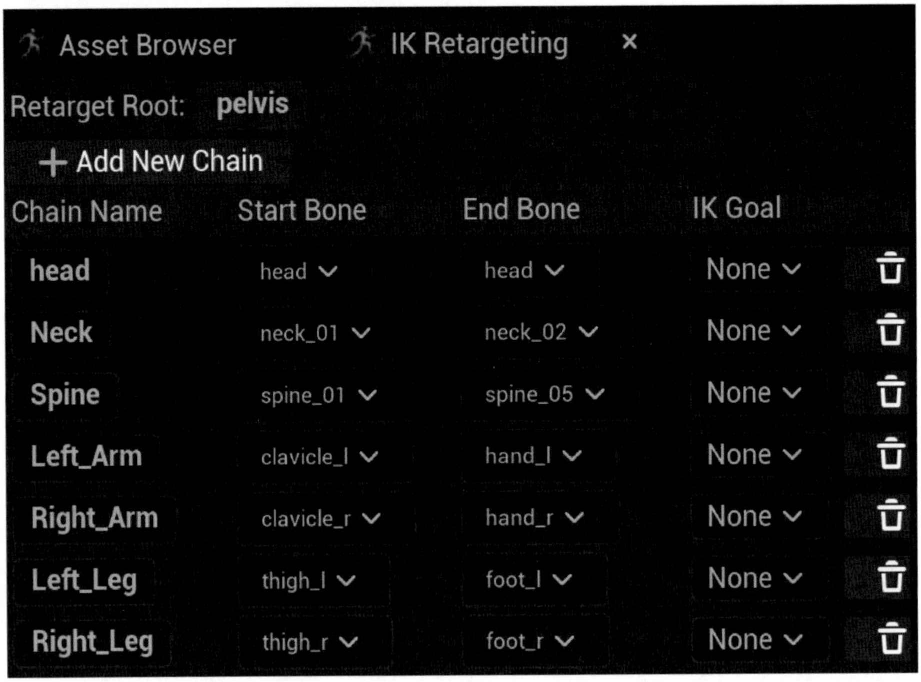
Asset Browser
IK Retargeting
Retarget Root: pelvis
+ Add New Chain
Chain Name
Start Bone
End Bone
IK Goal
head
head
head
None
Neck
neck_01
neck_02
None
Spine
spine_01
spine_05
None
Left_Arm
clavicle_l
hand_l
None
Right_Arm
clavicle_r
hand_r
None
Left_Leg
thigh_l
foot_l
None
Right_Leg
thigh_r
foot_r
None

Figure 18.42 – MetaHuman IK Retargeting list results

16. Save this IK Rig node setup by clicking **Save** at the top left of the interface.

Retargeting is now set up on both our Mixamo and MetaHuman skeletons. Now comes the fun part. Let's retarget some MoCap animation from the Mixamo source to our female MetaHuman

Retargeting Mixamo MoCap animation to the MetaHuman

All the hard work in the retargeting setup has been done now. Compared to the setup, the retargeting itself is the easy part.

To retarget the animations, we need the second kind of node called IK Retargeter. Let's create one:

1.   Still in the **Mocap_Retarget** folder, right-click on an empty spot to bring up the right-click menu and select **IK Retargeter**.

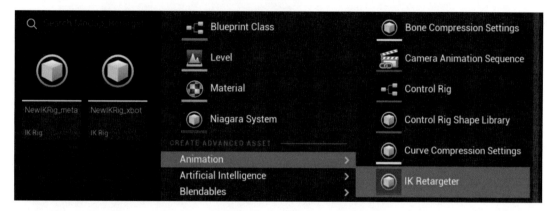

Figure 18.43 – Creating an IK Retargeter

2.   In the next window, it will ask you to **Pick IK Rig To Copy Animation From**. Since we're retargeting animations from the xbot to the MetaHuman, we need to select **NewIKRig_xbot** as shown in *Figure 18.44*.

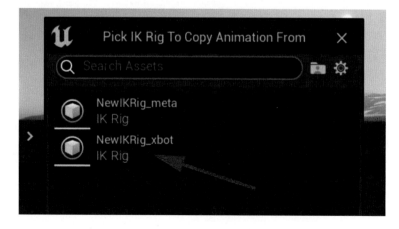

Figure 18.44 – Selecting NewIKRig_xbot

The new IK Retargeter is now created. Name it `xbot_retargeter` (see *Figure 18.45*).

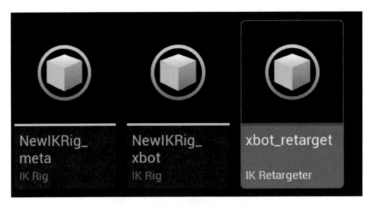

Figure 18.45 – Naming the new IK Retargeter

3. Double-click the **xbot_retarget** asset to open the IK Retargeter interface.

4. In the IK Retargeter interface, on the **Details** tab, find **Target IKRig Asset**. Expand the drop-down menu and select **NewIKRig_meta** as the target asset, as shown in *Figure 18.46*.

Figure 18.46 – Select target rig

The MetaHuman rig will appear next to the xbot rig. There's also an **Asset Browser** tab that lists all the animations associated with the xbot.

5.   In the **Asset Browser** tab, double-click on the **Button_Pushing** animation as shown in *Figure 18.47*.

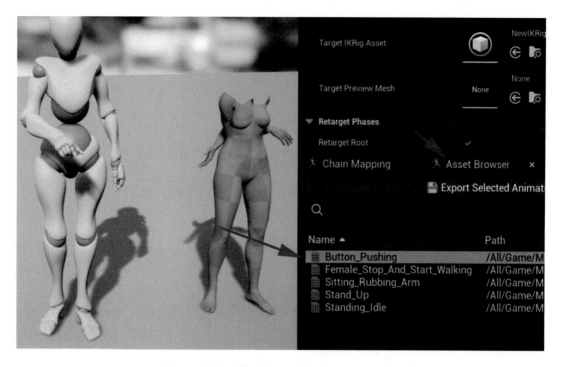

Figure 18.47 – Play Button_Pushing animation

You will notice that the animation is being retargeted to the MetaHuman rig, but the arms look incorrect. The first thing to check is **Chain Mapping**. Next to the **Asset Browser** tab is the **Chain Mapping** tab.

6. Open the **Chain Mapping** tab as shown in *Figure 18.48*.

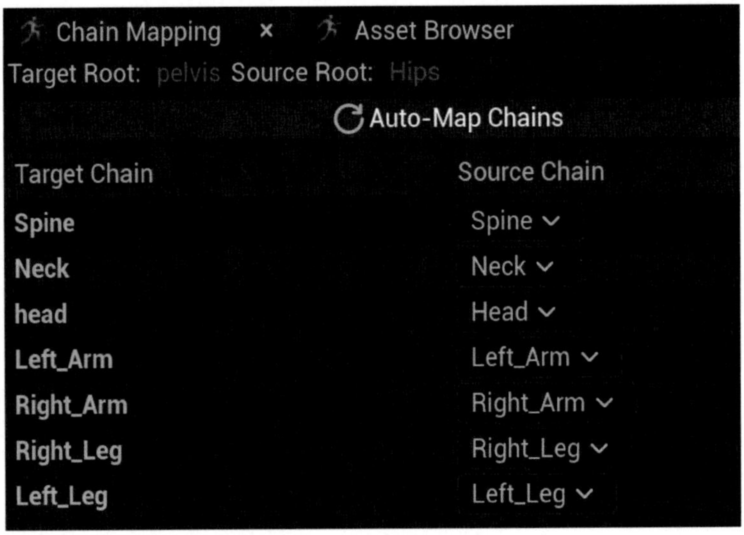

Figure 18.48 – Chain Mapping tab

In the **Chain Mapping** tab, you can see how UE matched up the body part IK chains we set up on the respective **IK Rig** assets. Sometimes, UE doesn't get it right, especially if the naming was not the same or close enough. If it is mismatched, you can fix it in the **Chain Mapping** tab by using the drop-down menus on the **Source Chain** side and selecting the correct match.

So, we know now that **Chain Mapping** is *not* the problem. The other thing it could be is the **retarget pose**. This is the initial pose UE uses to determine where the limbs are. However, if these poses are too different between the two rigs it is trying to retarget, it can cause problems.

To check and edit these poses, do the following:

1.   Click on the **Edit Pose** button on the top menu as shown in *Figure 18.49*.

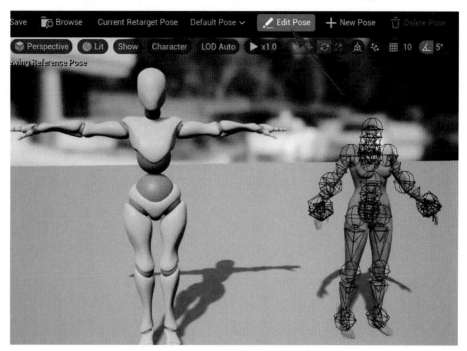

Figure 18.49 – Edit retarget pose

Here is our problem. The base retarget poses are too different. The xbot is in a T-pose (looks like a T) and the MetaHuman is in an A-pose (looks like an A) when it comes to the arms. No wonder UE is having problems calculating the retarget. Let's fix that.

2. With **Edit Pose** on, select the arm bones in the viewport and try to match the MetaHuman rig arm pose to that of the xbot by rotating them with the rotate tool as shown in *Figure 18.50*.

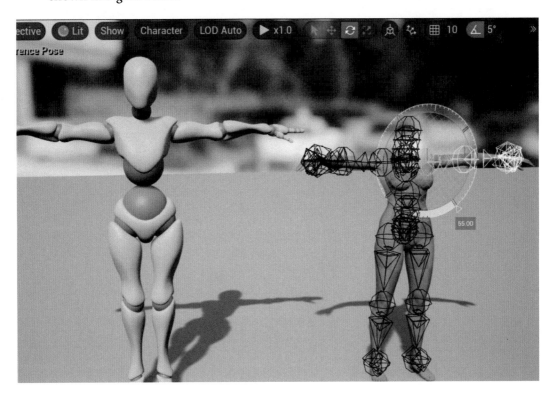

Figure 18.50 – Edit retarget pose

3. When you are finished editing the retarget pose, toggle **Edit Pose** off. Go back to the **Assets Browser** tab and select animations from the list by double-clicking on them, and see the results when you play them.

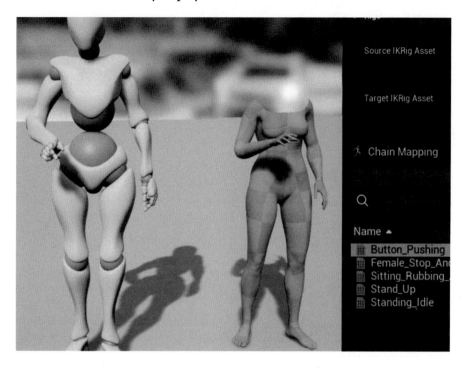

Figure 18.51 – Test retarget pose edit

As you can see, it is already much better, but you can go back and forth between **Edit Pose** and testing until you get the best possible results.

Bear in mind that what you are seeing in this editor is just a preview of the retargeting. Once you're happy with the retargeting preview, you can finalize the retarget by exporting the animations to the MetaHuman rig.

4. Select the animations you want to finally retarget in **Asset Browser** and click **Export Selected Animations** as shown in *Figure 18.52*.

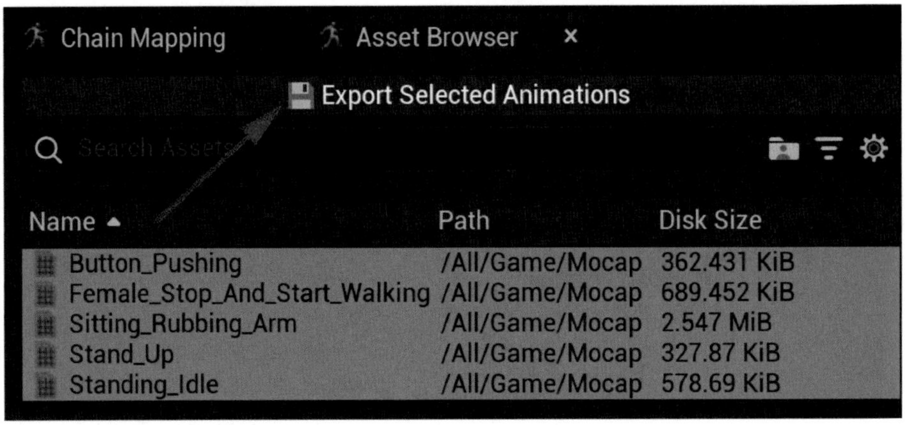

Figure 18.52 – Export retargeted animations

5. UE will then ask you to specify a folder. Export to the **MoCap_Retarget** folder to make sure you don't overwrite existing content.

You can follow the same process to set up retargeting on the UE Marketplace assets using the Mannequin skeleton or any other skeleton rig for that matter. You can even map a human arm motion to that of a spider leg if you get creative with this kind of retarget setup, so feel free to experiment.

Congratulations, you just retargeted a whole set of Mixamo MoCap animations to the MetaHuman skeleton.

Summary

In this chapter, we learned how to export free MoCap animations from the Mixamo library and import them into UE. We learned how to find some animation and MoCap assets on the Unreal Engine Marketplace and import them into our project. We then learned how to set up retargeting on both the Mixamo xbot skeleton and the MetaHuman skeleton. Finally, we retargeted a whole set of MoCap animations to the MetaHuman skeleton.

With this knowledge, you can find and share MoCap and other animation assets between different humanoid characters and you can let your creativity run free. Next, we will learn how to combine and edit this MoCap content on our female MetaHuman.

19
Motion Capture Editing and Cleanup Using Control Rig and Sequencer

In the previous chapter, we retargeted MoCap from Mixamo to our MetaHuman skeleton. In this chapter, we will learn how to bake it onto the MetaHuman Control Rig and, from there, edit it and combine it into one sequence.

Baking an animation between rigs is the process of transferring animations frame by frame from one to the other. This bakes a keyframe on every frame, so the target rig animation is an exact copy of the source animation in its relative world or local spaces. This will make more sense once you see practical examples as we progress through this chapter.

With the MoCap from the skeletons baked to the MetaHuman Control Rig, we can edit and clean up the animations. Editing MoCap well is a little bit of an art. In essence, what you're trying to do is keep as much of the subtle realistic core MoCap animation data as you can, while repurposing it for your own needs.

With MoCap cleanup, you try to work as *non-destructively* as you can. To work non-destructively means to keep the core of what you have, and make layered changes on top of it. In animation, you do this by layering additive layers of motion on top of your MoCap data to redirect it. For example, let's imagine you have a nice motion on your character's arm, but it clips through something at some point. Here, you can just add an additive layer of motion to redirect the motion so that the arm doesn't clip anymore.

Sometimes, you can just delete some MoCap frames and add your own, but you try to keep that for *ONLY* where needed. Sometimes, you can move or scale whole sets of keys or curves. There are many little methods and tricks to make MoCap do what you want it to do, without losing the realism that makes it great in the first place.

In this chapter and its *online only* bonus material, we will cover some of those methods and little tricks to effectively clean, combine, and repurpose MoCap.

In this chapter, we will cover the following topics:

- Planning your MoCap edit
- Baking the Stand_Up MoCap to the Control Rig
- Overview of the MetaHuman Control Rig
- Editing and cleaning the Stand_Up MoCap

Technical requirements

In this chapter, we will need to work with UE5 and the Mixamo website. You will need the following to complete this chapter:

- A computer that can run basic 3D animation software.
- Unreal Engine 5. You can download it from `https://www.unrealengine.com/en-US/download`.
- A basic understanding of how to navigate the UE 3D user interface. If you have skipped ahead, then please go back to *Chapter 6*, *Exploring Unreal Engine 5*.
- You must have completed *Chapter 15*, *Creating a Control Rig with Basic IK Controls for the Robot in UE5*, *Chapter 17*, *Creating Three Simple Animations for the Robot in EU5 Sequencer*, and *Chapter 18*, *Importing Motion Capture onto the MetaHuman Control Rig*.

The file related to this chapter are placed at `https://github.com/PacktPublishing/Unreal-Engine-5-Character-Creation-Animation-and-Cinematics/tree/main/Chapter19`

Planning Your MoCap edit

We have five pieces of MoCap: `Sitting_Rubbing_Arm`, `Stand_Up`, `Standing_Idle`, `Female_Stop_And_Start_Walking`, and `Button_Pushing`.

In this chapter, we want to clean them up and in *Chapter 20, Use Sequencer to Construct Your Final Scene*, combine them into one seamless animation. To make it easier to make them flow from one to the other when we combine them, we will edit them in such a way that they have a few specific poses where the animations can blend easily.

Animations can be blended in Sequencer so that they transition and blend smoothly between each other over time on the whole body, but issues usually arise with the feet. Imagine that you have two MoCap animations blending where the character is standing still, but in one of the MoCap pieces, the feet are wide apart, while in the other, they are close together. If we blend these two animations, the feet will slide over the ground when they're not supposed to during the blend. This kind of foot slide is very unnatural, so we must try to avoid that.

Another issue in blending can be the root bone. UE and most game engines normally like to have a root bone for the whole skeleton. It is normally on the ground between the feet of the character, at the origin of the scene. The child of the root bone in the skeleton is normally the hip/pelvis bone in a humanoid or animal rig. The most reliable point of reference for two animations to blend is the root bone.

The problem comes in if, say, in one animation, the hip bone is directly above the root bone and in the other animation, the hip bone is far away from the root bone, as shown in the following screenshot:

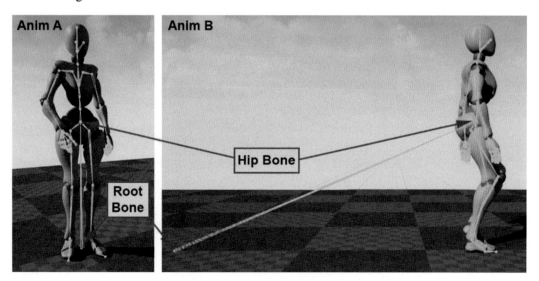

Figure 19.1 – Root bone and hip bone offset

When you try to blend from **Anim A** to **Anim B,** the character's hip position, relative to the root, is so different that the character will seem like it's flying off in a direction during the blend to compensate for the difference.

UE has ways of using a different bone as a reference point between blends, but this can get complicated and often has problems. Using the root bone as the blend reference between animations is the most reliable and easy way to set it up.

So, to combine our different MoCap animations and blend them easily, we need some consistent poses and root positions at the points we want to blend. After many years of doing this, I still prefer to do a little extra work in the beginning to sort this out before even attempting to combine and blend the animations. A little work and planning in the beginning can save you a lot of time and headaches later.

I think it might be helpful to set out exactly what we aim to achieve in this chapter in a visual way:

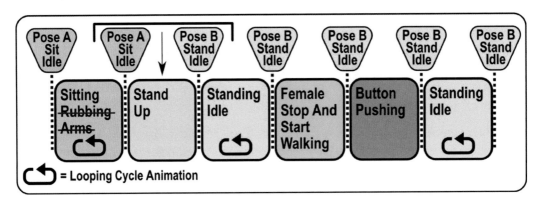

Figure 19.2 – MoCap edit plan

Our character will start sitting down, then get up, stand for a few moments, then walk forward a few steps, stop, press a button on her arm to activate the Robot Drone, and then keep standing, looking at the drone.

We will change the **Sitting_Rubbing_Arm** animation and remove the part where she is rubbing her arm. We could have kept this and cleaned it up, but it's a bit more complicated and time-consuming, so for this book, we'll just remove the rubbing arm part but keep it idle. We'll also make it an animation cycle, with the first and last frame being the same, so that we can loop it if we want to extend the time she is sitting down in the sequence.

However, the **Stand_Up** animation is probably where we want to start since it will have **Pose A Sit Idle** at the start before she stands up, and **Pose B Stand Idle** once she has stood up. Since it has both these poses, we may as well start with that animation first, then save the poses we create in that edit and take them to **Sitting Idle,** and then **Standing Idle** later.

With the **Standing_Idle** animation, we will take the **Pose B Stand Idle** pose we created and apply it to the **Standing Idle** animation at the beginning and end. This will turn it into an animation cycle so that we can also loop her standing still for as long as the sequence may require.

For the **Female_Stop_And_Start_Walking** animation, we will also edit and apply **Pose B Stand Idle** to the beginning and end. This is so that it can blend easily to the **Button_Pushing** animation, which, in return, blends back to **Standing Idle**. The **Standing Idle** animation can then play its cycle for as long as we want the character to stand there at the end of the sequence.

We will change the **Button_Pushing** animation so that instead of her pushing a button in the air in front of her, she lifts her left arm and pushes it on her arm.

So, now that we know what we want to achieve and have planned it out, we will start with baking the **Stand_Up** animation to the Control Rig for editing.

Baking the Stand_Up MoCap to the Control Rig

Before we can edit the **Stand_Up** MoCap animation, we need to bake it to our Control Rig. To do that, follow these steps:

1. In the **Content Drawer** interface, under **MoCap_From_Maximo | MoCap**, add a new folder by clicking + **ADD** in the top-left corner of the **Content Drawer** interface. Name it `CleanupSequences`, as shown in the following screenshot:

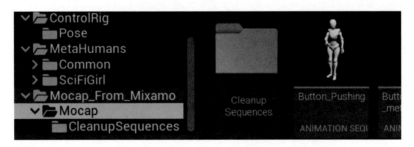

Figure 19.3 – Creating a folder for cleanup purposes

2. On the top bar of the main UE interface, create a new **Level Sequence** by selecting **Cinematics | Add New Level Sequence** and save it as StandUpCleanup in the CleanupSequences folder, as shown in the following screenshot:

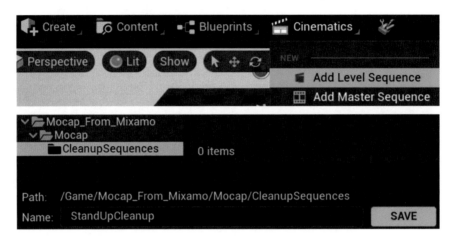

Figure 19.4 – Add Cleanup Sequence for Stand_Up MoCap

The new empty **StandUpCleanup** sequence will open in **Sequencer**. We will use this Level Sequence just to clean up and edit the **Stand_Up** MoCap animation.

3. In the **Content Drawer** interface, open the **Content | MetaHuman | SciFiGirl** folder. Drag the BP_SciFiGirl blueprint into the empty **StandUpCleanup** Sequencer timeline, as shown in the following screenshot:

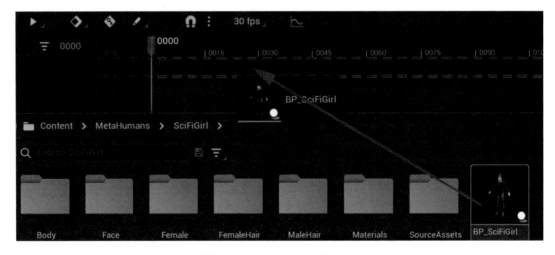

Figure 19.5 – Adding the MetaHuman blueprint to Sequencer

4. In Sequencer's **TRACK** window, under **BP Sci Fi Girl | Body**, find **MetaHuman_ControlRig** and delete it by selecting it and pressing *Delete* on your keyboard or by using the right-click context menu (the one that pops up if you right-click on the item), as shown in the following screenshot:

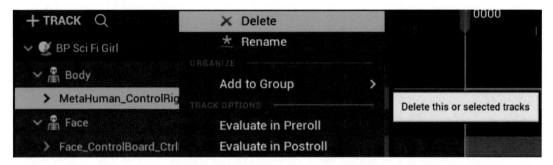

Figure 19.6 – Deleting the Control Rig

We are deleting this because it will override the raw skeleton animation that we will add next and stop it from playing.

At the time of writing this book, UE5 was still in early access and only the old retargeting tools were available from UE4. This redundant retargeting tool was used to retarget the original animations from Mixamo. This book has since been updated, but I based this lesson on those older retargeted animations since they teach better lessons about the MoCap cleanup process than the ones created with the new retargeting method.

You can download the **Stand_Up_meta** source animation that the following lesson is based on, as well as the bonus material animations, here: https://github.com/PacktPublishing/Unreal-Engine-5-Character-Creation-Animation-and-Cinematics/tree/main/Chapter19

You just need to add these to your UE project folders.

You can also find the old retargeted animations in the example final project file, which can be downloaded from here: https://github.com/PacktPublishing/Unreal-Engine-5-Character-Creation-Animation-and-Cinematics/tree/main/FullFinalUE5Project. Installation instructions have also been provided.

The animations can be found under **Content/Mocap_From_Mixamo/Mocap**.

1.   In Sequencer's **TRACK** window, under **BP Sci Fi Girl**, to the right of the **Body** item, select + **TRACK| Animation**. When you click on **Animation**, a list of compatible animations will appear that can be played on the MetaHuman skeleton. In the **Search Assets** field at the top of this list, type in `meta` to find our retargeted MoCap animations and select **Stand_Up_meta**, as shown in the following screenshot:

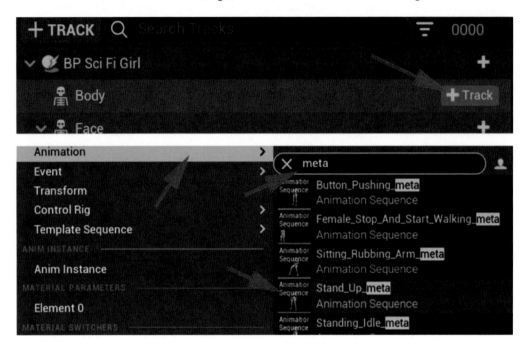

Figure 19.7 – Adding an Animation track

This will add the **Standing Up** MoCap to the MetaHuman skeleton, as shown in *Figure 19.8*.

2.   To make sure we know where the real floor level is, select the floor in the Viewport and make sure its **Location** is set to 0.0, 0.0, 0.0 in the **Details** panel to the right of the main UE interface, as shown in *Figure 19.8*. In newer versions of UE5, the default floor may already be on the ground plane, so you won't need to do this step.

3.   In the Sequencer timeline, set the active time range from **0000** to **0082**, which is the exact length of the **Stand_Up_meta** MoCap animation:

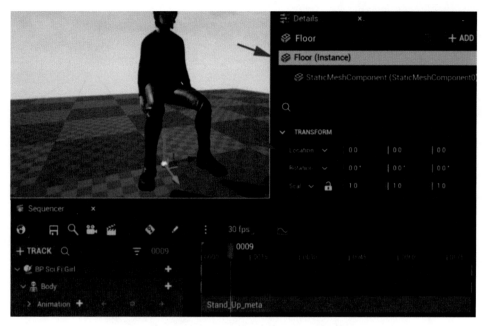

Figure 19.8 – Floor and timeline Active Range

> **Note**
>
> We now have the **Stand_Up_meta** MoCap animation playing on the
> MetaHuman skeleton. The skeleton animations play directly on the
> MetaHuman skeleton. This is different from the Control Rig animations.
> Control Rig animations play on the controllers, which, in turn, control the
> skeleton. In **Sequencer**, we can bake skeletal animations from the skeleton
> to the Control Rig or bake Control Rig animations from the Control Rig to
> the skeleton. We may do this several times back and forth during the cleanup
> process, depending on what we want to do.

As you can see, when we press play, there are some *issues*, such as the hands going
through the legs and she is floating off the floor. However, if we want to edit and
fix these issues, we need to bake this skeletal animation to the Control Rig. Let's
do that now.

4. In Sequencer's **TRACK** window, under **BP Sci Fi Girl**, right-click on the **Body** item. Select **Bake To Control Rig**; a list of available Control Rigs will appear. Select **MetaHuman_ControlRig**, as shown in the following screenshot:

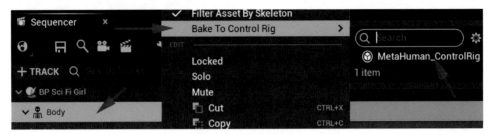

Figure 19.9 – Bake to Control Rig

5. The **Bake To Control Rig** setting window will pop up next. It's very important to uncheck **Reduce Keys**. We don't want to lose any of our MoCap data at this point. Then, click **Bake To Control Rig**, as shown in the following screenshot:

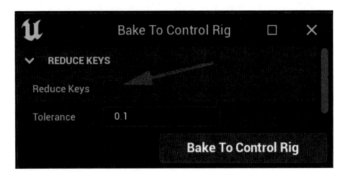

Figure 19.10 – Uncheck Reduce Keys

The skeletal animation will now be baked to the Control Rig. Once that's happened, the Control Rig controllers will appear in the viewport. Also, in the **TRACK** window under the **Body** item, there's now a **MetaHuman_ControlRig** track, just under the MoCap **Animation** track. We don't need this **Animation** track item anymore.

6. To keep our Sequencer timeline clean, we can delete the **Animation** track now by selecting it in the **TRACK** window and pressing *Delete* on our keyboard. It may get confusing otherwise since we may need to repeat this process a few times. Hence, it's a good habit to get rid of redundant tracks as we go:

Figure 19.11 – Deleting the redundant Animation track

7.   At this point, remember to save this sequence by clicking the **Save** icon on the Sequencer window top bar. Save frequently while you work on your sequence.

The animation is now on the MetaHuman Control Rig. Before we edit it, and since this is probably the first time you're using the MetaHuman Control Rig, let me give you a quick overview.

Overview of the MetaHuman Control Rig

The **MetaHuman Control Rig** is essentially very similar to our Robot Drone Control Rig, but with more controllers and more advanced features. Please make sure you have completed *Chapter 15, Creating a Control Rig with Basic IK Controls for the Robot in UE5,* and *Chapter 17, Creating Three Simple Animations for the Robot in EU5 Sequencer,* to understand how these controllers work in practice.

It has standard FK controls on the hips, spine, and head and IK controls on the arms and legs. However, one of the things that makes this MetaHuman Control Rig more advanced is that it can have both IK and FK on the arms and legs. You can switch between IK and FK on the arms and legs depending on your needs.

If you want to experiment with the MetaHuman Control Rig, you can view it in the main Viewport by dragging the MetaHuman's blueprint into a sequence, as we did in *Figure 19.5,* and then selecting one of the controllers in the **TRACK** window under **Body | MetaHuman_ContorlRig** or the **Anim Outliner** window (if the **Animation** window is not open, open it with the dropdown at the top of the main UE interface).

Anim Outliner is also where you can generally select your controllers, as well as just left-click on them in the Viewport, as shown in the following screenshot:

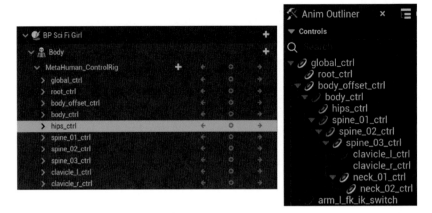

Figure 19.12 – Selecting the MetaHuman Control Rig controllers

When you first drag the MetaHuman blueprint into **Sequencer**, the rig controllers may not appear in the Viewport until you select one of them.

In the following screenshot, I have highlighted the different types of controllers that are available when the standard MetaHuman Control Rig is normally loaded first into a sequence:

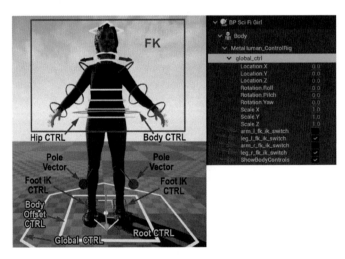

Figure 19.13 – The default MetaHuman Control Rig

The big six-sided yellow controller on the ground is **global_ctrl**. This controller is the overall parent and can move the entire character and all the controllers anywhere in your scene. This is also where you use the checkboxes to switch between IK and FK on the arms and legs.

If the box is unchecked, it's **FK**, while if it's checked, then it's **IK**. Under the FK/IK switches, there is the **ShowBodyControls** checkbox switch. Here, you can toggle how the controllers are displayed in the Viewport (either on or off). To get to these settings, simply expand **global_ctrl** in the **TRACK** window.

> **Note on IK and FK Switching**
>
> At the time of writing this book, the MetaHuman Control Rig has no IK/FK matching functionality. This means that if you're in FK mode on the arm and you animate or change it, none of those changes will be made to the IK controllers and vice versa. So, normally, the IK controllers and the FK controllers will get out of sync as you animate either of them. Some advanced animation rigs in some other 3D animation software programs have a matching feature where you can sync them back up if you want to switch from one to the other mid-animation.

Generally, try to decide at the beginning of the specific animation what you need to achieve and then decide whether IK or FK is the best way to go for the legs or arms. However, there is a workaround that we will cover later in this chapter, in the *Fixing the hands with the Snapper tool* section, if you want to use both in the same animation.

Next, we have a very useful controller called **body_offset_ctrl**. With this, you can also position the whole character and all the controllers, but crucially, it doesn't influence **global_ctrl** or **root_ctrl** and leaves them where they are when you move it. This is great for when you want to reposition the character relative to the root bone. You will see why this is important later in this chapter.

The next important controller to look at is **root_ctrl**. It is in the shape of an arrow in the MetaHuman control rig. This could be confusing since this normally controls the root skeleton bone of our skeleton, which is the parent of all the bones in the skeleton. You would think that this would do what **global_ctrl** does (move the entire rig), but this is not the case.

In a game engine and even with the kind of animation blending we want to do to combine the MoCap into one animation, we want exact control of where the root bone/controller is relative to the pelvis/hips bone. The root skeleton bone is rigged to the **root_ctrl** controller in such a way that it can be moved without influencing the other controllers (and the skeletal bones in turn) in any way, and vice versa. The root bone's motion is under complete control of the animator, who can do whatever they like with it without it affecting the position, rotation, or scale of the other controllers.

Because the IK box is checked, on the legs, we can see the foot IK controllers and their pole vectors. This works the same way as we used them in *Chapter 17, Creating Three Simple Animations for the Robot in EU5 Sequencer*, to animate the robot arms, only these are on the legs. The foot itself has some extra FK controllers to control the toes.

Because the FK box is checked, on the arms, we can see the arm FK controllers, as well as those for the fingers. On the MetaHuman Control Rig, the fingers are always FK controlled, even if the arm is switched to IK control. The body (the orange six-sided control around the hips), spine, neck, head, and clavicle controllers are all standard FK controllers too.

The **hips_ctr** controller has a special behavior (the round light orange control around the hips). This controller should just be rotated on the MetaHuman Control Rig. This can rotate the hips only, without influencing the body or spine position. This is useful if you have already made the perfect pose in the upper body and you just want to adjust the hip rotation to make it into a better shape for the pose.

With the **hips_ctr** controller set up the way it is, you can use this to make those tweaks to the hip rotation without the entire FK Control Rig above it following and ruining your pose. You can also use this in a walk cycle, where you just want the hips to swing a bit more without this offsetting your spine animation.

In the following screenshot, I switched the legs to FK and the arms to IK.

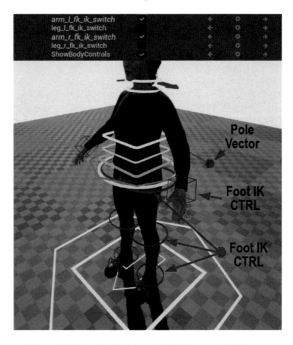

Figure 19.14 – Switching to FK legs and IK arms

Most professionally set-up humanoid animation rigs in most 3D animation software, such as Blender or Maya, are set up in this very similar industry standard way. So, if you get used to using this rig as an animator, it will feel very familiar to switch to other professional set-up rigs in a studio that uses Maya, for example.

With this basic understanding of how the MetaHuman Control Rig is set up and how to use it, let's continue and use this new knowledge to edit the **Stand_Up** MoCap animation in **Sequencer**.

Editing and cleaning up the Stand_Up MoCap

Now, let's edit the MoCap to suit our needs. Don't worry if you find this a little difficult and time-consuming. It does take a bit of practice to work your way around a rig with so many controllers as the MetaHuman rig has.

However, we need to set up a better near-clipping plane in UE to make posing the character easier in the Viewport display.

Changing the clipping plane in UE

In UE, the standard user camera in the Viewport has a clipping plane of 10 cm. This means that if you move the camera within 10 cm of an object in the Viewport, the parts of that object that are within the 10 cm won't appear in the Viewport. However, this is annoying if you want to get close to finger controllers to select and rotate them.

Let's adjust that while we animate. It's a good idea to switch it back to 10 cm after you've finished your animation since it could influence the way things render in the Viewport.

At the top of the main UE interface, select **Edit | Project Settings**. The **Project Settings** window will appear. Then, in the **Search** field at the top right, type near. In the search results, scroll down and find **Near Clip Plane**. Change that to 1.0 instead of 10.0, as shown in the following screenshot:

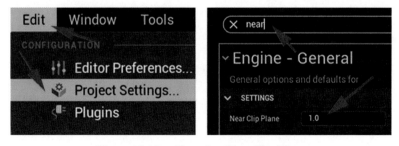

Figure 19.15 – Changing Near Clip Plane

Next, we'll offset the position of our MoCap so that it lines up with the ground and root.

Lining up the MoCap with the ground plane and the root

If the `StandUpCleanup` sequence is still not open in Sequencer, open it now by double-clicking on it in the folder you saved it in.

If you saved the sequence after completing the *Baking the Stand_Up MoCap to the Control Rig* section, then the MoCap should already be baked to the MetaHuman Control Rig.

If you look at our baked MoCap animation in the Viewport, you'll see that she is floating off the ground and away from her **root_ctrl**, as shown in the following screenshot. Let's fix that:

Figure 19.16 – Floating character animation away from the root

It would be better if, when she is fully stood up, her feet are on the ground and that the root is between her heels so that we can determine what we want this offset to be. This is frame **0044**, just at the point she is fully stood up:

1. Scrub to frame **0044** in the Sequencer timeline. Select **body_offset_ctrl** in the **TRACK** window and then left-click, hold, and box select all the keyframes on that controller only, before frame **0044**. Then, hold *Shift* on your keyboard and select all the keyframes after frame **0044** at the same time.

2. Press *Delete* on your keyboard to delete those keys, leaving the single frame on frame **0044**, as shown in the following screenshot:

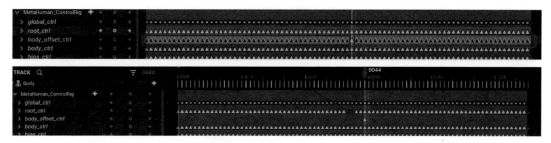

Figure 19.17 – Deleting extra keyframes from body_offset_ctrl

3. With **Automatic Keyframe** set to *on*, move **body_offset_ctrl** into the Viewport until the character's feet are on the ground and her heels are on either side of the **root_ctrl controller**, as shown in the following screenshot:

Figure 19.18 – Moving body_ffset_ctrl so that the character's feet are on the ground

Because **Automatic Keyframe** was *on*, the new position of **body_offset_ctrl** would be keyframed in this position, and since there are no keyframes before or after this keyframe, it will stay there.

The whole animation has now been offset so that the character's feet are on the ground... well – at frame **0044** anyway. For the rest of the animation, the feet are floaty. Let's fix that next.

Fixing floaty feet

With the offset keyed on **body_offset_ctrl** at **0044**, you can now scrub the Sequencer timeline to see what your animation looks like, all the way back to the beginning at frame **0000**, and after frame **0044** to the end of the animation.

Look at the feet of the character in the Viewport while you scrub the timeline or play the animation. It is very *floaty* (it doesn't stay in the same spot on the ground) and even clips the floor in places. This is because the whole animation is offset now, and sometimes, retargeted animations to differently proportioned characters can lose some accuracy in terms of where the feet should be. This is often the case with MoCap retargeting and a lot of time is spent by animators cleaning up the feet of MoCap animations.

In this case, we are lucky and it's an easy fix. The character in this original MoCap animation never really moves her feet during this animation. Where her feet position was while she was sitting is where they stay when she stands up. We know that on frame **0044**, her feet are perfectly aligned to the floor, so let's keep them in exactly that spot during the whole animation.

Just like we did in *Step 2* of the previous section, scrub to frame **0044**, select the keyframes before and after keyframe **0044** on both **foot_l_ik_ctrl** and **foot_r_ik_ctrl**, and delete them, leaving just the keyframe on **0044**.

With all the keyframes on the feet IK controllers deleted and leaving the one keyframe on **0044**, the feet will now stay in that position and not move and float when we play the animation.

If this animation was for an AAA game, I would have reanimated some micro-movements back into the feet to keep them *alive* during this animation, but for this tutorial, that is not needed. Next, let's look at the full body pose and improve it.

Improving the standing pose

Back on frame **0044**, have a look at your pose, as shown in the following screenshot:

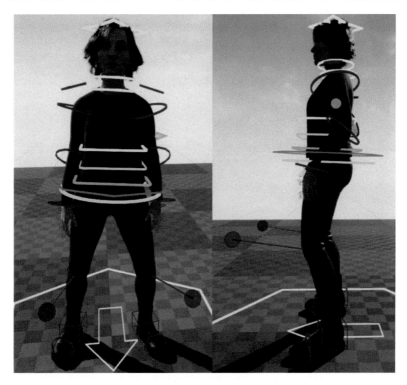

Figure 19.19 – Not a good pose

This is not a very appealing pose. The feet are too far apart, and the shoulders are drooping. Also, the hands are too close to the legs. This is also often the case when we retarget MoCap animations since the MoCap actor probably had different proportions from the final 3D model. Let's fix this now.

Here, we will make the change as an **Additive** layer since the MoCap keyframes are baked onto the rest of the body controllers and we don't want to lose that subtle core base MoCap data. Follow these steps:

1. On frame **0000**, in the **TRACK** window, to the right of the **MetaHuman_ ControlRig** track, select **+ Section | Additive** to add an **Additive** track:

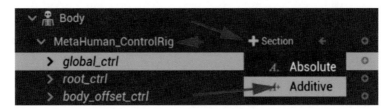

Figure 19.20 – Adding an Additive track

A complete duplicate **Additive** set of controllers will appear in the **TRACK** window.

2. On the original set of controllers, expand **global_ctrl** and check the boxes for IK on both the arms and legs, as well as **ShowBodyControls**. Delete all the keyframes on the IK/FK switch channels and **ShowBodyControl**, apart from the ones on frame **0000**. Make sure that the blue dashed **Additive** track is the whole active frame range in the timeline window. Left-click on the end of it and drag it to make it longer if needed, as shown in the following screenshot:

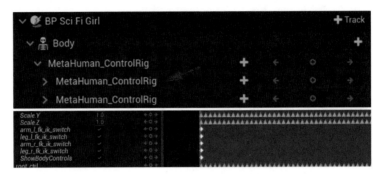

Figure 19.21 – Checking IK and extending the track

With **Additive** animations, I like to set the **anchor** keyframes. These keyframes can be used in several ways. Generally, the best way to judge where to put these **Additive** anchor frames is where we would have put a keyframe if we were to animate this from scratch. This animation would have three main poses in that case:

- **Sitting Pose** is the keyframe pose at the beginning of the sequence at frame **0000**. We will do this after **Stood Up Pose** because we want to determine where the feet will end up when she stood up first. Then, we can feed that back to **Sitting Pose**. We will do that later in this tutorial.

- **Stood Up Pose** is what we started with at frame **0044**.

- A **Stood Up Pose** would be placed at the end of the animation at frame **0082** to hold that stood-up position. We will do that later in this tutorial.

In this case, I want to anchor in the change on frame **0044** as the main offset across the whole animation. This is why I'm starting at frame **0044** and not **0000**.

Since we're now dealing with **Additive** animation layers, turn **Automatic Keyframe** off (so we don't accidentally key the base layer of the MoCap and not the **Additive** layer). In the timeline, scrub to frame **0044**, and then add a keyframe to the **Additive MetaHuman_CotrolRig** parent track. This will put a keyframe on all the controllers in this **Additive** set of controllers, as shown in the following screenshot:

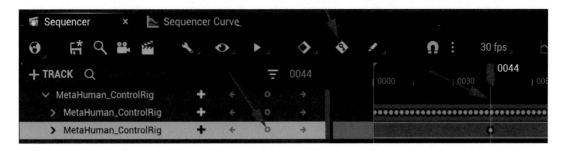

Figure 19.22 – Setting an Additive anchor keyframe on frame 0044

> **Reminder**
>
> With **Automatic Keyframe** *off*, if you don't set the keyframe directly after you move the controller, and then scrub the timeline or select another controller, you'll lose the change you just made. It will revert to previous keyframe values before you made the change since you did not keyframe the change.

On frame **0044**, adjust the pose. Bring the feet closer together by moving the feet with the foot IK controllers in the Viewport. Set + **keyframe** on the **Additive** versions of the controllers as you change them. You'll probably need to move the pole vectors on the legs too. Lift the shoulders a bit with the clavicle controllers.

Then, adjust the arms so that they're more natural with the hand IK controllers and their pole vectors. Look from the side and see if she leans backward or forwards too much and adjust if needed. The following screenshot shows before and after shots of what I did:

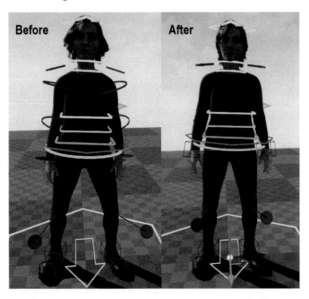

Figure 19.23 – Standing Additive pose at frame 44 – before and after

> **Some Help Needed?**
>
> If you are having some trouble, we also provide this pose in the final UE project file under **Content | ControlRig | Poses**. It's called `PoseB_Stand_Idle_tutor`. You can load this premade pose if you want to save some time.

If you decide to load this premade pose from the UE project files, then follow the steps numbered 1 to 5 in the following screenshot. Remember to be on the frame you want to paste the pose on and add a keyframe to the **Additive** layer controllers after to keyframe the pose:

Figure 19.24 – Pasting the pose

If you decide to keep the pose you created, save it to the **Pose** library under **Content |
ControlRig | Poses**. Select **All** the MetaHuman controllers while on frame **0044**. Then,
open **Poses** in the **Animation** window. Click **Create Pose** and name it `PoseB_Stand_
Idle` and click **Create Asset**, as shown in the following screenshot:

Figure 19.25 – Saving PoseB_Stand_Idle

Since we have this `PoseB_Stand_Idle` pose saved so that we can link the animations
together, as shown in *Figure 19.2* of our plan, let's paste it at the end of the animation.

With **Automatic Keyframe** still *off*, scrub to frame **0082** at the end of the animation.
Then, as shown in *Figure 19.23*, paste the `PoseB_Stand_Idle` pose from the **Poses** tool.
Remember to only add a keyframe to the **Additive MetaHuman_ControlRig** parent track
to set the keyframe on all the **Additive** controllers.

If this animation was for an AAA game standard, I would have created a new cleaned-up
pose at the end so that the **Standing Idle** pose doesn't repeat at frame **0044** and frame
0082 so soon after each other. However, that is more high-level cleanup and for this
exercise, it is fine to just reuse the same standing pose.

The standing pose is now keyframed on frame **0044** and at the end at frame **0082**. Next,
let's clean up **Sitting Pose** at frame **0000**.

Cleaning up Sitting Pose

Currently, the sitting pose doesn't look natural, and she is in an awkward pose. In this
section, we will clean up the sitting pose so that it feels natural and looks appealing.

If you scrub to frame **0000**, you'll see that our **Sitting Pose** needs a lot of work, as shown in the following screenshot:

Figure 19.26 – Current bad sitting pose

Follow these steps to clean it up:

1. As shown in *Figure 19.22*, set a keyframe on all the **Additive** controllers at frame **0000** to *anchor* in a keyframe.

2. Now that all the **Additive** controllers have a keyframe at frame **0000**, we can adjust the pose to something better.

   Here, using the controllers in the Viewport, I moved her hands onto her legs and positioned her fingers naturally. I moved her head up more and widened her knees so that they line up with her feet better in the sitting position with their pole vector.

   Remember to add a keyframe to the **Additive** set of controllers as you do this so that you don't lose your changes since **Automatic Keyframe** is *off*. The result should look similar to the following:

Figure 19.27 – Cleaned sitting pose

Some Help Needed?

If you are having some trouble, or want to save time, we also provide this pose in this chapter's UE project file under **Content | ControlRig | Poses**. It's called `PoseA_Sit_Idle_tutor`. You can load this premade pose if you want to save some time.

3. If you decide to keep the pose you created, save it to the **Pose** library under **Content | ControlRig | Poses**. Open **Poses** in the **Animation** window. Click **Create Pose**, name it `PoseA_Sit_Idle`, and click **Create Asset**, as shown in *Figure 19.25*.

   With that, we've cleaned up the **Sitting Idle** pose on the first frame. However, if you play back the animation now or scrub the timeline, you'll see that there's still a problem – her hands go through her legs as she gets up.

Let's fix that with the **Snapper** tool, which can be found in the **Animation** window.

Fixing the hands with the Snapper tool

The **Snapper** tool can be found in the **Animation** window to the right of the **Poses** tool. With the **Snapper** tool, you can make one object follow another while it bakes them into a separate keyframe animation. This is typically used if you just want one object to follow another temporarily and you don't want to create parent/child rigging just for that.

For example, let's say that we want a character to pick up a ball and then put it down. We can make the ball follow the hand, from the exact frame it picks it up to the exact frame it puts it down.

You can also use the **Snapper** tool to keep something in the same place by making it follow the world instead of another object. It will keep that object in the same spot in the world space during the snapped frames.

This is helpful if, say, an object is the child of another. The parent is moving, but we want to keep the child in the same spot for a certain number of frames. It's also really useful to get rid of foot sliding issues or to keep a hand on a fence while the character jumps over it.

In our case, I want to use the **Snapper** tool to keep the character's hands on her legs for a few frames in the beginning, as she stands up. We want her hands to follow her upper legs in this case. Unfortunately, the leg IK controllers don't track the upper legs. They track the feet; the pole vectors don't keep track of rotation – they only keep track of the position.

So, we need our upper leg FK controllers for the hands to track the upper legs accurately. We have been working with IK on the arms and legs. Furthermore, the IK and FK controllers are completely out of sync now since we made lots of changes to the animation of the IK controllers. Simply switching them to FK won't work.

Luckily, there's a workaround to get the IK and FK controllers' animations back in sync. Then, we can switch to FK or IK without losing our animation. Follow these steps:

1. Bake the MetaHuman Control Rig animation back on the skeleton as a separate animation with all the edits and cleanup we've done so far.

2. Bring that back into a fresh sequence.

3. Bake this new skeletal animation back on the MetaHuman Control Rig controllers. At this point, it will bake both the IK and FK controllers' animations according to the bone positions of the skeletal animation and the FK and IK will both be in sync again.

4. Now, we can switch to either FK or IK on the arms and legs and the animation will be the same on both again.

   Now, let's do what we've just outlined. You have already performed all these actions separately previously, but the following is a brief reminder of the steps.

5. Right-click on **Body** in the **TRACK** window and select **Bake Animation Sequence**. Name it `Stand_up_meta_cl_stage01` and save to the **Content | MoCap_From_Mixamo | MoCap** folder. Click on **Export To Animation** with the default settings, as shown in the following screenshot:

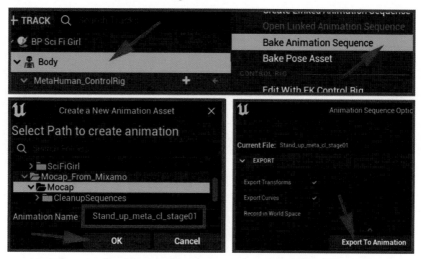

Figure 19.28 – Bake Animation Sequence

6. Now, create another new **Level Sequence** by selecting **Cinematics | Add Level Sequence**. Save it as `StandUpCleanup_Stage2` in the **CleanupSequences** folder. Open this sequence and drag the **BP_SciFiGirl** blueprint into it from the **Content Drawer** interface, as shown in the following screenshot:

Figure 19.29 – New Level Sequence

7. Delete the **MetaHuman_ControlRig** track under the **Body** track in the **TRACK** window by selecting the track and pressing *Delete* on your keyboard so it that doesn't override the skeletal animation. Click on **+ Track** on the **Body** track, select **Animation**, and pick Stand_up_meta_cl_stage01, as shown in the following screenshot:

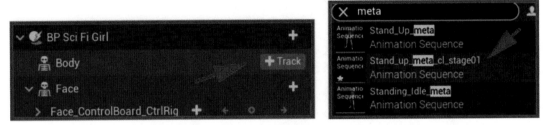

Figure 19.30 – Adding the skeletal animation track

8. Right-click on the **Body** track and select **Bake To Control Rig | MetaHuman_ CotrolRig**. Make sure that the **REDUCE KEYS** box is unchecked and press **Bake To Control Rig**, as shown in the following screenshot:

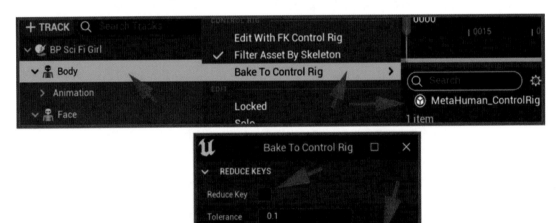

Figure 19.31 – Bake to Control Rig

Now, the FK and IK controllers both have the same animations and are back in sync. We can switch them to what we need them to be for the next part of the MoCap cleanup.

9. Since we're not on an **Additive** layer anymore, turn **Automatic keyframe** *on*. Expand the **global_ctrl** controller in the **TRACK** window. Delete all the keyframes on the IK/FK switch channels and **ShowBodyControl**, apart from the ones on frame **0000**. Check the box for **arms to IK** and uncheck the box for **legs to FK**, as shown in the following screenshot:

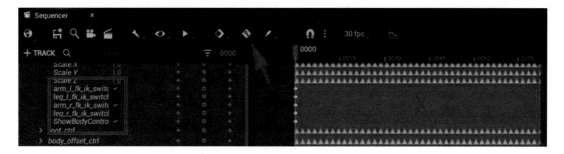

Figure 19.32 – Switching arms to IK and legs to FK

Next, let's use the **Snapper** tool.

10. Open the **Snapper** tool by going to the **Animation** window to the right of the **Poses** tool, as shown in the following screenshot:

Figure 19.33 – The Snapper tool

11. Select the left-hand IK controller (**hand_l_ik_ctrl**) then left-click on the gray box under **Children** in the **Control Rig Snapper** window, as shown in the preceding screenshot.

The left-hand IK controller (**hand_l_ik_ctrl**) is now set up as the child and it will follow what we set in the **Parent** field, in the **Control Rig Snapper** window. If you leave it set to **World**, it will bake the left-hand IK controller to stay in the same spot in the world.

12. Select the left thigh FK controller (**thigh_l_fk_ctrl**) then left-click on the gray box under **Parent** in the **Control Rig Snapper** window, as shown in the preceding screenshot.

The left thigh FK controller is now set up as the parent of the left-hand IK controller and the hand will follow the thigh during the frame range that we will set up next.

We want the left hand to follow the left thigh from frame **0000** to frame **0031**. Let's do this now.

13. Scrub to frame **0000** in the **Sequencer** timeline and click on the gray box around the first numbers field on the left. This will set the start of **Snapper frame range** to frame **0000**. Now, scrub to frame **0031** and click on the gray box around the second numbers field on the right. This will set the end of **Snapper frame range** to frame **0031**, as shown in *Figure 19.33*.

14. Check the **Keep Offset** box; otherwise, the **Snapper** tool will snap the left-hand IK controller's pivot to the thigh FK controller's pivot so that her hand will end up in her leg during the snap. We want to keep the same offset that we have now on frame **0000** when the range starts, as shown in *Figure 19.33*.

15. Check the **Snap Position** and **Snap Rotation** boxes, but keep **Snap Scale** *off*. It's not needed in this case. Then, click **Snap Animation**, as shown in *Figure 19.33*.

The left hand will now follow the leg exactly, from frame **0000** to frame **0031**.

Now, if you scrub the timeline, you will see that the hand follows the thigh well. However, when we get to frame **0032**, there's a sudden snap in the hand controller. The IK hand controller is now in a very different position at frame **0031** than it was before we used the **Snapper** tool. The next frame at **0032** is still the original animation.

To smooth this transition out from the new IK hand controller position at frame **0031** to the original animation afterward, we will simply delete some keyframes to aid the transition and let the animation curves take care of it. We generally try to delete as few keyframes as we can in cases like this, to keep as much of the MoCap data as possible.

16. In **Sequencer**, box select and delete all the keyframes between **0032** and **0042** on the **hand_l_ik_ctrl** controller, as shown in *Figure 19.34*.

The snap in the animation is now gone but when you scrub to frame **0037**, the elbow might be overextending and *locking out*. This doesn't look very good. Let's fix that.

17. With **Automatic keyframe** still *on*, in the Viewport, move the hand up and position it. Then, set an **in-between** keyframe to help the transition, as shown in the following screenshot. An in-between keyframe is a regular keyframe, but we call it an in-between keyframe since it's put in-between to help transition between two main keyframes or poses:

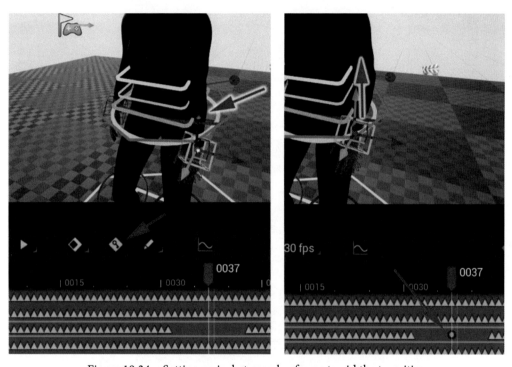

Figure 19.34 – Setting an in-between keyframe to aid the transition

To further help the transition, let's edit the animation curves. Since the animation is baked, it probably has linear curves that don't normally flow very well in transitions like this.

18. Select the **hand_l_ik_ctrl** controller and open the **Sequence Curve Editor** window. Left-click, drag, and box select all the keys around the transition and set the **Curve Handles** type to **Auto**, as shown in the following screenshot. Afterward, if you want to, you can clean up the other curves more by adjusting the handles on a channel-by-channel basis for position and rotation (XYZ):

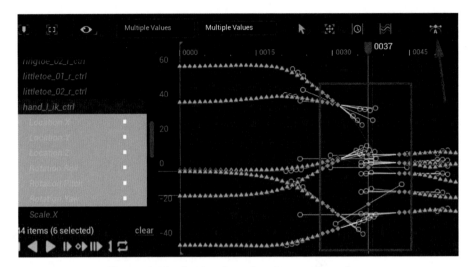

Figure 19.35 – Setting the animation curves to Auto

Another issue you may notice is that the character's fingers are clipping her legs as she gets up. This is because there's an animation on the fingers as they go from the pose of the fingers on the leg to the pose of the fingers while standing, as shown in the following screenshot:

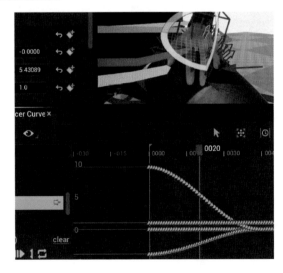

Figure 19.36 – Fingers clipping

We want the character's fingers to stay in the same position until she moves them off her legs at around frame **0032**. This will stop them from clipping the legs while her hands are on them.

19. In **Sequencer**, box select all the keys on the left-hand finger controllers, apart from the first and last frame, and delete them by pressing *Delete* on your keyboard, as shown in the following screenshot:

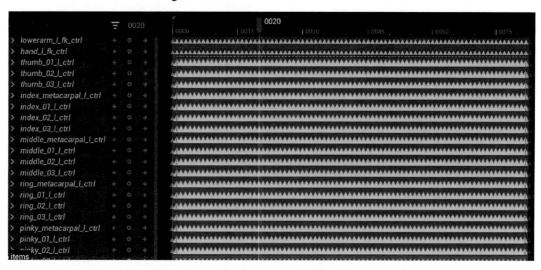

Figure 19.37 – Deleting the finger controller keyframes

20. Scrub to frame **0000**. In **Sequencer**, box select all the keys on the left-hand finger controllers, on frame **0000** (that you did not delete in *Step 19*). Press *Ctrl + C* on your keyboard to copy them, then scrub to frame **0032** and press *Ctrl + V* on your keyboard to paste them on that frame, as shown in the following screenshot:

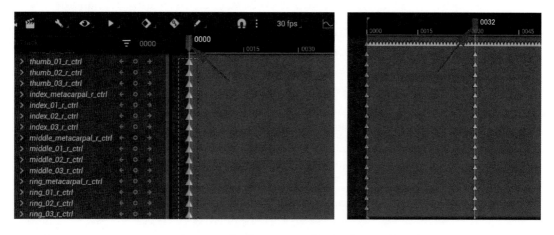

Figure 19.38 – Copying and pasting the finger controller keyframes from frame 0 to frame 32

The fingers should now stay in the same position from frame **0000** to frame **0032**.

Follow the same process with the **Snapper** tool to make the right hand follow the right thigh. However, there are some small differences and at the time of writing this book, there seems to be a bug in the early access version of UE5 concerning the **Snapper** tool, the right hand IK controller, and the left foot IK controller. If the same issue still exists when you're going through this chapter on your version of UE5, here is the fix.

When you use the **Snapper** tool on the right hand and right foot IK controllers, they may come out flipped in the opposite direction, as shown at the top of the following screenshot:

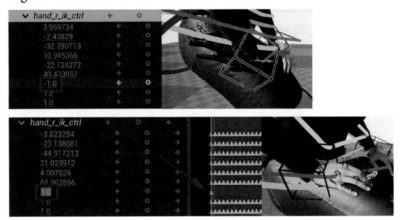

Figure 19.39 – Snapper bug on the L and R IK controllers

This is because the **Snapper** tool seems to bake a **-1.0** X scale value onto the controller's X scale channel. Delete these **-1.0** keys on the X scale channel and replace them with a +1.0 value and add a keyframe. This will fix the hand or foot, as shown at the bottom of the preceding screenshot.

Also, for the right hand to follow the right thigh, I found that I needed two keyframes to correct the transition from the snapped frames to the original, as shown in the following screenshot:

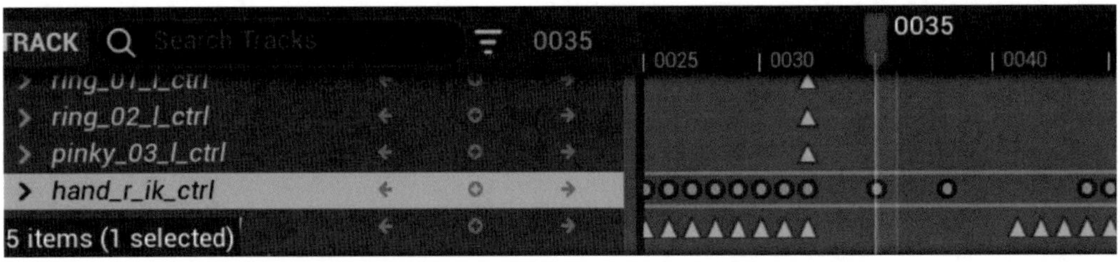

Figure 19.40 – The right hand IK controller snapped as it needed two in-between keyframes

Once you've finished making the right hand follow the right thigh at the beginning of the **Stand Up** animation and you're happy with your final animation, it's time to bake it to its animation asset.

21. Right-click on **Body** in the **TRACK** window and select **Bake Animation Sequence**. Save it as `Stand_up_meta_cleaned_final` in the **Content | MoCap_From_Mixamo | MoCap** folder, as shown in the following screenshot:

Figure 19.41 – Baking the final animation sequence

For those that want to explore MoCap cleanup in UE5 further, we have provided bonus online material on how to clean up the other four MoCap animations in this set. This will broaden your knowledge on the subject and teach you a few extra tricks of the trade on how to effectively clean up MoCap animation without losing too much of the core underlying MoCap data. This **bonus online content** can be found at `https://github.com/PacktPublishing/Unreal-Engine-5-Character-Creation-Animation-and-Cinematics/tree/main/BonusMaterial`.

In the UE project files that are provided with this chapter, I have included the cleaned-up MoCap files so that they can be used in the next chapter, including **Stand Up**, which we cleaned up in this chapter. You can find it in the accompanying UE project by going to **Content | MoCap_From_Mixamo | MoCap | CleanedMoCap_Final**. The final UE project can be downloaded from `https://github.com/PacktPublishing/Unreal-Engine-5-Character-Creation-Animation-and-Cinematics/tree/main/FullFinalUE5Project`.

Summary

In this chapter, we covered how to work with MoCap animation on the MetaHuman Control Rig in UE5 Sequencer. We planned what we wanted to achieve, then learned how to bake MoCap animation from the skeleton to the MetaHuman Control Rig. We had a good overview of the MetaHuman Control Rig itself and how to use its controllers. Then, we set up UE so that it's easier to animate within tight spaces by changing the **Near Clipping Plane** values.

We finished this chapter by cleaning up the **Stand Up** animation while using the **Poses** and **Snapper** tools in the **Animation** window. This chapter should have provided a good overview of how to edit MoCap in UE5. You should now be able to get the most out of all the free or paid-for MoCap libraries out there, as well as customize these MoCap animations for your own needs.

In the next chapter, we will combine all the assets we created in this book into our final movie scene in Sequencer.

20

Using Sequencer to Construct Your Final Scene

We now come to the end of this book, and I hope you have enjoyed the journey through all the topics with us. In the previous chapters, we created all the custom content for this final scene. All we need to do now is put it all together in our final scene using **Sequencer**. All our hard work is about to pay off. We will combine the character animations we created together to tell the story and we will work with camera animation and camera cuts in the same scene.

We will also learn to *migrate* our content from other project files we might have created or used in this book. The final project file is provided with this chapter if you want to study my setup afterwards at https://github.com/PacktPublishing/Unreal-Engine-5-Character-Creation-Animation-and-Cinematics/tree/main/FullFinalUE5Project

In this chapter, we will cover the following topics:

- Importing all the scene assets and positioning them in the scene
- Importing animations onto our characters
- Creating cameras and animating them
- Rendering our final scene

Technical requirements

In this chapter, we will need to work in **Unreal Engine** (**UE**) 5. You will need the following to complete this chapter:

- A computer that can run basic 3D animation software.
- You need to have installed UE5. You can download it from `https://www.unrealengine.com/en-US/download`.
- A basic understanding of how to navigate the UE 3D user interface. If you skipped ahead, this was covered in *Chapters 6, Exploring Unreal Engine 5*.
- You need to have completed *Chapter 17, Creating Three Simple Animations for the Robot in UE Sequencer*, *Chapter 18, Importing Motion Capture onto the MetaHuman Control Rig*, and *Chapter 19, Motion Capture Editing and Cleanup Using Control Rig and Sequencer*.

Importing all the scene assets and positioning them in the scene

If you used different UE projects files and folders to create the content in this book, we now need to combine them into one project for our final scene. It all needs to be available to us in a single project in UE. Luckily, UE makes that process easy with the **Migrate** tool. Even if you created all the content in this book in one UE project, it is still good to know how to migrate content between UE projects.

Migrating UE content between projects

We are going to start by creating a new project in UE5 for this last scene. If you already have everything in the same project, you can use this as a reference in the future, whenever you need to combine content from different projects into one.

For the purposes of this exercise, we'll migrate the content that we created in *Chapter 19, Motion Capture Editing and Cleanup Using Control Rig and Sequencer*, first:

1. Create a new UE5 project by opening UE5, then choose **Games** and **Blank**. Call it `FinalSceneChapter20`, as shown in *Figure 20.1*. Click **CREATE** and the new project will open in UE5:

    We use the **Games** profile instead of the **Film/Video** profile since the **Games** profile gives a better default blank scene to integrate our varied custom content.

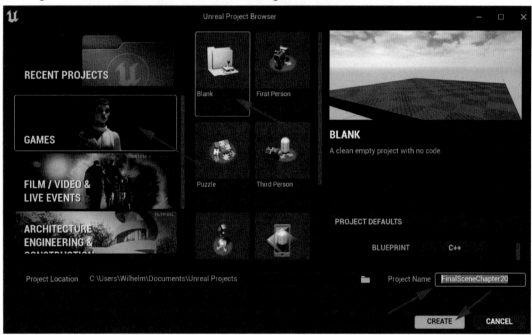

Figure 20.1 – Creating a new project for the final scene

2. With the new project for our final scene created, we can now close it again and then open the project we used for *Chapter 19, Motion Capture Editing and Cleanup Using Control Rig and Sequencer*.

3. Once that project is open, open **Content Drawer** and right-click on the Content parent folder. Then, select **Migrate…**, as shown in *Figure 20.2*:

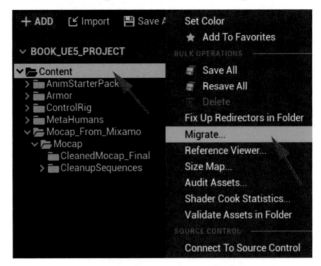

Figure 20.2 – Migrating UE assets

4. Once you select **Migrate…** in *Step 3*, a window will open where you can check the boxes for the folders and files you want to migrate, as shown in *Figure 20.3*:

Figure 20.3 – Choosing the asset folders to migrate

We don't need `AnimStarterPack` since that was just for demonstration purposes. We need the `Armor`, `ControlRig`, and `MetaHuman` content folders since they are needed for our female MetaHuman character in our final scene. However, in the `Mocap_From_Maximo` folder, we only needed the `Mocap` and `CleanedMocap_Final` folders and the final-stage cleaned Mocap animations for our scene, so I unchecked the rest.

> **Note**
>
> Generally, it's better to bring entire folders over so not to miss something that the content is reliant on. We call these **dependencies**. Say, for example, when we migrate the body **Armor** folder over, we don't want to leave out the texture and shader files. If we don't bring all the dependencies over, it might not load correctly in the new project and cause errors. Generally speaking, if you're in doubt, it's better to migrate *more* than you need, than less than you need for the assets to function correctly, with all its dependencies intact..

5. Once you have selected what you want to migrate, click **OK**, and you will then be asked to navigate to the `Content` folder of the project you want to migrate these assets to. Navigate to the `FinalSceneChapter20` project `Content` folder and click **Select Folder** at the bottom of the window, as shown in *Figure 20.4*:

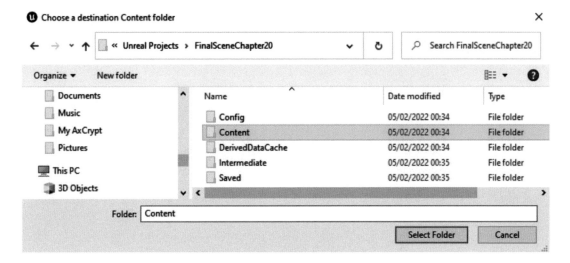

Figure 20.4 – Target Content folder selected

These selected assets will now be moved to the new project.

6. You can now close the project you're migrating from and open the FinalSceneChapter20 project and then the project's **Content Drawer**. You'll now see those assets in the new project for the final scene, as shown in *Figure 20.5*:

Figure 20.5 – Content migrated to a new project for the final scene

7. You can now use the same process to migrate all the other content needed for the final scene. This will include the Robot Drone and its animations, the Alien Plant and its animations, and the environment set and its effects. If you forget something, you can add it later as we go.

You have now learned how to migrate and move content between projects. Next, we can set up the body armor of the female character to follow her body during the scene.

Attaching the body armor to the MetaHuman Rig

Our custom body armor is a nice extra detail on our MetaHuman character. They have been created so that when they're perfectly aligned to her body and limbs, their pivots are at the origin of the scene at 0, 0, 0 position and rotation. Unfortunately, in my early access version of UE5 there's no way that I could find to maintain the default offset once you attach them.

When you attach items to the MetaHuman body parts they snap the pivot of the attached item to the pivot of the bone you're attaching it to. This may lead to them appearing in the wrong looking position once you attach them. Maybe there will be an easier way in the future, but I found a workaround that we can use in the meanwhile.

It is also better to do this right in the beginning before we load animation onto her. We want her to be in the default position when we attach these items.

Let's attach the armor to her body:

1. At the top of the main UE menu, select **Cinematics | Add Level Sequence**. Name it as `FinalScene`, as shown in *Figure 20.6*:

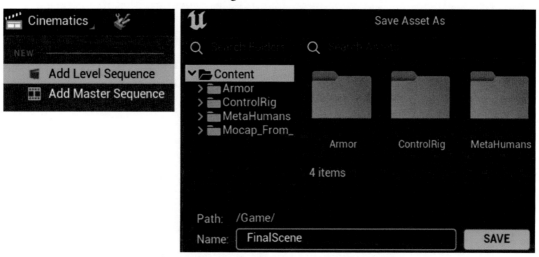

Figure 20.6 – New level sequence for the final scene

2. From the Content Drawer, drag **BP_SciFiGirl** into the **Sequencer** timeline as shown in *Figure 20.7*. You might get a plugin error since this is a new project and all the required plugins might not be loaded yet for the MetaHuman setup. If the errors come up, choose **Load Plugins**, after which UE might ask you to restart UE:

Figure 20.7 – Loading MetaHuman into Sequencer

3. If you have the old checker floor as default, select the floor and make sure the location translation is 0,0,0 in the **World Outliner** since, by default it seems to be 20 cm above the grid.

4. If the **Animation Mode** window for Control Rig on the top left is open, you can switch to **Select Mode** since it seems to interfere with the regular right click menus, we'll need to align the armor later. You can open it again after by clicking on the dropdown menu at the top of the main UE interface.

5. From the Content Drawer also select and drag all 16 the armor static meshes from the **Armor_Models** folder (`Content/MetaHumans/SciFiGirl/Armor`) into the **Sequencer** timeline as shown in *Figure 20.8*.

Figure 20.8 – Dragging armor into Sequencer

6. In the **Sequencer TRACK** window, select **ARMOR Chest Plate** and then click + **Track | Attach | BP Sci Fi Girl**. Choose **Torso** in the next pop-up window, and then **spine_04** in the next one, as shown in *Figure 20.9*:

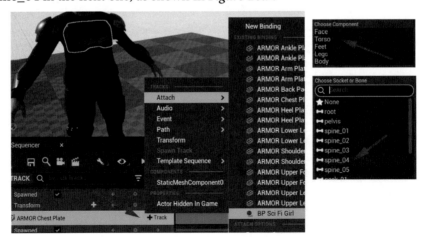

Figure 20.9 – Attaching the Chest Plate armor to the rig

As the **Attach** track attached the armor to the spine, it now also snapped the pivot of the armor to the pivot of the spine bone, so the chest plate armor is now in the wrong position on the character, as shown in *Figure 20.10*:

Figure 20.10 – Chest plate armor in the wrong position

Now, let's fix the chest plate armor.

7.   Right click on the **ARMOR Chest Plate** in the viewport and a context menu will appear. This is the menu that doesn't always work when the **Animation Mode** is active, and this is the reason why we switched to **Select Mode** in *Step 4*. From this menu, select **Transform | Snapping | Align to Floor** as shown in *Figure 20.11*:

Figure 20.11 – Aligning the armor pivot to the floor again

This aligns the armor pivot to the floor again like the original rotation before it snapped to the bone pivot. However, the position is still off. To get the armor pivot back to the original position at 0, 0, 0 in the world, we'll have to temporarily change it back to **World** space (its real position in the world) as opposed to **Relative** space (its position relative to the parent it's a child of, in this case, the spine bone).

We can only do this temporarily since only relative space works well with attached objects in **Sequencer**.

8. With the **ARMOR Chest Plate** selected, follow the steps below as also shown in *Figure 20.12*:

    I.   In the **World Outliner**, click on the **Location** dropdown and set it to **World**.

    II. Then change all the **Location** values to 0 , 0 , 0. After changing them all to 0, the armor's pivot will be back at the World origin at 0 , 0 , 0.

    III. Switch it back to **Relative** in the location dropdown.

    IV. You will see that the location values change, and are not 0 , 0 , 0 anymore.

    You now have the accurate relative location values that we can keyframe later in the armor's local Relative space:

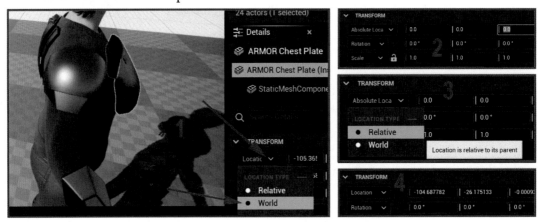

Figure 20.12 – Getting the Relative offset position

9. On some of these items, including this chest plate, you might have to repeat *Step 7*, as shown in *Figure 20.11*, to align this armor's rotation to the floor again to get the **Relative** offset rotation value.

10. Once the chest plate is back in exactly the right place on the body again, you'll know that you've done it right. With **ARMOR Chest Plate** selected in the **TRACK** window, create a keyframe on frame **0** on its track with these new relative position and rotation values after you have gone through this process. This will lock in and save these **Relative** transform values of the armor versus the skeleton bone it's attached to, as shown in *Figure 20.13*:

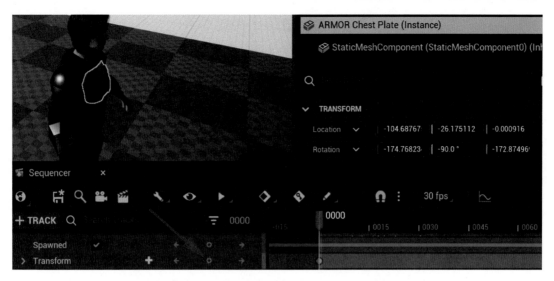

Figure 20.13 – Setting the keyframe with the Relative offset

11. Repeat this process for all the pieces of armor, with the only difference being the bone you attach it to; for example, the armor plates on the forearms should be attached to the forearm bones, and so on.

12. If you make a mistake and attach an armor piece to the wrong bone, you can simply delete the **Attach** track you created in the **TRACK** window under that item. Also note that it will only stay attached to the specified bone for the range set on the **Attach** track in the **Sequencer** timeline. In our case, make sure to make that range for the whole final scene length so they stay attached for all of it. You do that by left-clicking at the beginning or end line of the range, holding, and dragging it, making it longer or shorter, as shown in *Figure 20.14*:

Figure 20.14 – Attach range

Along with attaching the armor, we have also now learned how to attach items and props to any part of our MetaHuman or Control Rig character in **Sequencer**.

Next, let's prepare our other characters and the level for the final scene.

Preparing character and Level Assets

When we skinned and rigged our Alien Plant and Robot Drone, we might not have had the final textures on them inside UE. If not, assign the correct textures by double-clicking on their **SKELETAL MESH** files in **Content Drawer**.

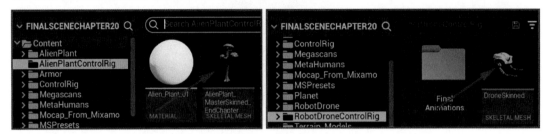

Figure 20.15 – Opening Skeletal Mesh by double-clicking

Once the asset opens, the **Asset Details** panel should open by default on the left of the interface, instead of the right-hand side where it normally opens.

If you can't see it, in the main UE interface menu, at the top, click on **Window | Asset Details** to turn the window display back on, as shown in *Figure 20.16*:

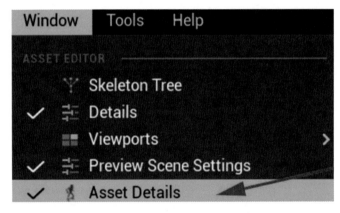

Figure 20.16 – Opening the Asset Details window

In the **Asset Details** window, under **MATERIAL SLOTS**, use the dropdown to select the correct final textures for the Alien Plant and Robot Drone, as shown in *Figure 20.17*:

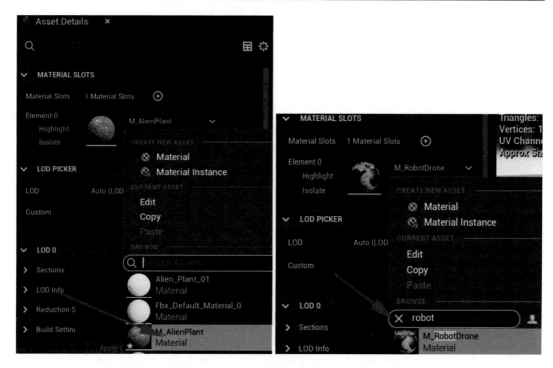

Figure 20.17 – Loading final textures on the Alien Plant and robot characters

Afterward, it might have to calculate the Shaders again, so give it a bit of time to complete the process.

Currently, we have a **Level Sequence** in **Sequencer** for our final scene, and then we also have the **Level** (Virtual 3D movie set) you created at the end of *Chapter 9, Let's Build a Virtual 3D Movie Set*, and *Chapter 10, Adding Lighting and Atmospheric Visual Effects in UE5*.

We'll use both these assets in combination. Let's play it safe and make a **Duplicate** of the **Main** level with the set, background, and lighting. If we delete the wrong thing, we can then always go back to the original.

To do that, right-click on the **Level** containing **Virtual 3D Movie Set** in **Content Drawer**, select **Duplicate**, and call it MovieSetFinal, as shown in *Figure 20.18*:

Figure 20.18 – Duplicating the movie set level

Now, open the new duplicate MovieSetFinal level and delete the placeholder **MetaHuman** and **Robot Drone** if you have them in there. You do that by selecting them and them in the **Level** viewport and pressing Delete on the keyboard. (Do not delete them in the Content Drawer, delete them only in the **Level** itself). Deleting it in the **Level** viewport will only delete them out of the **Level**, and your assets will still be in your Content Drawer for when you want to use them again.

We are simply cleaning up the movie set to only have what we want in it. We need to add the skinned Robot Drone and Alien Plant in our final scene later, so they can animate. So, these unskinned placeholder objects are not needed anymore.

You can also delete anything that you don't want on your movie set but be careful to leave all the wonderful backgrounds, environments and lighting you did. I left the Alien Plant static meshes for now as placeholders, so I know where to place my animated ones later, as shown in *Figure 20.19*:

Figure 20.19 – Just the movie set with the placeholders removed

Save the `MovieSetFinal` level and everything else at this point by selecting **File | Save All** in the UE main menu at the top.

Once you have a movie set with only the background environment and lighting, we can combine it with our **Level Sequence** called `FinalScene`. This is the one where you attached all the armor to her body in the *Attach Body Armor to MetaHuman Rig* section of this chapter.

With the `MovieSetFinal` level you just prepared still open, double-click on the `FinalScene` **Level Sequence** in **Content Drawer**.

She will appear in the level with all her armor as you set it up earlier, as shown in *Figure 20.20*:

Figure 20.20 – Final scene Sequencer in Level

We have now, in a sense, combined our `FinalScene` **Level Sequence** and our `MovieSetFinal` **Level**. In fact, it's more like our `FinalScene` **Level Sequence** is playing *inside* the `MovieSetFinal` **Level** with it acting as its backdrop or movie set.

Now, from **Content Drawer**, drag **SKELETAL MESH** for **Robot Drone** and **Alien Plant** into the **Sequencer** timeline, one after the other. They will then appear in the scene at the origin, just like the MetaHuman with her armor, as shown in *Figure 20.21*:

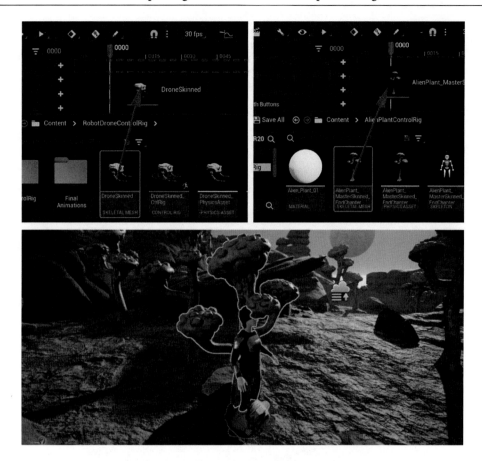

Figure 20.21 – Adding actors to the movie set

> **Note**
>
> Since the Robot Drone and Alien Plant have a simple setup and we prebaked all
> their animations, we do not need to bring the Control Rig versions of them into
> this scene. If you do want to create new animations for them in this sequence
> itself, then you can bring the Control Rig versions in if you choose to. With the
> MetaHuman's complex setup, it's far easier to just bring the whole blueprint
> into the sequence to make sure everything loads correctly.

Finally, we just need to change a setting on the character's hair. At the moment, it has
Levels of Detail (**LODs**). LODs are more for games that will display less detail of an
object, for example, the number of polygons, depending on how far the game camera is
away from it. For our scene, we don't need it, and we don't want to see lower-detail hair if
the camera is further away. There's also a bug in the current release of UE5 surrounding
hair thickness. This might be fixed in later releases of UE5, but for now, we need to change
the default thickness to display it better.

Select the **BP Sci Fi Girl** MetaHuman Blueprint in the viewport or **World Outliner**. In the **Details** window, select the **Hair (Inherited)** item, then under **GROOM**, double-click on the box next to **Groom Asset**, as shown in *Figure 20.22*:

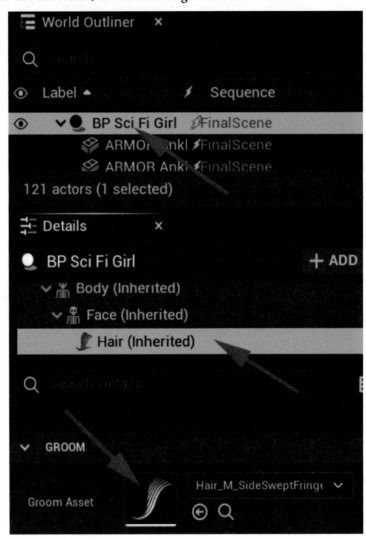

Figure 20.22 – Selecting the Hair item for editing

This will open the hair asset. In the **LODS** window on the right. Change **Thickness Scale** to 3.0. Then, delete the other LODs by clicking the **X** on the right, until only **LOD 0** is left. You might have to do that a few times since the next LOD in the sequence renames itself to **LOD 1**; so if you have four LODs, repeat this three times so only **LOD 0** is left, as shown in *Figure 20.23*:

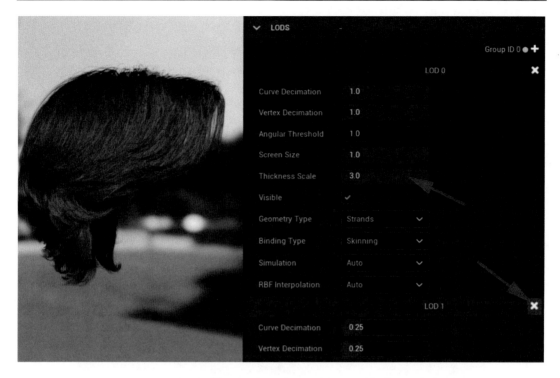

Figure 20.23 – Deleting extra LODs and setting Thickness Scale

We have now loaded and prepared our movie set and added the main actors to it. We are now ready to make our movie. Next, we will load the animations we created onto our characters/actors and bring them to life.

> **Note**
>
> On my current version of UE5, the hair physics tends to do strange things at times in my **Sequencer** scenes. You can disable the physics simulation by unchecking **Enable Simulation** under **Solver Settings** present in the **Physics** tab, which is to the right of the **LOD** tab at the top. This problem might be fixed in future updates of UE5.

Importing animations onto our characters

Importing animations onto the skeletal meshes of our characters is the next step in **Sequencer**. This will add the cleaned Mocap for the human character and the animations we created for the Robot Drone and Alien Plant to the characters in **Sequencer**.

Importing Mocap animations onto the MetaHuman

First of all, we probably need to discover how long our sequence will roughly end up being. That is why we'll import our animations onto our human character first:

1. For now, move the **Alien Plant** and **Robot Drone** out of the way, by selecting them in the viewport and moving them. This is just so that we can have a clear view of our human character. You'll notice that her feet are going through the floor, as shown in *Figure 20.24*:

Figure 20.24 – Moving the robot and plant out of the way

2. Delete the **MetaHuman_ControlRig** track under the **BP Sci Fi Girl** item in **Sequencer** by selecting it and pressing *Delete* on the keyboard, so as to prevent an override of the animation we're about to load, as shown in *Figure 20.25*:

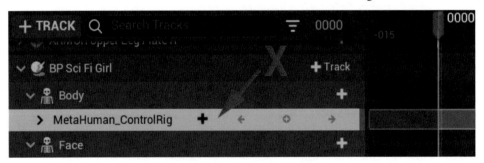

Figure 20.25 – Deleting the Control Rig track

3. Add an animation track by clicking + **Track** | **Animation**, then search for sit and choose Sitting_Idle_meta_cleaned_final, as shown in *Figure 20.26*:

Figure 20.26 – Adding a sitting idle animation

The sitting idle animation will now play on the character.

Figure 20.27 – Sitting animation cycle playing on the human character

4. Next, on frame **0000**, select her in the viewport and lift her up about 20 cm so her feet are on the ground. Set a keyframe on the **BP Sci Fi Girl** item **Transform** channel in the **TRACK** window to lock that position in, as shown in *Figure 20.28*:

Figure 20.28 – Moving the character on the Transform track and keyframe

On close inspection, we now realize something. The hands are clipping the armor we attached earlier, as shown in *Figure 20.29*:

Figure 20.29 – Clipping hands

This kind of thing happens very often in a production environment where items are added later or models are updated. We can now fix this with all the methods we learned about in *Chapter 19, Motion Capture Editing and Cleanup Using Control Rig and Sequencer*. For the purposes of this chapter, I included the fixed animation. If you want to use that instead, load the `Sitting_Idle_meta_cleaned_final_armorFix` and `Stand_up_meta_cleaned_final_armorFix` animations from the project file provided with this book.

Fix hands clipping armor

If you want to do this yourself for practice, here's a very brief description of the steps, covered in detail in the previous chapter. There's nothing really new in here, just a repeat of the steps we've already covered in *Chapter 19, Motion Capture Editing and Cleanup Using Control Rig and Sequencer*:

1. Set the range in the timeline from **0000** to **0238** (the length of the sitting animation).

2. Right-click **Body | Bake To Control Rig | MetaHuman_ControlRig**. Don't reduce keys.

3. Add an **Additive** animation layer, check the arms and legs controllers **IK** box to switch them to **IK**, and on `head_ctrl`, check the **Local** box, if it looks like it is at an odd angle.

4. Set a keyframe on all the **Additive Controllers** on frame **0000**. Make sure **Automatic Keyframe** is off since we're working with an **Additive** layer.

5. Create a new pose on the hands and fingers, not clipping the leg armor, and keyframe it on frame **0000** on the additive layer.

6. Select all the Control Rig controllers and save this new pose at frame **0000** to the **Poses Library** and call it `PoseA_Sit_Idle_ArmorFix`.

7. Right-click on **Body** in the **TRACK** window, select **Bake Animation Sequence**, and name it `Sitting_Idle_meta_cleaned_final_armorFix`.

8. Delete the **MetaHuman_CotrolRig** track from **BP Sci Fi Girl**, so we can adjust the Stand Up animation with the same changes.

9. On **Body** in the **TRACK** window, select **+ Track | Animation** and choose the `Stand_up_meta_cleaned_final` animation.

10. Set the range in the timeline from **0000** to **0082** (the length of the sitting animation).

11. Right-click on **Body | Bake To Control Rig | MetaHuman_ControlRig**. Don't reduce keys.

12. Add an **Additive** animation layer, check the arms and legs controllers' **IK** box to switch them to **IK**, and on `head_ctrl`, check the **Local** box, if it looks like it is at an odd angle.

13. Load the `PoseA_Sit_Idle_ArmorFix` pose from the **Poses** tool and key it on frame **0000** on all the **Additive** controllers.

14. If you scrub the animation, everything looks fine from frames **0** to **20** on the hand, so set an **anchor** keyframe on all the **Additive** controllers.

15. At frame **0044** and frame **0082** at the end of the animation, load and keyframe the `PoseB_Stand_Idle_tutor` pose from the **Poses** tool to get it back to the correct standing position and end pose at the end.

16. At frame **0031**, the fingers and hand clip badly, so make a correction with in-between keyframes on the hand IK controllers to stop the clipping.

17. Right-click on **Body** and in the **TRACK** window, select **Bake Animation Sequence**, and name it `Stand_up_meta_cleaned_final_armorFix`.

18. Delete the **Animation** and **MetaHuman_ControlRig** tracks in the **TRACK** window for **BP Sci Fi Girl**.

We have now fixed the hands clipping the armor on the Stand up animation. Next, we can load them into Sequencer.

Loading animations into Sequencer continued

We can now start again, loading animations where the hands don't clip with the upper leg armor:

1. Load the `Sitting_Idle_meta_cleaned_final_armorFix` animation by repeating *Step 2* (*Figure 20.26*) and *Step 3* (*Figure 20.27*), only now loading this fixed animation at frame **0000**.

2. Go to the end of the Sitting Idle animation at frame **0239** in the timeline and click **+ Animation** on the existing **Animation** track. Search for `stand` and select the fixed `Stand_up_meta_cleaned_final_armorFix` animation, as shown in *Figure 20.30*:

Figure 20.30 – Adding a fixed standing up animation

3. It will appear on a second **Animation** layer. However, blending animations is easier if they're on the same **Animation** layer, so left-click and hold in the middle of this track and drag it to the same layer as our sitting idle animation, as shown in *Figure 20.31*:

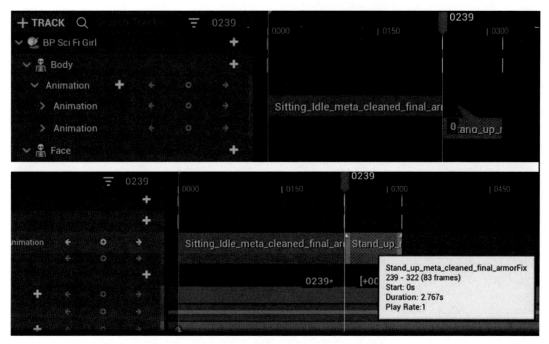

Figure 20.31 – Dragging the animation to the same track

If your animations don't flow seamlessly one to the other, you can blend animations together to smooth the transition by left clicking and holding, in the middle of these tracks, and dragging them over each other. The section where they overlap will blend one animation to the other as shown in *Figure 20.32*:

Figure 20.32 – Blending animations

Because we matched our start and end poses exactly in our Mocap cleanup, we don't need to do that between the Sitting Idle and the Stand Up animations in this case. Just line the end up with the beginning of the next one with no gap in-between.

4. Next, in the same way as the ones before, add the `Stand_Idle_meta_cleaned_final` animation. However, it turns out that there's a small glitch in the head going from the end of stand up animation to the beginning of the stand idle animation. So, drag them over each other to blend between the two for a few frames to get rid of the glitch, as shown in *Figure 20.33*:

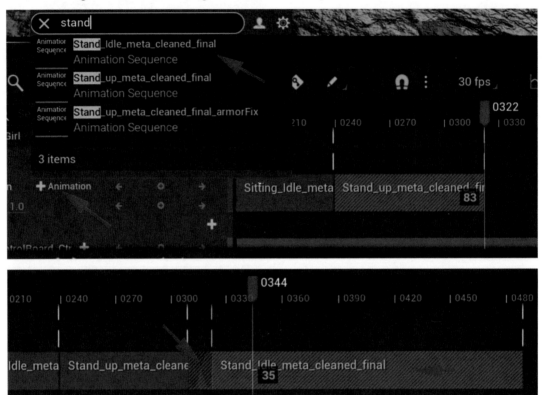

Figure 20.33 – Adding the Add Stand Idle and Small Blend

Playing back our sequence at this point, it feels like she stands still for too long in the stand idle animation after she gets up. Let's make it shorter.

5. Hover the mouse at the end of the `Stand_Idle_meta_cleaned_final` animation track on the timeline and click, hold, and drag it shorter to about frame **0400**, as shown in *Figure 20.34*. You can also call this **trimming** the animation:

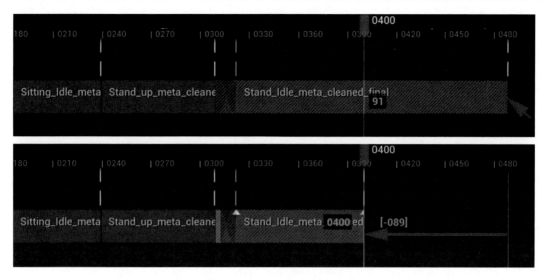

Figure 20.34 – Trimming the animation

6. Now, at frame **0400**, add the `Walk_start_stop_meta_cleaned_final` animation. Since we're not completing a full cycle of the stand idle, the pose at the beginning of the Walk animation won't match exactly. So, drag the Walk animation track a few frames to the left for a little bit of blending, as shown in *Figure 20.35*:

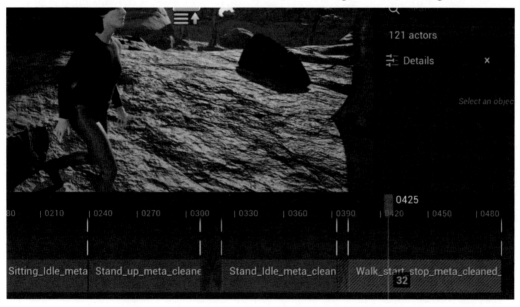

Figure 20.35 – Adding a walking start-stop animation

After she stops walking, we want her to push the button on her arm to activate the Robot Drone.

7. At the end of the walk animation, around frame **0496**, add the `Button_push_` `meta_cleaned_final` animation and also drag it to the same animation track as the others.

    However, we have a problem. When you scrub or play the timeline, when it transitions from the Walk animation to the Push button animation, at frame **0497**, she snaps back to the origin of the scene.

    This happens because during the Walk animation the character and its root moved several meters forward, whereas during the other animations she was still in the same spot. The Push button animation was animated at the origin, so when it starts playing it plays it back at the origin.

    Luckily, we animated the root of the character in the Walk animation to follow the character so that as she stops again the root is exactly between her heels, like the main stand pose. This root position is our relative reference point of where our character is in the world. We can use this root position to tell the Push button animation where the character is in the world and then play the animation there, instead of at the origin where it was animated

8. Right-click on the `Button_push_meta_cleaned_final` animation clip in the **Sequencer** timeline, then select **Match With This Bone In Previous Clip | root**, as shown in *Figure 20.36*:

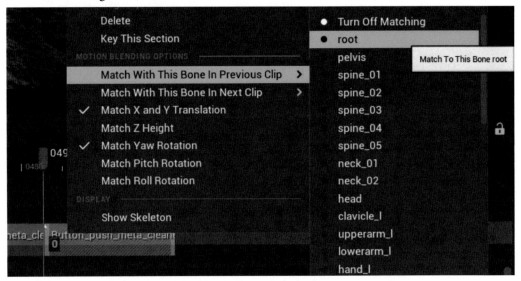

Figure 20.36 – Matching with root previous clip

9. Between the end of the Walk animation and the beginning of the Push button animation, it felt a bit abrupt, so I added a 16-frame blend in-between the two animations.

10. At the end of the `Button_push_meta_cleaned_final` animation, add the `Stand_Idle_meta_cleaned_final` animation again, so she can stand there in her stand idle cycle for as long as needed for the movie scene. Have a little bit of blending between the two animations.

11. Drag and extend the end of the `Stand_Idle_meta_cleaned_final` animation track to frame **1000**.

Because it's a seamless cycle, it will just keep repeating without any glitches. You can see where the beginning and end of each cycle is in these extended animation tracks by the thin white vertical line, as shown in *Figure 20.37*:

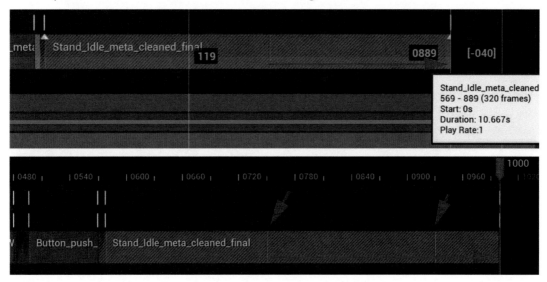

Figure 20.37 – Extending standing idle to frame 1000

12. Set the active range (thin vertical green and red line) from frame **0000** to **1000**.

13. One by one, extend all the **Attach** tracks for all the armor pieces so they're longer than the active range by clicking, holding, and dragging them at the end of the track in the timeline till they're longer than frame **1000**, as shown in *Figure 20.38*. They should now stay attached during the whole sequence:

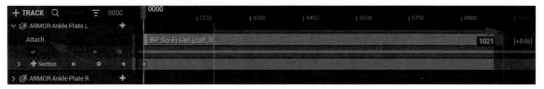

Figure 20.38 – Attaching the track range

Congratulations, you have now added the full Mocap animation sequence to our MetaHuman character! We now know roughly how many frames our scene is and can time the Robot Drone animations. Next, let's import our animation onto our Robot Drone in our movie scene.

Importing Mocap animations onto the Robot Drone

The timing of the animations on the Robot Drone depends on when the female character pushes the button on her arm to activate it. But first, let's position it in our scene.

When you add assets to **Sequencer**, in the case of the Alien Plant and the Robot Drone, they will automatically get a **Transform** track, as shown in *Figure 20.39*. Normally, it's the last track on the item. This **Transform** track can be used to position the asset in the scene, and we can even animate that position. This **Transform** track is like the overall parent of the world position of the asset in **Sequencer** and the scene:

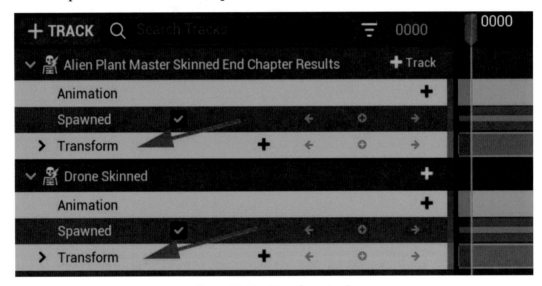

Figure 20.39 – Transform track

This is separate from the **Animation** tracks or **Control Rig** tracks of the items where you play the skeletal or Control Rig animations. This is very useful since you can play a skeletal animation on the item that has been animated at the origin of the scene and then use the **Transform** track position to play that animation in a different location in the scene, and even animate that position over the course of the scene.

We will use this **Transform** track to control the world position of our Robot Drone and also use it to animate it flying around the scene. We know we want the drone to be un-activated until she pushes the button on her arm. In my Sequencer, it is at frame **0530** (yours might be different).

This is a good starting point for our Robot Drone animation before it starts moving when she pushes the button:

1. On frame **0530** (in my case), select the drone in the viewport and move it to its starting position when it activates. I put it in front of the human character within her perspective on the ground. After you move and rotate the drone to sit perfectly on the ground with its main body, set a keyframe on the Robot's **Transform** track at this frame, as shown in *Figure 20.40*:

Figure 20.40 – Moving the robot to the starting position and setting the keyframe

2. On frame **0000**, add an animation on the **Animation** track and choose `Robot_Action_Unactivated`. Extend this animation cycle till just before the point that the human character pushes the activation button in the usual way, by clicking, holding, and dragging the end of the track, as shown in *Figure 20.41*:

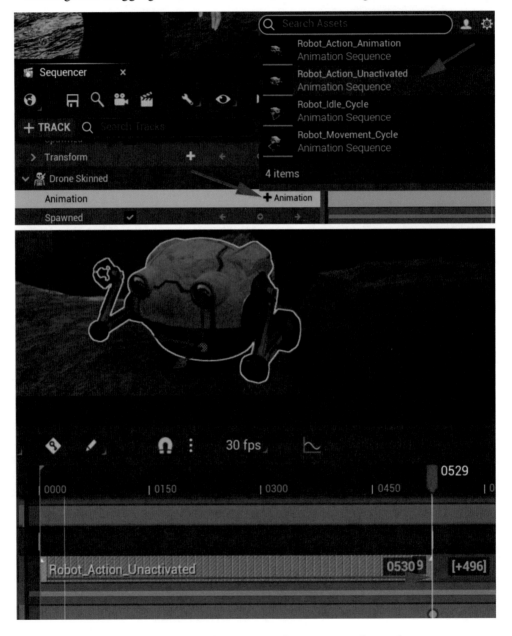

Figure 20.41 – Adding the unactivated animation and extending

3. At the point that the human character pushes the activation button, in my case frame **0530**, add `Robot_Action_Animation` (in my case, it's the salute) with + **Animation** on the **Animation** track. Make sure there is no gap between this and the previous track. Add a keyframe to the **Transform** track at the beginning of `Robot_Action_Animation`. Then, when it's fully activated, in my case, 50 frames later at **0580**, lift the robot off the ground in the hovering position and set another keyframe on the **Transform** track at this position, as shown in *Figure 20.42*:

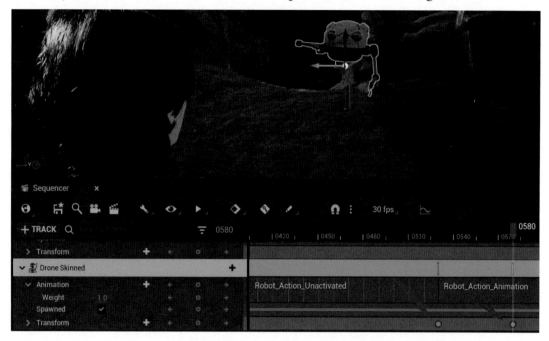

Figure 20.42 – Adding an activate action and keyframe position

After this, it's up to you what you want the Robot Drone to do next. If you want an example, you can study what I did in the `FinalScene_tutor` level sequence (included with this chapter's resource UE project). Have fun with this and be creative. Experiment with the tools and timing. Remember that you can also use the Graph Editor to edit the animation on the Transform track.

In summary, this is what I did with my `FinalScene_tutor` level sequence:

1. I added the `Robot_Idle_Cycle` and `Robot_Movement_Cycle` animations to my Robot Drone **Animation** track.

2. After the salute action (in my case), I put the `Robot_Idle_Cycle` animation, which I then trimmed to be shorter, and then I blended that into the `Robot_Movement_Cycle` that I extended for several cycles.

3. Then, I used the **Transform** track to animate the Robot flying off into the environment to explore it, as shown in *Figure 20.43*:

Figure 20.43 – Example robot sequence

4. Finally, I decided my sequence at the beginning is too long while she is sitting down, so I set the active range of the sequence to start at frame **0200** and end at frame **0800**, as shown in *Figure 20.44*:

Figure 20.44 – Active range adjustment

Our animation is now on our Robot Drone, and it has come to life in our movie scene. Next, let's get some movement into the movie set background by making the Alien Plants play the swaying animation we created in *Chapter 16, Creating a Simple Swaying Animation Cycle in UE5 Sequencer*.

Importing animations onto the Alien Plant

After everything we've done in this chapter, you might be happy to hear that this is probably easier part. Let's make our Alien Plants come to life:

1. Add `AlienPlant_Sway_Animation` to the **Alien Plant Master Skinned** item's **Animation** track by clicking **+ Animation** at the beginning of your active range in the timeline, as shown in *Figure 20.45*:

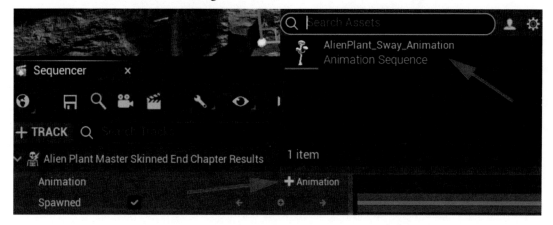

Figure 20.45 – Adding a sway animation to Alien Plant

2. Extend the `AlienPlant_Sway_Animation` track to be several cycles longer than the active range of the timeline, by clicking, holding, and dragging it at the end of the track, as shown in *Figure 20.46*:

Figure 20.46 – Extending the Alien Plant sway animation

3. Move, rotate, and scale it into the position of one of the Alien Plant static mesh placeholders in the viewport, and then delete the placeholder and keep the new animated one. We've now replaced the placeholder with an animated Alien Plant, as shown in *Figure 20.47*:

Figure 20.47 – Replacing the static plant with an animated Alien Plant

4. Right-click on the **Alien Plant Master Skinned** item and select **Duplicate** in the **TRACK** window. This will duplicate both the item and the **Animation** track, as shown in *Figure 20.48*:

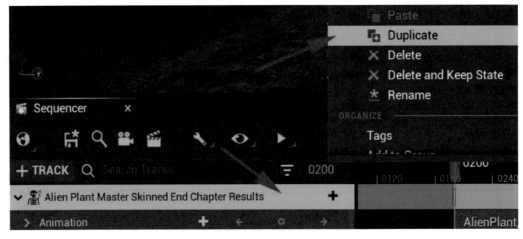

Figure 20.48 – Duplicating the Alien Plant track item

We now have two animated Alien Plants in **Sequencer**, but their animation plays at the same time and is perfectly in sync since the animation track was also duplicated as it was. This will look odd in a natural scene. We'll offset each Alien Plant's animation a little bit, so they don't play perfectly in sync.

5. Move the duplicated Alien Plant to the position of the next static Alien Plant you want to replace. Now move the `AlienPlant_Sway_Animation` track a few frames earlier to offset the timing of the animation, so it's not in sync with the original animated Alien Plant anymore, as shown in *Figure 20.49*:

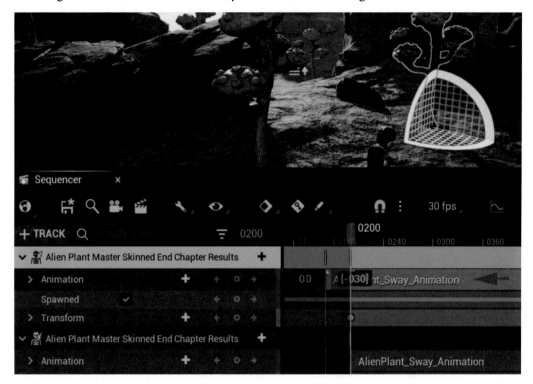

Figure 20.49 – Offsetting the duplicate Alien Plant animation track

However, still make sure that the `AlienPlant_Sway_Animation` track covers the whole active range, so the swaying animation plays for the whole sequence. You can drag and extend them to make them longer if needed.

6. Repeat *Step 4* and *Step 5* until you have replaced all the static Alien Plants with animated ones and offset their animations, so they don't play in sync.

All our animations have now been implemented for the *actors* on our movie set. Next, let's work with the cameras to film them.

Creating cameras and animating them

As far as the cameras are concerned, I will leave it up to you. Do whatever you want with them. However, if you want an example, you can study what I did in the `FinalScene_tutor` level sequence (included with this chapter's resource UE project).

But you probably want to know how to work with cameras in **Sequencer** in the first place. Here's how to set up multiple cameras and then create camera cuts between them in **Sequencer**. These are just the basics, but you can do most things you would ever want to do with cinematic cameras with these simple tools. There's much more that you can do with a camera and shots in **Sequencer**, but that is beyond the scope of this book.

To create a camera and animate it, please execute the following steps:

1. First, we need to add a **Camera Cut Track** to our sequence to store and manage our cameras and camera cuts. You do this by clicking **+ TRACK** at the top of the **TRACK** window and then selecting **Camera Cut Track**, as shown in *Figure 20.50*:

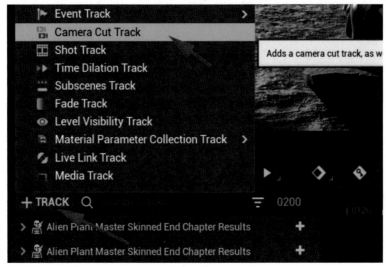

Figure 20.50 – Adding Camera Cut Track

2. Then, to create a new cinematic camera, click on the camera icon on the top menu of the **Sequencer** window, as shown in *Figure 20.51*:

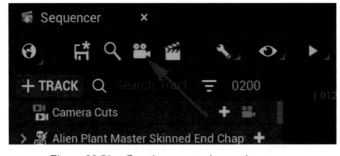

Figure 20.51 – Creating a new cinematic camera

The new **Cine Camera Actor** will appear in your **Sequencer TRACK** window and timeline. You can create as many of these cameras as you want. Later, you can create one for every camera cut.

3. If you select this **Cine Camera Actor** in the **TRACK** window, a small viewport will appear overlayed over your regular viewport. This is looking through the viewpoint of this cinematic camera, as shown in *Figure 20.52*:

Figure 20.52 – Cinematic camera selection

This is useful for when you move, animate, or change settings on the camera in the main working viewport, but you want real-time feedback on its effect on the cinematic camera. You can animate and set keyframes on this camera's position on its own **Transform** track.

> **Note**
>
> Make sure to animate the **Cine Camera Actor** and not the **CameraComponent**. This might cause issues. Like in this case it's also sometimes best to keep your animation keys on one of the objects in the hierarchy if they serve the same child. If you do some keyframes on one object in the hierarchy and then some on the other, they become more difficult to clean up. Try to keep it simple.

There's another very useful way to control these cameras and that is in **Pilot Mode.** If you click on the camera icon on the right of the new **Cine Camera Actor** track to switch it *on*, your main viewport becomes what this cinematic camera sees, as shown in *Figure 20.53*:

Figure 20.53 – Pilot cinematic camera

Here, you can use your regular viewport navigation to pilot the camera position to get the exact view you want from this camera. If you want to go back to the regular perspective camera and viewport, just click on this camera icon to turn it *off*.

The other three most frequently used important settings on the camera that are on **CameraComponent** in the **TRACK** window are **Aperture, Focal Length,** and **Manual Focus Distance,** as shown in *Figure 20.54*:

Figure 20.54 – Camera settings

These have the same function as a film camera in the real world. **Aperture** is how wide the aperture is and it effects the depth of field (things in background more or less out of focus). **Focal Length** is the type of lens and can also be used to zoom in and out. **Manual Focus Distance** is the distance at which the subject will be perfectly in focus.

Don't worry about this too much if you don't know what these settings should be. Next to **Current Aperture, Current Focal Length** and **Manual Focus Distance**, of the camera item in the **TRACK** window, there's a grey number, if you left click, hold, and drag left or right on this number, and it will go up or down.

Simply drag these values left or right until you get the desired result. With the camera selected, in the **Details** window of the main UE interface there are more advanced camera settings that you can experiment with if you want to, but most of the time, these three settings will be all you'll need.

Next, we'll look at how to use multiple cameras and cut between them.

Using multiple cameras and cutting between them

In UE5, we can create multiple cameras with different positions, angles, and settings and cut between them, just like a real movie set. These camera cuts are controlled through the **Camera Cuts** track. Here is how to use it:

1. Set up and animate your first cinematic camera, for the first cut, the way you want it.

2. On frame **0000**, in the **Sequencer Track** window to the right of the **Camera Cuts** track, click + **Camera** and select the first camera you want to cut to in the sequence.

    This cinematic camera appears in the **Camera Cuts** track. You can adjust the length and timing of this track in the same way as you adjust any track in **Sequencer**, by dragging the end or clicking and holding, then dragging in the middle to move it.

3. Trim it to where you want your second camera cut, as shown in *Figure 20.55*:

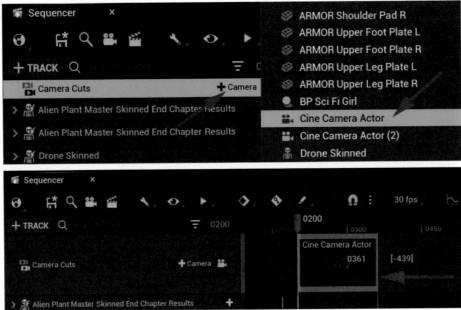

Figure 20.55 – Adding the first camera cut

At this point, you can create another cinematic camera by clicking on the camera icon at the top of the **Sequencer** menu for your second camera cut.

4. Animate and set it up the way you want your second camera cut to look, at the timing you want. Then, add it to the **Camera Cuts** track at the time you want it to cut to this camera by clicking the + **Camera** on the **Camera Cuts** track, as shown in *Figure 20.56*:

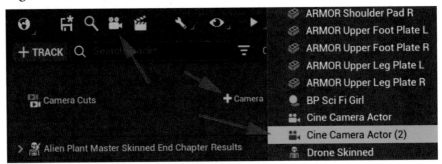

Figure 20.56 – Adding a second camera cut

5. If you want to see your sequence camera cuts in the viewport, to see what will be rendered to your movie at the end, click on the camera icon on the **Camera Cuts** track.

This is not like the Pilot Mode on the individual cinematic cameras since you can't edit the camera with the viewport navigation in this mode. It is simply for viewing the camera cuts and the final result, as shown in *Figure 20.57*:

Figure 20.57 – Viewing the camera results in the Viewport

6. You can exit this viewing mode again by clicking the camera icon to turn it *off*.

You can create as many of these camera cuts as you want to film this scene. Have fun and try different things. Present the hard work you put into this book in the best possible way. Once you're happy with your camera cuts and are ready to render your final movie, we can move on to the very last step of this book.

Rendering our final scene

You'll also be happy to learn that this last step is the easiest one. In this last step, we will render an AVI movie file of our scene that can be uploaded and shown to your friends on social media if you want to:

1. Next to the camera icon on the main **Sequencer** menu is a film clapperboard icon. Click on that to open **Render Movie Settings**, as shown in *Figure 20.58*:

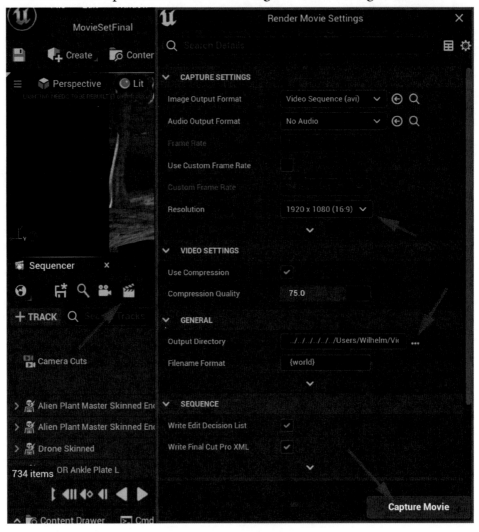

Figure 20.58 – Render Movie Settings

2. The **Resolution** is **1920 x 1080**, which is full HD, but you can render it bigger or smaller if you want to. Select an output directory for the movie to be saved to, and then click **Capture Movie**.

This will render the active time range of your sequence from the **Camera Cuts** track point of view. It might take several minutes for this process to complete, depending on the speed of your computer.

3. Once completed, navigate to the folder you specified as the output directory to find your rendered final movie. Watch it and enjoy the result of all your hard work.

Huge congratulations to you for reaching this point in your journey and finishing this book!

We provide the final UE5 project file that can be downloaded here with installation instructions: `https://github.com/PacktPublishing/Unreal-Engine-5-Character-Creation-Animation-and-Cinematics/tree/main/FullFinalUE5Project`.

You can explore this project with examples of everything we've done in this book.

We also include the example final render of the final scene here: `https://github.com/PacktPublishing/Unreal-Engine-5-Character-Creation-Animation-and-Cinematics/blob/main/FullFinalUE5Project/FinalScene.mp4`.

Summary

In this chapter, you learned how to migrate content from different projects into each other. You learned how to attach different objects and props, such as armor, to character animations. We prepared character and level assets for our final scene. We also imported a cleaned-up Mocap onto our MetaHuman character and stitched them together into one sequence.

We did the same for custom animations on our Robot Drone character and made the background come to life with the swaying animation on our Alien Plant. We then covered how to work with multiple camera cuts in **Sequencer** and how to edit and animate them. Finally, we rendered the result into a final AVI movie file.

With the skills you learned in this book, you can now create your own custom 3D content and animations and create your own stories inside UE5. You can let your imagination run wild and your only constraint is the time and work it requires.

We feel so honored that you took this journey with us. If this is the start of your computer animation journey, we wish you all the best and we hope that what we covered in this book will lay a solid foundation for you to build upon.

If you're already established as a computer artist, I hope we provided some good alternatives in using the UE5 pipeline instead of the classic ones, especially when it comes to rigging and animation.

Index

L

M

Packt.com

Subscribe to our online digital library for full access to over 7,000 books and videos, as well as industry leading tools to help you plan your personal development and advance your career. For more information, please visit our website.

Why subscribe?

- Spend less time learning and more time coding with practical eBooks and Videos from over 4,000 industry professionals

- Improve your learning with Skill Plans built especially for you

- Get a free eBook or video every month

- Fully searchable for easy access to vital information

- Copy and paste, print, and bookmark content

Did you know that Packt offers eBook versions of every book published, with PDF and ePub files available? You can upgrade to the eBook version at packt.com and as a print book customer, you are entitled to a discount on the eBook copy. Get in touch with us at customercare@packtpub.com for more details.

At www.packt.com, you can also read a collection of free technical articles, sign up for a range of free newsletters, and receive exclusive discounts and offers on Packt books and eBooks.

Other Books You May Enjoy

If you enjoyed this book, you may be interested in these other books by Packt:

Game Development Projects with Unreal Engine

Hammad Fozi, Gonçalo Marques, David Pereira, Devin Sherry

ISBN: 978-1-80020-922-0

- Create a fully-functional third-person character and enemies
- Build navigation with keyboard, mouse, gamepad, and touch controls
- Program logic and game mechanics with collision and particle effects
- Explore AI for games with Blackboards and Behavior Trees
- Build character animations with Animation Blueprints and Montages
- Test your game for mobile devices using mobile preview
- Add polish to your game with visual and sound effects
- Master the fundamentals of game UI design using a heads-up display

Blueprints Visual Scripting for Unreal Engine 5

Brenden Sewell, Marcos Romero

ISBN: 978-1-80181-158-3

- Understand programming concepts in Blueprints
- Create prototypes and iterate new game mechanics rapidly
- Build user interface elements and interactive menus
- Use advanced Blueprint nodes to manage the complexity of a game
- Explore all the features of the Blueprint editor, such as the Components tab, Viewport, and Event Graph
- Get to grips with OOP concepts and explore the Gameplay Framework
- Work with virtual reality development in UE Blueprint
- Implement procedural generation and create a product configurator

Packt is searching for authors like you

If you're interested in becoming an author for Packt, please visit `authors.packtpub.com` and apply today. We have worked with thousands of developers and tech professionals, just like you, to help them share their insight with the global tech community. You can make a general application, apply for a specific hot topic that we are recruiting an author for, or submit your own idea.

Share Your Thoughts

Now you've finished *Unreal Engine 5 Character Creation, Animation and Cinematics*, we'd love to hear your thoughts! Scan the QR code below to go straight to the Amazon review page for this book and share your feedback or leave a review on the site that you purchased it from.

https://www.amazon.com/review/create-review/
error?asin=1801812446&

Your review is important to us and the tech community and will help us make sure we're delivering excellent quality content.

Made in the USA
Coppell, TX
19 November 2023

24466104R00364